★ SESQUICENTENNIAL COLLECTOR'S EDITION ★

# TexasMonthly®

## Texas, Our Texas

# TexasMonthly®

## Texas, Our Texas

150
Moments
That Made Us
The Way We Are

★

**TexasMonthlyPress**

Texas Monthly Press, Inc.
P.O. Box 1569
Austin, Texas 78767

A B C D E F G H

Library of Congress Cataloging-in-Publication Data

Texas, our Texas.
    1. Texas—History—Addresses, essays, lectures.
I. Burka, Paul, 1942-      . II. Texas monthly (Austin, Tex.)
F386.5.T485    1986    976.4    85-28890
ISBN 0-87719-051-8(hc)
ISBN 0-87719-043-7(pbk)

# THE GREAT MYTHS

## 1

## The Republic

## The Open Range

## Oil

COVER ILLUSTRATION BY ALEX MURAWSKI

# CHARACTER AND CULTURE

## 43

# Coming of Age

## 105

# BEHIND THE LINES

## BY PAUL BURKA

... AND MANY HAPPY RETURNS.

THIS BOOK IS OUR birthday present to Texas. In honor of Texas' sesquicentennial year, it is entirely devoted to a single theme: "One hundred and fifty moments that made us the way we are."

The material in this book originally appeared in the January 1986 issue of *Texas Monthly* magazine. It represents the combined effort of 98 authors. Most are Texans; the rest know us well. Never before has the work of so many of the best Texas writers been assembled between two covers.

What they have given us is a character study of Texas. It is not a chronology; the moments are arranged by topics rather than by dates. Neither is it exactly a history. Some profound historical events are not represented here–the Great Depression, for example, or World War II, or the sit-ins of the early sixties–simply because they were not unique to Texas. This book is an impression rather than a record, a portrait rather than a photograph. It is an attempt to discover who we are and how we got that way.

Along the way we considered more than four hundred moments. Some fell off the list because they just weren't of sufficient consequence. Such was the fate of "the beginning of Texas League baseball in 1888" and "the first chili cookoff." Some posed insurmountable research problems. That is why you will not find "the arrival of the first planeload of pot" on our final list. Some weren't unique to Texas. So much for "the last bear sighting." And some moments, while interesting, didn't have much to do with the way Texas is today. Scratch "Texas approves pari-mutuel betting in 1933."

The 150 moments that made the final cut are the chromosomes of modern Texas. Some belong in any history of Texas: Travis at the Alamo, the gusher at Spindletop, Jack Ruby shooting Lee Harvey Oswald, to name a few. But many others are drawn from everyday life, small incidents that multiply themselves into history: a farmer runs out of water, a stewardess goes to work for a neophyte commuter airline, a Vietnamese refugee becomes valedictorian of his high school class. In our scheme, barbecue at Kreuz Market is as important as oil at Spindletop. Come to think of it, maybe more so.

This book is also a reflection of the way we as Texans see our state today. It is far different from the way Texans saw themselves fifty years ago as they prepared to celebrate the state's centennial. Here, for instance, is a newspaper editorial from 1935: "The coming century will see the state slowly change from a cotton growing region to one in which there is wide diversification of"–Guess what comes next. Industry? Natural resources? Guess again– "crops, in large part stimulated by the growing demand of general and local industries for the products of the soil."

At the time of the centennial, Texas was a poor Southern state made poorer by the Depression. It was a rural state, too, with bad roads and worse schools. The major asset of that Texas was neither soil nor oil, but its mythic past. "The Alamo, Goliad, San Jacinto–wherever lives a man of the white races, these names accelerate the blood flow and bring thrills of pride." Those words were part of a commentary on the appointment of Jesse Jones to plan the centennial celebration. They appeared in a short-lived journal of the day called *The Texas Monthly.*

A state that saw its future only as the slow diversification of crops naturally preferred to look backward. No wonder it produced one Theophilus Fitz, whose contribution to the centennial was *Tejas,* an opera, with a libretto by two women from Brownwood. A musical called *The Cavalcade of Texas* played in Dallas; the *Morning News* called it "an expression of Texas, by Texans for Texans." The *News* wrote, "Texas is possibly less than expert in the art of pageantry. The work, then, must not be judged by the standard of Salzburg, Chicago, or Baltimore spectacles, but as a sumptuous achievement of our young but ambitious theater." This kind of patriotic extravagance was matched in the political arena by a legislator who pleaded for the state to build a monument in Gonzales, where the first shot of the Texas Revolution was fired. "We want no pageants to blow away with the wind," he said, "but something enduring that the world may know our wonderful history and be reminded of our heroes."

Today Texas is a different place. It isn't poor any more–its per capita income exceeded the national average in 1981 for the first time–and it isn't Southern, either. It's certainly not rural. Unlike the generation of 1936, we can be proud of the present as well as the mythic past, and we aren't afraid to be judged by the standards of Salzburg, Chicago, Baltimore, or anywhere else.

But have the wrenching changes that have occurred in the last half-century separated us from our past? A lot of Texans would say yes. Texans have not taken kindly to change since statehood ended the Republic. The lament was even put to music in a cowboy doggerel that was popular at the turn of the century:

*I'm going to leave old Texas now.*
*For they've got no use for the Long-*
*horn cow;*
*They've plowed and fenced my*
*cattle range,*
*And the people there are all so*
*strange.*

Here we are, 86 years later, and the cowboy is still a Texas mythic hero, and the first thing any Texan does when he gets a little money is to go buy himself a ranch and run a few cattle on it. Texas may change, but Texans never will.

# AUTHORS

PETER APPLEBOME is a senior editor of *Texas Monthly.*

JIM ATKINSON is an associate editor of *Texas Monthly* and coauthor of the best-selling *Evidence of Love.*

DON BACON is the assistant managing editor of *U.S. News & World Report* and coauthor of a forthcoming biography of Sam Rayburn.

DONALD BARTHELME is the author of twelve books of fiction. He teaches at the University of Houston.

FREDERICK BARTHELME's most recent book is *Tracer.* He teaches creative writing at the University of Southern Mississippi.

PETE BARTHELME is a writer who lives in Houston.

WILLIE BROWN is the Speaker of the California Assembly.

DOMINIQUE BROWNING is the executive editor of *Texas Monthly.*

WILLIAM BROYLES, JR., was the first editor of *Texas Monthly.* He was born in Baytown and lives in New York. His book on a veteran's return to Viet Nam, *Brothers in Arms,* will be published in 1986.

PAUL BURKA is a senior editor of *Texas Monthly* and the editor of the sesquicentennial issue.

FRYAR CALHOUN grew up on his family's farm near Plainview. He is coauthor of *California White Water: A Guide to the Rivers.*

BENJAMIN CAPPS is a novelist and historian who lives in Grand Prairie.

GARY CARTWRIGHT is a senior editor of *Texas Monthly.* He is the author of five books, the most recent being *Dirty Dealing.*

CATHERINE CHADWICK is an assistant editor of *Texas Monthly.*

SUSAN CHADWICK is a writer who lives in Houston.

ALISON COOK is a senior editor of *Texas Monthly.*

GREGORY CURTIS is the editor of *Texas Monthly.*

TOM CURTIS is the Houston bureau chief for the *Dallas Times Herald.*

CARMINA DANINI is a staff writer for the *Laredo Morning Times.*

JOHN DAVIDSON is a senior editor of *Texas Monthly* and the author of *The Long Road North.*

ANNE DINGUS is a contributing editor of *Texas Monthly* and a freelance writer living in Austin.

ROBIN DOUGHTY is an associate professor of geography at the University of Texas at Austin. He is the author of *Wildlife and Man in Texas* and coauthor of *The Amazing Armadillo: Geography of a Folk Critter.*

RONNIE DUGGER publishes the *Texas Observer.* His most recent book is *On Reagan.*

PETER ELKIND is an associate editor of *Texas Monthly.*

MICHAEL ENNIS is an associate editor of *Texas Monthly.*

JAMES FALLOWS is the Washington editor of the *Atlantic* and a former associate editor of *Texas Monthly.*

DEBORAH FANT is a copy editor at *Texas Monthly.*

JOHN HENRY FAULK is a Texas humorist and the author of *The Uncensored John Henry Faulk.*

T. R. FEHRENBACH is the author of *Lone Star.* The most widely read history of Texas, it is the basis for a current PBS miniseries.

LAURA FISHER is a writer who lives in Dallas.

CHET FLIPPO is a former senior editor of *Rolling Stone* magazine whose most recent book is *On the Road With the Rolling Stones.*

STEPHEN FOX is a fellow of the Anchorage Foundation of Texas.

JOE B. FRANTZ is a professor of history at the University of Texas at Austin and the author of *Forty-Acre Follies.*

SAUL FRIEDMAN is a special writer for *Newsday* and teaches journalism at Columbia University.

LISA GERMANY, a native of Eastland, is a freelance writer who frequently writes about architecture.

ALICE GORDON, a former associate editor of *Texas Monthly,* is an editor at *House & Garden.*

DON GRAHAM is an associate professor of English at the University of Texas at Austin and the editor of the forthcoming *South by Southwest: Stories From Modern Texas.*

JOHN GRAVES, of Glen Rose, is a contributing editor of *Texas Monthly.* His books include *Goodbye to a River, Hard Scrabble,* and *From a Limestone Ledge.*

A. C. GREENE is a contributing editor of *Texas Monthly,* a Texas historian, and an author. He lives in Dallas.

KATHERINE GREGOR is a writer who lives in Austin.

EDWARD EVERETT HALE was a Unitarian clergyman who wrote *The Man Without a Country* in 1863.

J. EVETTS HALEY is the author of *Charles Goodnight, Cowman and Plainsman,* and many other books about Texas, including *A Texan Looks at Lyndon.*

STEPHEN HARRIGAN is a senior editor of *Texas Monthly.* His latest novel is *Jacob's Well.*

SHELBY HEARON is the author of nine novels, including *Group Therapy* and *A Small Town.*

WILLIAM J. HELMER is a senior editor of *Playboy* and an expatriate who maintains his Lone Star citizenship by writing for Texas publications.

JOHN H. HERNDON, a native of Kentucky, arrived in Texas in 1838, when he was about 25 years old. He was a successful lawyer, who "dallied in politics, war, corporate business."

ROLANDO HINOJOSA-SMITH is the Ellen Clayton Garwood Professor of English at the University of Texas at Austin. His latest books are *Mi Querido Rafa* and *Partners in Crime.*

HARRY HURT III is a senior editor of *Texas Monthly.* He is working on a book about the Apollo moon missions.

MOLLY IVINS is a columnist for the *Dallas Times Herald* and a former editor of the *Texas Observer.*

JAN JARBOE is a columnist for the *San Antonio Express-News.*

CHARLIE JEFFRIES was an amateur historian whose writings appeared in the *Southwestern Historical Quarterly.* Asked by the *Quarterly* for his credits, he wrote the following: "I have been living around Winkler nearly all my life; I have never been anywhere much; I have never seen anything much. . . . As for writing, I have been doing a little of that for a good many years. I have inherited a taste for history, all my folks having been that way as far back as I know anything about them."

DAN JENKINS is an author whose latest book is *Life Its Ownself.*

MIKE KELLEY is a columnist for the *Austin American-Statesman.* A collection of his columns titled *My Name's Kelley, and That's My Opinion* was published last year.

ELMER KELTON is the author of 26 books, including *The Time It Never Rained,* and the associate editor of *Livestock Weekly,* published in San Angelo.

LARRY L. KING's latest book is *None But a Blockhead: On the Writing Life.*

AARON LATHAM is the author of *Urban Cowboy* and writes frequently for national magazines.

TOM LEA is a painter and writer who lives in El Paso. He is the author of *The Wonderful Country* and *The King Ranch.*

NICHOLAS LEMANN, a former executive editor of *Texas Monthly,* is national correspondent for the *Atlantic.* His most recent book is *Out of the Forties.*

FRANCIS L. LOEWENHEIM is a professor of history at Rice University.

BEVERLY LOWRY is a novelist who lives in San Marcos. Her latest book is *Daddy's Girl.*

SCOTT LUBECK is the director of Texas Monthly Press. He writes frequently on computer-related subjects.

PRUDENCE MACKINTOSH is a contributing editor of *Texas Monthly.* Her most recent book is *Retreads.*

LARRY MCMURTRY's latest book is *Lonesome Dove.*

WILLIAM MARTIN is a contributing editor of *Texas Monthly.*

WILLIE MORRIS is a writer in residence at the University of Mississippi at Oxford.

JOSEPH NOCERA is a senior editor of

*Texas Monthly.*

KAYE NORTHCOTT is a Texas-based journalist who edited the *Texas Observer* during the seventies.

DANIEL OKRENT is the editor of *New England Monthly.* His most recent book, *Nine Innings,* will be issued in paperback this spring.

FREDERICK LAW OLMSTED was a New England journalist who wrote *A Journey Through Texas* in 1857.

WILLIAM A. OWENS is a writer and folklorist who was born in Pinhook. His books include *Tell Me a Story, Sing Me a Song . . .* and *This Stubborn Soil.*

E. J. PALMER was born in England in 1875 and came to Missouri at the age of three. He was a botanist and an amateur poet.

JOE NICK PATOSKI is an associate editor of *Texas Monthly.*

DREW PEARSON is the assistant receiving coach of the Dallas Cowboys.

PAULA PHILLIPS left Southwest Airlines last August to start Cathy and Paula's Cater Parties with another former flight attendant.

DICK J. REAVIS is a senior editor of *Texas Monthly.*

JAN REID is a contributing editor of *Texas Monthly.* His most recent book is *Deerinwater.*

T. R. REID is the author of *The Chip,* a book about the inventors of the microchip.

AL REINERT is a contributing editor of *Texas Monthly.* He is working with photographer Geoff Winningham on a book about Houston's 150th birthday.

ARNOLD ROSENFELD is the editor of the *Austin American-Statesman.*

PATRICIA SHARPE is a senior editor of *Texas Monthly.* She edits Around the State and Touts and writes consumer articles.

MARK SINGER is a staff writer for the *New Yorker* and the author of *Funny Money.*

GRIFFIN SMITH, JR., is a contributing editor of *Texas Monthly.* His most recent books are *Forgotten Texas* and *The Great State of Texas.*

LIZ SMITH is a syndicated columnist for the *New York Daily News,* a television commentator for NBC in New York, and a 1949 graduate of the University of Texas.

MIMI SWARTZ is an associate editor of *Texas Monthly.*

W. L. TAITTE is a contributing editor of *Texas Monthly.* He is also critic-at-large for WRR-FM in Dallas.

ALAN TENNANT is an Austin writer whose books include the award-winning *The Guadalupe Mountains of Texas.* He is working on a book about falcons.

MARSHALL TERRY is the director of the creative writing program at Southern Methodist University and the author of *Dallas Stories.*

TERRY TOLER is a writer who lives in Austin.

JOHN EDWARD WEEMS, who lives in Waco, is the author of *A Weekend in September,* about the 1900 Galveston storm. His most recent book is the forthcoming *If You Don't Like the Weather . . .*

RICHARD WEST is a former senior editor of *Texas Monthly* and the author of *Richard West's Texas.* He has written for *New York* and *Newsweek* and is an associate editor of *D* magazine.

TOM WICKER is the political columnist of the *New York Times.*

GARY CLEVE WILSON is a writer who lives in Austin.

SUZANNE WINCKLER was born in Colorado City. She is the coeditor of *The Bird Life of Texas* and is a former senior editor of *Texas Monthly.*

JAMES WOLCOTT is a contributing editor of *Texas Monthly.*

BRYAN WOOLLEY is a novelist and a feature writer for the *Dallas Times Herald.*

LAWRENCE WRIGHT is a contributing editor of *Texas Monthly.* He is working on a memoir titled *In the New World.*

EMILY YOFFE is an associate editor of *Texas Monthly.*

RICHARD ZELADE is a writer who lives in Austin.

# ACKNOWLEDGMENTS

"Where the Lambs Come Down to the Slaughter," page 16, is from E. J. Palmer, "Notes and Documents: Texas," ed. B. C. Tharp, *Southwestern Historical Quarterly* 67, no. 1 (July 1963): 78–85. Reprinted with the permission of the Texas State Historical Association.

"Greetings From Sour Lake," page 35, is excerpted from Charlie Jeffries, "Reminiscences of Sour Lake," *Southwestern Historical Quarterly* 50, no. 1 (July 1946): 25–35. Reprinted with the permission of the Texas State Historical Association.

"Texans Are Lusty!" captions, pages 44–47, are excerpted from "Texas Is Big," *Life* magazine, vol. 6, no. 15, April 10, 1939, pp. 64–75. © 1939. Reprinted with the permission of *Life* magazine, Time Inc.

"The Legislature Starts to Earn Its Reputation," page 51, is reprinted from John H. Herndon. "Notes and Documents: Diary of a Young Man in Houston, 1838," ed. Andrew Forest Muir, *Southwestern Historical Quarterly* 53, no 3. (January 1950): 276–307. Reprinted with the permission of the Texas State Historical Association.

"The Handshake Deal," page 51, is adapted from J. Evetts Haley, *Charles Goodnight, Cowman and Plainsman.* New edition © 1949 by University of Oklahoma Press. Used by permission.

"The Royal Treatment," page 59, is excerpted from Dan Jenkins' columns in the *Fort Worth Press,* Sunday, October 12, and Monday, October 13, 1958. Reprinted with the permission of Scripps Howard Newspapers.

"That Old-time Religion," page 66, is from William A. Owens, *Tell Me a Story, Sing Me a Song . . .,* pp. 235–38. © 1983 by William A. Owens. Reprinted with the permission of the University of Texas Press.

"The Organization Man," page 111, is from Willie Morris, *North Toward Home,* pp. 250–52, published by Houghton Mifflin Company, Boston. © 1967 by Willie Morris. Reprinted with permission.

The song lyrics on page 118 in "The Midnight Special" are from "Governor Pat Neff," words and music by Huddie Ledbetter. Collected and adapted by John A. Lomax and Alan Lomax. Published by TRO-Folkways Music Publishing, Inc. Used by permission.

The lyrics on page 156 in "Where Have All the Young Folks Gone?" are from "Detroit City," by Mel Tillis and Danny Dill, published by Cedarwood Publishing Company, a division of Musiplex Group, Inc. © 1962. Reprinted by permission of the publisher.❧

★ SESQUICENTENNIAL COLLECTOR'S EDITION ★

# TexasMonthly®

## Texas, Our Texas

STEVE CARVER

# THE GREAT MYTHS

**THE REPUBLIC** Why, 150 years later, do we still remember the Alamo? Why do we still think like Travis, or fight about the same things Lamar and Houston did? Because what matters most about Texas is that it's a state that was once a nation. **THE OPEN RANGE** The cattlemen built empires that they thought would last forever. But there were too many homesteaders and not enough water. The land began to play out, and the great ranches had to be rescued by the oil beneath them. **OIL** The oil patch has been our twentieth-century frontier. Like the Old West, it was a place where a man could live by his own rules and enjoy the illusion that providence had singled him out for riches—until, alas, the oil began to run out.

1

# THE FIRST TEXAN

## BY GREGORY CURTIS

1836 "VICTORY OR DEATH," TRAVIS WRITES FROM THE ALAMO, TRANSFORMING HIMSELF INTO A HERO— AND TEXAS INTO A CAUSE WORTH DYING FOR.

ON SUNDAY, MARCH 9, 1834, NEARly two years to the day before he would die at the Alamo, William Barret Travis wrote in his diary: "Started to Mill Creek waters all swimming & prairie so boggy—could not go—*The first time I ever turned back in my life.*"

Only eleven months of Travis' diary survive, but what makes the passage leap out—other than Travis' own underlining—is that it is the one entry in which the Travis of fact and the Travis of legend seem perfectly joined. Otherwise the diary is simply a daily log of his law practice and personal expenses, a document by an obsessive counter. He lists his shirts and socks, and he lists his sexual adventures. (Someone named Susanna is recorded as his fifty-ninth conquest. He was then 24.) That brief underlined passage is the only moment of personal assessment in the entire document, and there is in those words Travis' unstated reproach of himself for letting nature dominate his intentions. He was a vain, moody man, idealistic and romantic. He worked hard by day, and at night he gambled or consorted with prostitutes or sat alone reading Sir Walter Scott. He was brainy and ambitious and filled with passionate energy. He spent all his short life seeking a stage upon which to play out his self-appointed destiny. The only thing he understood about himself was that he would not turn back. He wanted to be a hero and a patriot, and he became a hero and a patriot. He wrote his famous letter from the Alamo proclaiming his new role, and the world listened. He had, with a few strokes of a pen, made his dreams real. He had invented himself and invented Texas as well.

Texas is a place where family means very little, where awards and degrees and other kinds of official certification mean very little, and where a person's past outside Texas means very little either. Here a person can truly invent himself, and he will be believed and accepted as long as he manages to do a reasonable job of living up to his own invention. This truth of our place and character has made the state, then and now, a ripe tree for plucking by carpetbaggers, shysters, promoters, and confidence men of all descriptions who get away with claiming tc be what they are not. But they are overshadowed by the people who have come here or been born here and worked to become something far better than they or anyone else might have expected. Travis, whether he understood all this or not, was the first Texan because he made the world accept his vision of himself.

WHEN THE HIGH WATER forced him to turn back, Travis was going to Mill Creek to see Rebecca Cummings, with whom he was conducting a passionate romance. Travis hoped to marry her. He was a fervent, courtly suitor who brought her jewelry and requested in return a lock of her hair. Rebecca, for her part in this courtly drama, knew how to tease and provoke him just long enough before yielding some degree of her favors. (Travis writes in another diary entry that she was cold

to him early in the evening but later "*muy caliente*"—very hot.) Travis might have pressed his suit with even greater passion except for two inconvenient legacies from his past. One was the wife and two children he had left behind in Alabama. The other was a nagging venereal disease that he was treating with an elixir made of mercury.

Travis, born in South Carolina, was the oldest of eleven children, although his father, Mark, had had an illegitimate son before his marriage. Travis' mother was named Jemima. When Travis was nine, his father moved the growing brood to Alabama, where he farmed a tract of land. Travis' uncle Alexander lived nearby. This uncle was a man of considerable local reputation, a circuit preacher, founder of Baptist churches, mediator of disputes, and organizer of small towns. Travis spent time in his company, and Alexander seems to have had more influence on the boy than Travis' own father had. At sixteen or seventeen, most likely through the devices of his uncle, Travis left home to attend school in a nearby boomtown named Claiborne. He never returned to farming or to live with his family. Soon he was reading law with Judge James Dellet, a former Speaker of the Alabama House and United States congressman. At the same time, he taught school. In October 1828 he married one of his students, and nine months later his first child was born. Travis was nineteen years old. In the coming months he joined the Masonic lodge, got commissioned as an adjutant in the Alabama militia, and founded a newspaper, the *Claiborne Herald*, whose inscrutable motto was "Thou shalt not [ CONTINUED ON PAGE 37 ]

> TRAVIS AS IDEALIZED MILITARY HERO: HE WAS A FRONTIER LAWYER WHO SOUGHT A STAGE UPON WHICH TO PLAY HIS SELF-APPOINTED DESTINY.

3

# 1832 A VISIONARY GENERAL NAMED MANUEL DE MIER Y TERÁN GIVES UP HOPE FOR A MEXICAN TEXAS.

# "TEXAS IS LOST"

BY JAN REID

AS MEXICAN INSURGENTS OVER-ran Oaxaca in 1812, routed soldiers loyal to Spain holed up in a Carmelite convent protected by a moat. Twenty-three-year-old Manuel de Mier y Terán directed rebel cannon fire from the drawbridge. In a show of bravado, another young officer decided to swim the moat. The dark water was mostly mud and slime, he found out. Instead of throwing the man a rope, Mier y Terán watched from the bridge and guffawed.

In the fast careers of powerful men, small slights have lasting magnitude. Twelve years later, that day's floundering knucklehead, Guadalupe Victoria, assumed the Mexican presidency. Even he recognized the indispensable talents of Mier y Terán. He was a brilliant, loyal, educated, politically astute general, and in the violent truculence that accompanied the new republic's endless factional squabbles, any president had need of those qualities. Still, Guadalupe Victoria desired nothing but miles between himself and the inherited minister of War and Navy. Senators blocked the general's diplomatic mission to England, so in 1827 the president sent him off to survey Mexico's boundary with the United States. If there couldn't be an ocean of distance, the empty and remote province called Texas would do.

Loaded with scientific instruments and reference books, the general's caravan crossed the Rio Grande in early 1828. Mier y Terán found the military garrison in sad shape. A few hundred unsupplied soldiers hoarded rice and scavenged buffalo meat and venison. To communicate with other travelers, soldiers would kill a hawk, tie a message to its wing, and hang it in a tree. The expeditioners thought Texas was bizarre. They had never heard bullfrogs before. Illiterate frontiersmen located underground water with quivering forked sticks; the fascinated general wondered if North American scientists had explained these water witches.

Mier y Terán spent two weeks with Stephen F. Austin. Kindred spirits, they began a correspondence that remained warm even in adverse times. Austin's colonists bred mules for export to the British and French West Indies and raised astonishing crops in the Brazos River valley. The farmers told him that because of the mild winters, they could work longer in Texas and thus not so frantically and hard. They pressed him for tariff concessions, a port at Galveston, and an exemption from Mexico's revolutionary ban of slavery.

During those thirteen months he didn't exactly fall in love with Texas. The ratio of lawyers, he noted, was unseemly high. The climate nearly killed him. The feverish general couldn't believe the summer heat and ordered improved thermometers from New Orleans to verify his readings. He diligently mapped and recorded, but Spanish troops dispatched from Cuba cut the mission short when they invaded Tampico in mid-1829. The mapping would be completed three decades later by other scholarly gentlemen officers—who wore the uniforms of the United States.

The Veracruz governor, Santa Anna, took credit for the Mexican victory at Tampico and became a national figure, but military analysts give more credit to the artillery siege of Mier y Terán. Aides said he directed the cannon fire with a sword in one hand, a cup of chocolate in the other. Based in Tamaulipas, he then completed his report on Texas.

The visionary general anticipated an overpopulated Mexico with insufficient arable land. Texas, he had seen, was an agricultural bounty—and a matter of national security. Politicians in Mexico City were debating whether to let Nicaragua and Guatemala join the federation after the Spaniards' expulsion. Forget about Spain, he urged, and look north.

"The department of Texas is contiguous to the most avid nation in the world," he wrote. "The North Americans have conquered whatever territory adjoins them." If Mexico surrendered Texas, "it would degenerate from the most elevated class of the American powers to that of a contemptible mediocrity, reduced to the necessity of buying a precarious existence at the cost of many humiliations." Any Mexican citizen "who consents to and does not oppose the loss of Texas is an execrable traitor who ought to be punished with every kind of death."

He begged for more troops and influenced legislation in 1830 that restricted American immigration. Colonists on the order of Stephen F. Austin were welcome but must be outnumbered three to one. He wanted to recruit German and Swiss settlers and send Mexican convicts to Texas. Every Mexican governor was supposed to recruit 450 families for Texas; a total of one family signed up.

Mier y Terán was only 43, but the illness that began in Texas had ruined his health. Weary of his depression and a bleak life on the frontier, his wife left him and returned to Mexico City. An abrasive garrison commander at Galveston Bay drove even Austin to civil disobedience. Fighting broke out when a subordinate jailed some settlers, including William B. Travis, without charges.

Trying to quell that disorder was the last straw for Mier y Terán. "I am an unhappy man, and unhappy people should not live on this earth," he wrote a friend while staying in the village of San Antonio de Padilla. "I have studied this situation for five years, and today I know nothing, nothing, for man is very despicable and small; and—let us put an end to these reflections, for they almost drive me mad. The revolution is about to break forth, and Texas is lost."

The next morning, July 3, 1832, he put on his dress uniform and added a gay silk scarf. He spoke to a sentry, walked behind a roofless church, propped his sword against a rock, and drove it through his broken heart.✦

> HE WAS BRILLIANT, LOYAL, AND POLITICALLY ASTUTE. IN THE END, TEXAS BROKE HIS HEART.

KAREN BARBOUR

## 1700: THE COMANCHES DISCOVER HORSE POWER

In the history of early Texas, the first Comanche horse raid ranks in importance alongside the invasion of Mexico by Cortez. The acquisition of the horse changed the Comanches from inconsequential nomads into the fiercest and deadliest of the Plains Indians—a warrior tribe capable of keeping the Spanish out of the Texas interior for a century and slowing the westward advance of the frontier for half of another. Of all the feats of Comanche horsemanship, the one that most astonished eyewitnesses was "a stratagem of war, learned and practiced by every young man in the tribe, by which he is able to drop his body upon the side of the horse at the instant he is passing, effectually screened from his enemies' weapons."

—PAUL BURKA

## THERE GOES THE NEIGHBORHOOD

### 1 8 4 5

*If Texans don't think much of Yankees, well, Yankees have returned the favor. Edward Everett Hale, a leading American author of his day, was one of many Northerners who strenuously opposed the annexation of Texas. In his 1845 tract "How to Conquer Texas, Before Texas Conquers Us," Hale proposed a solution to the Texas menace that may yet win out.*

**G**ood men and true have now to labor in and on Texas, to avert the dangers of annexation. Those dangers were manifold. They included

• The introduction into the Union of an un-principled population of adventurers, with all the privileges of a State of naturalized citizens.

• The creation of an enormous State, in time to become the real Empire State of the country. Texas, with three hundred and ten thousand square miles of territory, is admitted as one State, into the Union. If she remains such, she will prove the Austria of the confederacy, to overrule all opposition.

Must it prove true, however? May not northern men—northern capitalists, northern emigrants, northern fathers and mothers, northern teachers and pupils—change this condition? May not the north pour down its hordes upon these fertile valleys, and bear civilization, and Christianity and freedom into their recesses? Northern energy has peopled and civilized southern countries heretofore—may it not again?

## DOUBLE VISION

*Lamar denounces Sam Houston.*

### 1838

Mirabeau B. Lamar, the champion of Texas nationalism, was not made for the part. Nervous and high-strung, Lamar could not even deliver his own inaugural address when he became the second president of the Republic of Texas, succeeding his arch-enemy, Sam Houston, in December 1838. The speech had to be read by his secretary.

But the message was unmistakably Lamar's.

Houston had been desperate for statehood. But Lamar had a different vision for Texas. "I cannot regard the annexation of Texas to the American Union in any other light than as the grave of all her hopes of happiness and greatness," the secretary read. Before Lamar's term was up, he had reversed almost every policy of his predecessor. Houston had favored giving the Indians legal title to land. Lamar made war on them. Houston had tried to avoid a confrontation with Mexico. Lamar sent a military expedition to Santa Fe and thought Texas should extend all the way to the Pacific. Houston had located the capital in the city that bore his name. Lamar moved it to Austin.

Ancient history? Hardly. Is Texas tied to the rest of America, or is it a place apart? Does it look east or west? Must it live by society's rules, or does it have its own code? The issues are as old as Houston and Lamar's time and as new as our own.     —PAUL BURKA

## 1836: In the Heat of Battle, Sidney Sherman Remembers the Alamo

It was first uttered as a savage cry for vengeance. For six weeks, since the fall of the Alamo, Sam Houston had been leading his rebel army in a series of feints and retreats, searching for some tactical advantage over Santa Anna's superior forces. But Houston's elegant dodges were lost on his volunteers, who found them humiliating and wanted to fight. When finally the time came for them to emerge from the live oak mottes at San Jacinto and attack the dozing Mexican encampment, they were primed with frustration and rage.

The left flank of the Texan line was commanded by a thirty-year-old Kentucky businessman who had come to Texas with 52 volunteers he had outfitted himself. Colonel Sidney Sherman was not without a sense of grandeur, but he was more direct than Houston and impatient with his commander's Zen-like strategy. When, a few hundred yards from the Mexican lines, he shouted, "Remember the Alamo!" the fury of the attackers was instantly pulled into focus.

Remembering the Alamo, the Texans were filled with slaughter. They attacked the enemy with bowie knives, tomahawks, and rifle butts, killing those who begged for mercy. Finally they did take prisoners, but treated them shamefully and left the dead Mexicans on the field to be eaten by coyotes.

As the carnage of that day receded into history and Texas became a tamer place, the phrase "Remember the Alamo" began to stand more for remembrance than for vengeance. Sidney Sherman died penniless in 1873, but he bequeathed to Texans a splendid verbal talisman. "Remember the Alamo" reminds us, when we're feeling ordinary, that somehow we have the right to feel special, even prideful, and that destiny is still on our side. —STEPHEN HARRIGAN

## LAST REQUEST

**"Discharge your doubts," a dying Moses Austin commands his son.**

**1821** Moses Austin knew that he was dying. He called his wife to his bedside and, as Maria Austin later wrote her son Stephen, made "a considerable exertion to speak." His message was directed to Stephen, and it had but a single thought: that his son should carry out Moses' plan to colonize the province of northern Mexico known as Texas. "He called me to his bed side and with much distress and difficulty of speech, beged me to tell you to take his place," Maria wrote to her son. "He prayed [God] to extend his goodness to you and enable you to go on with the business in the same way he would have done."

Stephen took his father's death hard, but he was reluctant to commit himself to carrying on the work. Twenty days before Moses died, he had written his son about his plan to bring three hundred American families to Texas, as well as his own, and had admonished Stephen to "discharge your doubts." Now, from beyond the grave, he insisted once more. Finally, Stephen could not find it in himself to disobey his father's last request. By that November he had picked out the land between the Colorado and the Brazos for his colony, and the first settlers were arriving.

Possessing special qualities that Moses Austin lacked, Stephen was far better equipped than his father to act as impresario. Good schooling in Connecticut and Kentucky had honed the social skills so essential to dealing with Spanish and Mexican officials. His experience as a territorial legislator and judge on the Missouri frontier had produced political skills, tact, and flexibility that enabled him to govern his colonists. Most important, Stephen F. Austin was interested in far more than merely selling land. To his father's ambition of recapturing the family's lost financial status, which had fallen in the panic of 1819, the son added a vision of building a new civilization out of the wilderness.
—ROBIN DOUGHTY

C. F. PAYNE

# 1845 TEXAS JOINS THE UNION BUT WISELY REMAINS SOVEREIGN OF ITS VAST PUBLIC LANDS.

# PRIVATE PROPERTY

## BY T. R. FEHRENBACH

PEOPLE FROM OTHER parts are sometimes surprised to learn that there are no public lands in Texas. That has disgruntled many a deer hunter moved here from Western states, and it has endangered a few Yankees and others who never learned to respect fences or to understand that almost every inch of Texas is private property.

Because Texas entered the Union as a sovereign nation, the only state to do so, it retained title to all unappropriated lands within its borders under the terms of annexation. The feds got nothing; everything they have got since they bought, like Fort Hood, or had donated to them, like Big Bend National Park. Meanwhile, Texas disposed of all that property, once half the state, keeping almost nothing for itself, so that now it faces the same problem as Washington when it wants a piece of ground for public purposes. That seemingly minor historical fact has had vast economic, political, and social effects upon modern Texas.

To begin with, the western portions of Texas developed differently from similar regions in the western United States. If all that land had come under the federal Homestead Act or had remained under the control of Washington until today, there would be no Permian Basin oil royalties puffing up the Texas school funds, Texas government would have been far poorer, and we probably would not have a state capitol slightly taller than the national one. And Austin would today be totally embroiled in the sagebrush rebellion flaring in western states like Nevada, where the federal government owns 86 per cent of the land, or Utah (64 per cent), fighting over federal restrictions, reclamation, and land use, while West Texas would not have emerged with its aura of vast private

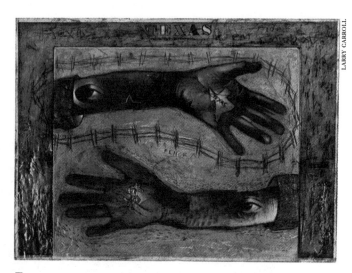

TEXAS KEPT ITS PUBLIC LANDS; THE FEDS KEPT THEIR HANDS OFF.

landed empires. The ramifications are endless. However, perhaps equally important to the development of our state, Texas' experience with public lands played a large role in the emergence of modern Texan attitudes toward private right and private property.

The Texas experience is unique among the states. At the beginning of modern history–the Anglo colonization –Mexico granted generous portions of land to immigrants on far better terms– in effect, free–than the United States government has ever sold or granted its own public domain to American citizens. At the start, most people came to Texas for one purpose: to acquire landed property, and if they could cut it on this raw, still-dangerous frontier, they prospered.

Although the policy backfired strategically for Mexico, it fostered colonization so excellently that the new republic continued it. With a conscious goal of creating a Jeffersonian society of freeholders, the Republic instituted the famous headrights, an entitlement program that assured every head or potential head of a family willing to live in Texas a substantial piece of ground. The state kept up the practice, one way or another, both

before and following the Civil War, though it soon ran out of good, wellwatered lands in the east. No government elsewhere equaled it; the heralded federal Homestead Act of the 1860's, still in effect, was much more niggling and bound up with hedges and restrictions.

As late as 1876 Texas still owned 61 million acres, mostly in the west, as well as 20 million acres set aside as school lands, earmarked to foster public education. There had been problems giving it away– the Indians disputed title and still held possession, and no one knew how to develop this country in an orderly fashion. But with the coming of the cattle kingdom and, soon thereafter, barbed wire and windmills, there were plenty of buyers, from pioneer cattleman Charles Goodnight, with his eye on Palo Duro Canyon, to scores of investors from Chicago to the British Isles. And Texans were eager to dispose of everything. Texas had always traded land for people; it was land poor, and there was no notion of saving land as a public patrimony. That idea even went against the Texan grain; history had already created a Texas orientation toward private landed property and every owner's right to do with it as he pleased.

So the land went fast, at prices from 25 cents to $1 per acre. The XIT deal, trading 3.05 million acres to a British cattle syndicate to finance construction of the state capitol, is the most famous, but there were many such grants, among them the Spur, Hanford, and Matador transactions. They did arouse opposition, not to the sale itself but to the sale in large blocks, thus "creating principalities, pashalics, and baronates among a few capitalists."

The state government, with its East

Texas orientation, tried to prevent big ranchers from buying the school lands, believing the cry of one farm child more civilizing on the prairie than the "bleating of ten thousand calves." It didn't work. Cattlemen still acquired the land, through agents, fraud, perjury, and misrepresentation that often delayed clear titles for decades. Still, they got it; ecology if not the law was on their side. Ideology aside, the small family farm couldn't last in the arid country beyond the 100th meridian.

Nesters were no problem on the Texas plains; the real range wars were between two sets of cowmen. The first were the old hands who simply appropriated former Comanche range without bothering to seek title. The second bought up the range and fenced the pioneers out. That led to an epidemic of shootings and fence-cutting, quelled with great difficulty in the 1880's. Again, the big ranchers won, this time with the law on their side. So the business of consolidation and the making of principalities and baronates went on apace.

The real developers of western Texas saw ranching not as a way of life but as a business. They felt no regret at the passing of roundups and trail drives. They helped bring rails in; they sold sections for townsites; they even took up farming when irrigation and power machinery made it feasible to plow the plains.

For better or worse, West Texas land development went faster and was more profitable than it would have been had Texas' public domain fallen to the federal government. Had Texas followed the usual Western pattern, few if any great farms would have sprouted while politicians tried to reserve the land for a mythical yeoman class of family farmers—impossible in the water-starved West. Today vast stretches of Texas would still be federal lands, leased by grousing cattlemen or goat ranchers.

And the nature of the disposal of public lands, concurrent with wire fencing, enhanced the strong bias toward private domain in the Texas ethos. Ranchers still had to fight for their empires—clearing titles took years, and meanwhile, property had to be guarded and patrolled. The sense of empire, or private kingdoms, took deeper root, affecting not just owners but the whole society itself.

Soon, to cross a fence line broke the code, if not of the West at least of most of Texas. And what a man did behind his own fences was his business. That ethos, not frontier but immediate-postfrontier bred, is still one of the strongest in Texas. And the feeling for property rights has forged the strongest laws against trespass in the nation.

Unlike the public lands of the United States, the public lands of Texas are long gone. But the influences of that history will probably be around for another century. ♣

# So Long, Little Dogies

BY LARRY MCMURTRY

## 1890 THE ERA OF THE GREAT TRAIL DRIVES ENDS.

THE IMPORTANCE OF THE TRAIL drives, vast enough commercially, was no less vast psychologically. In Texas in the last half of the nineteenth century, cattle were what oil was to become in the first half of the twentieth: a seemingly infinite resource that quickly bred not merely fortunes but also imagery and identity—though in the realm of the image, oil has never been able to compete with cattle, one reason so many oilmen become cattlemen manqué. Within ten years of its inception, the cattle trade had established an appealing and enduring body of imagery and provided Texans as a people with the reputation for dash and extravagance that they cherish to this day.

Before cattle began to spill out of Texas, what were we, to the nation? Commercially, a minor adjunct to the Cotton Kingdom; politically and psychologically, the American equivalent of the Balkans. The violent animosities that Serbs and Croatians took centuries to refine were, like so much else, spontaneous developments in Texas. Freebooters had only to arrive within our much-disputed borders to become patriots and freedom fighters;

> THEIR HISTORY WAS BRIEF, BUT THE TRAIL DRIVES LIVE FOREVER IN THE MYTHS OF THE COWBOY AND THE BOUNDLESS WEST.

they swarmed in like Turks and quickly wrenched the whole state loose from the Indians and the Mexicans.

When the dust of what was, comparatively, a short conflict settled, it was found that cattle were swarming even more prodigally than freebooters in the southern part of what had become the state of Texas.

One of the marvels of American commerce is the rapidity with which certain industries mature. Computers provide an example from our own day: the home-computer business became the behemoth that it is in less time than it takes to wear out a good adding machine. Technologically, the oil business had a fairly slow gestation, but its myth—by which I mean its power to seize and hold the public's imagination—was established in an afternoon, at Spindletop. Wells are rarely allowed to gush nowadays, but the image of the gusher is still the most potent the oil industry has produced; its undiminished power can be seen in the recent Russian film *Siberiade,* whose final sequence recalls *Boom Town* and many other movies on the same subject.

The cattle trade flowered no less sud-denly. No one knows how many cattle ran free in South Texas at the time of annexation, but by the 1860's their numbers had swelled to between three and four million—a free resource, waiting to be exploited.

Despite that extraordinary abundance of product, the beginnings of trail driving as a marketing practice were casual and intermittent. Markets existed, and the early cattlemen knew it. But the markets

were very far away, and the routes to them rich in hazard. The arrival of either beasts or masters could not be guaranteed. Nonetheless, a few proto-Texans made drives in the 1840's; one or two headed for Illinois, but the more reachable markets then were New Orleans and Mobile. Mosquitoes lay thick along the Gulf trails, and many coastal cattlemen preferred to ship from Matagorda Bay rather than drive overland; "ship-

ping" is a term still in use in the cattle business, though what it usually describes nowadays is the movement of cattle by truck from pasture to feedlot.

Certain early drovers, keen for profit, considered no market on the continent beyond the reach of their beeves. Tom Candy Ponting and Washington Malone drove a herd of Longhorns to Muncie, Indiana, where boxcars were secured. In 1854 the cattle were taken to Manhat-

tan, driven through the streets, and sold at the Hundred Street Market. New Yorkers, unflappable even then, seemed to regard the presence of Texas Longhorns in their boulevards as nothing to get excited about.

More remarkable still were the first drives to California. As soon as word of the Gold Rush reached Texas, a man named W. H. Snyder, excited by the thought of all [ CONTINUED ON PAGE 38 ]

11

# 1950 BEFORE THE END OF TEXAS' LONGEST DROUTH, A GENERATION IS FORCED OFF THE LAND.

# BONE DRY

## BY ELMER KELTON

IN 1947, A YEAR AFTER I RETURNED home from World War II, my father lost his Crane County ranch lease. Like me, the owner's sons had come back from service and understandably wanted to ranch the place themselves. Unable to find another suitable lease nearby, my father reluctantly sold his cattle. He felt that luck had turned against him.

Sometimes we know not what we pray for. That ranch turned desperately dry soon after he vacated it, and ten years were to pass before enough rain fell to grow good grass again.

Most people consider that the longest Texas drouth within living memory began in 1950 or 1951, but ranchmen in some areas along the Pecos River and to the south in Mexico had full use of it at least three years earlier. Accustomed to protracted periods of cloud failure, they were several years in admitting they had a full-fledged drouth on their hands, not just another dry spell. The word "drouth" is used with respect in West Texas and not lightly conferred. Not until thin and dirt-cheap Eisenhower calves were following Harry Truman cows to the dusty feed grounds every day did ranchers concede that this one might be in a league with those rock dehydrators the garrulous old men on whittle-and-spit benches kept talking about.

When I was a kid on the McElroy Ranch in Upton and Crane counties, the 1918 drouth was the benchmark against which all others were measured and found wanting. Now a later generation of oldtimers tells my grandchildren about the fifties and relates the story with awe.

It *was* awesome, and in many respects it marked a turning point for Texas ranches and farms. Old ways, taken for granted since the settling of the country, failed in the face of that unprecedented challenge, and those operators who survived were forced to innovations sometimes simple, sometimes bizarre.

I remember a year when dryland fields around San Angelo made what the farmers called bumblebee cotton, stalks about a foot tall and just a few stunted bolls to each one. Migrant Hispanic pickers from the lower Valley took one look at the miserable crop and pulled out for the irrigated plains. Some farmers improvised sledlike strippers to salvage what they could. The Eggemeyer family just north of town salvaged theirs with a long wooden ladder dragged behind a pickup. While the father drove down the rows as slowly as the engine would allow, his wife and children sat on the ladder and pulled bolls as they passed.

Much of the rangeland west of San Angelo is dominated by tobosa grass, palatable to livestock when green and succulent but dry as old bedstraw once it matures. Hoping to entice cattle to eat it, an Ozona ranchman sprayed water-thinned molasses over a tobosa flat, all but ruining a sprayer. The cattle just licked the sweet molasses from the grass.

Drouth in Texas terms did not mean a total absence of rain; it simply meant that the effects of one rain did not carry forward to the next. On the land, men gave full rein to their ingenuity, trying to catch and hold whatever rain did fall. Ranchers who had never had a plow on the place pitted and chiseled rangeland, trying to coax some response from whatever grass roots still clung to life. Farmers who had resisted the contours and terraces first popularized during the thirties' Dust Bowl days finally signed up with their local soil conservation district. Ranchers grasped at every new miracle grass that came along, especially those from the desert areas of Mexico or Africa. Most failed. They just *thought* they had come from a desert.

Faith and hope were both curse and salvation. Because of them, many people clung to herds too large too long, trusting that rain would come tomorrow or next month or next spring, because it always had. Farmers wasted high-priced seed in powdered ground, partly because of faith and partly because of foolish federal regulations that for years forced them to plant or lose the historic base upon which their acreage allotments were calculated.

Ownership of cattle has always been considered prestigious in Texas, but that prestige carried a price tag heavy as a millstone for most of the drouth years. Sheep were better, but not a lot. The only animal that more than paid its way was the much-maligned goat. As cowboy cartoonist Ace Reid once said, a goat could live on nothing and a man could live on goat. Angora goats bought and paid for millions of dollars' worth of cattle and sheep feed and never got a bite of it.

During those long years—seven for a major part of West Texas, fewer for other areas of the state—I was an agricultural reporter for the *San Angelo Standard-Times,* watching friends and relatives fight their long war a day at a time. Many took outside jobs, as did their wives, trying desperately to stay. The times were harder on lessees than on landowners because they had no land equity to fall back upon. Even some landowners, those fortunate enough to live where the derricks grew, were saved only by oil and gas royalties. I shared their sorrow as one rancher or farmer after another played out his string and left the land, especially young war veterans who had not had time to root down, just as today's farm crisis is wiping out so many young families unable to build a solid equity. I watched stockmen build feed debts of $25 and $30 on ewes that would not sell for $15. Few lenders foreclosed; they could not afford to swallow the loss. Like the rancher and the farmer, they had to bet on the future.

I wondered sometimes why anybody stayed, knowing that in their place I probably would not. But the answer must have been in an inherited pioneer

> HOPE WAS CURSE AND SALVATION FOR WEST TEXAS FARMERS. THEY TRUSTED THAT RAIN WOULD COME BECAUSE IT ALWAYS HAD.

spirit, sturdy and resilient, and a stubborn sense of humor that let them laugh when it would have been easier to cry. They took strength from classic jokes, some on the dark side, like the one about how when Noah built his ark and it rained for forty days and nights, Texas got half an inch.

In January 1957 President Eisenhower came to view the drouth situation. I watched him tear his fine camel-hair coat on Earl Byrd's barbed-wire fence. But the president promised to do something. By March a fine Republican rain was fall-ing. It rained all spring, all summer, all fall. Even Democrats made a good crop, though some lost much of it because they couldn't get it out of muddy fields. Where ranchers had been sure all the roots were dead, grass came up in good solid stands. Everything seemed on its way back to normal.

But not really. Much would never be the same. Many people were gone and would never be back. Those who remained tended to operate larger tracts than before because commodity prices and lower livestock carrying capacity dictated that they get larger or get out. They had learned bitter but lasting lessons about the limitations of the land, the grass, the water. They had learned about cropping to stretch the moisture. They had learned about rotation grazing and stocking within the capabilities of the range. Because the fifties drouth taught them of the land's fragility, most Texas farmers and ranchers are better caretakers than before. It was a war of attrition, and like a war it taught them that they were tougher than they knew.❧

13

# WHEN MYTHS COLLIDE

### BY DON GRAHAM

EDNA FERBER, CASTING ABOUT for a suitable title for her novel about Texas, settled on what seemed inevitable: *Giant*. Though Texans hated the book—too exaggerated, too muckraking, they said—they loved the George Stevens film, released in 1956. And why not? *Giant* gave Texans —long insecure, long self-victimized by a colonial mentality—a consoling secular myth that emphasized everything good about Texas and suggested that everything bad was fixable; it would just take time. Yes, about a hundred years, said Leslie Benedict, wife of *Giant*'s empire builder, Bick Benedict.

The cattle empire story was irresistible to local and national audiences. Cotton and timber had once been kings in Texas, too, but neither of those ways of life held the glamour and romance of the cattle trade. For Texas historians and moviemakers alike, real Texas was cowboys, vast ranches, and pastoral beatitudes. *Giant* repackaged and updated the myth, bringing *Red River* into the twentieth century, where the old beloved ranching tradition was pitted against a newer, rawer Texas myth: oil.

*Giant* set up a simple equation. The cattleman, because he worked with living creatures and had roots in the land and the primal Texas frontier experience, was good; the oilman, because he succeeded as much on luck as hard work, was bad. The cattleman was a member of the landed aristocracy, while the oilman was an insolent upstart without family, breeding, or attainments. Bick Benedict has class, and what he doesn't already possess as nature's nobleman, he acquires by marrying the fairest flower of Old South gentility, plucky Leslie Lynnton of Maryland.

Bick's adversary, Jett Rink, is a threat to the movie's official ideology in more ways than one. The hungry young wildcatter, in a consummate performance by James Dean, nearly steals the movie, and the morality, out from under Bick and the cattle barons. (Dean is so right in this role that it comes as a shock to

DEAN, NEWMAN: THEIR MOVIES PROVED THAT THE OLD-TIME CATTLEMAN WAS FINISHED.

learn, from Stevens' papers, that Frank Sinatra was a contender for the part.) Jett is a have-not, and the haves are mighty smug about what they've got. When Bick and his good-ol'-boy associates try to sugar-talk Jett into selling them the little shirttail piece of ground willed him by Bick's ornery sister, Jett reads their intentions right down to the last iota of power and greed and brushes them off with that little sliding motion of his hand that every- **[ CONTINUED ON PAGE 40 ]**

## 1933
# KING'S RANSOM

### OIL SAVES THE KING RANCH.

One of the abiding notions of Texas folklore is that ranchers greeted the arrival of the oil age with hostility. Ranchers, the myth holds, lived in a pure association with the land, which was forever defiled when the drilling began. Hostility there may have been, but the truth is that ranching was saved by oil. The King Ranch is the most striking case in point. In 1933 the great ranch was in danger of being broken up and sold. It was more than $3 million in debt, a hopelessly large burden considering that even in its best years the cattle operations seldom cleared more than $200,000. Instead of resisting the oilmen, as Bick Benedict had in *Giant,* ranch patriarch Bob Kleberg sought them out—at first, to no avail; Gulf, Shell, and Texaco turned him down. Finally Humble said yes. In exchange for a loan to pay off the ranch's debts, Humble received what was then the largest oil and gas lease in the country. Humble did nothing but explore the ranch for six years; for another six it drilled only near fields adjacent to the ranch. In 1945 Humble risked a wildcat well. It came in. Within eight years, so did 649 more. Oil not only saved the King Ranch; it made it richer by far than it had ever been. —PAUL BURKA

## THE OPEN RANGE
# R.I.P.
## 1866–1884

AUSTIN, JANUARY 31, 1884. THE Open Range died here today after a brief life of less than twenty years, far from the Staked Plains where it was born. It had been in ill health ever since the introduction of barbed wire in 1876. Death was attributed to a law, enacted here today by the Texas Legislature, that made fence-cutting a felony.

As befitted its rugged reputation, the decedent had made a valiant fight for survival. When wealthy cattlemen fenced off pastures and water—cutting off schools, churches, even the seat of Archer County in the process—the free-grassers, who couldn't afford fences, let alone land, brought out the wire cutters. The chaos was front-page news as far away as Chicago: HELL BREAKS LOOSE IN TEXAS! the headline read. WIRE-CUTTERS DESTROY 500 MILES OF FENCE IN COLEMAN COUNTY. But the patient never had a chance to recover in Austin, where the Legislature was dominated by unsympathetic East Texas farmers. Even concealment of wire cutters was made a crime.

The Open Range is survived by the sanctity of property rights, the concept that a man crosses another man's fence at his peril, and also by the most powerful of all the Texas myths. —PAUL BURKA

# RANGE WARRIOR
## 1902: Cattlemen hire a gunslinger.

WESTERN HISTORY COLLECTION/UNIVERSITY OF OKLAHOMA

*A gunslinger's fate: Killin' Jim Miller (left) ends up on the wrong end of the rope.*

The High Plains was still grazing land in 1902, the year cattlemen paid Killin' Jim Miller $500 to assassinate the nesters' mouthpiece, James Jarrott. The murder was supposed to put the fear of God in the nesters and send them back where they had come from. But it didn't work out that way.

Twenty-five families had crossed the plains in covered wagons in the winter of '02. Despite cattlemen's threats of a range war, they began buying state-owned land that had previously been leased to ranchers along a strip of grassland extending from just west of Lubbock to the state line. Jarrott, a former legislator who was acting as their agent and lawyer, had successfully defended the nesters' claim in several lawsuits. The patience of the cowmen was about exhausted. They had taken the plains from the Indians and considered it morally if not legally their property forever. That's when they decided to practice a little six-gun justice.

The cowmen hired Miller, a onetime Texas Ranger turned prolific professional killer. More a bushwhacker than a gunfighter, he preferred to shoot his victims in the back. That was how he supposedly nailed Pat Garrett. As was his style, Miller waited behind a windmill tower and, when Jarrott stopped to water his team of horses, pumped the lawyer full of lead. It took five shots to kill Jarrott. "He was the hardest man to kill I ever shot," Miller admitted later.

After gunning down at least a dozen people, Miller ran out of luck in 1909 when he was lynched along with three Oklahoma cowmen who had commissioned him to kill a rival. The cattlemen who financed the murder of James Jarrott didn't fare much better. Jarrott became a martyr, and the nesters became some of Lubbock's richest and most respected pioneers. —GARY CARTWRIGHT

# BARBED WIRE MAKES ITS POINT

DOUG SMITH

J. W. GATES

John Gates had a problem. Though San Antonio was a trade center for cattlemen all over Texas in the 1870's, the 21-year-old barbed-wire salesman from Illinois couldn't find any customers in town. Barbed wire would make "the finest fence in the world," he told the cattlemen who arrived with their great herds of Longhorns to buy supplies for the trail drive to Kansas. It was "light as air," "stronger than whiskey," "cheaper than dirt."

To the suspicious cattlemen, barbed wire looked like something dreamed up by a Yankee inventor who had never seen real live cattle. Finally, Gates took the kind of chance that later in his life would earn him the nickname "Bet-a-Million." He talked city officials into letting him build a corral in Military Plaza—and made them keep his purpose a secret. On the afternoon that his corral was finished, Gates challenged cattlemen to bring their

## 1876

steers inside, where he would prove that "the cattle ain't born that can get through."

After a crowd gathered, the cattle were driven in. Immediately they charged the wire. But after getting pricked by the barbs, they retreated. They charged again. And again and again. The fence held. At last the steers backed off, bellowing in frustration from the center of the corral. That night, it is said, Gates couldn't fill orders fast enough.

On the plains and prairies of Texas, where wood and stone were not available for fencing, men had let their cattle roam free. But barbed wire gave cattlemen a reason to buy land: they could protect their water holes and their grasslands. In 1876, the year of Gates's demonstration, fewer than 3 million pounds of wire were sold in the entire country. The next year the figure rose to almost 13 million. By 1880 it was over 80 million, and the open range was doomed.

—CATHERINE CHADWICK

## "WHERE THE LAMBS COME DOWN TO THE SLAUGHTER"
### 1919

*Speculators hawk the High Plains.*

The first reliable irrigation pump, installed on the High Plains in 1910, was the most important invention in West Texas since barbed wire. It turned the Panhandle from ranch country into farm country and, by luring cotton from the tenant farms of East Texas to the Llano Estacado, weaned Texas from Dixie. It also touched off an orgy of land speculation, much to the bemusement of one E. J. Palmer of St. Louis, who was inspired by the arid landscape to write these verses while on a train near Amarillo.

### Texas

*Oh, a thirsty land of dust and sand*
*Is the Panhandle Plains of Texas*
*Where the coyotes howl and the*
*    panthers prowl*
*And the rattlesnakes strike and*
*    vex us!*
*And the people are strange who*
*    ride the range—*
*For they went to the legislature*
*And voted the towns all "dry" by law*
*Tho the rivers were dry by nature.*

*Oh, the wonderful size of the*
*    enterprise*
*Of the State and the folks of Texas;*
*Tho how they contrive to live and*
*    thrive*
*On the desert may perplex us!*
*For little they raise but milo maize*
*And cattle and cain and sand;*
*But when the grass is dry and the*
*    cows all die*
*They live by selling the land.*

*The land sharks bask in dusty*
*    pools*
*Where the lambs come down to*
*    the slaughter;*
*And they tell 'em the cows dried up*
*    on the range*
*Were drowned in the last high*
*    water.*
*'Tis the breeding place of a strong*
*    fit race*
*For the strenuous life that waits*
*    them*
*With their long-horned steers thru*
*    the long dry years*
*And the "dry" long-whiskered*
*    statesmen.*

# A Panhandle Farmer Runs Out of Water

## 1960

When the water first arrived, it seemed endless. The ancient sand and gravel beds of the Ogallala Aquifer stretched from the Texas High Plains to the Dakotas, often just a hundred feet beneath the surface. Some believed it was an underground river replenished every year by runoff from the Rocky Mountains. Local legend told of eyeless fish sucked up by pumps from the dark subterranean waterways. By the end of the fifties, when irrigated farming on the Texas High Plains was approaching its zenith, 3.6 million Panhandle acres were producing nearly a fifth of the nation's cotton.

But all was not well with the wells; the Ogallala was beginning to run dry. S. R. "Pockets" Heard of Petersburg was one of the first to notice the change. Pockets Heard drilled the first well on his Hale County farm in 1934. His water was drawn from crevices on the edge of the aquifer, near the Caprock. When one crevice ran dry, he had to find another. In the early sixties, wells that had once filled his ditches to overflowing began to peter out. He deep-

*For Pockets Heard of Petersburg, the water that had once seemed endless didn't last.*

ened the shafts, to no avail. There was enough water for spring irrigation, but in the dog days of summer he would hear his well motors speed up as they lost suction and began to pump air instead of water. "There was nothing to do but turn 'em off, go home, and kick the cat," he recalls. Today his wells pump scarcely 10 per cent of the water they delivered back in the fifties, and Heard is once again, for all intents and purposes, a dryland farmer—a fate that sooner or later will befall the rest of the farmers on the High Plains.

—FRYAR CALHOUN

## HOME ON THE RANGE

### A CITY BOY BUYS A RANCH.

**1981** On October 1, 1981, Andy Lear bought a ranch. It was small, as Texas spreads go—a mere 310 acres—but that was all right. What he loved about the property was how much it looked the way he had always imagined a Texas ranch should look. And oh, yes, he liked the location. Brenham, in Washington County, was less than two hours from downtown Houston. That was important because he lived in downtown Houston and had no intention of moving.

Andy Lear, to be blunt, was a city boy. So why did he, a successful urban developer at age 37, feel so compelled to buy a ranch? He shrugs and smiles. "When I first got here from the East"—he was born in Connecticut and educated at Yale and Harvard Business School—"I figured I would make a bunch of money and leave. But the longer I stayed, the more I liked it here, and somehow, I acquired a certain acculturation, I guess you could call it. It got so that I really, really wanted to buy a ranch. I just did. I can't explain it exactly."

Who can? Is there any instinct more primal than the desire of every Texan to have a little plot of land he can call his own? No doubt the urge is rooted in frontier days, yet it remains strong today, even as Texas has become citified. For city boys, buying a piece of Texas is a way of reclaiming (or acquiring) their essential Texanness. Lear is not the first city boy to buy a ranch, or the most famous. What he is, when he jumps in his Mercedes every Friday night and heads for his ranch, is thoroughly representative. "Hell, ninety per cent of Washington County is owned by Houstonians," says Andy Lear, Texas rancher.

—JOSEPH NOCERA

## THE GREAT DIVIDE

### 1921

Before his death in 1919, Christopher Columbus Slaughter controlled more acres than any individual Texas rancher before or since—at one time, 1.4 million acres, more than half again the size of today's King Ranch. His holdings stretched from near Big Spring to beyond Plainview and as far west as the New Mexico line. His legacy, he wrote his son, was a spread "undivided and indivisible until the death of the last one in my family." But the age of the cattle baron was at an end. The 3-million-acre XIT had been sold in pieces; Charles Goodnight, old and broke, had lost his empire; the lease laws favored the farmer over the rancher. Within a year of Slaughter's death, his children had run the ranches into debt and were quarreling among themselves. In 1921 his widow and nine children drew from ten lots in a hat, representing equal shares of the empire, and the spread "undivided and indivisible" was no more.

—PAUL BURKA

17

# WHERE THE BUFFALO ROAMED

BY ALAN TENNANT

THEY WERE JUST TOO big—too big and vulnerable and bawling loud to live even on the edge of the white man's world. By the 1870's the last of the southern bison herd was gone, just as the first Panhandle ranchers were staking out their enormous spreads. Charles Goodnight had seen the herds that stretched from horizon to horizon, though, as a Ranger scout during the Civil War, and he rounded up the last four calves on the Llano Estacado in the summer of '78.

The Plains Comanche went out about the same time, grown so weak by the days of their final raids that even a confederation of Comanche, Kiowa, and Cheyenne was unable to defeat a heavily armed troop of hide hunters at Adobe Walls on the Canadian River. By the turn of the century, both Indians and buffalo were historical curiosities in Northwest Texas.

The Goodnight bison, periodically crossbred with Herefords to produce Cattalo, had thrived, however, and by the onset of World War I numbered around two hundred, a tenth of the continent's remaining population. Then myth entered the story and, as it's supposed to do, for once distilled from the facts a deeper truth.

John Graves isn't sure when he first heard the legend of the last buffalo hunt, but what matters is that he wrote it down, and he did it with enough truth to make it part of our heritage. In *The Last Running* old Tom Bird, weakened by a failing liver "speaking loudly now of

THE INDIAN AND THE BUFFALO WERE REAL. BUT "THE LAST BUFFALO HUNT" WAS A POIGNANT FAKE.

long-gone years of drinking at plains mudholes and Kansas saloons," clumps irascibly out onto his porch to find nine braves, one of whom, Starlight, carries the half-century-old scar of Bird's musket ball. For a long time the Comanches under Starlight look at the buffalo, "studying the cows and the one calf and . . . old Shakespeare, who had

killed a horse once and had put innumerable men up mesquite trees and over fences." Then they demand one of Bird's animals to run in the old way.

Because Bird and Starlight share the understanding of lifelong foes—besides his scar the Indian carries the recollection of having faced down Bird on an early trail drive through Comanche territory

18

—the rancher cuts loose his big bull before the Indians' ponies. Finally one of the braves pulls ahead and, "with the long bubbling shriek . . . which deadly exultant men on horseback have likely shrieked since the Assyrians and long, long before," jams his lance just behind the buffalo's ribs. "The bull skidded to his knees, coughed, and rolled onto his side." Then "they rode off down the road toward Oklahoma, past the fences of barbed steel that would flank them all the way."

The actual running of the bison that occurred in Armstrong County in the fall of 1916 didn't have anywhere near as clean a conclusion, but it spelled the end of the West with even greater finality. The Last Buffalo Hunt, as it was billed by both the *Childress Index* and the *Panhandle Herald,* was an ersatz Western extravaganza staged for 11,000 of Charlie Goodnight's guests, whose 1462 automobiles—guarded by riflemen in case the buffalo went astray—ringed his front pasture. There a four-year-old cow that had been kept in a pen behind the house was pursued, on saddled ranch ponies, by four reservation Kiowas in cowboy getup, followed by a back-up gunner with a .30-30 and a Model T carrying a newsreel crew. After a ten-minute chase the Kiowas brought down the cow—an event reckoned to be such a sight that Goodnight staged it again for a commercial movie called *Old Texas.* Three years later the spectacle was reenacted as part of a ranch-warming gala hosted by W. J. McCalister, an oilman who had bought the Goodnight place. This time the hunt was merely a sideshow, along with buffalo riding and Indian war dancing, that culminated in an elaborate scramble after a young bull bison by one of the original Kiowas and flying ace W. P. Erwin in his taxiing biplane, flanked by a phalanx of mounted cowboys and an automobile caravan filled with newsmen and photographers.

Even in 1919 Panhandle ranchers seemed close to the frontier, as near in time as we are to World War II, with as many veterans—trail drivers and Indian fighters—still on the scene. But those cowmen and reporters and filmmakers were as far removed from the old ways as death is from recent life, for once the livid coal of wildness is snuffed out, in an animal or a way of life, it is gone for good. To many of those at the buffalo carnivals, the world of the wild High Plains—Graves's chief calls it liberty ("Liberty was grass, and wind, and a horse, and meat to hunt, and no wire")—was still a recent memory, but a memory of a cosmos they could not, even then, reach back and touch themselves or, except in wild West parody, pass on to their younger kin.

"Damn you, boy," Tom Bird fumes to his city-bred nephew at the end of Graves's tale. "Damn you for not ever getting to know anything worth knowing. Damn me, too. We had a world, once." ♣

# 1936 OVERGRAZING AND DROUTH PRODUCE THE TERRIBLE ORDEAL OF THE DUST BOWL.

# THE EXHAUSTED LAND

## BY JOHN GRAVES

A REGION'S DECLINE from virgin status is generally a gradual and subtle process, so that even people who have witnessed great alteration in their personal landscapes may often be unable to say just when specific changes took place—when the wolves or the antelopes ceased to exist, say, or when the creek quit running all year round, or when mesquite took over the pastures. But there can be moments of crux, more or less, when human activities and natural forces combine to implement change, or sometimes just to commemorate change that has become inevitable.

In terms of the Texas landscape, insofar as its breadth and its varied nature will let us see it as a unit, I think there have been two main moments of that sort in the past century and a half. The first one, the ranching crisis of 1886, came about when a period of reckless overgrazing was followed by drouth and severe winter weather, and it rather definitively underlined the collapse of the open-range cattle industry hereabouts, the demise of that ebullient frontier Texas that "grew from hide and horn." But the second crux, in my opinion, had a great deal more significance. It can be centered handily at just about the state's centennial year of 1936, a time when catastrophic drouth, a hundred years or so of casually brutal use of the land, and a worldwide depression merged to create the horror of the Dust Bowl. Texas didn't face those things alone, of course, but did face them fully. In that short, miserable era both the condition of the

VISITORS WAXED LYRICAL ABOUT THE LAND IN GOOD TIMES, ESPECIALLY IF THEY WERE CATTLEMINDED.

land and the lives of the people on it reached an all-time low point, and from low points come realization, new direction, and maybe even improvement.

By and large, civilization is rough on countryside, and civilization of one sort or another has been around Texas long enough that it is not possible now to know precisely what things were like in primitive times. You can work up an argument in certain circles, for instance, about whether the brush country southward from San Antonio had been a thickly grassed oak-and-mesquite savannah

before Spanish and Mexican ranchers reached it with their beasts, or just the scrub-infested expanse that Anglos found when they got there. Such fleeting glimpses as we can get of virgin Texas by no means show us a uniformly idyllic region. The climate with its well-known extremes was much the same as at present. Drouths stalked the future state's central and western reaches periodically, enforcing nomadism and frugal living patterns on Indians and wild beasts alike, and were broken by unreasonable torrents of rain. Huge winds scoured the land, and the hot sun baked it. Individual rivers might run muddy much of the time, carry big loads of natural pollutants like salt and alkali, or fail to flow in dry spells. Certain areas were steamy and malarial, while others were desert. All of which is to say that Texas was Texas, even then.

It did all *work* much better, though, in part because the vegetation and the animals and men of these parts had over long time adapted themselves to the way things were, but chiefly because the country as a whole had immense resilience, springing back to productivity after drouths, storms, prairie fires, or bitter winters with a swift healthy vigor that much of it no longer possesses. In sections where climatic extremes were less common—the East Texas woods, the tall-grassed blackland prairies, the humid upper coast, and so on—descriptions of the land in average times that have come down to us from civilized frontiersmen do often have an idyllic glow. Even westward, where dwindling rainfall nourished ever shorter grasses and runtier trees, if any trees at all, early visitors who saw the land in good seasons could sometimes wax lyrical about it, especially if they were cattle-minded. Tom Lea's finest book takes its title from an epigraph passage that he found in the reminiscences of an old-time Ranger named Gillett: "Oh, how I wish I had the power to describe the wonderful country as I saw it then."

Most of the wonderful country west of the solid forests was in grass, and the main reason for its resilience was its enduring sod rooted in topsoil laid down by ancestral grasses. That humus-laden soil held mineral richness and held water too, doling it out to the grass's roots for new growth and to branches and creeks and rivers in all but the worst of drouths, when the sod would go to sleep, still alive, waiting for rain to wake it to new growth. Fibrous and spongy and mat-covered, the soil could not wash or blow badly, and though the wild ruminants of the region ate the turf down to stubble from time to time, they moved along elsewhere before doing lasting damage to its crowns and roots. Even in rain-scant places where streams had always been intermittent, many of them still had good holes of water in the driest of times, and in my battered, hilly part of North Central Texas I can show you dry stony washes that once were timbered, perennially flowing creeks full of fish, with vanished soft bottoms of sand or mud from which the Indians scooped mussels, leaving telltale shell middens along high banks where they can still be seen.

It pretty much went, all that. It went chiefly as a result of sod destruction through plowing and overgrazing, and the consequent erosion of topsoil by water and wind. In East Texas the felling of woods by lumbermen and by farmers wanting field land had much the same effect. The trouble progressed but slowly in flattish areas with good rain, where water ran off gently and new growth, whether of crops or grass or brush or weeds, was always springing up to cloak naked dirt. Hence the upper coast, parts of the blacklands, and many riverbottom strips still possess much reasonably productive soil after a century to a century and a half of economic use. But in steeply rolling places like the Hill Country or in the big, dry, windy expanses of the west, both subject to infrequent but inevitable wild deluges, soil could move with terrible speed.

Its principal agents were cotton and cattle, which bared the soil and let it be washed or blown and were produced for money rather than subsistence, mainly for the use of people far from Texas. The process was thus another instance of large-scale nineteenth-century exploitation of a resource, the price that some thoughtful people say had to be paid for progress. Cotton, along with a few other cash crops, got most of the plowable land where adequate rain could be expected—and, west of the 98th meridian, quite a lot where it couldn't be expected. The cattle, abetted by sheep and horses, got the rest, which in the days before barbed wire, when many a master of thousands of cows had title to little or no land, meant just about every accessible square inch.

The farmers filled up the humid prairies and flowed west into ever dustier realms, whole families laboring at the manifold tasks of plowing and harrowing and planting and chopping and weeding and picking that cotton demanded, playing hell with the soil all the way so that yields diminished decade by decade or sometimes year by year. The pattern was a tough one, but these were stubborn folk, and many of them kept on battling through the bitterness of Populism's defeat, the advent of boll weevils, and market surges and crashes, enduring well into the drouthy and catastrophic Depression, which put a harsh stop to many things. Hence a good many friends I've had of my own generation, in their sixties now, remember clearly the names and quirks of individual plow mules, who in their family could pick how many pounds of bolls per long autumn day, and how a bad growing season or low lint prices could lead to a winter without new shoes for school or even enough food in the house. One recalls a year when his mother made the family's bread from homegrown milo maize but cautioned the kids against mentioning it to friends because that was animal food. It is perhaps no wonder that cotton-farming rural Texas, what was left of it, was a hotbed of military volunteerism as World War II drew near.

Rather neatly and without much straining, the history of cattle-grazing since the Republic's birth can be seen as comprising three periods of just about fifty years each. The first period, that of longhorned beasts on unfenced free range, is familiar to all in at least a mythic way, through the novels and movies and boots and belt buckles that it has not yet ceased to engender. Its formative years during the two and a half decades before the Civil War saw consolidation of Anglo-American control of the settled regions, a slow expansion of the frontier against fierce Plains Indian resistance, the blending of Southern and Mexican ways into a distinctively Texan system of handling range cattle, and sporadic attempts to find means of marketing the incredible numbers of nearly wild, fast-multiplying Spanish kin inherited or appropriated from their erstwhile owners. No reports that I've seen detail the impact of cattle on rangeland during those times, for nobody then fretted about such things, but since there were around five million of them running loose in the eastern and southern parts of the state, that impact must have been fairly dramatic.

So, of course, was the epic expansion that followed the war's hiatus, the twenty years of high Western romance. Indians and buffalo were destroyed or shoved off the Great Plains in short order; cowboys and bovines flowed west and north in trail herds. By the late seventies Eastern and European markets had an unfailing supply of meat by way of the Kansas railheads, and ranching and cowboying had established themselves up the unfenced plains to Montana and the Dakotas. West Texas filled up too, those parts of it that had adequate natural water for cows, and shared in the brief glory days of the Beef Bonanza, when cattle prices were rising sharply season by season and not only experienced ranchers but also domestic and foreign corporations, English milords, Northern financiers, and many other sorts of folk were scrambling to acquire huge herds and get in on the free grass and the profits that would continue forever.

Terrific overstocking thus quickly prevailed, and records pertaining to the classic rolling ranch country below the Caprock in the Panhandle show that even in the early eighties, a relatively wet period, grass ran short and once-dependable springs started to dry up. As was inevitable, drouth in Texas and great blizzards farther north brought major "die-ups" of cattle and halted the fun in the middle eighties, just a hundred years ago. The market collapsed, the boom was over, the open-range system had played out. Henceforth—though the change took place over a decade—those who kept on ranching would own or lease their grass and wrap it up in barbed wire, providing stock water with dams or windmills where necessary.

As for the land, it had already begun to suffer, and it had more suffering ahead. The old, wild, resilient days were gone, all over Texas. In theory, fences and ownership could have led to wiser, gentler use of grass, just as they did lead quickly to the improvement of cattle through introduced British bloodlines, impossible before when somebody else's randy and aggressive Longhorn bull was always waiting around to seduce your heifers. And in practice it does seem that some of the larger outfits, especially family-owned ones, saw the portents, achieved some understanding, and even in the late nineteenth century did not load their ranges with beasts to what was then seen as the limit. But the limit was ill-defined in those days, and a lot of people still didn't think there was one, or care. Absentee owners, corporate or individual, stayed interested in annual profits, and so through necessity did many small ranchers living at the economic brink.

The end result of enclosure in most grazing sections was that the land was used even harder, on the whole, than in open-range times, and the cattle couldn't move off of it to better places during bad spells as the buffalo and even the Longhorns had. Grass cover in many places went from sod to gnawed clumps scattered across bare dirt, wildlife thinned out, streams dried up, gullies appeared and deepened and widened, hillsides turned to naked rock or clay, and mesquite and cedar and other brush moved thickly in. In the older and moister parts of the state those things had been happening for a long while, but in general less quickly and drastically. Dry West Texas was especially vulnerable to damage from hard use, and during the half century running from the Beef Bust to the mid-thirties it became as we know it today.

Or, really, worse than we know it today. In that troubled decade when the Great Depression ruled, soil exhaustion and major drouth combined to create unprecedented dust storms and erosion and a landscape with little visible usefulness left in it, and both cattlemen and dryland farmers saw the bottom of things. Lots of them went totally broke and had to quit, especially marginal small-timers, which included most West Texas farmers and a good many ranchers too. World War II when it came sucked them into its vortex and cast them up later in other places and other roles. The urban-rural population figures tell a little of the story. In 1930 our countryside outside of cities and larger towns held about 3.4 million Texans constituting 59 per cent of the state's whole population. In 1950, after the drouth and the winnowing and the war, there were 3.1 million country folk comprising 40 per cent. Other vast forces were at work, true, and still are, but in that first shrinkage of the rural populace since the Texas census began in 1850, disillusionment with the exhausted land was a chief one. Few looked back with nostalgia at small dusty fields with skimpy cotton worth a dime or so a pound at best, or at chewed-down pastures full of cows with hipbones like hat racks.

There being hardly anywhere to go but up, many who really wanted to stay on the land and hadn't been wiped out at the bank started trying to do things better. Knowledge to help them accomplish that was at hand. The rural devastation of the Depression years had by no means been confined to Texas, and it had inspired a quasireligious movement, centered in the Midwest but powerful elsewhere too, to dispel frontiersmanly ignorance, restore some of the soil's productivity, and stave off further ruin. It involved a lot of practices such as terracing, contour plowing, cover-cropping, clearing invasive brush, reestablishing grass on fields that should never have been tilled, planting windbreak trees, and carefully managing grazing not only through stocking rates but through cross-fencing, rotation of animals in pastures, and distribution of water.

Not that any real revolution has occurred, that virginity is back with us, or that the lessons of the thirties and the fifties remain sharply clear in all rural minds. West Texas is still West Texas, closer in aspect to its horrible Depression self than to what the Comanche and the buffalo knew, though much of the flat High Plains section has grown lushly agricultural in the past three decades on the basis of irrigation from wells—depletion of the state's groundwater being, of course, a large topic in itself. Marginal terrain that was truly wrecked long ago by cotton and cows can only be partially restored; this beloved hilly rock pile I live on, for instance, has not sprung back to primeval resilience despite my noblest efforts when younger, nor would it with less than ten thousand years of utter human absence. Although in general all over the map farming is more diversified and wisely conducted and cattle-grazing less severe than of yore, greed is yet with us and manifests itself in such practices as plowing up sloping rangeland for wheat when wheat prices rise and overstocking by some types whenever the feeder-calf market stays favorable for a couple of years in a row. Soil in consequence is still flowing merrily Gulfward or traveling across our skies on the wind.

Yet in the countryside the knowledge of good and evil does now exist where it didn't really before, with effects that are visible in spots and patches just about anywhere you go. Whether in the long run it will keep us from turning most of our landscape into something resembling those stretches of North Africa and the Near East and the Balkans that once furnished sustenance for empires is something that can't be foretold. I have no urge to don the cloak of Jeremiah, but one needs only a minimal awareness of historical human tendencies to see that ruin could quite easily prevail, and that in a densely peopled future when all sources of food have become crucially dear, the burgeoning masses of Texans predicted to us by boomers might well have a relationship to their home region like that which Ethiopians have sadly achieved.

Or maybe the available good knowledge will win out. I for one find comfort in knowing it is at least on hand. In truth it was a long time coming. ❧

# HUGH ROY CULLEN'S LAST HURRAH

### BY GARY CARTWRIGHT

1954 HUGH ROY CULLEN HAS THE WILDCATTER'S DELUSION: THAT GREAT WEALTH BRINGS GREAT WISDOM. BUT WHEN HE STAGES A RALLY FOR HIS HERO JOE MCCARTHY, HE FINDS NO ONE IS LISTENING ANYMORE.

WHEN THE NAMES ARE CALLED of the legendary wildcatters who gave Texas its wealth and, for better or worse, much of its character –H. L. Hunt, Clint Murchison, Sr., Sid Richardson–Hugh Roy Cullen will be at the top. Roy Cullen was one of a kind. The estimated $175 million contributed by the Cullen Foundation built the University of Houston and much of the Texas Medical Center and sustained many lesser known causes. Like all the old wildcatters, Cullen suffered from the malady of the era, a psychotic fear of socialism, but nobody in Texas ever gave more money to the general betterment or, for that matter, had more to give.

Blunt, stubborn, impulsive, at times vindictive, Roy Cullen seemed born to create ripples, and he created ripples every time he opened his mouth, which in his late years was constantly. He became something of a political godfather and a human propaganda machine, using his millions to finance ultraright-wing causes, not only in Texas but all across the country. Cullen was a rarity among wildcatters in that he equated wealth with social responsibility. But he also shared in the wildcatter's grand delusion, that wealth bestows wisdom. Few men who have made vast fortunes by finding oil in the ground have been able to resist the notion that they are among the chosen. Finding oil is a testament to character, not to luck. Wildcatters, in

their hearts, want more than riches. They want to guide destiny and shape the image of their time.

Though not as radical as H. L. Hunt, who, it was said, thought the country went communist when the government started delivering mail, Cullen adamantly believed that the Red hordes, disguised in their nefarious costumes as foreigners, one-worlders, and practitioners of creeping socialism, were just offshore or, in some cases, had already landed. In 1952 he was the largest single contributor to the campaigns of notorious U.S. Senator Joseph McCarthy, who was also getting money from Murchison and Hunt and became known as Texas' "third senator."

Cullen thought Franklin Roosevelt was a dictator and warned that the New Deal would mark the end of free speech. He vehemently opposed any American association with the United Nations ("the most dangerous movement this country has ever embarked on") and assailed the Marshall Plan as "a handmaiden of World Union." It was his suggestion that the billions being sent to refugees in Europe and Asia be used instead to buy atomic bombs and long-range airplanes.

More than once Cullen demanded that Harry Truman and Secretary of State Dean Acheson be arrested and tried for

> OILMAN HUGH ROY CULLEN WANTED TO SAVE AMERICA FROM THE RED MENACE. HE GAMBLED ON JOE MCCARTHY AND HIT A DRY HOLE.

treason. In his mind there was no fundamental difference between a communist, a socialist, and a liberal, and even some conservative Republicans were suspect. On learning that John Foster Dulles, Eisenhower's secretary of state, favored an international alliance, Cullen labeled him a rat and a crook.

A basically simple, self-made man–a fifth-grade dropout who went on to advise presidents (whether they wanted advice or not)–Cullen had a faith in the American dream that was paramount and untainted by cynicism. He really believed that with hard work, discipline, and a little help (albeit not from the government) anyone in America could become successful. He wrote his first check to the fledgling University of Houston (it was barely more than a junior college at the time) after reading a fundraising pamphlet describing how a "typical student" woke at first light, boarded the 7:18 a.m. Southmore bus in his dark suit and short-brimmed hat, ate a 29-cent lunch at Walgreen's, and worked and studied until he fell into bed at 11:15 p.m. "That's the kind of young man I'd like to help," Cullen told Dr. Walter Kemmerer, who later became president of the university. Preeminently of the there's-no-free-lunch philosophy, Cullen never pretended he wouldn't run the university his way. Some years later he summarily fired Dr. Kemmerer.

He could be as sentimental as he was strong willed and vindictive. It was reported that he gave $1 million to Houston Baptist Memorial Hospital after

hearing the hospital superintendent play and sing Cullen's mother's favorite hymn, "Beckoning Hands." That same week he gave million-dollar gifts to three other hospitals. He gave generously to the Warm Springs Hospital for polio victims in Gonzales—but only after making certain it wasn't associated with the Warm Springs Hospital in Georgia, where Franklin Roosevelt took the waters.

There is an apocryphal story that he once gave $20,000 to the Houston Symphony on the condition that it play "Old Black Joe." He was an unabashed racist, of course—it would have been nearly impossible fifty years ago to find a rich, self-made Texan who wasn't. But he wasn't as reactionary as, say, Herman Brown, one of the Brown and Root brothers. LBJ biographer Robert Caro writes that Brown hated Negroes and labor unions, believing that Negroes were lazy and unions encouraged laziness in white men. Cullen gave $100,000 to Houston College for Negroes (but more than $75 million to U of H) and with it a speech on how well the South had treated the black race and how far the race had come because of that treatment. After the Supreme Court's 1954 ruling against racial segregation in public schools, Cullen wrote to President Eisenhower, declaring that the court's decision had "done more to destroy individual freedom than any government action since the founding of this nation."

Cullen was a rabid supporter of the States' Rights party in the late forties, "states' rights" being for some a euphemism for "keep the darkies in their place." He constantly railed against Truman's "so-called civil rights program." But he was as unpredictable as he was opinionated. Unlike Herman Brown, he was considered pro-union, at least by the union leaders of Houston, many of whom were also ardent states' righters. Cullen favored free enterprise but opposed free trade. He believed that the two principles that kept America strong were free enterprise and high tariffs. In a letter to Republican presidential hopeful Thomas Dewey he argued that the only way to stem social revolution was for "labor to 'sit on the same side of the table' with capital," sharing profits as well as management responsibilities.

It would kill the old man to read this today, but that sentiment could have come straight out of a handbook for socialists.

THEY SAID CULLEN HAD A NOSE FOR oil, but what he really had was a nose for money and opportunity. He quit school at age twelve to help support his mother and the other children, and by his early twenties he was a successful cotton buyer in western Oklahoma. Cullen was not from a backward or unlearned family. His ancestors were major landholders in Virginia in the 1670's, and his grandfather Ezekiel Cullen fought in the Texas war of independence and served in the Republic of Texas' first legis-

lature, writing the bill that created the state's first public school system and made provisions for a permanent university fund.

The panic of 1907 ruined many cotton buyers, but not Roy Cullen. Though he was forced to sell his cotton at a loss to repay bank loans, his sacrifice enabled some banks to stay in business and established his integrity and credit. Cullen always insisted that the insights he had gained during the panic ultimately prompted his fierce opposition to the "so-called economic reforms" of FDR's New Deal. They certainly prompted him to hightail it out of Oklahoma.

It was his nose for opportunity that led Cullen to Houston. A great believer in the wisdom of charts and maps, Cullen studied maps of the United States and observed that although there were many seaports east of the Mississippi, there were few west of the river. One was Houston, a mosquito-infested swamp of 78,000 that had once been the capital of Texas and might have remained so except for a fire-eating speech made by his grandfather seventy years earlier. Ezekiel Cullen had spoken of Houston as "that abominable place—that wretched mudhole—that graveyard of men" and had been so convincing that the Legislature moved the capital to Austin.

The overriding factor in Roy Cullen's decision to relocate was Houston's newly dredged ship channel. The port was a gateway to one of the world's richest areas, the Mississippi and Missouri river basins, which covered one third of the continent. Cullen researched material from one hundred of the world's largest ports and discovered that most, like Houston, were man-made—Liverpool, Hamburg, Shanghai, even New York, which was a shallow bay until a channel was dug through the Narrows. Houston was destined to be one of the world's great cities, and Roy Cullen decided that was where he belonged.

Cullen arrived in Houston with his family in 1911 and immediately set himself up in the real estate business by purchasing a tract of land on the Ship Channel. In no time he was embroiled in a political struggle with real estate tycoon Jesse Jones, who was to become his lifelong enemy. At issue was where to locate city-financed wharves and harbor facilities. Jones, who was chairman of the harbor board, wanted them close to downtown, where he already owned considerable property and later would own much more. Cullen wanted the wharves downstream where he and some friends owned land. Cullen fought with all his resources, including money for a full-page ad in the *Houston Post* that appealed to blue-collar workers. His side prevailed. Though Cullen never owned a newspaper, he learned early in his career how to use money and prestige to attract headlines. Over the years his press releases were invariably published

by all the Houston newspapers.

Cullen never liked or trusted Jesse Jones, and the bad feelings between them intensified when Jones accepted an appointment as secretary of commerce in the Roosevelt administration. Cullen wrote to Jones that the policies of the New Deal were poisoning the doctrine of free enterprise expressed in the Bill of Rights. Jones wrote back (somewhat facetiously, one imagines) that the nation would no doubt survive. He didn't bother to add that the Bill of Rights is silent on the doctrine of free enterprise.

By the time Cullen and Jones tangled again on an issue central to Houston, Jones had bought the *Chronicle* and turned it into his surrogate voice. This was the bitterly fought battle over zoning in 1948. Jones and his 8-F Crowd (named for the suite in Jones's Lamar Hotel where they met for cards and politics), favored zoning as a way to stymie the decentralization of the downtown business district. Cullen, whose stubborn and unsophisticated independence was anathema to the 8-F circle, thought zoning was socialistic and un-American. Advertising campaigns heavily financed by Cullen actually argued that zoning was the first step to socialized medicine.

The campaign hit its low point when Cullen whipped off a letter to Houston's three newspapers charging that Jesse Jones and "a bunch of New York Jews" were trying to run the city; Cullen threatened to resign from all his boards and chairmanships and move out of town. Cullen won again. Houston still isn't zoned.

ROY CULLEN WAS IN HIS THIRTIES before he got into the oil business, and he was forty before he made his first strike in 1921. It came at Pierce Junction southwest of Houston, in a field that the large oil companies had abandoned after drilling 52 dry holes. By the start of World War II Cullen was worth hundreds of millions of dollars.

Cullen revolutionized the oil industry and established himself as king of the wildcatters by sheer force of will. He leased fields that had been abandoned by large oil companies and drilled deeper than anyone had dared drill before. Digging deeper was like a religion to Cullen. A drilling contractor once remarked, "When they say the last rites over Mr. Cullen, and get ready to lower him into the ground, I'll bet he'll look over the side of the casket and say, 'Better dig a little deeper, boys!'"

Though Cullen was constantly thumbing through the few books available on oil geology and though he made use of such technological breakthroughs as gravity meters, seismographs, and electromagnetic surveys, he credited his success to his study of "creekology." By observing how the course of creeks and rivers bent and flowed around certain hard surface formations, a [ CONTINUED ON PAGE 40 ]

# 1919 LIFE IN THE BOOMTOWNS IS SO SQUALID THAT A JURY FREES A WOMAN WHO KILLED HER HUSBAND. THE VERDICT? JUSTIFIABLE HOMICIDE. AFTER ALL, HE WAS THE ONE WHO BROUGHT HER HERE.

# DIAMONDS AND GALOSHES

## BY ANNE DINGUS

LIVING IN A BOOMTOWN, AN ELEC-tra woman recalled, she felt like the scrawny bridegroom whose hefty new wife sat on his lap: it hurt at first, till the numbness set in. For women in the teens and twenties, towns like Ranger and Wink were a far cry from the El Dorados they had imagined. They found the eaves of houses sawed off to make room for derricks and the streets so boggy that mules drowned in the muck. Filthy, boisterous men crowded the streets, and an acrid stink filled the air. The whole aspect was so dismal that an Eastland lawyer named H. P. Brelsford once defended a boomtown wife charged with the murder of her husband by arguing that it was justifiable homicide; the husband deserved it for subjecting her to such a squalid life. She was promptly acquitted.

The most pressing problem for new arrivals in any boomtown was finding accommodations. Most men with families took up tent living—cool enough in the summer but miserable in the winter—unless they found shelter in a real house where an enterprising native turned a spare room into profit. Of course, with the princely oil-field salaries, easily $5 a day even during the Depression, a family lucky enough to find a vacancy could afford the tab. If tents or rooms were unavailable, men slapped together shanties of scrap metal and tar paper and told their unhappy wives that oil riches would soon buy them a mansion. New houses were nonexistent. The oil patch paid so much better than construction that there were no workers to build anything. By the thirties the established oil companies were moving in on new booms and building housing for transferred workers, but the inrush of temporary help still lived in clusters of cheap shacks that Humble employees called Poor Boy Camp.

Locals often looked down on the boomers. Nearly every citizen in a boomtown made money off his leased land or increased business; they were less desperate and less impressed by the prospect of sudden wealth. When the John McClesky well came in near Ranger, Mrs. McClesky's first reaction wasn't delight but dismay; the oil had stained her pretty white chickens. Told by her husband that she could have anything she wanted, she requested a new ax. One Beaumont widow leased her farmland for a huge sum but continued to make daily trips into town to collect the garbage from the hotels and cafes for her hogs. Daisy Bradford, the farm wife who lent her name to Dad Joiner's discovery well for the East Texas field, cooked and cleaned for the crew even after the well hit and made her rich.

Tent wives and town wives shared many miseries. Groceries were in scant supply; staples like flour and sugar quadrupled in price, and fresh foods like milk and eggs simply weren't to be had. Salt water spewing from wells killed farm wives' vegetable gardens. Everywhere there were long lines as overburdened businesses abandoned regular hours and struggled to meet the demands of a zooming population. (Ranger went from 800 people in 1917 to 30,000 two years later—never, the residents were fond of saying, the same 30,000 from one day to the next.) A woman's life was mostly waiting: all morning to pick up the mail, half the afternoon to see if the general store had any matches or beans left. Women avoided the public cafes, where grimy men straight from the rigs waited two or three deep behind each diner and used napkins left by their predecessors.

Sickness was a constant danger. The tents and shacks had no plumbing; families often threw their garbage into the streets. Most water had to be shipped in at a nickel or dime a gallon, because well or cistern water was so polluted that it was useless even for bathing or laundry. Drinking water cost a nickel a glass, the same as Coca-Cola. In 1918 a flu epidemic swept Ranger, and the lack of a hospital or quarantine rooms meant the infection spread everywhere. Ten years later at Wink the typhoid rate was ten times the national average, dysentery four times. Gas poisoning was always a threat; anyone living near a well grew accustomed to inflamed eyes and nausea. Women learned to avoid lighting matches when the stench was especially bad, serving cold meals instead. Often they couldn't cook anyway, because stovepipe, an easy substitute for well casing, was frequently confiscated or stolen. The roar from the gushers assailed everyone's ears. "The roar is so great in Desdemona," the local paper reported, "that conversations are shouted and gesticulated. Talking over the telephone is almost impossible. Mothers can't coo to their babies and lovemaking is a problem."

Housecleaning was the bane of women's lives. In Ranger, where Main Street was an oily morass, women had to hoe the mud off their plank flooring before they could even think of mopping. In the Permian Basin the scourge was sand and grit, which blew into the family's dinner or the baby's crib. One Sour Lake woman recalled, "Gas and oil from the wells made everything black. You had to scrub silver every day." Laundry was the most laborious chore. Oil-stained clothes had to be treated with gasoline to remove the oil, then rubbed on a washboard and boiled to remove the gasoline. Only then could they be washed with soap and hung out to dry. It's a wonder women attempted to fight the conditions at all, and yet the attempt to do so marked the sole class distinction in a boomtown, separating the decent people from—a new term that had cropped up—oil-field trash.

Most women dreaded going to town. In Ranger fistfights and shootings were so prevalent that residents rechristened the *Daily Times* the *Daily Crimes*. An-

> BOOMTOWN WOMEN DRESSED IN FINERY, BUT LIFE IN THE OIL PATCH OFTEN MEANT SAWED-OFF HOUSES, GRIMY MEN, GRITTY STREETS, AND MOST OF ALL, MUD.

other reason for avoiding the streets was the presence of prostitutes. To protect respectable ladies, a beauty shop in Wink placed a magazine on the seat of any chair vacated by a woman of questionable virtue.

Boomtown wives had little opportunity for fun. Churches (if there were any; Batson Prairie had none) kept their ladies busy with missionary and charity work. Celebrity-watching was a pastime in Ranger, which attracted the likes of former heavyweight champ Jess Willard, evangelist Billy Sunday, circus owner John Ringling, and former president William Howard Taft. A Ranger woman handed a silver dollar to a raggedly dressed man and drove off without discovering that he was former governor O. B. Colquitt. By the twenties bridge clubs had preempted the more traditional sewing circles. Women with money shopped at the expensive clothing and jewelry stores that followed the booms. It wasn't unusual to see a woman elegantly turned out in diamonds and furs sloshing through the streets of Ranger in rubber galoshes. Even among women, oil dominated conversations and entertainment. A must for everyone was an expedition into the country to view the latest gusher. Eventually the thrill played out along with the oil, but it lasted long after the money vanished and the mud dried up and the chickens turned white again.🍂

# HUMBLE PIE

BY JOSEPH NOCERA

THERE ARE PEOPLE who will tell you that the ultimate triumph of the Exxon Corporation –a triumph not just of size but also of intelligence and foresight, two qualities sorely lacking in a lot of corporate boardrooms of late– can be traced directly to that fortuitous day in 1917 when nine Texans shook hands on a deal to merge their individual oil companies into one corporate entity, which they called the Humble Oil and Refining Company. The people who make this extravagant assertion are almost always old Humble hands, and while they can respect Exxon in a distant, cerebral way, it is Humble they still clasp to their breasts. Twenty-six years after it was absorbed by Standard Oil of New Jersey, fourteen years after its name vanished from the Texas landscape, it is Humble Oil they still love. To a man, they will proclaim (extravagantly) that the Humble Oil and Refining Company was, quite simply, the greatest Texas oil company there ever was. Talk to these fellows a while, and you quickly realize that never was a company so woefully misnamed. What is one to make of their claims? They all hold shards of truth, but they all hold elements of delusion too. And in both the truths about Humble and the delusions can be found something supremely Texan.

The essential delusion was this: "the greatest Texas oil company there ever was" was truly a *Texas* company for a very, very short time. For most of its corporate life, the majority of its stock was owned by Yankees. And not just any Yankees, but robber baron Yankees, Yankees who could bring out xenopho-

"IT WAS THE SADDEST DAY IN TEXAS HISTORY" WHEN THE EXXON TIGER GULPED DOWN HUMBLE OIL.

bia in the most sophisticated Texan–the Yankees of John D. Rockefeller's Standard Oil of New Jersey. The very company that was run out of Texas after Spindletop for antitrust violations. For more than forty years the most curious anomaly in Texas business was not just that Standard owned Humble but that most Texans were so ready to avert their eyes from that fact.

The original Humble name came from an oil boomtown north of Houston. And the original founders–including some of the most famous names in oil, among them Sterling and Blaffer, Fondren and Farish–were all men who had made their fortunes in the boom. Their intent from the beginning was to form a company in the Standard Oil mold, an integrat-

ed company that could explore for oil and then drill for it, produce it, transport it, refine it, and sell it at gas stations. There were several glitches in the plan, however. First, Texas law specifically disallowed integrated oil companies. Not a big problem. Shortly after the men agreed to pool their companies, the Legislature conveniently passed a law lifting the ban. Ostensibly the law was passed at the behest of Texaco, but the Humble founders were the first to take advantage of it. The second problem was money. The founders soon realized that they desperately needed cash to build the huge refinery they envisioned, to set up a marketing operation, to get big the way they all wanted to get big.

The cash [ CONTINUED ON PAGE 42 ]

28

## 1901
# GUSHER!

"**O**n this spot on the tenth day of the twentieth century a new era in civilization began." So reads the monument at Spindletop. There was oil before Spindletop, but Spindletop brought to oil the ineradicable image of the gusher and the irresistible lure of gold. Before this single well could be controlled, it poured 800,000 barrels of oil onto the plains south of Beaumont in just nine days, producing more oil by itself than any *field* had produced before it. Only the Battle of San Jacinto has had more influence on the course of Texas.
—PAUL BURKA

# PERMIAN ENDOWMENT
### *UT Strikes Oil.*

# 1923
Before the oil came in, the plight of Texas' two leading universities was desperate. In 1905, for example, the University of Texas library was confined to a part of the college chapel, most of the faculty was without offices, and the gymnasium had a dirt floor. Things were even worse at Texas A&M, which Governor Joseph Sayers described as "a travesty upon agricultural and mechanical education." In some years the Legislature provided no funding, forcing the universities to scruff along on student fees and income from grazing rights.

On May 28, 1923, the regents offered the presidency of UT to a former professor named Herbert Bolton. He later gave the regents a two-hour lecture on how far short of excellence the university actually fell and then turned down the job. But on that same day an event was taking place out in empty Reagan County that would change the entire educational picture in Texas. At 3053 feet, a well called Santa Rita No. 1 showed the presence of petroleum in its oil sand. The next day the well blew in a gusher.

For the universities, finding oil was a little like inheriting a bushel basket of Confederate money and discovering half a century later that gold coins lay at the bottom of the basket. In 1858 state lawmakers had endowed the future University of Texas with rich state-owned farmland, but in subsequent years the gift was revoked and two million acres of seemingly worthless West Texas desert substituted.

Santa Rita was not a great well in itself. Its importance was symbolic; it freed two schools from the limitations of legislative budget-making in a state that had never emphasized superior education. Today the oil endowment is $3 billion. Santa Rita turned two struggling schools into near-great universities that have uplifted the Texas image as much as anything in the state's history.          — JOE B. FRANTZ

# U-TURN...
### 1973: Texas starts importing oil.

**H**E REMEMBERS THINKING, "THIS IS A BIG deal," and he remembers realizing how unusual that was. It is not often in this life that you instantly understand the significance of the events you're involved in. But May 2, 1973, was different; Sam Hunnicutt, a big strapping man who is vice president of the American Petrofina Pipeline Company and runs its Big Spring operation, knew—absolutely knew—he was making a little history. Precisely at noon, Fina's Big Spring refinery began receiving a shipment of 354,854 barrels of oil. Throughout its life, the Fina refinery had taken its crude from Texas and the surrounding states through a series of pipelines. The same pipelines also sent Texas crude to Fina's Harbor Island Terminal in Aransas Pass, where it was shipped to Philadelphia for refining. But this time the flow from the pipeline had been reversed; the crude had been sent up the pipeline from a tanker called the *Monticello Victory*. The crude had come from Iraq.

In reversing the pipeline and buying foreign crude, Fina was prescient. When other oilmen heard about the pipeline, they were incredulous—they never, ever thought Texas would run short of oil. But within six months the oil embargo had hit and every American refinery was scrambling for foreign oil. In 1974 and 1975 as many as seven foreign tankers at a time would line up outside the terminal, waiting for a chance to unload their cargo into the Fina pipeline. As for Hunnicutt, he filled a half-dozen bourbon bottles with the first few gallons of crude that came out of the pipeline. He gave most of the bottles away to friends, but he kept a fifth of the Iraqi crude for himself. Today it stands on a shelf in his office, a souvenir of the day when everything changed.
—JOSEPH NOCERA

# ...DOWNTURN
### 1981: The drilling bonanza ends.

**A**ND THEN THERE ARE THOSE MOMENTS that barely enter the consciousness when they take place but seem with the passage of time to be loaded with ominous significance. Take the last week of December 1981, for example. The Hughes Tool Company rotary rig count—the chief measure of drilling activity in the United States—hit 4530 that week, up from 4522 the previous week. But how was that newsworthy? The annual rig count had been climbing steadily since 1976, when it bottomed out at 1549. In 1981, with the oil boom in full frenzy, another increase seemed just the natural order of things.

But of course it wasn't. A week later the rig count fell to 4467. An aberration? More like the beginning of the end. In March it dipped below 4000. By June it was in freefall (2931), and every oilman and his banker knew the party was over. The last week of December had been the exact moment when boom turned to bust. Today the rig count hovers around 1900, right where it was in 1979.          —JOSEPH NOCERA

JEFF SMITH

# H.L. HUNT AND DAD JOINER MAKE A DEAL

It was the most famous deal in the history of the Texas oil business and the most controversial. It provided the cornerstone for one of America's biggest private fortunes. And it has had a lasting impact on Texas.

The date: November 26, 1930. The place: suite 1553 at the Baker Hotel. The principals were Columbus Marion "Dad" Joiner and Haroldson Lafayette Hunt. The terms: H. L. Hunt bought Dad Joiner's five thousand acres of oil leases in Rusk County for $1.3 million—$30,000 in cash and the rest in promissory notes and future oil payments.

Joiner's leases turned out to be in the heart of the giant East Texas field, then the largest oil

## 1930

reservoir ever discovered—a forty-mile-long ocean containing more than four billion barrels. Even more than Spindletop, it forever linked Texas in the public mind with oil. Hunt went on to drill more than six hundred wells on the Joiner leases, netting the first $100 million of a family fortune estimated at anywhere from $3 billion to $5 billion at the time of his death in 1974.

What is and always has been in dispute is, what did Dad Joiner know and when did he know it? Even as Joiner and Hunt were sequestered in the Baker,

a well called Deep Rock No. 1 came in, proving that Joiner's original Daisy Bradford No. 3—the first well drilled in the East Texas field—was not a fluke and that the field was the real McCoy. Later, Hunt would assert that he had told Joiner about Deep Rock No. 1. Joiner later said that Hunt had lied and told him it was a dry hole; Joiner sued, then changed his mind and dropped the suit in midtrial. In any case, the two men's fortunes were irrevocably set at that moment. Hunt became the richest and most famous oilman of them all, while Joiner spent the rest of his days trying to find another East Texas field and died nearly broke and surely broken.

—Harry Hurt III

# 1931: BIG OIL WHUPS LITTLE OIL...

## ...and a fifty-year feud begins.

I T WASN'T A HURRICANE OR A TORNA-
do, but in Texas it qualified as a disaster nonetheless: cheap oil. Ten-cents-a-
barrel oil. The East Texas field was just too
bountiful. In 1931 its crude so flooded the
market that other fields in Texas shut
down, unable to compete. Big companies
like Humble, with operations that went far
beyond East Texas, were screaming for
production controls, known as prorationing. But when the Railroad Commission
tried to impose limits, independent producers, whose whole livelihood rested on
how much they could take out of that one
field, simply ignored the orders and ran
their wells wide open.

Governor Ross Sterling knew a disaster
when he saw one—after all, he had been
one of the founders of Humble. So he did
what governors have always done when
faced with disaster. He sent in the National
Guard to enforce the limits. It was the moment in Texas history when politics and oil
merged, never to part again. By the time
the prorationing was finally accepted, in
the mid-thirties, the oil industry had been
changed forever. The Railroad Commission's hard-won control over supply enabled it to set the world price of oil until the
rise of OPEC.

The battle over prorationing was to oil
what the open range was to the cattle business. The independents, like the free-
grassers of the 1870's, lived by their own
rules and, on a massive scale, ignored
those imposed by others. They lost the
fight, but they linked oil to the Texas frontier myth.                        —PAUL BURKA

# 1948

## Boy Scouts And Slant Holes: No Place But Texas

I n 1948 a Longview oilman
gave the Boy Scouts an oil
lease. When the well came in
the following January, Scout
officials and civic leaders
gathered on a platform in the
East Texas oil field for a
ceremony dedicating it as East
Texas Boy Scout Foundation
No. 1. Unknown to the Boy
Scouts, however, their well
was a slant hole, drilled at an
angle to reach deep into producing territory owned by someone else.

That was just the way things were done
in the East Texas field in the forties and
fifties. As the field was drained, en-
croaching underground water forced the
remaining oil to the east, toward leases
owned by major oil companies like Humble and Shell. To the independents in the
western part of the field, it didn't seem
fair that the big boys should get bigger.
Slant holes weren't cheating; they were
just a way to recoup oil that God had put
under their leases. The complicity of the
local oil service industry, from roughnecks to well servicers, was essential. No
one wanted to see the area stop producing. Slant holes were an open secret, an
oil-field version of populism.

When the scandal finally broke in
1962, a grand jury returned 386 indict-

TOM CURRY

ments. The first case involved a district
judge on trial in his own courtroom. (The
district attorney couldn't try the case; he
owned a working interest in a slant well.)
A fellow judge found his colleague not
guilty. That set the pattern. Not a single
oilman was convicted; juries sided with
the locals against the majors. Civil suits
fared no better. After Humble lost a suit
to recover $475,000 from a slant-well
operator, a visiting judge described the
jury's verdict as a "rank miscarriage of
justice." In the end the scandal's main
result was to give the world a rare
glimpse into the strange psyche of oil.

—PAUL BURKA

31

# BOOMTOWN BRETHREN

## BY JOSEPH NOCERA

CHARLES FRASER HAD A DREAM. Oh, yes, he did! Brother Fraser was a banker, but he was not a stuffed-shirt, pin-striped, put-up-your-first-born-for-collateral kind of banker. Brother Fraser was a banker with a dream, and that made him an entirely different species.

Brother Fraser's bank was the First National of Midland, and in the era of the holding company, it was the largest independent bank in Texas. But Brother Fraser wanted more. Oh, yes, he did! He wanted his bank to get bigger and bigger and bigger, until finally it was the biggest independent bank in the nation. Lordy, how that Brother Fraser could dream!

And Brother Fraser wasn't the only banker with a dream. Over in Abilene, there was Brother Don Earney, dreaming of turning his little Abilene National into a regional power. In Dallas Brother Elvis Mason, king of the InterFirst holding-company empire, dreamed of leaving archrival Texas Commerce Bancshares behind once and for all. And in Oklahoma City, in a small shopping center called Penn Square, Brother William Patterson dreamed of transforming his dinky bank into a major commercial center for the oil and gas industry.

As to how these brethren would turn their dreams into reality, well, goodness gracious, man, there was an oil boom on –oh, yes, there was!–and they were going to ride the boom for all it was worth. There were wells to be drilled! There were rigs to be built! Everywhere you looked there were multimillion-dollar deals to be financed! The dreams were going to be fulfilled by oil. Sure, you could get technical and say that maybe the collateral was a little shaky, and maybe some of these young whipper-snappers you were loaning money to didn't know an oil log from a fire log. You could say that, but you'd be missing the point. The price of oil was going up, up, up–all the brothers said so!–and that made everything okay. Oh, it was a lovely dream while it lasted!

OIL GIVETH, BUT THE FDIC TAKETH AWAY.

And then the price of oil started to drop, and just like that, the dreams were dead. The Federal Deposit Insurance Corporation showed up one day at the Penn Square Bank and began slashing away at the bank's loan portfolio. The examiners crossed out one loan after another from the "Don't worry, this guy promised he'd pay as soon as he gets the money" side of the ledger and put them on the "Let's stop kidding ourselves" side. Slash, slash! In July 1982 Penn Square, which had gone from nothing to a $2 billion lender overnight, closed its doors. Brother Patterson, indicted for fraud and the like, began dreaming of

ways to stay out of jail. Then the FDIC showed up at Brother Earney's bank. Slash, slash! The feds practically gave the bank to MBank out of Dallas, and Brother Earney was indicted for embezzlement and a few other things. Then in 1983 it was InterFirst's turn to report hundreds of millions in "uncollectible" loans–slash, slash!–as Brother Mason bid adieu. And in October 1983 the biggest independent bank in Texas was independent no more. Though under Fraser First National of Midland had grown to nearly $2 billion in assets, the FDIC found more than $600 million in bad oil loans, declared the bank insolvent, and sold it to RepublicBank of Dallas. By then, however, Brother Fraser had long since left the scene.

Now, some people will tell you that the moral of this sermon is that bankers shouldn't dream on quite so extravagant a scale. But I am here to tell you, their problem was that they didn't dream big enough. At the same time Brother Fraser was dreaming his dream, the really big dreamers were in places like New York. There was Brother Rockefeller, for instance, and Brother Wriston. They too wanted their banks to get bigger and bigger and bigger, and they too hitched their dreams to the oil economy. They loaned money not to oil companies but to oil-producing nations–entire nations! –like Mexico and Argentina and Brazil, and they handed out not mere millions but billions upon billions of dollars. Oh, how they could dream! Well, of course, now Mexico owes the banks $96 billion, and Brazil owes $108 billion, and Argentina owes $50 billion, and with the price of oil in the dumps, no one expects ever to see that money repaid. But do you see the FDIC showing up at the doors of Citibank and Chase Manhattan, sharpened pencils at the ready? Not at all. You start putting some of those loans on the "Let's stop kidding ourselves" side of the ledger, and just like that, there goes the international banking system as we know it. Life can be unfair, sometimes–eh, Brother Fraser?♣

# FRIDAY NIGHT RINGERS

### BY LARRY L. KING

THERE WAS A TIME when recruiting football talent in Texas was almost as common, if not as socially acceptable, among high schools as among colleges. Outlaw football practices seemed to be at their peak during big oil booms. Whether that proves that oil money actually passed hands, or merely that boomtowns attracted working families likely to have big kids, might be argued forever. The pattern was such that I suspect boomtown leaders of chicanery. If you establish a tent-and-tin-shack city, you may want to give it instant recognition and a quick history, and what better way to do that, in a land where football is almost a religion, than to import youths who are agile, mobile, and hostile?

My suspicions might have something to do with the games I had to play against tough old boys like Byron "Santone" Townsend, who led Odessa to the state championship in 1946. Townsend got his nickname because it was alleged that he had been spotted by Odessa scouts while a junior high stud in San Antonio and rapidly spirited west. In the three years Townsend was a starter for Odessa, the Broncos defeated Midland by a combined score of 149–0; as a member of two of those Midland squads, I believed anything anyone wanted to tell me about how Odessa got Townsend—whatever he might have been paid wasn't too much.

Bill Shoopman, a commercial photographer in Odessa who photographed Townsend in action, recalls, "There was

HOMEGROWN LOCALS DAMN SURE DIDN'T HAVE CARS AND MONEY.

open talk his daddy had been lured to Odessa because of the boy's football ability, but of course, nobody ever proved it." Shoopman himself had played for the Eastland Mavericks in the thirties, and "every year or two, maybe four strangers would show up and play for us. If you hung around long enough, you might find yourself playing against them later on. There was kind of a gentleman's

agreement, I guess, that you wouldn't blow the whistle on them.

"One year a guy named Rex Clark suddenly showed up to play for us. He was a hell of a back, but nobody knew where he came from. Rex drove a good car, wore good clothes, and had money to rattle, so we all assumed somebody was paying him pretty good. The homegrown locals damn sure didn't have cars and money."

The Ranger Bulldogs of that era housed a goodly percentage of their squad in a local fire station. Town merchants fed them and supplied walking-around money. In 1934–35 tiny Haskell had a heck of a fullback named John Kimbrough. In mid-season of '35, Kimbrough magically appeared in Abilene. There was gossip and sniping from Haskell fans about under-the-table money, but Abilene partisans said they didn't know what those Haskell malcontents were talking about. Kimbrough went on to become an all-American at Texas A&M, but he never admitted more about his high school transfer than that Abilene had seemed like a nice town to live in.

High school football recruiting finally ended in the late forties when the Interscholastic League sternly enforced a rule, much maligned in recent years, that a student moving to another town couldn't compete in varsity sports for a full calendar year. Maybe it was just a coincidence that the wilder oil booms quit at about the same time. ♣

# 1937 ALGUR MEADOWS FIGURES OUT HOW EVERY OILMAN CAN GET RICH AT THE EXPENSE OF THE FEDS.

# THE ABC'S OF OIL

## BY MARK SINGER

ALGUR H. MEADOWS, his many admirers agreed, was a gifted trader. If a deal could be shaped to suit a fellow who had an oil property to sell, Meadows would find a way to shape it. Above all, he enjoyed the game.

The evolution of Meadows' brightest idea—the ABC method of oil-and-gas financing—can be traced to the early thirties, when H. L. Hunt and his fellow folk heroes wildcatted in the East Texas oil field. As the boom percolated, it became evident that just about anything you drilled would discover oil, if only you could raise the cash to drill. Often an operator would promise a drilling contractor twice the usual price—say, $20,000 to do a $10,000 job—if the driller would accept his payment in future oil rather than in current dollars. Many drillers—who, after all, felt more comfortable making holes than making loans—would in turn try to sell those oil payments at a discount to anyone who had cash. Al Meadows happened to have some cash.

In Shreveport, Meadows and a partner had created a syndicate of small-loan companies called the General American Finance System. The Depression seriously depleted the loan companies' capital, but there were some funds available the day in 1933 that a drilling contractor named Blondy Hall showed up, bearing a promised future oil payment valued at $105,000. Meadows and his partner agreed to buy it for $35,000.

Within three years the General American Finance System had become the General American Oil Company of Texas (GAO). A year later Meadows moved to Dallas and set up offices in the Republic Bank building. GAO grew rapidly

REPUBLIC BANK'S EXECUTIVES, 1955: AL MEADOWS FINDS A FRIEND.

and steadily, and—following the pattern of the Blondy Hall deal—it owed its growth less to exploration than to the acquisition of proven reserves.

For GAO to continue acquiring new reserves, though, took cash. Lots of cash. Meadows could always borrow the money from a bank, of course, but then he'd have to pay the bank lots of interest. That's when Algur Meadows had his great idea. Why not borrow the money and pay it back—principal and interest—in oil? All he needed was to find a friendly and imaginative banker.

Meadows found his man right there in the Republic Bank building: Fred Florence, who guided Republic from the twenties through the fifties. Their brainchild—the ABC method (so named because it involved three parties designated A, B, and C)—was the device that enabled Meadows and hundreds of

other Texas oil and gas operators to transform respectable holdings into huge fortunes. It worked this way:

A was an oil producer in need of cash—usually an independent oilman who, like every purebred oilie that ever punched a hole in the ground, had somehow overextended himself. Let's say that A had a property that he would sell for $1 million.

B—an operator like Meadows—would pay $250,000 down. And a bank would lend the balance to a carefully selected third party, C.

C was the key to the deal. Meadows used to refer to C as the elevator boy. He would ask a banker, "How much will you lend me with these properties as collateral?" Upon hearing the answer, he would say, "Okay, now how much would you lend the elevator boy on the same collateral?" He put it that way because the banker had to be willing to make, in effect, a nonrecourse loan.

The $750,000 that the bank loaned C —at an annual interest rate of, say, 5 per cent—would be passed on to A, and C would acquire from B an oil production payment (a species of royalty) with a face value of $750,000.

ABC worked the way it did because all the parties involved—especially B—had an aversion to taxes. If B received $25,000 each month in oil production revenue, or "runs," he would typically keep about $5000 to cover his operating expenses. The rest would go toward the oil production payment, which was structured in a way that allowed C to earn half a per cent more in interest than he was paying the bank. According to the tax codes, C—not B—had received the $20,000 in net oil and gas runs. The result: A got his hands on $1 million in cash and paid a comparatively painless long-term capital gains tax. B spent $250,000 to acquire a $1 million property (which actually had a long-term worth of much more) and was not required to pay tax on the income that provided three quarters of the purchase price. C paid taxes, but only on the difference between what he received in interest from B and what he paid in interest to the bank—in this case, half a per cent of $750,000. Anyway, C didn't mind paying his tax bill, because all along he had been a little ol' shell company with only $1000 in capital. Making that half a per cent spread in interest was just like finding money lying on the sidewalk. Besides which, C typically happened to be a feeder for charity. There was one C entity called AMC, whose profits flowed to the ex-students' association of Texas A&M. Another, Tex-Ex, benefited the University of Texas alumni association. At Southern Methodist University, Ponies Oil did very well, thank you, by ABC.

General American bought property everywhere—Texas, Oklahoma, the Gulf Coast, California, Wyoming, Canada, *everywhere*—and Republic financed a great deal of it. In 1951 General American paid $20 million—but only half a million in cash—to acquire North American Oil Consolidated of California. Republic was one of three institutions that banked the $19.5 million production payment. Then General American sold one of the North American properties for enough to pay off the entire deal. After that, Meadows got in the habit of doing five or six ABC deals a year. As the tax rate increased, ABC financing became even more attractive. By the midfifties, two fifths of Republic Bank's loan portfolio was invested in oil and gas, and those assets generated half the bank's interest income. ABC became the lifeblood of trades among independent operators, and it was a boon to petroleum engineers because a banker's willingness to finance an ABC loan depended upon accurate reservoir analysis. Mobil and Conoco started to get the hang of it, as did, in time, bankers and insurance companies from exotic places like New York.

The fun lasted until the Tax Reform Act of 1969 required B to become a taxpayer. C became a useless relic.

In 1978 Meadows died in an automobile accident, and the acquisition of General American Oil became inevitable. The Meadows Foundation, founded in 1948, held the largest block of the company's stock. When Phillips Petroleum bought GAO in 1983, the foundation traded its stock for $298 million in cash. Thus did the Meadows Foundation and its prudent fiduciaries get out of the oil business—presumably forever—and into the rather less innovative business of clipping coupons. The foundation's assets now total $340 million, and its bylaws restrict its gifts to the people of Texas, which is how the charms and dividends of the ABC method live on and on.◆

# GREETINGS FROM SOUR LAKE

### BY CHARLIE JEFFRIES

*At its height, the legendary Sour Lake oil field yielded 50,000 barrels a day. For those infatuated with the new allure of oil, it was a magnet. But, as Charlie Jeffries wrote in his 1946 article "Reminiscences of Sour Lake," it was not a nice place to visit, and you wouldn't want to live there.*

CORSICANA PUBLIC LIBRARY

**SHOESTRING WAS THE MOST DANGEROUS PART OF THE MOST DANGEROUS OIL AND GAS FIELD IN TEXAS.**

DURING THE FIRST week of October, 1903, I went to Sour Lake. Boll weevils had ruined the cotton in my part of the country, and, like thousands of others, I went to the oil field to tide over a hard time. By pawning my fiddle and my six-shooter and borrowing fifty cents from a friend, I scraped up enough money to buy a ticket; I got there without a cent. . . .

For surging energy, unrestrained openness, and diabolical conditions otherwise, Sour Lake was head and shoulders above anything Texas had seen up until that time or perhaps has seen since. The site is on low ground. At that time little effort was made at drainage; and a short while after operations began, a large part of the field was worked up into such a mess of mud as can hardly be imagined.

One thing that made the mud so bad and rendered the place such an inferno in other ways was the crowded condition. There were few, if any, laws governing oil field operations; no such thing as restrictions on drilling existed. Landowners sold their land to anyone who came to buy it and in as small amounts as the buyer's purse spoke for. . . . In many instances land in as small amounts as one-sixteenth, or even one-thirty-second, of an acre was sold. The result was that the greater part of the field was

soon a forest of derricks. As quantities of water are required to run a rotary drill, the slush which spread from these hundreds of wells and which was stirred up by the men working in it made the place a sight to behold.

As the oil field was the important feature of the Sour Lake scene as a whole, so was Shoestring the center of interest of the oil field. Shoestring was a long narrow strip of land in the middle of the oil-bearing district, where development was most intensified. In many ways it was the pulsing life center of the oil field. Here the wells were thickest; here the mud was deepest; here the gas was strongest; here the boilers roared the loudest; here the efforts of men had the fullest play. Things of magnitude went on in other parts of the field, in the Cannon tract, and in outlying leases, but they were overshadowed by the activity at Shoestring. This was the place with

which men with pride of action liked to identify themselves. As the elect viewed it, no one was deemed worthy of being connected with Sour Lake unless he had undergone his period of seasoning in Shoestring. . . .

The constant effort to stay clear of the mud added no little to the interest of the scene. The derrick floors were high, if not always dry; and other places absolutely essential to the drilling, like the ground around the boiler and engine, were by a never-ending effort kept comparatively clear. But always near by, even on the holdings of the larger companies, was the waste from the overflowed slush pits, giving the place the appearance of a freshly drained pond.

The struggle between mud and men was close-locked. There were no roads, that is high, dry roads in Shoestring. The only way of getting around in that part of the field was by whatever means one could devise. A network of large pipes, not unlike a badly constructed spider web, ran about over the field. They had been laid without any regard to system, but they were usually up out of the mud, and these, to some extent, served as causeways. The pipes, together with the derrick floors and the little islands about the boilers, served as foundations for more bridging; the bridges usually consisted of two-by-twelve planks thrown down wherever the crying need of some little piece of work demanded. On these frail structures the traffic of the field was conducted. . . .

Another highly noticeable feature of the field was the gas. The region is sulphurous, and the gas that comes out of the wells is highly impregnated with the mineral. As the pressure was enormous, forcing out millions of cubic feet of the fumes daily, it rendered the place highly dangerous. In the early days little effort was made to dispose of the gas; generally it was allowed to escape at the mouth of the wells, spread, and do such mischief as it would. On damp, still days it could be smelled a mile or more from the field. It had a scent something like rotten eggs and at first was quite offensive; but, strange to say, when a person got used to it, he rather liked it. This particular kind of gas was . . . called "rotten" gas. While it was disagreeable to be in, it was not the kind that was dangerous.

It was the gas fresh from the wells, less diffused and more highly impregnated with sulphur that the workers dreaded. This kind had hardly any scent, but it was as deadly as a murderer. . . . If a person, or any other living animal, inhaled a few strong breaths of it, he would fall over unconscious; and if he lay in it and continued to breathe it, he would die as surely as if chloroformed. . . .

In saloons, Sour Lake ranked high. These were of all sizes and quality. . . . There was the House of Lords, a place where the big boys gathered and played pool and rowdied around. There was the Derrick Saloon, and there was the Big Thicket Saloon, and there was Dad's Saloon; this last was a noted hangout for blacklegs and cutthroats. . . . It is almost a waste of words to say that the saloons were well patronized; but the extent to which the patronage sometimes went was an eye opener to even an old denizen. After payday, when a gang of pipe-liners came to town, especially if it happened to be a chilly, drizzly evening, the sidewalk for a block or more would be filled with jabbering, reeling men.

Apology may be due for so little being said of the gentler side of the picture; for a gentler side there indubitably was. Friendships were strong; generosity flourished; and deeds of noble conduct in many ways were to be seen constantly. But it is not these softer things that the old-timer usually recalls when his mind runs back on . . . Sour Lake in the boom days.♣

[ CONTINUED FROM PAGE 2 ] muzzle the ox that treadeth out the corn." Then in 1831, having made such an auspicious start in life, he abruptly left his son and pregnant wife and came to Texas. He believed she had been unfaithful. It is possible he had murdered the man he thought was her lover.

Once in Texas he immediately asked Stephen Austin to recommend him as consul from the United States. Astonishingly, Austin did. Travis spent his time going back and forth between San Felipe, the principal town of the Anglo settlements, and Anahuac on Galveston Bay near the mouth of the Trinity River. There he conspired with various others to resist customs laws. For that he was arrested and imprisoned in the spring of 1832, which in turn caused disturbances to arise among the discontented Anglo settlers. At one point Travis was staked to the ground and surrounded by Mexican soldiers pointing their rifles at his head. An armed group of Texans had approached the garrison. The commander announced that at the first shot from the Texans Travis would be killed. Travis told the Texans to shoot anyway, but the rebels held their fire and eventually dispersed. Soon enough Travis was released.

From then until the outbreak of the revolution Travis practiced law in San Felipe. He was a busy and probably capable lawyer, although he was prone to try to settle certain cases with his fists. He was tall and rawboned, with dark, curly red hair and a ruddy complexion. At a time when wearing socks could be considered an effete affectation, Travis paid careful attention to the buying, sewing, and washing of his clothes. And he doused himself with lavender water. He read books; he courted ladies, both virtuous and otherwise; he went to balls and parties, such as they were on the frontier. Still, he was known for his gloomy temperament. He walked about the town or sat down to the gambling tables at night in his fancy clothes, a lonely, brooding figure, set apart from everyone else by his dress, his education, his aversion to farming, his dark brow, and his sudden, awesome temper.

DURING THE 1830'S, ANGLO IMMIgrants had been flooding into Texas. Those victims of Texas fever, having left behind whatever they had in Tennessee, Carolina, or Mississippi, had a tremendous stake in Texas' turning out to be everything they had hoped. Thus it was often with wild expectation and racing emotion that they first saw their new home. "We're here all united together, bound together by an indissoluble tie," one wrote back home. "As the past has been full of bitterness, we of

course look forward to future happiness." Those emotions were combined with exalted notions of liberty and romance. Lord Byron and Sir Walter Scott were the most popular authors of the age, and their romanticism inflamed their readers. Sam Houston's maiden speech as a congressman from Tennessee had supported the Greeks who were fighting for their independence; so were the Poles, and suddenly, in 1835, so were the Texans. Daniel Cloud, who would later die at the Alamo, wrote home, "If we succeed, a fertile region and a grateful people will be for us our home and secure to us our reward. If we fail, death in the defense of so just and so good a cause need not excite a shudder or a tear." Macajah Autry, who also died at the Alamo, wrote, "I go the whole Hog in the case of Texas. I expect to help them gain their independence and also to form their civil government, for it is worth risking many lives for."

Yet such inflamed emotions can crash as quickly as they arise. In the weeks before the Alamo, Texas was all discouragement and disillusion. The provisional council, which had been called together to set up a government, fired the existing governor, Henry Smith. But Governor Smith refused to be fired and instead fired the council. So at the top, instead of leadership, there was nothing but squabbling and confusion. The Texans had captured San Antonio from the Mexican army in December 1835 – in effect winning the first battle of the Alamo – only to have two ambitious commanders strip the fortress of its supplies and munitions for an expedition against Matamoros. Then Jim Bowie and thirty men arrived in San Antonio on January 19, 1836, to join the Texans who had remained there. Bowie had orders from Sam Houston to blow up the Alamo and to abandon the town. He did neither. Just over two weeks later, on February 3, Travis arrived with thirty men. On the way, truculently, he had written a letter to Governor Smith threatening to resign his commission if his orders to go to San Antonio weren't changed. Travis had sulked in camp waiting for Smith's reply, which never came. Eventually he had no choice but to trudge on into San Antonio. Only a few months before, he had been a lawyer in private practice with little military experience. Now he was Lieutenant Colonel William B. Travis of the Texas cavalry.

The revolution had captured his spirit. He had learned that he was to be offered a commission in the artillery, but before official word even arrived he refused it and wrote a letter extolling the virtues of a cavalry, in which he finally did receive a commission. He immediately ordered a uniform made, but his orders for San Antonio arrived before it could be completed. He spent his own money to equip the men he had recruited, and he left with them to meet his destiny dressed in jeans. As soon as he reached San Antonio, he began squabbling with Bowie over who was in command. Travis longed to leave San Antonio, but once Davy Crockett arrived on February 8, Travis began to see the place in a different light. "It is more important to occupy this post than I imagined when I saw you last," he wrote to Governor Smith. "It is the key to Texas." Abruptly, for reasons lost to history, he and Bowie ended their differences and agreed to a joint command. Nine days later, at the start of the siege, the agreement was made moot. Bowie was struck by a mysterious disease. From time to time he lapsed into incoherency, and throughout the rest of the siege, he lay on his cot. A 26-year-old lawyer with no qualifications but his own will had assumed command. Even the famous Crockett accepted his authority.

Travis had found his stage in the Alamo and his destiny in the form of thousands of Mexican troops. Now he needed to present his vision of himself to the world. He sat down to write his letter. "To the People of Texas & all Americans in the World," he began. He described the forces besieging him and how he had answered their call for surrender with a cannon shot. Then, as in his diary, he underlined a sentence: "*I shall never surrender or retreat.*" He ended with a call for aid. "If this call is neglected," he continued, "I am determined to sustain myself as long as possible & die like a soldier who never forgets what is due to his own honor & that of his country—*Victory or Death.*" News of the letter and of the battle inflamed America, and troops of volunteers set out to join the fight. The war was over before they could arrive, but still they came. Travis had changed Texas from an impoverished Mexican farming colony to a great cause worth dying for, to a country born of heroic blood, to a noble idea.

During the thirteen days of the siege, Travis' men did not see him much. He stayed in his room, waiting. At night, like Hamlet, he paced along the fortress walls. He constantly wrote for reinforcements and supplies. Only 32 men arrived. James Butler Bonham, who had grown up only a short way from Travis' birthplace in South Carolina, carried one of the messages out of the Alamo, but he rode back through the Mexican lines and into the Alamo to cast his fate with them all.

On the night of March 5, it was clear that the main attack would come the following day. The fortress walls were finally crumbling from the Mexican cannon fire, but the cannon were silent now, gathering for the attack. Legend—not historical evidence—says he drew a line in the dust. But he did address his men and gave them a choice of leaving or meeting certain death within the Alamo. All stayed but one. When the attack began the next morning, William Barret Travis, the dandified, impetuous country lawyer, rushed to the north wall at the point of the fiercest attack and died like the hero he had willed himself to be, at the head of his men. ♣

[ CONTINUED FROM PAGE 11 ] the beefsteak a state full of rich miners could consume, made up a herd and set off at once for San Francisco. He reached it a couple of years later, having decided to go north along the Rio Grande to the Continental Divide before turning west. At about the same time, Jack Cureton crossed a herd along the more difficult southern route. The Apache were not then so angry as they were to become, but the desert was the real problem with the southern route. Raphael Pumpelly, one of the keenest observers to travel the border country of Arizona, left a vivid description of the cattle corpses he passed on a trip through the Sonoran Desert a little more than a decade after Cureton's drive:

> The routes over these wastes are marked by countless skeletons of cattle, horses, and sheep, and the traveller passes thousands of the carcasses of these animals wholly preserved in the intensely dry air. Many of them dead, perhaps, for years, had been placed upright on their feet by previous travellers. As we wound, in places, through groups of these mummies, they seemed sentinels guarding the valley of death.

Little wonder that the southern route never became really popular, though Cureton was by no means the only cattleman to attempt it.

The drives of the 1840's and 1850's were false starts. The markets existed, and the cattle existed, but the difficulty of getting the latter to the former, across such distances, was evidently discouraging. Two years on the trail could exhaust an entrepreneur sufficiently to make him seek less arduous sources of profit. The energies were gathering, but conditions were not ripe. The country was still unsettled, and many of the bolder spirits who were to become pillars of the new industry—Charles Goodnight, for example—had their hands full fighting Indians, clearing out bandits, and generally making the country safe for the settled folk with whom they had so little in common.

The Comanche resistance lasted a good deal longer than anyone expected it to, and before it was blunted the Civil War came, a terrible, exhausting war. The drain on human resources was so great that one might expect that a generation would have been required for full recovery, but the American temper was evidently at its most resilient then. The guns had scarcely fallen silent before the robber barons got to work.

At that same moment, when veterans of the conflict were still straggling home, a flood of Texas cattle began to flow north, initially to Sedalia, Missouri. But Missouri didn't really welcome the trampling herds; drovers were attacked and harassed by vigilantes. Baxter Springs, Kansas, proved not much better, and the much-advertised threat of Texas fever did nothing to improve the situation for cattlemen.

At that point Joseph McCoy, an aggressive buyer for Chicago packing interests, mounted a strong lobbying campaign in Abilene, Kansas, a community easily reachable from Texas along a trail that had been worked out a few years earlier by a Cherokee trader named Jesse Chisholm. McCoy convinced Abilene that its destiny lay with cattle; facilities on the order of loading pens and drover's hotels were established, and none too soon, for the cattle were now coming in the thousands.

The annus mirabilis was 1866. Some think as many as a quarter of a million Texas cattle were driven north in that year, some eighty to ninety herds. Kansas felt the brunt of all those hooves—a mixed delight—but Kansas was not alone. In that year Charles Goodnight and Oliver Loving, with an eye to the Colorado rather than the Kansas markets, made their famous drive across the Pecos and opened the Goodnight-Loving Trail.

No less daring was Nelson Story, who, the same year, defied the U.S. Army and a number of Indian nations and took the first herd into Montana. It was soon apparent that Mr. Story had gotten ahead of his time, or at least of his place. Not for almost a decade and a half, until Custer had fallen and been revenged, did driving cattle to Montana become practical and popular.

From 1866, for slightly more than a score of years, the Great Plains were alive with cattle, most of them Longhorns pushed out of the South Texas brush. Abilene and Dodge City were the Athens and the Rome of that migration, but tributaries of cattle were constantly breaking loose from the central channel, and most of the tributaries flowed north, to the fresh pastures of Nebraska and the Dakotas, Wyoming, Montana, or into Canada.

Twenty years is not long; the mid-sixties soon became the mid-eighties, at which point the flow of cattle was unabated. In 1886 John Blocker, the business-minded brother of the famous trail boss Ab Blocker, was said to have an interest in 82,000 cattle, all of them on the move at once, in various herds, along various trails.

A mere four years later it was over. A few herds were trailed north after that, but the activity had already become a romantic anachronism. By 1890—the year of Wounded Knee—trail driving on any serious scale had become as much a thing of the past as Indian fighting. The speedy twentieth century was in sight. Railroads spanned the continent, and barbed wire spanned the Great Plains. The open range, that world of grass of a limitlessness that forever held the imagination of all who saw it, moving observer after observer to oceanic imagery in their attempts to describe it adequately, closed abruptly behind the last straggling herds, never to open again. The golden age of cowboying had passed, and its long silver age began.

The trail drives, and the wide-open cow towns they spawned, were almost solely responsible for the myth of the cowboy—perhaps one should say of the Westerner—which remains potent to this day. (The Westerner merges two figures, the cowboy and the gunfighter, in real life rarely the same breed, though most cowboys wore guns and many gunfighters herded cattle at one time or another.) A hundred years have now passed since the great herds filled the plains. The range closed, the cow towns became sedate; an urban age ensued. Yet even now movie studios are still releasing major westerns. A year or two ago President Reagan presented the first Congressional Gold Medal ever given a writer by our government to Louis L'Amour, author of more than a hundred westerns. Even more recently, *Fortune* magazine singled out the Marlboro man ads as being, from an advertiser's point of view, the most successful set of images ever presented to the buying public.

This vigorous and tenacious myth didn't grow out of ranch life, with its repetitive and largely unromantic round of calving and fencing, feeding livestock and doctoring them. It grew out of those brief years when the West was unfenced and cattle, men, and horses were on the move. Few enough of the tens of millions of words and images that have been devoted in the last hundred years to depictions or dramatizations of Western life describe trail driving per se, but the drives were the generative activity without which most of the words would not have been written or most of those images cast.

Mining was also a potent activity in many parts of the West for many years, and yet the scattering of books and films about mining seem minute when compared with the vast corpus of work that accrued around the cowboys and the gunmen who followed them along the cow trails and into the cow towns.

The growth of the myth undoubtedly owed much to the birth of the film industry even as the range was closing. The eminent film historian Siegfried Kracauer, in his *Theory of Film*, argues that chases are one of the most intrinsically cinematic of all subjects; in support of his argument he quotes Robert Flaherty, who said, "People never get tired of seeing a horse gallop across the plains." The success of hundreds of crudely acted, clumsily plotted westerns, offering little more than the innate eye appeal of speeding horses juxtaposed against a vast plain, would seem to bear Flaherty out.

Without the romantic conception of the cowboy engendered by the drives, there would have been less occasion for the careers of William S. Hart, Tom

Mix, John Wayne, Clint Eastwood, and a host of other actors who rode to fame in the westerns. Without the drives we would not have had *The Long Trail*, John Ford's silent masterpiece; would have had no *Red River*, no *Rawhide* no *Gunsmoke*; no Johnson County or Lincoln County war; no gunfight at the OK Corral.

The rich iconography of the gunfighter derived from the marshals and outlaws who filled the cow towns; behind Marshal Dillon were such colorful men as Bear River Tom Smith (first marshal of Abilene), James Butler "Wild Bill" Hickok, the Earps, Bat Masterson, and others. The romance of outlawry in America owed much to the range wars; Billy the Kid, the Wild Bunch, Tom Horn, and a host of minor banditti whose exploits are all but forgotten left legends that have fed our popular culture for a century now.

Curiously enough, most of the great gallery of cattlemen who peopled the industry in the golden years of trail driving have been largely ignored by the films, the television series, and the pulp westerns. Charles Goodnight's career would have made a great role for John Wayne—any stage of his career, at any stage of Wayne's—but it didn't happen. Little has been done with Shanghai Pierce, Charles Siringo, Teddy Blue, Uncle Dick Wootten, the Marquis de Mores, or Teddy Roosevelt's cowboy years. That colorful talker Ab Blocker, who in the judgment of his contemporaries drank water out of more cow tracks and pointed more cattle toward the North Star than any other man, survives only in a short sketch by J. Frank Dobie and a few brief tributes in *The Trail Drivers of Texas*—by far the most important collection of firsthand narratives by the trail-driving cowboys.

The places, or at least the place names, have fared better. Some fairly ordinary rivers and some distinctly meager villages have enjoyed a resonance, in legend, far out of proportion to their size or appeal. Place names are all in the way of poetry that many people ever experience, much less create, and the West produced some wonderful ones: the Pecos, the Cimarron, the Purgatoire (or, to many cowboys, the Picketwire), the Red, Powder River, Crazy Woman Creek, the Stinking Water, Dodge City, Abilene, Ogallala, Deadwood, Tombstone, and many more. Whoever thought up "Boot Hill" as a name for a cemetery had the poetic spark. The power of place names is a mostly unstudied literary phenomenon, but writers from Homer on have felt it; in this regard, if in no other, western writers are well equipped.

In attempting to assess how it is that the trail-driving experience produced a romantic model—the Westerner—whose potency lasted a century, we should hearken for a bit to the trail hands themselves. What did they think about their time on the trail?

Almost unanimously, they regarded it as

the happiest and most satisfying experience of their lives. Over and over again, in memoirs, they speak of how wonderful it was: the beautiful, unspoiled country, the excellent horses, their fine comrades; they mention the loyalty they felt for their outfits, the excitement of crossing the endless plains, the trivial nature of their hardships in the light of all the fun they had, the thrill of arriving at some prairie Sodom where their small wages were usually quickly squandered.

Few of these memoirists were eloquent; instead they were grindingly sincere, even sanctimonious. The last quality particularly irked Teddy Blue, never sanctimonious himself. He thought the cowhands who contributed to *The Trail Drivers of Texas* sounded like a bunch of preachers, which was not how he remembered them. Just reading the table of contents of that book reveals the sober attitude with which the contributors approached their task: "A Thorny Experience"; "Seven Trips up the Trail"; "The Good Old Cowboy Days"; "Made a Long Trip to Wyoming"; "Trail Driving to Kansas and Elsewhere"; "Preferred to Take Older Cattle up the Trail."

For all the sobriety of its short, prosaic accounts, the book is irreplaceable, and invariably the most eloquent passages in the for the most part homely literature of the trail are expressions of regret that it all ended, that the open range closed, that the settlements came, that their comrades are gone. Teddy Blue's valediction at the end of *We Pointed Them North* (1939)—in my view the single best book about the trail-driving experience—is better-put than most but identical in its imagery to many others on the same theme.

A man has got to be at least seventy-five years old to be a real old cowhand. I started young and I am seventy-eight. Only a few of us are left now, and they are scattered from Texas to Canada. The rest have left the wagon and gone ahead across the big divide, looking for a new range. I hope they find good water and plenty of grass. But wherever they are is where I want to go.

Many of the trail-driving cowboys were, in Olaf Stapledon's phrase, last and first men; that is, the last to do the work they did and also the first to do it. Most of the cowboys were poor teenagers from Texas or other Southern parts, youths whose prospects were dim until the cattle drives saved them from the slavery of the plough. Those who went at fifteen or sixteen with the drives of '66 or '67 were only in their thirties when, twenty years later, the life began to die. Some of them saw both the beginning and the end, and then lived for forty or fifty years in the shadow of what they felt to be an unmatchable experience. For their male children, the shadow of that experience was often heavy. No matter how skilled they got as cowboys, they could never go up the trail. The primal experience of their craft—and it was a craft they cherished deeply

–had also been, in some haunting way, a terminal experience.

Extremely intense experience is almost by definition brief, and so it was with trail driving. The cowboys well knew that the open country couldn't last. They saw the railheads moving west, saw the settlers moving with them. The paradox of their experience–a paradox of which the more thoughtful among them were keenly aware–was that in entering the open range they hastened its closing. It was indeed their fate to be the men who killed the thing they loved.

Of course the plains were only virgin in *their* eyes; the Indians had lived on them for many generations. But by the time the trail drives were finished, so too were the Indians, and the movement of people and animals on the Great Plains would never again be easy and unobstructed as, for so long, it had been.

The movement of people and animals is evidently a pleasing thing to be part of, also a pleasing thing to contemplate and to watch. Robert Flaherty's simple remark, that people never get tired of watching a horse galloping across the plains, is surely one of the keys to understanding the vitality of the Western myth. The cowboys didn't walk those cattle north. They were not true nomads, but they benefited from the romance that attaches to nomadism, particularly if the nomads are horse people. The identification of cowboys with horses was immediate; in 1874 Joseph McCoy wrote that "the reputation of Texas for horsemanship is national and needs no eulogiums in this place." The cowboy swiftly joined the ranks of renowned horse people, which include the Huns, the cossacks, the bedouin, and the Plains Indians, all of which have been good box office in romantic art, fiction, and film.

The trail drives produced a body of imagery that speaks of movement without constraint. Images of movement on horseback suggest a degree of freedom for which a great many hemmed-in people yearn. There is no evidence that cowboys were more free or more emotionally effective than anyone else; in many respects they were patently ineffective and not at all free. But that is realism, and the cowboy belongs to romance. However they may have felt as living men, they function in our urban and suburban culture as symbols of freedom, of a simpler, more satisfying, less constrained way of life. As the cities spread, urban figures –space cowboys à la *Star Wars*, superagent gunfighters à la James Bond–may partially replace them. But the replacement will only be partial. The trail drives only began to end one hundred years ago. The thunder of all those hooves, the jingle of all those spurs, has not entirely faded. For a while yet the cowboy, his hat thrown back and his spurs still a-jingling, his face filled with a "glow and a glee" as he contemplates the sea of grass, will go on riding through our lives. ♣

THE OPEN RANGE
## WHEN MYTHS COLLIDE

[ CONTINUED FROM PAGE 14 ] body remembers. Then he goes out and strikes oil on that land, and from then on Jett Rink, J.R., has his brand on half of Texas. In *Giant* we are supposed to take the side of cattle against oil. But oil, it turns out, makes a fine subsidy for raising cattle, and Bick can't afford a landscaped lawn or a swimming pool until he, too, enters the oil game.

If *Giant* presented the Texas myth at its fullest, most glorious moment, *Hud,* just seven years later, turned it upside down. Dark, bleak, ironic, *Hud* is a drastically scaled-down version of *Giant.* The shimmering vistas of *Giant* have become in *Hud* a flat, closed-in wasteland. The cattle grazing on the open plain are now diseased, and in the film's most powerful visual moment they are driven into scooped-out pits where they are executed, covered with quicklime, and buried by bulldozers. The cattle drive and ranching era closes grimly. Shot in Oscarwinning black and white, *Hud* looks like World War II footage.

Like *Giant, Hud* sets up a stark contrast between the good (ranching) and the bad (selfish oil interests). Homer Bannon, the elderly rancher who remembers the trail-drive days, is supposed to carry the moral message of the film, but instead he comes across as a pious, didactic old-timer whose defeat, while pathetic, is also inevitable. Standing against the old man is his hard-driving, unprincipled son, Hud, and Paul Newman, taking the Jett Rink role one step farther, completely steals the movie. When the old man says he's not going to let any oil companies ruin his land by drilling holes in the ground, Hud is furious. He'd drill and he'd sell the diseased cattle to unsuspecting buyers. In 1963, Hud's argument had a very contemporary ring to it when he said, hell, the rest of the country is crooked; look at those rigged game shows on TV. The real message of *Hud* came through loud and clear and caught director Martin Ritt by surprise: "It shocked me the first time I got a letter and it said that the old man is a pain in the ass and that Hud is right!"

Mythically, the day of the cattleman was over, and in Texas film mythology Jett Rink and Hud have achieved a powerful merger in the figure of J. R. Ewing, oil baron, wheeler-dealer, and sexual gunfighter par excellence. In *Dallas* the ranch setting is just a prop, a place for the Ewings to have breakfast in the morning and bourbon and branch water in the evening. The moral tensions between ranching and oil, so evident in the earlier films, have been resolved: oil is king, and money is the sole measure of value. ♣

OIL
## HUGH ROY CULLEN'S LAST HURRAH

[ CONTINUED FROM PAGE 25 ] wildcatter could surmise that the geologic pressures that had formed the various rises had also formed faults and traps where deposits of oil collected. In South Texas, where Cullen made most of his major discoveries, the clue was salt domes. Cullen learned early that the smart move was to locate a salt dome and drill near the flank. His guiding principles were "Flank the old domes and drill deeper." Using those principles, he tapped the supposedly worn-out fields at Pierce Junction, Blue Ridge, and Humble for millions of barrels of oil.

"The trouble with this business," Cullen once explained, "is that everybody expects to find oil on the surface. If it was up near the top, there wouldn't be any trick to find it–and it wouldn't be worth much."

One of the reasons oil companies didn't drill deeper in those days was the problem of heaving shale. Below three thousand feet soft, shifting layers of shale would crumble and close in on the well. For three decades drillers had been unable to solve the problem, but in 1927, in the Humble fields near Houston, Roy Cullen developed a method of conquering the shale. The breakthrough was called thinning up, meaning that drillers cleared the shale with water instead of the usual mud mixture. The University of Pittsburgh later awarded Cullen an honorary degree for "originality of thought, daring, and vision," but it forgot to mention unmitigated mule-headedness. What Cullen really did was force the drill bits through the shale. His method in fact remained a secret. It was five years later that Michel Halbouty mixed mud with chemicals and invented the method used today.

Cullen spent days and sometimes weeks at a drilling site, seldom bothering to sleep or, when he did, napping on sacks near the drilling platform. His wife, Lillie, was constantly after him to slow down and spend more time with his family, but Cullen couldn't do it.

In 1930 Cullen and his partner Silver Dollar Jim West (so named because he liked to scatter handfuls of silver dollars around airports to see how the rabble responded) bought up some leases around Rabb's Ridge, a tract of swampland in Fort Bend County that other geologists and engineers had pronounced worthless. Cullen had noticed that the Brazos River east of the ridge had been shoved on its present course by subterranean pressures that had created a telltale salt dome. Drilling in the swamp was frustrating and backbreaking. A road had to be built across the slough to carry machinery, and the first few loads sank in quicksand. The heat must have been insufferable, not to mention the mosquitoes, but one night the derrick began to heave convulsively. When it blew, most of the roughnecks scattered for cover, leaving Roy Cullen to wrestle the control wheel and shut down the gusher. It was one of the great gushers of Texas.

Cullen used his profits from Rabb's Ridge to found Quintana Petroleum, which his grandchildren still operate. In 1932, Cullen brought in the most sensational discovery of his career, the mile-deep fields beneath the O'Connor Ranch in Refugio County. The Tom Thompson Field, as it came to be called, made Roy Cullen one of the richest men in the world.

ROY CULLEN HAD SPENT THE FIRST 50 years of his life relentlessly accumulating a fortune, and he would spend the final 25 warning against the Red menace. Starting shortly after FDR's election in 1932, Cullen assumed a benevolent protectorate over the political affairs of his state and country. He devoured right-wing literature, wrote in doomsday-prophet strokes, and flooded newspaper offices and the halls of Congress with letters—demanding, denouncing, threatening. Cullen didn't deliver opinions, he delivered manifestos.

By the start of World War II, ultraconservative politicians from Texas to Washington were looking on Roy Cullen as a political godfather. He backed Pappy O'Daniel for governor of Texas in 1938, mainly because the former flour salesman denounced New Deal socialism. In the climate that followed the war, a paranoia gripped the country, nowhere more than in Houston. During the fifties, the final decade of Roy Cullen's life, crazies came in multiduplicates. It was the age of the Red menace, the decade when demagogues shouted "Jump" and millions of feet went into action.

As Don E. Carleton points out in his book *Red Scare!* some of Houston's more moderate (and more cynical) conservatives, like Jesse Jones, Judge James A. Elkins, and the Browns and the Hobbys, used the scare as a mere tactic to discredit liberals who were sticking their noses into such sacred areas as the oil depletion allowance, labor relations, corporate tax reform, medicine, education, and race relations. They feared, as *Houston Post* reporter Ralph O'Leary wrote, that "the rest of us are going to take their money away from them." Theirs was the simple ideology of greed.

But the voice that many ordinary people heard was the voice of the true believer, Hugh Roy Cullen. Many demagogues and Red-baiters talked about the little people and rugged individualism and communist infiltration of the PTA, but only Cullen backed his diatribes against government socialism with bucks—millions of bucks, for education and medicine and a lot of other things Houston would have otherwise gone without.

Cullen's money and influence also gave sustenance and legitimacy to the Minute Women and other right-wing extremist groups. When one of those groups managed to ban a popular civics textbook from the Houston school system, Cullen replaced the banned book, free of charge, with a right-wing screed that taught that Reds in the State Department had given China to Mao Tse-tung and tricked the United States into the Korean War. Members of the Minute Women led a crusade that successfully prohibited free lunches in the school system. Teaching children to beg, one River Oaks housewife rationalized, would make "this rich community the laughingstock of the East."

Politically, Cullen managed to muddy the waters in the mainstreams of both parties. Thwarted in 1948 when his Texas Regulars tried and failed to capture the Democratic party—and were later pulverized in the general election when they joined forces with J. Strom Thurman's Dixiecrats—Cullen began to organize a grass-roots campaign for the midterm election in 1950 and the presidential election of 1952. He spoke of purging members of the New Deal politburo and drew up a list of congressional candidates that met with his approval, including Richard Nixon, who was running for the Senate in California. In all, Cullen poured money into the campaigns of at least fifty candidates in twenty states, and at least a dozen of his candidates won.

Cullen already had his candidate for the 1952 presidential election. He was grooming Dwight Eisenhower, who had been his houseguest in Houston several times and with whom Cullen had kept up a running correspondence. All the old wildcatters liked Ike that year.

But by the spring of 1954, just three years before Cullen died, he was having second thoughts about Ike, and presumably Ike was having second thoughts about Cullen. To the mind of the old oilman, the president wasn't moving fast enough to restore free enterprise. Eisenhower was becoming less tolerant of Cullen's drone of advice, especially his insinuations that the Reds were making a fool of the president in Korea. On top of everything else, Cullen's favorite politician, Senator Joe McCarthy, was giving everyone in Washington fits. Now he was attacking the U.S. Army and, by implication, Ike himself. Into the middle of the political maelstrom stepped Hugh Roy Cullen with an invitation to McCarthy to speak at the 1954 San Jacinto Day celebration at the historic battleground in Houston.

No one knew it at the time, but the San Jacinto Day controversy would be a last hurrah for Cullen. He was in his seventies, semiretired except for his flurry of political activities, and in poor health. Cullen had issued the invitation on behalf of the Sons of the Republic of Texas, and he must have realized almost from the start that it

was a mistake. Publicly, Cullen called McCarthy the greatest man in America, but privately he expressed doubts concerning the senator's methods. So did Sid Richardson and Clint Murchison, Sr., as well as Jesse Jones and the 8-F Crowd. McCarthy had been acceptable as long as he was going after unnamed commies, but now that he was sniping at Ike and the Army, the man was an embarrassment.

On the campus of the University of Texas, students demonstrated, and 1571 of them signed a forty-foot petition protesting McCarthy's appearance. Two of the students, including former *Daily Texan* editor Ronnie Dugger, took the petition to Houston and personally presented it to Roy Cullen.

But something happened in Washington that momentarily took the heat off Cullen. A Senate subcommittee scheduled hearings on the Army's accusations against McCarthy on the same day that McCarthy was supposed to speak, thereby confirming the wildest conspiratorial theories of the Sons of the Republic of Texas. A rumor spread that Oveta Culp Hobby, who was serving as secretary of Health, Education, and Welfare in the Eisenhower administration, had somehow persuaded the subcommittee to sabotage the San Jacinto Day affair. Cullen got on the telephone. First he called senators Karl Mundt, Price Daniel, and Everett Dirksen. Getting the runaround, Cullen went finally to the Senate minority leader himself, Lyndon B. Johnson.

"This whole state is roused up," Cullen told LBJ. "Figure it's a double cross and figure Oveta Hobby has done it. People don't like it." Lyndon said he would see what he could do and promptly arranged to reschedule the hearing so McCarthy could speak in Texas.

The rally, when it finally came, was a humiliating failure. Cullen had estimated that 100,000 would hear the speech, but only about one tenth that many showed up. Houston mayor Roy Hofheinz refused to proclaim Joe McCarthy Day and suddenly remembered that he had a prior commitment, as did the city council members. Even members of the Texas Legislature avoided McCarthy. One by one, the old wildcatters distanced themselves from McCarthy, until the only one that remained was Cullen.

Three years and three months later, Roy Cullen died at age 76. An estimated 93 per cent of his fortune had been given away to charity or placed in trusts for his five children and fifteen grandchildren. But finally, his legacy is more complex and poignant than the wealth and the monuments he left behind. He was a self-made man who wanted his country to be as self-made as he was, a man whose beliefs, though sometimes rabid, were always pure. In the end he was left alone because the world was becoming a place where a cantankerous wildcatter like Hugh Roy Cullen could no longer muscle his way into acceptance as a statesman. ❧

# HUMBLE PIE

[ CONTINUED FROM PAGE 28 ] came from Standard Oil of New Jersey, still hankering for a foothold in Texas. In 1919 Standard paid a generous $17 million for 50 per cent of Humble's stock. One old Spindletopper, upon hearing of the deal, proclaimed (extravagantly), "They aren't paying that much for any property; they're paying it for those boys! They don't have men like that up there. Before you and I die, those boys will be running Standard Oil!" Partly delusion? Sure; what Standard mostly wanted was Humble's reserves. Partly true? As it turned out, Humble sent many of its most promising executives to Standard (though this pipeline never went the other way), starting with Will Farish, the first president of Humble to end his career as head of Standard.

For the next forty years the relationship between the two companies resembled a carefully choreographed pas de deux. On the one hand, Standard continued to buy up Humble stock; on the other hand, it went to great lengths to appear almost disinterested in Humble. Standard hadn't forgotten its earlier rude treatment in Texas and wasn't about to risk getting thrown out again. So what evolved over the years was a rather odd set of corporate rituals. The two companies' boards of directors were completely separate. The two staffs never cooperated or consulted. When a man left Humble for Standard, he was not transferred; he resigned from the former on one day and was hired by the latter the next—though he retained whatever seniority he had built up in Humble. Although the giant Humble refinery in Baytown served almost no other purpose than to refine crude destined for Standard's Esso gas stations, the refining executives were under the strictest of orders to maintain an arm's-length relationship with Standard. In the twenties an ambitious attorney general tried to make an issue out of Standard's ownership of Humble, but he failed utterly, for he simply could not prove that Standard pulled the strings.

The thirties through the fifties were the glory years for Humble. Bankrolled by Standard, run by men of genuine vision, Humble was, unquestionably, a first-rate oil company—perhaps the best big oil company there ever was. It had the Texas instinct for the audacious roll of the dice; oilmen gasped when, during the height of the Depression, Humble paid out $3 million to lease the mineral rights on the King Ranch (which turned out to be enormously lucrative for both Humble and the King Ranch). It had that Texas distrust of bureaucracy; Humble district managers had nearly as much autonomy as if they had been in business for themselves.

The old Humble hands remember it so fondly for quite another reason, one that has little in common with the myth of the rugged entrepreneur that Texas oilmen hold so dear. Humble provided security. The pay was the best in Texas. Humble company towns were the best. The jobs were the most secure. The benefits were in a class of their own (in the thirties Humble would match, dollar for dollar, any money its employees salted away in a savings account). In an industry filled with companies whose regional names had long ago lost any significance —Standard of New Jersey, Standard of California, Standard of Indiana, Gulf, Texaco—Humble remained distinctly, deliberately Texan. It sponsored Southwest Conference radio broadcasts ("Go to the game with Humble"), contributed liberally to state and local historical societies, and devoted its corporate magazine to Texana, not oil. When you said you worked for Humble, you said it proudly.

But the glory days ended abruptly, on December 1, 1959. On that day Standard Oil of New Jersey completed a tender offer for the remaining stock in Humble and effectively took hands-on control. Humble was taken over not because it had done anything wrong—on the contrary, for much of the previous decade it had supplied the bulk of Standard's profits—but because it got caught up in the business fad of consolidation then sweeping the country. Half a century earlier, Humble's disappearance would have provoked outraged editorials in the papers and storms of protest in the Legislature. This time, nothing. Times had changed; Texans still resented the East, but theirs was a more complicated resentment, having more to do with envy than fear.

One of the first moves made by Standard Oil was to swap numerous executives between the two companies so that Humble people would begin to absorb the Standard culture and vice versa. Bureaucracies and committees mushroomed. The Humble board of directors was phased out. In 1966 Mike Wright became the first Standard Oil lifer to run Humble, and by the time he retired in 1976, most of the old Humble hands were long gone. When, in 1972, the Humble name was replaced with "Exxon" (as were the names of all the Standard Oil companies), the change simply affirmed an arrangement that had long since been in place.

Still, those few old Humble hands who remained recall that day with mist in their eyes. "It was the saddest day in Texas history," one of them told me (extravagantly), "when we walked into that conference room and heard we were being named Exxon. They gave us all that bull about how the name came from a computer. A computer! I retired a few months later." Just a few months before, the man had reached his thirtieth anniversary with the company, and in the old Humble tradition, he had been given a gold watch. As he sat across from me in his parlor, he took the watch off and handed it to me. "Yes," he said, "I retired from Exxon. But I got my watch from Humble." ❧

# CHARACTER AND CULTURE

**THE TEXAS STEREOTYPE** ⋆ Rich oilmen and poor Aggies. Bluenoses and bluebonnets. Barbecued beef and mechanical bulls. Open spaces and closed minds. That's us, all right. The trouble is, sometimes other folks think that's all of us there is.

**THE CIVILIZERS** ⋆ We got manners from Miz Hockaday, we got chicken-fried steak cooked by a real Frenchie, we got Western art and J. Frank Dobie, and for the highfalutin we got the Metropolitan Opera, so by golly, we ain't hicks no more.

**THE MEXICAN PRESENCE** ⋆ "Poor Mexico," the saying goes. "So far from God, so close to Texas." The first Mexicans in the state knew only poverty, prejudice, and paternalism. In time, the two cultures arrived at a rich, if uneasy, understanding.

43

# TEXANS ARE LUSTY!

## PHOTOGRAPHY BY CARL MYDANS

**1939** *LIFE* TAKES ITS LIFE INTO ITS OWN HANDS AND VENTURES INTO TEXAS, THE LAND OF THE "BOOGER-ROOGER," WHERE MEN ARE ROWDY, WOMEN ARE BEAUTIFUL, AND HORSES ARE "VERY USEFUL."

IN 1939 *LIFE* MAGAZINE PAID TEXAS a goggle-eyed visit and reported to its readers certain astounding facts. It discovered, for instance, that "Texas Is Big." That, in fact, was the title of the article. Subsequent pages bore such headings as "Texas Is Rich," "Texas Is Booming," "Texas Is an Empire," and "Texas Has a Heroic Past." After watching a group of jowly men cozying up to mannequins and engaging in some friendly gunplay, *Life* was moved to conclude that "Texans are lusty." "The typical Texan is big and breezy," readers were told, "fond of strong language and strong drink. . . . Above all, Texans are lusty he-men."

And what brought *Life* to Texas? Was it our size? ("It is larger than New England, plus New York, Pennsylvania, Ohio and Illinois. It is so big that one out of every twelve acres in the U.S. is in Texas.") Was it to determine how, by *Life*'s lights, we had whipped the Depression? ("For rich, self-sufficient Texas, industry is simply jam on its already well-buttered bread.") Well, no. It seems that some Texans were making mischief in Washington. "The Vice President of the U.S. is a Texan. Majority leader of the House is a Texan. Chairman of the House Judiciary Committee is a Texan. Chairman of the House

Agriculture Committee is a Texan. With Jack Garner and his cohorts leading the Democratic opposition to the New Deal, the Lone Star State bulks every bit as large in national consciousness as it does on maps of the nation."

Everywhere it looked, *Life* found its suspicions confirmed. Men wear cowboy boots and tote guns, women drift about in Neiman-Marcus gowns, and cattle bellow along through "the Bad Lands." Texans, the magazine found, routinely drive two hundred miles for lunch, but in the final analysis horses "are very useful because a Texan never does anything on foot that can be done on a horse." Texas does not need skyscrapers but builds them anyway because we like to show off. Other startling observations: We are "near Latin America." We like elbow room. We have no use for swank, and yet we are serious about our culture. Why, there's even a bookstore in Dallas!

No doubt there were many Texans who greeted this stereotypical image with yucks, but their viewpoint has not prevailed. Over the years, the Texas stereotype has been refined some, but it hasn't changed. We're still lusty, booming, big, and rich, and since people refuse to see us any other way, we might as well learn to like it.✦

AND HOW DID *LIFE* KNOW TEXANS ARE LUSTY? IT ATTENDED A "BOOGER-ROOGER" PARTY GIVEN BY ATHENS COTTON BARON ARCH UNDERWOOD. ABOVE: "SHOOTING STUNTS WERE PERFORMED BY SHERIFF JESS SWEETEN OF HENDERSON COUNTY WHO PINKED THE END OFF A GUEST'S CIGAR." RIGHT: "SHOOTING BETWEEN HIS LEGS, SWEETEN HIT A CIGARET STUCK IN GRASS. HE IS CALLED THE BEST U.S. 'DRAW AND SHOOT' MAN."

## Texans Are Lusty

"THE PRESIDENT OF THE
MERCANTILE NATIONAL
BANK OF DALLAS, ROBERT
L. THORNTON, STROKES THE
PLASTER CHIN OF ONE OF
THE TWO MANNEQUINS WHO
WERE THE BELLES OF ARCH
UNDERWOOD'S PARTY," SAID
*LIFE*. "ONE MODEL IS CALLED
SADIE HENDERSON. SHE IS
USUALLY PLACED IN THE MEN'S
WASHROOM TO EMBARRASS
GUESTS. THIS IS SADIE'S SIS-
TER, KEPT AS A SPARE IN CASE
SADIE IS ABDUCTED."

## Texas Is Rich

"FINE CLOTHES LIKE THIS $225
NUMBER ARE BOUGHT AT DAL-
LAS' SMART NEIMAN-MARCUS,"
SAID *LIFE*. FOR THE MOST
PART, HOWEVER, *LIFE* VIEWED
TEXAS' WEALTH AS STRICTLY
RURAL. ITS PICTURES SHOWED
TEXANS AT WORK PRODUCING
CATTLE, COTTON, SHEEP,
TURKEYS, SULFUR, AND OIL —
ALL CATEGORIES IN WHICH
TEXAS LED THE NATION.

## Texas Is Big

HAS ANYONE EVER TALKED ABOUT TEXAS' SIZE WITHOUT MENTIONING THE KING RANCH? CERTAINLY NOT *LIFE*. "BIGGEST RANCH IN THE U.S. IS THE 1,250,000-ACRE KING RANCH, WHICH IS FOUR-FIFTHS THE SIZE OF DELAWARE," SAID THE MAGAZINE. "HIGHWAYS COME TO A DEAD END AT ITS BORDERS." THE ROAD WAS FINALLY COMPLETED IN 1940.

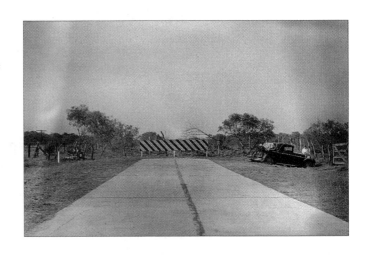

## Texas Is Booming

"HOUSTON'S BUILDING BOOM JUMPED CONSTRUCTION 35% IN 1938," SAID *LIFE*. "THE CITY SPENT $25,000,000 ON CONSTRUCTION, WAS FIFTH IN BUILDING IN THE U.S. AN AVERAGE OF 77 FAMILIES MOVED INTO TOWN DAILY, BRINGING THE POPULATION UP TO 400,000. THIS HOLE IS FOR A SIX-STORY CONTINENTAL OIL & GAS BUILDING."

## Texas Is an Empire

THE BIG BEND COUNTRY, WHICH *LIFE* CALLED THE BAD LANDS, DOESN'T LOOK MUCH DIFFERENT TODAY. "BARE, ERODED AND STONE DRY, THEY DESERVE THEIR NAME," SAID *LIFE*. "NOTHING BUT CACTUS AND BRUSH GROWS THERE. FEW PEOPLE LIVE THERE. YOU CAN GO ALONG A ROAD A HUNDRED MILES WITHOUT SEEING A SINGLE TREE."

# HOW OTHERS SEE US

BY WILLIAM BROYLES, JR.

**1961** IN *THE SUPER-AMERICANS* JOHN BAINBRIDGE DEPICTS A RAW, VITAL, BOORISH STATE. IF WE DON'T LIKE THE IMAGE, WE HAVE ONLY OURSELVES TO BLAME.

EVERY NOW AND THEN, AN OUT-sider comes close to getting it right. Here is John Bainbridge, writing about Texas in *The Super-Americans*, back in 1961: Texas is "the frontier of America—the land of the second chance, the last outpost of individuality, the stage upon which the American Drama, in all its wild extremes, is being performed with eloquence and panache, as if for the first time." That's us, all right, Americans with the energy and optimism the rest of America forgot was its birthright. Bigger, better, taller, and just plain more than anybody else.

There was just one little problem. Bainbridge filled his book with examples of oilmen throwing huge, tasteless parties, with oilmen donating gorillas to the zoo on the condition they be named Eleanor and Franklin, with oilmen's wives flying to Paris for four days of shopping. In his Texas the timpanist fires off a pistol to punctuate *Bolero,* a blind driver is arrested seven times for DWI, and restaurant menus offer son-of-a-bitch stew.

It was that image again, the boorish rich Texan, the one formed unforgettably a few years before by James Dean in *Giant.* Dean plays Jett Rink, the redneck ranch hand on Rock Hudson's ranch who is hopelessly in love with Hudson's wife, played by Elizabeth Tay-lor, who has brought the civilization of the East to benighted West Texas. Dean makes her a cup of tea in his tiny shack, and when she leaves, her boots sink deep into the mud. Dean, spurned, watches the footprints fill slowly up with water and . . . oil. Dean then uses his new wealth to impress Taylor. He opens a garish hotel and—what else?—throws a huge, tasteless party.

The myth of the rich Texan draws its power from the fact that so many of our richest men were poor the night before their well came in. We were a state filled with lottery winners, ordinary people not overinclined to display their sudden wealth with what passes in the East for class and dignity. Texas was to the rest of America what America had once been to Europe, a great bounty inexplicably bestowed on knaves and bumpkins. *The Super-Americans* showed the world that Jett Rink was real. It was a sensation, and you didn't have to be a discriminating reader to suspect that we were being held up for amusement. To hell with the nice platitudes about being "the last outpost of individuality." We were being laughed at. Made fun of. Ridiculed. What could be worse?

> BEING A TEXAN MEANT BEING UNDER CONSTANT SCRUTINY. WE WERE UN-FINISHED, WE LIVED IN THE REALM OF POSSIBILITY.

All over Texas book reviewers sprang to the defense. Andrew Forest Muir in the *Houston Post* accused Bainbridge of traveling "the length and breadth of Texas—between Dallas and Preston Hollow, with an occasional sortie into the wilds of Midland and Athens." A. C. Greene, in a devastating parody in the *Dallas Times Herald,* suggested that Bainbridge had been taken in, "lis'nin' where he should have been laughin'."

Texas, our gallant defenders argued, wasn't like that. Why, Texas was a whole lot more than a bunch of rough-edged Jett Rinks, newly rich rednecks tossing silver dollars out the windows of their limos. We had schools and libraries and civilized folks who read books—even rubbish like *The Super-Americans.* We had Jews and Catholics and contented Negroes and Latin Americans. Some of us didn't even own a horse or an oil well. We were, our defenders seemed to insist, just like everyone else.

The furor over *The Super-Americans* marks a watershed of sorts in the Texas myth. Bainbridge recognized the good things about the myth, that everything was possible, that success, not defeat, was the American destiny, that the past was nothing, the future everything, that any person with enough gumption and determination could earn his dreams. But he went farther. He showed that the myth had a dark side, that the price for all that indi- [ CONTINUED ON PAGE 98 ]

48

# 1963 LBJ HAS A LITTLE DO FOR THE WEST GERMAN CHANCELLOR. "WHAT WILL PEOPLE THINK," LADY BIRD ASKS, "IF WE TREAT MR. ERHARD LIKE HOME FOLKS?"

# LYNDON 'N' LUDWIG

## BY TOM WICKER

MAYBE IT WAS THE president of the United States fitting what he called a forty-liter hat on the head of the chancellor of West Germany that made the events of December 29, 1963, so memorable. Some would say stunning. Maybe it was Cactus Pryor, the master of ceremonies, lamenting that no way had been found to barbecue sauerkraut. Maybe it was the sight of Ivy League McGeorge Bundy, briefcase in one hand, plate of spareribs in the other, forty-liter hat on his head. Most likely it was the 42-voice mixed chorus of St. Mary's High School in Fredericksburg singing, while Lyndon Johnson and Ludwig Erhard joined in the traditional four hand claps, "*Die Sterne bei Nacht/ Sind gross und klar/Tief in das Herz von Texas!*"

Lyndon Johnson, after all, had been president for only five weeks. The nation was just emerging from the trauma of John Kennedy's assassination, and it was getting its first real look at the new president in his natural habitat—the Texas Hill Country, the LBJ Ranch, the never-ending West under its expansive sky. The contrast was extreme: from the high-style Kennedys of the East, with their glittering black-tie parties at the White House, to the down-home Johnsons of the West entertaining their first foreign visitor with a barbecue in a high school gymnasium.

Lady Bird Johnson, for one, had been worried about it. "What will the people think," she had asked Phil Potter of the *Baltimore Sun* and me, as she served little squares of cheese impaled on tooth-

*TIEF IN DAS HERZ VON TEXAS:* LBJ'S DOWN-HOME DIPLOMATIC DEBUT.

picks, "if we just treat Mr. Erhard like home folks? Will the country think we don't know the right way to do things?" Potter reminded her that Franklin and Eleanor Roosevelt had served hot dogs to the king and queen of England, and FDR had won four terms.

The Erhard conference and barbecue climaxed a remarkable Johnsonian sojourn on the ranch. On Christmas Day he had left Mrs. Johnson, his daughters, and 23 guests waiting for their turkey

dinner for more than an hour while he gave reporters a fast tour of the LBJ Ranch, including the main house and master bedroom; distributed souvenir ashtrays; showed off the Muzak system he'd had piped in from Austin, 65 miles away; and offered a lengthy, dazzling LBJ monologue replete with historical lore, tips on cattle raising, facts on an executive order reducing government employment, a description of his latest land deal, hints about his forthcoming State of the Union address, several Sam Rayburn stories, and anecdotes about his contemporaries highlighted by Johnson's excellent, often cruel mimicry.

The days preceding the chancellor's arrival featured more of the same. The day after Christmas Johnson shot a buck deer from the back seat of his Lincoln Continental. The next day, entertaining the press and a gaggle of Washington officials at a warm-up barbecue beside the Pedernales River, LBJ outdid himself. He held a news conference over a bale of hay set up as a podium, then mounted a black Tennessee walking horse named Lady B. and rode off into the sunset. Beside him, portly press secretary Pierre Salinger clung desperately to a red and white paint.

The ranch had been transformed into the only Texas White House in history. Army helicopters stood waiting on the tiny airstrip where LBJ, as a vice presidential candidate three years earlier, had forced his pilot to land a huge Lockheed Electra. A new communications tower rose above [ CONTINUED ON PAGE 99 ]

## 1838
### The Legislature Starts To Earn Its Reputation

*Judging from this diary entry by John H. Herndon, a newcomer to Texas, the Legislature even then was the best show in town. In this case, however, the town was Houston— capital of the Republic until 1840.*

Saturday, April 14. Warm, clear day. House convened at 10 a.m. Ladies began to assemble soon after and by 11½ the house was full, at which time the President entered in a very dignified, graceful manner and took his seat. After having sat a few moments and surveyed the audience he arose and in a clear and impressive style addressed both houses for one hour, giving satisfaction to every auditor. But the meeting was not permitted to pass off in this happy manner. As the crowd were dispersing, Ward made an attack upon Lubbock, Comptroller, who after being knocked down and arising shot at Ward without effect. Thus ended that matter for the present. Two hours afterwards Seavy and Armstrong fell out and fought. After they had been separated Seavy went out and provided himself with a pistol, returned and shot Armstrong in the back of the head from which he died immediately. Seavy is in jail and will unquestionably be hung and thus endeth this affair. I am just informed all the justices in town are now employed in the investigation of crime: One for Murder, another for Counterfeiting and others for petit larceny. What a den of villains must there not be here?

## 1944: BRAGGING RIGHTS

John Randolph didn't invent Texas braggadocio, but he did make it famous. *Texas occupies all of the continent of North America except for a small part set aside for the United States, Canada, and Mexico.* Just before World War II he developed a bus broadside advertising campaign in Houston for Jax beer that he tagged "Texas brags." *Fold Texas northward and Brownsville will be 120 miles into Canada.* In 1944 he was stationed with the 124th Horse Cavalry in Marfa, when he had a brainstorm. *Fold it eastward and El Paso will be 40 miles into the Atlantic.* He wrote his wife to send him his advertising files of notes and clippings. *Fold it westward and Orange will be 215 miles into the Pacific.* Writing after hours for four months, he produced what was to become Texas' best-selling souvenir of all time, a 62-page booklet of fact and fancy with the same name as his old ad campaign. *If Texas oil wells were opened to capacity, they would produce more oil in a day than the U.S. could use in a month.*

The response was a Texas brag in itself. *If all the hogs in Texas were one big hog, he could dig the Panama Canal with three roots and a grunt.* By the time Randolph returned to Houston in 1945, the booklet had sold 100,000 copies. *The King Ranch is so big that there is a month's difference in seasons between the northern and southern parts.* When he died in 1972, total sales were close to one million. *Said a Texas father to his son going East, "Son, it is very rude to ask a man where he is from. If he is from Texas, you will find it out, and if he's not, don't embarrass him."*

— TERRY TOLER

### BLUEBONNET SCENE, 1910

*And seen, and seen, and seen.*

**Has any artist been imitated more than Julian Onderdonk of San Antonio, the painter credited with creating the art form that hangs over half the sofas of Texas? Onderdonk painted *Bluebonnet Scene,* thought to be the first of the genre, around 1910 and spent the remaining twelve years of his life producing rich, atmospheric Texas landscapes, like the one above. They earned him the tag "the bluebonnet painter," which he thoroughly disliked. Nonetheless, Onderdonk is the undisputed master of the genre, and it was he who inspired generations of Sunday dabblers to set up their own easels in fields of blue.**
— **KATHERINE GREGOR**

# THE HANDSHAKE DEAL

## 1866

*The following account of the Goodnight-Loving partnership is adapted from J. Evetts Haley's book,* Charles Goodnight, Cowman and Plainsman.

The firm of Loving and Goodnight came into being in a dugout at Bosque Grande in the New Mexico wilderness. No papers were executed and no instruments drawn, yet its conditions bound its parties as strongly as the threads of life.

The handshake deal between Oliver Loving and Charles Goodnight was consummated during an early cattle drive to Fort Sumner in 1866. It was soon put to the test. Loving was on his way to Santa Fe the next year when he was shot by Comanches. He made it to Fort Sumner, but the wound became gangrenous. Loving knew he was dying and sent for Goodnight. He told his partner that he had gone deep into debt to supply the Confederate government with cattle for which he was

never paid. He asked Goodnight to continue the partnership for two years until all debts were satisfied and his family provided for. Goodnight agreed. After a time, Loving said, "I regret to have to be laid away in a foreign country." Goodnight assured him that he would bring his remains back to Texas.

Loving died a few days later and was buried at Fort Sumner. Goodnight took their herd on to Colorado, established a ranch there, and returned for Loving's body. Down the relentless Pecos and across the implacable plains the strangest and most touching funeral cavalcade in the history of the cow country followed the Goodnight and Loving Trail east to Loving's home in Weatherford. Though Goodnight was then 31 years of age, until his death nearly 63 years later his vibrant voice would mellow with reverence as he would slowly say, "my old partner," and raise his eyes to the picture that hung on the ranch-house wall.

*AMARILLO ART CENTER*

C. Barsotti
AFTER GEO. HERRIMAN

## THE UNKINDEST CUT

*A cuckold goes to jail.*

**1922** For those who find Texas primitive and its mores even more so, nothing confirms the prejudice like the discovery that Texas law until very recently permitted a man to kill his wife's paramour. This statute was one of the vestiges of the frontier mind-set that dominated Texas long after the frontier had vanished.

Pity, then, one J. O. Sensobaugh of Dallas, who, upon interrupting his wife and another man in flagrante delicto, produced a gun, some rope, and a razor and proceed-

ed not to kill his rival but to render him incapable of further offense. The victim survived to testify in court, where Sensobaugh was convicted in 1922 of aggravated assault and sentenced to a $300 fine and sixty days in jail. He appealed, citing his statutory right to vengeance. The appellate court didn't buy it, saying in essence, "If you wanted immunity, you should have killed him." Moral: In Texas, murder may occasionally be forgiven, but emasculation, never.

—PAUL BURKA

## A TOUGH OLD GAL
### 1871

AUSTIN HISTORY CENTER/PICB0991

*Lizzie Johnson*

Texas, it has been said, is hell on women and horses. An inscription on a grandfather clock given by Charles Goodnight, the rancher who was the first settler of the Panhandle, to his wife aptly sums up the plight and place of women on the Texas frontier:

IN HONOR OF
MRS. MARY DYER GOODNIGHT
PIONEER OF THE TEXAS PANHANDLE

*For many months, in 1876–77, she saw few men and no women, her nearest neighbor being seventy-five miles distant, and the nearest settlement two hundred miles. She met isolation and hardships with a cheerful heart, and danger with undaunted courage. With unfailing optimism, she took life's varied gifts, and made her home a house of joy.*

Mary Goodnight was tough, but the toughest of all was cattle queen Lizzie Johnson. After the Civil War she started rounding up unbranded Longhorns whose owners had been forced to abandon ranching. She put together a respectable herd, and by 1871, at age 28, she had registered her own brand.

Lizzie married late, at 36, to a rancher cum preacher named Hezekiah Williams. Recognizing in him a fondness for drink and a certain naiveté in business, she persuaded him to sign, long before it was in vogue, a prenuptial agreement that her property and profits during the marriage would remain solely hers. Eventually she amassed a quarter of a million dollars, while Hezekiah lost money time and time again. Lizzie bailed him out, but she made him sign a note for each loan.

Obviously Lizzie couldn't trust such a man to see her herds safely up the Chisholm Trail, so she decided to make the trip with him. That was unheard of; women never went on trail drives. Lizzie made the trip several times, traveling with her husband in a buckboard behind the two herds, which, at her insistence, were kept separate. And if there is any doubt left as to Lizzie's toughness, consider this: her cowhands were under standing orders to steal Hezekiah's unbranded calves and brand them as her own.

—ANNE DINGUS

## KREUZ BARBECUE MEETS NOUVELLE CUISINE AND SURVIVES

**1982** "Texas is a place where they barbecue everything but ice cream," a turn-of-the-century traveler is said to have observed. At about the same time, Charlie Kreuz first stoked his pit near Lockhart's courthouse square, one of hundreds of well-tended fires perfuming the Texas air. Eighty-odd years later Kreuz Market has outlasted them all, and barbecue is not merely lunch, it is culinary art.

As recently as the mid-sixties, when the small-town meat markets where Texas barbecue was born were already becoming curiosities, the meal still outweighed the mystique. The *Houston Chronicle* went to Kreuz's and photographed a grizzled old nester hunched over a mess of beef. "Shore good eatin'," he said, an explanation that for generations had been the only one necessary.

By 1982 the Texas Tourist Development Agency was photographing Kreuz's owner and carvers by a butcher block laden with beef and sausage. It juxtaposed the result with a similar shot of Dallas' *grand luxe* French Room and ran them as an advertisement in *Gourmet, Bon Appetit, National Geographic,* and a dozen other national magazines. "Haute cuisine," said one caption. "Hot cuisine," said the other. Twenty-three thousand people wrote back wanting to know more about Texas.

Despite its new-won fame, Kreuz's goes on as it always has, serving succulent slabs of shoulder, prime rib, and pork loin on red butcher paper—no plates, no forks, no sauce. "People come from all over the country and act like they're here to see a shrine," says Rick Schmidt, whose family bought Kreuz's from old Charlie's descendants in 1948. 'I've got to take a picture,' they say, 'because my friends back home won't believe this.'"

—GRIFFIN SMITH, JR.

◄ *Still life with barbecue.*

# HOW MANY AGGIES...

## BY JOHN HENRY FAULK

PEOPLE WHO ATTEND Texas Agricultural and Mechanical University are called Aggies. Aggies are noted for their fierce school spirit—also for their devotion to something they call Tradition. One of the Aggie traditions in years past was to be ferociously male. Another was that Aggies should not marry other Aggies.

Much of that has changed in the past quarter century. Aggies now can be either male or female. Not at the same time, of course. Aggies can now marry each other and frequently do. The greatest change that has come to the once-proud Aggies, however, is the public humiliation and humbling that they have received at the hands of the Aggie jokesmiths. The Aggie joke has flooded across Texas like a tidal wave, treating Aggies as a class of lunatic bumblers. The Aggie joke is now embedded, as firmly as a mesquite thorn in a bare heel, in our Texas folk culture.

Texas folklorists, who have been studying Aggie jokes for years, say that their research has established the time, date, and place of the first Aggie joke. It seems that at 5 p.m. on April 18, 1920, an Aggie named Tom returned to his dormitory room on the A&M campus to find his roommate, an Aggie named Will, in bed with bandages over both ears. "What the hell happened, Will?" Tom asked.

"I was ironing my shirt. The phone rang. I picked up that hot iron instead of the receiver," Will explained.

"But what happened to the other ear?"

"I had to call the doctor!"

Last month I was standing in a camera shop, down in deep East Texas, when an old, old man came in leaning on a cane. I quickly approached him, having been

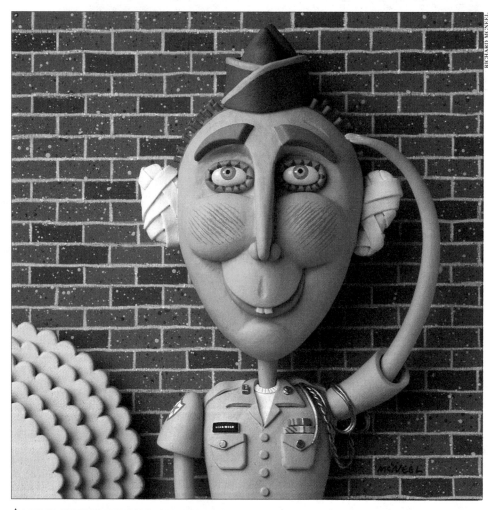

AGGIE TRADITIONS DIE HARD, AND THE ONE THAT DIES HARDEST IS THE VENERABLE AGGIE JOKE.

alerted by his request to *rent* flashbulbs. "Excuse me, sir! Were you ever a Texas Aggie?" I asked.

"Betcha boots I am," he snapped. "Still am! Once an Aggie, always an Aggie."

"When did you attend A and M?"

"Started in the day it opened, 1876! Was there four happy years."

"How old are you, sir?" I gasped.

"One hundred and thirty next birthday," he said proudly.

"Do you remember the first Aggie joke you ever heard?" I asked breathlessly.

"Well, yes. It was the first day of school. I asked my professor, 'Sir, is it all right to take off my shoes? I can't count to twenty with my shoes on.' I was serious about it, but everybody laughed. Without intending to, I had told the first Aggie joke."

"Then Aggie jokes are as old as A and M is," I ventured.

"Of course!" he snorted. "Where you think we got our Aggie traditions?" ✦

# BANE OF THE BAPTISTS

BY GARY CLEVE WILSON

BRANN BECOMES A CASUALTY IN HIS OWN WAR WITH THE BAPTISTS.

"IN THE YEAR OF OUR Lord, 1891, I became pregnant with an idea. Being at the time chief editorial writer on the *Houston Post*, I felt dreadfully mortified, as nothing of the kind had ever before occurred in that eminently moral establishment. Feeling that I was forever disqualified for the place by this untoward incident, I resigned and took sanctuary in the village of Austin. As swaddling clothes for the expected infant, I established the *Iconoclast,* which naturally gravitated to Waco, the political ganglion and religious storm centre of the state."

Thus did William Cowper Brann, the most controversial and widely read Texan of his day, write of the founding of the *Iconoclast,* a journal that by the end of 1894, its first year of publication, had a circulation of 100,000. To call Brann a polemicist is akin to calling a jalapeño hot. Either completely for or completely against, he held no middle ground. Political boss Mark Hanna was "the Avatar of Greed, the Scourge of God." The United States Senate was an "asylum for senility." But what readers relished most was the *Iconoclast*'s running war with Waco, Baylor, and the Baptists.

To Brann that countrified Trinity exemplified Victorian hypocrisy in its most splendid combination. When local preachers thundered against prizefighting, Brann wrote, "If Corbett and Fitzsimmons were to fight in Dallas to-day—without admission fee—Waco, the religious hub of the world, would be depopulated. Half the preachers of Texas would go early to secure front seats."

From issue one, Brann was on the attack. Religious leader T. DeWitt Talmadge was one of the first victims of Brann's corrosive satire: "The man who

can find intellectual food in Talmadge's sermons could acquire a case of delirium tremens by drinking the froth out of a pop bottle." Not surprisingly, Talmadge christened Brann "Apostle of the Devil." The name stuck, and Baptists began to pray for deliverance from that journalistic scourge.

Brann, who half seriously believed that the only thing wrong with Baptists was that they weren't held underwater long enough, never let up. No *Iconoclast* was without an exposé of some religious quackery or foolishness that Brann would righteously flay. Then Antonia Teixeira came along. She became to Brann what Helen became to Troy: the cause of an epic disaster.

A Brazilian missionary student at Baylor, Antonia boarded with Baylor's president, the Reverend Dr. Rufus C. Burleson. While there, she became pregnant. In the summer of 1895 H. Steen Morris, a relative of Burleson's, was arrested and charged with her rape. Brann put two and two together, and it came up "Baptists and a despoiled innocent." He could

ask for no better cause.

Baylor, Brann wrote, would "stink forever in the nostrils of Christendom—it is damned to everlasting fame." It was as if the university itself had committed the rape. Baptists and Baylorites tried to defend their honor while Brann exploited the issue for two years. He was selling papers.

He was also raising hackles. It was only a matter of time before Baylor sympathizers would act. When Brann proposed the erection of a monument commemorating Baylor's taking "an ignorant little Catholic as raw material" and getting "two Baptists as the finished product," Baylor loyalists figured they had had enough.

On a Saturday afternoon in October 1897, Brann was abducted at gunpoint and driven to the Baylor campus for a lesson in humility. Beaten and threatened with worse, He was chased off campus. A week later he was caned and horsewhipped by a father-and-son team of Baylor partisans. Brann began to carry a gun and took shooting lessons. Six months later he got his chance.

Brann was to take a well-earned vacation in the spring of 1898. He and his business manager were downtown buying railroad tickets when from behind them stepped Tom Davis, a local real estate investor and vocal detractor of Brann. Davis drew his pistol and shot at the lanky editor. Brann whirled, returning fire. The two emptied their sixshooters into each other as the late afternoon crowd stampeded. Moments later Davis was lying in a pool of blood, and Brann—shot in the groin, foot, and back —slid to the ground. He died early the next morning. Davis, hit six times, died soon after Brann. No one has given Texas Baptists much trouble since.

# 1955 DALLAS' CULTURAL ASPIRATIONS TAKE A BEATING WHEN CITY FATHERS REJECT A SCULPTURE.

# "A BUNCH OF JUNK"

## BY A. C. GREENE

THE MURAL COMMISSIONED BY ARCHITECT DAHL INCITED DALLAS TO CULTURAL PECKERWOODISM.

ON A MONDAY IN June 1955, before the weekly council meeting at city hall, Dallas mayor R. L. "Uncle Bob" Thornton and members of the city council strolled across Commerce Street to view the three-thousand-pound metallic mural that had just been installed in the unfinished $2.5 million public library building. The 24-by-10-foot sculpture by Pennsylvania artist Harry Bertoia consisted of hundreds of gilded multishaped pieces of steel roughly welded to a framework some four feet in depth, which made the gleaming work vibrantly three-dimensional. It stretched its stunning length above the library's main desk. Bertoia himself had been in Dallas the Friday before to supervise the installation.

The council members gazed up, and in the words of a *Dallas Morning News* writer, "Although all had been prepared by descriptions of the $8,700 'object d'art' . . . there were some surprised expressions." The mayor was the first to voice his surprise: "It looks to me like a bunch of junk painted up," he said. "Besides, that's a cheap welding job." Councilman W. H. Harris asked, "I wonder just what he was thinking about when he made it. He must have had the whole family working on it, including the children." Mayor Pro Tem Vernon A. Smith protested, "People will come in and forget what they came for when they see that collection of junk," and Councilman J. R. Terry was quoted as saying with a sigh, "I guess I just haven't been educated up to it." The mayor did see a bit of silver lining. "It has advertising possibilities. It'll attract attention."

Then some unidentified council member asked the question that was undoubtedly foremost in everyone's thoughts: "Have we paid for it yet?" Standing there, casting their eyes on the modernistic artwork, the Dallas City Council felt the chill winds of a latent political cyclone.

Mayor Thornton's comments and the council's reaction made the local front pages, then were spread across the nation by the wire services. Local philistines had a carnival. Letter writers to both newspapers opened fire, sight unseen, on the Bertoia mural, which, incidentally, was not a mural at all. It was called that because the official library building specifications–approved by the council–had stipulated "a mural painting on the plaster wall" to the right of the entrance.

The attack against the Bertoia sculpture was led by *Morning News* columnist Lynn Landrum. Landrum was famous as a reactionary against almost anything arty that came within range of his typewriter. The Columntator, as he referred to himself, admitted he'd not seen the piece but explained, "The proper viewpoint for surveying non-representational art is the non-representational viewpoint. In this case, the viewpoint is approximately one mile west of the masterpiece. The view is even better from Fort Worth." Landrum suggested titles for the metallic screen: *Billy Goat Fodder; Cancan at the Crematorium; Think, Thank, Thunk.* Letters to the editor, as published, ran 80 per cent against the artwork.

Within two weeks of its hanging, the mural was down. The council privately called in library architect George Dahl, who had commissioned the Bertoia metal screen in place of a traditional painted mural, and told him he would have to pay for it, that they wouldn't. Dahl, a man of strong opinions and statements, said if he paid he'd by God take it with him. So, on Friday, July 8, a truck backed up to the library's front entrance; the metal screen was dismantled, put under wraps, and hauled off to an undisclosed destination. Dahl was disgusted. "I hope everybody who had a part in getting the mural removed is proud of himself," he said.

Harry Bertoia was deeply incensed. A major designer, he was enjoying immense national success. He had executed sculptural screens for such clients as General Motors, Manufacturers Trust Company of New York, and the Massachusetts Institute of Technology. (In 1956 he would win the American Institute of Architects' Craftsmanship Medal.) "I think I gave the city of Dallas one of my very best efforts," he told Bob Stanley of the *Times Herald.* "The judgment is beyond me. Perhaps, in time to come, Dallas might even repent of having done such a thing."

To the gleeful antis, the removal of the mural ended the controversy. The council issued a pious official statement. "We think to buy more books and things of that character for the benefit of most people would be a much wiser investment for the taxpayers than a mural which only a limited number would understand and enjoy."

To this point this story has been based on articles and columns published at the time. The writer will now reveal his never-before-disclosed role in the chain of events, a role that was minor but turned out to have a somewhat more than minor impact.

Although I had spent some prior years as a journalist, in 1955 I was the owner of a bookstore in Abilene. When I read about the much-abused mural that had been banished by the Dallas city fathers, an idea occurred to me. The Citizens National Bank was erecting a new office building, the first in Abilene since the Wooten Hotel was constructed in 1929. Knowing that bank president Malcolm Meek was an ambitious, public-relations-conscious executive—and a contemporary of Thornton, who was a banker as well as mayor of Dallas—I suggested that he offer to buy the Bertoia and install it in his new building to show that Abilene was cognizant of the importance of Bertoia and his sculptural art, even if Big D wasn't.

Malcolm Meek immediately liked the plan. He first contacted Dahl, saying his certified check for whatever amount Dahl needed was ready to be cut. He called Uncle Bob, sympathetically suggesting that letting Abilene have the mural would be the best disposition of the affair. He was also going to call the *New York Times,* which had been spotlighting the Dallas art assault. I am not sure that Malcolm Meek was any more appreciative of modern art than was Uncle Bob, but he knew a publicity windfall when he saw one.

Whether the Abilene offer was the thing that turned the tide, the tide got turned,

and quickly. The *Times Herald* reported in a front-page story that an effort seemed to be under way by a group of Dallas private citizens to buy and restore to the library the controversial mural if the library board would guarantee its acceptance. Boude Storey, president of the library board, said he knew of no reason why it would not be accepted as a donation. Mayor Thornton quickly announced that the city had no objections "if someone will sponsor it privately." By the beginning of August the citizens' group had announced that it not only had collected enough to buy back the mural but probably might even donate a few hundred excess dollars for books (the city having chopped the library book budget by 40 per cent).

The formal opening of the new library was set for Sunday, September 25. It was the most spectacular day the Dallas library had known, thanks to the Bertoia screen. Even Uncle Bob Thornton said he had decided he liked the device since he found out it was not a mural but a metal screen. "That makes more sense," he said.

The Bertoia screen became a much-loved feature of the library, remaining over the main desk for 27 years, until that new library became the old library. The screen was moved in 1982 to the new central library where today it hangs, its tribulations forgotten, over an outdoor walkway.

The contretemps over the screen didn't end attempts at public censorship in Dallas, but it marked a swing in civic sentiment. Dallas was no longer a village, guided by outspoken rural anti-intellectualism. Dallas felt that it had become a more sophisticated place and expected better of its officials than the embarrassment of calling the work of a respected artist "a bunch of junk," even if that might be their personal view. After the Battle of the Bertoia, newspaper columnists and editorial writers quit automatically taking the peckerwood side of every cultural question. In 1976 Councilman William E. Cothrum protested the Henry Moore bronze scheduled for the new city hall plaza. By the time it was installed in 1978, Cothrum's views had changed enough for him to escort Henry Moore to a Dallas Cowboys game.

Dallas continued to go through artistic yahooism, but it was political, not cultural. Earlier in 1955 the Dallas Museum of Fine Arts had been pressured to remove paintings by Picasso, Diego Rivera, and others. The pressure came from citizens who thought that the artists were communists. But the Bertoia incident gave arts supporters enough spunk to fire back at the philistines, and in December 1955 the museum board announced that it would acquire and exhibit items "only on the basis of their merit as works of art." On the other hand, there is no record of whether Uncle Bob Thornton ever again looked at the badly welded bunch of junk. ◆

# 1920 THE ORIGINAL POOR LITTLE TEXAS RICH GIRL GOES ON A LEGENDARY SPREE AT NEIMAN-MARCUS.

# ELECTRA GOES SHOPPING

## BY SUSAN CHADWICK

ONE DAY IN DALLAS, AS THE country raced into the roaring twenties, a fashionably plump, middle-aged woman, elegantly dressed and draped with jewels, entered the Neiman-Marcus store. The staff knew her, of course. She was one of the store's wealthiest and most eccentric customers. But on this day she astounded them all—and bought $20,000 worth of beautiful clothes.

Incredibly, what she bought wasn't enough. And so the next day she came again and bought another $20,000 worth of fine things, spending in two days the equivalent of almost a quarter of a million in today's dollars.

So goes the tale, chronicled by *Dallas Morning News* columnist Frank X. Tolbert, of Electra Waggoner, the first and most famous of all the Texas rich girls. What she saw, she wanted; what she wanted, she bought. For a brief but dazzling year or two, Electra Waggoner, with her shopping sprees and lavish parties, stunned the world with her exquisite taste, her style, and her wealth and established the precedent that oil money was meant to be spent conspicuously and extravagantly.

The only daughter of land and cattle baron Tom Waggoner, pretty little Electra grew up in palatial splendor at El Castile, the family estate in Decatur north of Fort Worth. With her violet eyes, long dark lashes, fair skin, and sweet disposition, young Electra was the object of many a cowboy's dreams, but she gave her heart to an Easterner, A. B. Wharton of Philadelphia, whom she met while on a tour of Europe. They were married in 1902, when Electra was twenty years old. Her father built her a mansion in Fort Worth as a wedding present, and the citizens of Waggoner in North Texas formed a new town and named it Electra.

For nineteen years Electra lived a relatively quiet, private life, though it included shopping trips to Europe and the Orient and seasons spent in Palm Beach and at the summer home in

ELECTRA: WHAT SHE WANTS, SHE BUYS.

Spring Lake, New Jersey. But by 1921 Electra was ready to move her family to Dallas, so she bought a redbrick Georgian mansion there and named it Shadowlawn.

Alas, Electra's marriage foundered, and she moved into her new home a divorcée and single mother. It was then that Electra burst upon the world social scene and set the standard by which big Texas spenders are still measured. Shadowlawn, at 4700 Preston Road in the Turtle Creek area, was three blocks long and had a backyard lake. Electra furnished it with half a million dollars' worth of new drapes, lace bedspreads, billiard

tables, Chinese chairs, French sofas, Persian carpets, marble chests, and Venetian cabinets with made-to-order matching banquet table and chairs, as well as with objets d'art, cloisonné, and other fine items she had collected on voyages around the world. By that time, it should be noted, the Waggoners were not just well off; they were very well off, oil having been discovered all over their half-million acres.

At Shadowlawn Electra had a closet. More than a closet, it was a warehouse. One room was devoted to furs—only furs. Another was filled with the latest fashions delivered directly from Paris and New York. Another room held 350 pairs of custom-made shoes, almost enough to wear a new pair every day, and indeed it was reported that new shoes from New York and Neiman's were delivered daily.

And, oh, did Electra entertain. The wealthy Texans of her time were in the habit of throwing a pretty good party now and then. But none did it like Electra. Her guests included kings and queens of society from around the world, Morgans and movie stars. They feasted on stuffed pheasant and strawberries in the middle of winter, all served on plates of fourteen-karat gold or sterling silver. Weekend parties began at Shadowlawn and ended in a caravan of Electra's cars at her ranch, Zacaweista. On occasion Electra hired a private train to move her parties across the country.

In the summer of 1922 Electra married again, to Weldon Bailey of Gainesville. Shadowlawn was sold, and the extravagant parties ended. The marriage was not a happy one; it lasted only two and a half years. Several months after the divorce, her health beginning to fail, Electra tried again, but this marriage was even shorter than the last; it was annulled after only a few months. On Thanksgiving Day, 1925, at the age of 43, Electra Waggoner died in a New York hotel room on Park Avenue, of complications, it was said, resulting from a broken heart. ♣

# 1958

A NEW COACH LEADS THE LONGHORNS TO A LONG-AWAITED VICTORY OVER OKLAHOMA AND REMAKES TEXAS FOOTBALL IN HIS OWN IMAGE.

# THE ROYAL TREATMENT

## BY DAN JENKINS

*Texans have always taken their football seriously, but in the late fifties almost no one else did. The Southwest Conference hadn't produced a national champion in more than two decades. In 1956 UT, once the conference's flagship school, won just one game—by one point. Oklahoma drubbed UT with embarrassing regularity. Then Darrell Royal came to coach the Longhorns. Soon everybody was taking Texas football seriously. Royal won his first big game, breaking the domination of Oklahoma over Texas, in 1958, and Dan Jenkins, who at the time was a young sportswriter with the soon-to-be-defunct* Fort Worth Press, *filed this report on the creation of a football dynasty:*

DALLAS, OCTOBER 11, 1958—Those plans of substituting Wayland's College of Women for Oklahoma on the University of Texas football schedule were abruptly cancelled here today by a Longhorn team that wouldn't accept defeat from the Sooners in any kind of crazy package.

You'd have to go back to the grassy knolls of San Jacinto to find more Texas heroes on one field. Some might compare it to the Alamo, but who wants to talk about a loser?

If there was a secret weapon in the 15–14 upset of Oklahoma Saturday it was Vince Matthews, the obscure junior passer from Houston whom Coach Darrell Royal had saved for the occasion.

But Matthews had no more to do with the victory than all of those University of Texas defenders who stopped Sooner drives at their own 13, 23, 5 and 24 yard lines.

It may be trite to say so, but the Big Day was the result of a team effort, an organization effort, actually.

Royal's scouts had pegged the Sooners so accurately that those weird formations of Bud Wilkinson were no more effective than a grammar book in a Tennessee Williams play.

At times, in fact, you got the impres-

BOB BRYANT CATCHES THE PASS THAT TOPPLES OKLAHOMA FOR COACH DARRELL ROYAL.

sion that Texas had invented them and just lent them to Oklahoma for the afternoon.

Royal substituted beautifully all day, changing his men as Casey Stengel changes relief pitchers. The best example was in the winning drive when he let Matthews sweep the Longhorns downfield into position at the OU seven, then sent in Bobby Lackey for the clincher.

Spirit won it for the Longhorns, a spirit that has been lacking on Texas'

part in the intersectional game for years.

It has been instilled in the Orange by Royal, who has a way with young men. The modern Southwest Conference has yet to see a team as suicidal as these Longhorns who can't wait to hit you, get up, and start trying to hit you again.

It's been ages since this correspondent saw a football team wrench victory out of so much adversity, battling time, a top-level opponent and the sting of a succession of disheartening blows. ✦

# LOCO MOTIVES

### BY FREDERICK BARTHELME

*On September 15, 1896, the Missouri, Kansas, and Texas railroad, in a nationally publicized event designed to generate cash and goodwill for the company, intentionally crashed two locomotives together at ninety miles per hour in a field outside Waco. Fifty thousand people from all over the country attended. The collision and explosion sent scalding water and hunks of metal whistling through the crowd, killed at least two people, wounded dozens, and contributed mightily to the idea that Texans are hugely, almost divinely stupid, not to mention universally crude, insensitive, and morally corrupt. Herewith, our reporter's eyewitness account.*

MARBIGALE GETS ME UP EARLY because she wants to go to the train wreck, a rollerball thing they're doing out by Waco. We have special tickets on the MK&T, tour sponsor on the deal, so we head for Crush Town, the tent city where they're colliding the trains. I want to see this wreck, too, I mean, a really wonderful wreck–this is America, right? This is Texas.

So we're in this pasture and it's four in the afternoon, the sun's bending people over right and left, and what we have is five acres and 50,000 human beings in running shorts. Talk about beauty. They have loudspeakers playing "Nuages" everywhere. One guy has Confederate gear on, so I know the crowd isn't local.

We get us a spot in this mesquite tree onto which the promoters have pasted orange blossoms, trying to pretty up the place. It's a scrawny thing, but it's good for us. Suddenly, out of nowhere, comes a howling, and this real slow train comes onto the track, and then another one comes from the other direction, also slow, and Marbigale turns around with a disappointed look and says, "Say, Bilbo, you hungry?"

So then 35 dozen young men in foreign-made buggies drawn by foreign-born horses come in. These people have a lot of foreign mannerisms–vests,

**THE CRASH AT CRUSH: ONLY IN TEXAS WOULD PEOPLE PAY TO SEE TWO TRAINS COLLIDE.**

for example, and temple-high sideburns, and degrees in smiling and similar. Then E. Power Biggs shows up with the biggest organ I ever saw, and he's looking for Scott Joplin, who's around somewhere working up some rags. The locals are all snake charmers, flying jennies, freaks of nature–regulars. They're booing and hissing and throwing tripe at the trains, because the trains are going so slow, and at these foreigners, because they're so foreign.

"Spine-tingling!" Marbigale yells, and she tosses some tripe we bought at Tripe Country on the way up.

The trains stop an inch from each

other, guys climb down from opposing engines to shake hands, and at this juncture the jeers reach big proportions. There's a speech that begins, "Throughout all of my clangorous hours," which I believe is made by Pat Robertson, practicing. Marbigale hollers at Pat, "Yo, Devil's Food! Why don't you call *me* for a change?"

So the trains back up, out of the pasture, and we wait an hour watching Leo Wolfson, of Dallas, make his fortune in lemonade, and the foreign-born folks, who are sitting around with their hands in their pants. We watch their hands, to see what they do with them in there.

After a time here come the whistles again. The tree we're in starts shaking, and there's this rumbling, real quiet, like you got your head underwater in the bathtub and somebody's thumping on the porcelain with a sock of rabbit pellets. And on the extreme left and right we got fierce columns of black smoke whisking up into the green Texas sky, and the rumbling gets crazy, like an earthquake or something, and the folks are unnerved—they're moving around real jerky in this way they don't ordinarily do, as if they're from New Jersey or something, and can't even move their legs far enough apart.

There's a guy under our tree wearing a checkerboard suit, so he must be from California. He turns to this Texas boy alongside him and says he bets the red engine wins, and the Texas boy, he looks at this other for a long time, I mean a *long* time, and then he says, "Wins?" as if he's a stranger to the concept.

The trains slither across the prairie like black lightning, and this boy's trying to get his bet amidst all the rollin' and tumblin', the earsplitting roar, the curls of smoke curling away from the locomotives like topknots. As if by magic, Lord John Whorfin (evil pure and simple from Planet 10 in the Eighth Dimension, a little-known section of the state north of Marfa), steps up and breaks the California kid's neck, snaps it right in two. There's applause.

There's no stopping the trains. They're hurtling at one another at the advertised speed, they hit, there's an explosion ("Boilers," I tell Marbigale), pieces of metal the size of human heads ricochet everywhere—a guy in the next tree gets a seventy-pound steel chain in the face, splitting his skull like a red-centered honeydew. This stove bolt zings right past Marbigale and me and plugs up this photographer's eye. Out-of-staters are screaming and causing trouble. Suddenly it doesn't even *look* like Texas around there anymore; it looks like I don't know what—some lesser state. There's debris everywhere, and people falling down. This one fella gets cleaved right in two by the extraordinary silver hair of the beautiful owner of the Crush Gallery, made airborne by the blast.

Marbigale is restless. She says, "This is a fool way to spend a day, Bilbo. It's only the invention of bumper cars, a moment in history." She gets up, ready for home. "I've been thinking about dinner," she says. "What do you like for dinner?"

I look around us—steam, and burst pop-off valves, burst drive-wheel valves, a lot of valves. I stare at the wounded, maimed, sick, and dead. My heart thumps in my throat. I'm too shocked to scream. I say, "Marbigale, what about the dead and the dying?"

She takes a look, waits a minute, then shakes her head, and starts down the tree. "Nah," she says. "We'd have to clean 'em first."❧

# 1977

THANKS TO AN ORNERY MECHANICAL BULL, A PASADENA HONKY-TONK BECOMES THE STOMPING GROUNDS OF THE URBAN COWBOY.

# BRAVE NEW BEAST

BY AARON LATHAM

ONE DAY IN 1977 A FLATBED TRUCK pulled up in front of Gilley's Saloon in Pasadena loaded with a pile of nuts and bolts and leather. A crossbreed of beast and machine, it had been fathered by a Brahma bull, but its mother was a motorcycle or an oil-well pump or a jackhammer or a cement mixer or maybe even a Cuisinart. This "animal" seemed as unlikely to go down in any kind of history as that scrawny-looking horse without a tail that carried Sam Houston to victory down the road at San Jacinto. Yet it became a symbol for the plight of the urban cowboy, imprisoned in a mechanized world, a small cog in a vast urban machine, trying to recapture the unreachable past.

"It's a bucking machine, what they train rodeo riders on, a damn mechanical bull," explained Sherwood Cryer, the boss at Gilley's. "Unload it." Steve Strange and Gator Conley, veteran Gilley's hands, jumped to do what the boss said. They used a piano dolly to roll it into Gilley's and plugged it in. Nobody thought about bolting it to the floor.

"Who's going to be the first one to ride it?" asked Sherwood. When nobody volunteered immediately, he turned to Steve Strange and said, "Well, you talk about being a goddam rodeo hand, let's see you get up there."

"But, but," Steve stuttered.

The last time Steve had gotten on a bull, it had cost him one of his testicles. The bull caught him in the chute, and when he got out of the hospital part of him was plastic. He had not been on a bull since.

"Go on, get up there," Sherwood ordered.

Trying not to think about his last encounter with a bull, Steve tied a bullrider's rope around the middle of the mechanical bull. Then he crawled aboard. From his perch on the back of the bull, Steve stared down at the concrete floor, which looked a lot harder seen from on high. No one had thought to gather up any mattresses to land on.

Sherwood sat down at the remote con-

FOR URBAN COWBOYS, GILLEY'S MECHANICAL BULL IS A WAY TO RECAPTURE THE PAST.

trols that ran the bull. He pushed a button, and the bull started to buck up and down. He twisted a lever, and the bull started to spin and buck at the same time, like a cement truck on a roller coaster track—which is what makes a bull so hard to ride, the up and down combined with the round and round.

"I kept looking at the cement and wouldn't let go," Steve remembers. "I kept saying to myself, 'Steve, you can do this. You can do this. Don't let go.'"

He kept expecting Sherwood to stop the bull, but no such luck. Both the bull and the man running it seemed to have hearts made of steel, prison hearts. The bull just kept spinning and bucking and bucking and spinning.

And then Steve Strange was flying through the air. He says he jumped, but others say he was thrown. In any case, he was the first would-be cowboy to be launched into the air by the mechanical bull.❦

# 1974

A CARTOON TEXTBOOK THAT INFLUENCED
GENERATIONS OF TEXAS SCHOOLCHILDREN FACES
CHARGES OF RAMPANT RACISM–AND IS FOUND GUILTY.

# Classic Comics

BY ARNOLD ROSENFELD

I WAS ONE OF THE LAST GENERATION that swam regularly in Houston's bayous. I say that not so much out of pride–even then, skinny-dipping in the bayou was not considered all that great a thing to do–but out of some necessity to identify the times.

"Pollution" was a word none of us had heard, and corrosion was something that happened to a car. You got corrosion on weekend trips to Galveston, when your father parked the family car for long hours out on West Beach in the sun and the sand and the salt air. You had to be careful to hose the old jalopy down when you got home, or else you got corrosion. Nobody I knew ever got corroded in the bayou, or even sick, although it was the polio epidemics of the time that finally caused the authorities to close down bayou swimming for good.

The bayou was a killer, nevertheless. Kids were all the time diving off the side and banging their heads on the bottom or on sunken logs or getting caught beneath underwater snags. The bayou could reach out and get you. We went swimming in it anyhow. We talked about it more than we did it. It was a rite of passage, just like *Texas History Movies.*

That was, I'd say, about 1946. I was–and wasn't–a student at James S. Hogg Junior High School. The closest I got to actually studying was *Texas History Movies.* When I saw a copy of this strange volume a few months ago in an Austin bookstore specializing in Texana, my heart leapt. For the uninitiated, *Texas History Movies* represented all that most of us knew in those times–or were willing to know–about the history of our state. Texas history was a required course in junior high school and, therefore, one of the most detested. The Houston school board insisted that every student have at least a working knowledge of state history.

For most of us, that seemed unnecessary. Everyone knew about Texas history. We had beaten the Mexicans at San Jacinto. We even had a high school named for it, and all of us had been out

*TEXAS HISTORY MOVIES* REPRESENTED ALL WE WERE WILLING TO KNOW ABOUT OURSELVES.

to the nearby battleground at least twice. What did they want of us? My parents had gone to San Antonio on a vacation once and had seen the Alamo. They had told me about it. Wasn't that enough? The Houston school board was filled with such strange enthusiasms. A few years later they would have us all studying the Hoover Commission's recommendations for reorganizing the federal government. Talk about boring.

For those bored out of their skulls with the school board and its required history texts, there was *Texas History Movies,* the *Classics Illustrated* of state history. Published originally in 1926

as a comic strip in the *Dallas News,* it was converted into a little paperback booklet and distributed free to hundreds of thousands of Texas schoolchildren by Magnolia Petroleum, later Mobil Oil.

I paid $20 for a copy in good condition at the Austin bookstore. It took me at least half an hour at home that night to explain to my wife why such a purchase was worth twenty perfectly good dollars. She never understood. She's from Boston. Self-righteously, I settled down to read *Texas History Movies.*

I hated it. Over the years, something had happened to both of us.

For one thing, as far as *Texas History*

63

*Movies* was concerned, Texas history had somehow come to a screeching halt sometime around 1885, when a guy with a beard suggested putting a horny toad in the cornerstone of the new state capitol at Austin. All further history is summed up with an enigmatic "And Texas has reached the estate of 1928," which is like summarizing the history of the United States since 1900 by saying, "And lots of terrific things happened after that." I used to write junior high school book reports like that. You know, lots of emphasis on the first 20 pages you did read, then the briefest of summaries of the 275 you didn't.

Perhaps especially because of the excitement of discovery, the finding of a long-lost friend, I felt ill-used by *Texas History Movies*. Lots of us, unfortunately, thought that *was* history. The cartoon Indians are fond of saying things like "White brother heap good feller" and "Ugh" when they are not being chased by spirited and patriotic colonizers eager to settle their land the right way. Mexicans are referred to as tamale eaters. Cartoon black people, when they are not otherwise occupied singing things like "Aw wish ah wuz way down souf in Africa," are found to be declaring, hat in hand, "Ah wants to go wit' Marse Woolridge."

I wondered how many of us were still around who thought that was Texas history. Others, apparently, have wondered the same thing. When the *Houston Chronicle* decided to reprint *Texas History Movies* in 1974, the Texas State Historical Association (which had obtained the rights from Mobil Oil in 1961) organized an advisory board with black and Hispanic members to make racially sensitive corrections. For the sesquicentennial, two new editions of *Texas History Movies* have been issued by a Dallas firm, PJM Publishers. They include an exact replica of the original book and a paperback abridgment representing about 35 per cent of the original. The abridgment has been carefully revised by historians and teachers who, according to the publisher, have researched every cartoon and caption from the standpoint of accuracy, story value, humor, and sensitivity.

Still, the revised versions may never quite catch up with *Texas History Movies,* not for those of us who read it in the original—however it influenced us. *Texas History Movies* remains an artifact, like arrowheads, of our past. Says George B. Ward of the Texas State Historical Association, "Every generation rewrites history according to its own experience, and most history reflects the values of its day. Therefore *Texas History Movies,* with its biases and caricatures, is a valuable historical tool that lets us see how we used to understand ourselves and our history." All true, and one of the major tests of the sesquicentennial will be whether it brings us closer to our mutual history, the guilt as well as the glory, than did *Texas History Movies.*◆

# Icing on the Cake

BY ALISON COOK

**1893** MISS ALICE O'GRADY OPENS THE ARGYLE IN BUMPTIOUS SAN ANTONIO. WITH HER PASTEL-TINTED CABBAGE AND SPUN-SUGAR WONDERS, SHE SERVES TEXANS THE STYLE AND REFINEMENT THEY YEARN FOR.

ONE SUMMER SATURDAY IN 1981, an elegantly thin and mournful-looking fellow named Mel Weingart boarded a flight from San Antonio to Washington, D.C. His baggage contained not clothing but papayas, San Antonio–grown mint, and Explorateur cheese, all destined for the Monday luncheon that Beryl Bentsen was tossing for Nancy Reagan. Like hundreds of well-bred South Texans before her, the senator's wife had turned to San Antonio's select Argyle club—and to Weingart, its longtime manager and arbiter extraordinaire—when things had to be, well, perfect. Weingart could be trusted to take care of everything in that ever-so-comfortable but unmistakably upper-class Argyle style, from ordering the right flowers to securing the right help to baking those trademark Argyle cheese straws. All day Sunday, Weingart labored in Bentsen's kitchen, prepping his menu of fresh lobster and homemade mayonnaise garnished with papaya, lime, watercress, and tiny roses, followed by lemon-buttered veal and a raspberry soufflé so bedecked in spun sugar that Bentsen's worldly guests broke into spontaneous applause. The First Lady, to the Texans' gratification, lingered longer than expected.

Weingart is no stranger to such command performances. When Anne Armstrong was appointed ambassador to the Court of St. James's in 1976, she summoned Weingart to London to set her staff and kitchen in order and to establish the proper haute-Texas tone for her official residence, Winfield House. It was only fitting. For 127 years, through several incarnations, the pillared, deep-verandahed building that is the Argyle club has been an exemplar of the style by which upper-class San Antonio identifies itself. And for much of that time, it has been an exemplar of something larger—the civilizing impulse at work. In big cities and hamlets, in the crassest boomtowns and the brawlingest frontier towns, there was always that handful of people who took it upon themselves not just to tame the land but to smooth its rough edges. Every log-cabin musicale, every reading society, every museum poked and prodded into existence, attested to the fact that there were standards in this world—manners and culture and values—and, more to the point, that there were people determined to bring those things to Texas. They were the sort of people who invariably held forth in the San Antonio homestead that came to be known as the Argyle.

Although today the Argyle houses a private dining club so exclusive that certain newly moneyed San Antonians would betray their sainted mothers to

MEL WEINGART, THE ARGYLE'S ARBITER EXTRAORDINAIRE: IS THE CLUB A BASTION OF CULTURE OR A FORTRESS AGAINST THE NEW MONEY?

gain admission, the structure began life in 1859 as the headquarters of a vast horse ranch. Presiding over its cool rock walls, thick cypress floors, and lofty ceilings was lawyer and horse breeder Charles Anderson, who endowed his tough Texas sorrels with such biblical names as Jehoshaphat and Nebuchadnezzar. In the interests of selling his beasts to the Army gentry stationed nearby, he mounted lavish hunting parties with the aid of a large staff and counted such luminaries as Robert E. Lee among his guests. After Anderson's pro-Union sympathies caused him to be run out of town by a secret secessionist order called the Knights of the Golden Circle (when last heard from, Anderson was governor of Ohio), he was succeeded at the ranch by another man of parts. Hiram McLane not only bred horses but collected violins and penned Southwestern epics, his most celebrated effort being a historical tragedy of the Alamo with prologue in blank verse.

But it was Alice O'Grady, the daughter of an Irish innkeeper from Boerne, who firmly established the Anderson-McLane homestead as a bastion of fine Southern manners. Wearing a corsage of cow clover, Miss Alice opened the place as the Argyle Hotel on St. Patrick's Day, 1893, with her brother Bob as host. The hilly, wooded surrounds that were to become the blue-chip neighborhood of Alamo Heights boasted only a few houses then, but Miss Alice's cornucopian table quickly became the talk of the town. Not only did she [ CONTINUED ON PAGE 99 ]

65

# THAT OLD-TIME RELIGION

## BY WILLIAM A. OWENS

*In his book* Tell Me a Story, Sing Me a Song . . . , *published in 1983, William A. Owens painted a timeless portrait of that East Texas cultural mainstay, the revival meeting.*

IT WAS AUGUST, THE DOG DAYS, hot, dry, and dusty, the time for protracted meetings in the country. It was a dull time, between the last plow down a furrow and the first cotton sack down that same furrow. People needed this time, for rest and for gathering together with their neighbors. So they came, walking the road at dusk, meeting other families, at times moving aside to let a car bound for the meeting go by. I waited till there were no longer the sounds of people coming in—of mumbling voices and shoes on hard-packed ground. Then I took a seat on a back bench. The people around me had tired eyes, tired faces, tired, but not unfeeling. Like the faithful of their people who had gone on before, they were looking up at the preacher, waiting for him to bring the light and spread it among them. Only then would their quietness give way; only then would they sound their own prayer and praise. . . .

It was going to be a good meeting, I heard from people around me. They meant that it would reach some emotional peak. The night before had, in their words, been "a good'un." Two women had gone into trances, one of them so deep that they had to labor over her all night and only "this e'enin," too late for her to leave her house, had they been able to bring her out of it.

At a pause in the singing the preacher

THE TIMELESS REVIVAL: A WOMAN GIVES A SHOUT AND THROWS HER HEAD BACK, MOVING WITH OTHERS, SIGHTLESS IN THEIR REJOICING.

came down to the mourner's bench and stretched out his arms. Then in a voice more emotional than tuneful he began a song that stretched back to early seekers, people who wanted the touch of God not through a priest but through their own reaching out:

*Come you sinners, poor and needy,*
*Weak and wounded, sick and sore;*
*Jesus ready stands to save you,*
*Full of pity, love, and pow'r.*

It was his song and prelude to his sermon. No one raised a voice with him as he slowly trod the sawdust. This was as much sermon as song—a part of an appeal for sinners to seek salvation. The sad pleading of the stanza changed to a tone of comfort in the refrain:

*I will arise and go to Jesus;*
*He will embrace me in his arms;*
*In the arms of my dear Savior,*
*Oh, there are ten thousand charms.*

His sermon carried the same burden of thought, with elaboration after elaboration on human frailty, the need through Christ's blood to be born again, and the final resting place in hell for those who continued on the downward path with sin and Satan. Deacons said, "Amen and again amen." Women wept softly. Workers pleaded in soft voices with those who had not yet "given themselves to the Lord." A man laid his hand on my arm and leaned close: "You been born again?" I nodded. He moved on. Then the preacher reminded them of the saints who had gone on before.

Suddenly a woman started toward him, singing in a high-pitched voice. He shouted "Glory!" and jumped up on the mourner's bench, singing with her, beckoning others to join in until half the people were on their feet, rejoicing:

*I have a mother in the Promised Land,*
*I have a mother in the Promised Land,*
*And I hope some day we'll all be there,*
*Away over in the Promised Land.*

By the time they had started "I have a father in the Promised Land" a woman gave a shout and moved in a slow dance toward the mourner's bench. Her head thrown back, her eyes closed, she bumped into benches, and into men and women sightless in their own exulting.

Almost without missing a beat the singers ended one song and took up another, omitting the stanzas, beating out the refrain over and over:

*Oh, you must be a lover of the Lord,*
*Or you won't go to heaven when you die.*

On and on they went, singing, shouting, dancing, praying, but no one came to the mourner's bench, no one fell into a trance. When it was clear the meeting was trailing off to an end the preacher asked that they give each other the right hand of fellowship before departing. The people formed two lines and, in a ritualistic manner, met to shake hands with him and with each other, singing together their inner peace:

*What have I to dread, what have I*
*to fear,*
*Leaning on the everlasting arm?*
*I have blessed peace in my*
*Savior dear,*
*Leaning on the everlasting arm.*

They sang the stanza and then repeated the refrain over and over, loath to leave each other, the comfort of the words:

*Leaning, leaning, leaning on the*
*everlasting arm;*
*Leaning, leaning, leaning on the*
*everlasting arm.*

As I walked toward my car I could hear a woman's voice, high above the others, singing "thribble," a wavery, plaintive tenor, the plaint of a spirit consoled yet unconsolable, a plea from the persuaded to the almost persuaded. ❧

# 1948 HURRY UP AND BRING US A MESS OF THEM ESCARGOTS, WILL YA, HON?

# CLASSY EATS

## BY PATRICIA SHARPE

YOU CAN'T PRONOUNCE FISH *EN PAPILLOTE*? TRY CAMILLE BERMANN'S CHICKEN-FRIED STEAK INSTEAD.

CAMILLE BERMANN fondly refers to his new Maxim's restaurant as the Taj Mahal. Considering the fortresslike glass building it occupies on Bermann's own piece of Greenway Plaza real estate, the luxuriously swaddled dining room, and the high-tech kitchen with its army of cooks, he hasn't overstated the matter by much. Maxim's is the bastion of Houston's old guard, the secure haven of the River Oaks plutocracy. Wildcatter Glenn McCarthy, now 77, eats there three or four times a week. Attorney for the defense Percy Foreman has his own table with ever-present telephone.

With all its pomp and circumstance, the present Maxim's seems a bit too cream-fed and fat to reflect its pioneering role in Houston's past. The legendary Maxim's started downtown in 1948 on Fannin Street, moving ten years later to the corner of Lamar and Milam. There, in three narrow Moulin Rouge rooms plastered with red-flocked wallpaper and crammed with reproductions of French impressionist paintings, the new restaurant dazzled a wet-behind-the-ears populace whose idea of a fancy dinner was a steak and a baked potato washed down with bourbon and branch water. (As if to symbolize that its purpose was to civilize the wilderness, Maxim's was located in a corner of the Foley's parking garage.)

The Houston that existed when Maxim's first opened hardly seemed like the ideal setting for a classical French restaurant. Houston was still an industrial city, not an international one, and some of its richest citizens were onetime roughnecks who still acted the part. Dallas and San Antonio were regarded as far more sophisticated. And if fine dining was desired, why, New Orleans and New York were the only places to go. Houston had only a dozen or so viable restaurants—places like Kaphan's, Ye Olde College Inn, and the Rice Hotel—and whatever their virtues, a delicate touch in the kitchen was not among them.

Bermann had met his share of Texans when he was headwaiter at the Beverly Country Club, one of the many posh casinos that flourished in New Orleans before the Kefauver Commission cracked down on crime. He had watched Houstonian oilmen win and lose $100,000 in a night. Moreover, he had contributed to the education of their palates; the strategy of any casino is to wine and dine its clients, putting them in an expansive and generous frame of mind. Bermann knew that those men were accustomed to New Orleans' finest cuisine and that they were not getting anything resembling it when they went home to Houston. As the idea of opening a fine restaurant began to dawn on him, he realized that what wealthy Texans wanted above all was class. That was definitely something he could provide.

His restaurant was like nothing Houston had ever seen before. The rooms were intimate, as in a bistro, and at the entrance was [ CONTINUED ON PAGE 101 ]

# SIC TRANSIT CHILI
## 1936: San Antonio dethrones the chili queens.

D.R.T. LIBRARY

Sadie Thornhill was a chili queen. In the late 1800's, wearing flowers in her hair, Sadie worked Military Plaza in San Antonio. She worked hard, all night long, competing with other beflowered queens for business and fame. Chili was Sadie's product; beauty, her come-on.

Until late afternoon the square was jammed with produce wagons and ribbon salesmen, doctors, dentists, patent medicine shows. As the sun set, the merchants rolled on home. In no time, makeshift chili stands were set up: three tables in a U, some benches, a portable kerosene stove, a lamp. The queen stood in the dust beside the stove, striking glamour poses and dipping up bowls of chili.

Not just chili. Enchiladas, frijoles, homemade tortillas, tamales. From sundown until dawn, mesquite fires burned, lamps flamed, pots were stirred, dance hall ladies danced the fandango, traveling vaudeville acts performed, and music played, as night owls roamed among the chili stands, dancing, eating, taking in the show. Actors, politicians, evangelists—whoever had come to San Antonio was taken to Military Plaza for a late-night supper. William Jennings Bryan was charmed. In 1893 the world's fair in Chicago had a booth called the San Antonio Chili Stand.

City hall was erected in 1890 where once Sadie's chili fires had burned, an appropriate replacement to be sure. The stands disappeared from the plaza, though for many years after that they were tolerated in Haymarket Square. As San Antonio grew, the demand for public health regulations increased. Nobody knew what went into the chili. In 1900 the proprietor of a chili stand was put on trial for slicing meat from a dead horse. Dogs were also mentioned, and birds flying over. Finally, in 1936, health officials banished the establishments for good. The stands—along with Sadie and the rest of the chili queens—passed, from Military Plaza to Haymarket Square, into memory.          —BEVERLY LOWRY

# 1886: Queen of Clubs

No sooner had Texas become synonymous with freedom and adventure than along came the womenfolk trying to civilize it. The men of that era being beyond salvation, the women concentrated on their own minds and their daughters'. Most girls' schools combined the lofty with the down-to-earth; Holley Hall, an early Dallas academy, used as its motto "Yearn for the Infinite and don't wiggle your feet." Baylor maintained a "female department" from the beginning and even offered a Maid of Philosophy degree.

The chief cultural instrument was the women's club, of which there were hundreds, like the Quid Nunc Club in Tyler, the Wednesday Club in Fort Worth, the Up-to-Date Club in Colorado City. They offered women everything from self-improvement, in the form of discussions on history, poetry, and literature, to civic involvement. Women's clubs were responsible for the first public kindergarten in the state, the public libraries in 85 per

*Mrs. Henry Exall.*

MRS. PETER STEWART

cent of Texas towns, and the petticoat lobby, which during the twenties pressed the Texas Legislature for better health and education laws.

Most women's clubs have gone the way of the corset—but not the Dallas Shakespeare Club. Its official history notes that Dallas women have a "sophistication and vitality" different from "the more typically Texas women." Its founder, Mrs. Henry Exall (no one dared call her by her first name), did what she could to keep them that way during her 52-year reign as president from 1886 to 1938. She judged the club's quotation contests from memory and decreed that secretaries keep minutes in verse. So great was her stature that when she died, the membership limped along with two vice presidents rather than replace her. Two of her granddaughters are the club's current co-presidents. "We're an old-fashioned club now," said one, Mrs. Peter Stewart, "but she was a little ahead of her time."          —ANNE DINGUS

# THE MASTER BUILDER
## 1872: Galveston is graced with a great architect.

Nicholas J. Clayton was Texas' supreme High Victorian architect. He came to Texas from County Cork, Ireland, by way of Cincinnati, and to architecture from marble carving and other building trades. In 1872 he settled in Galveston and embarked upon a career that was in utter harmony with Galveston's stature as the most civilized city between the Mississippi and San Francisco.

RICHARD PAYNE

THE COLOSSAL ARCHES OF OLD RED.

In one of his best buildings—Old Red, the University of Texas Medical Department Building (1891)—Clayton adroitly balances horizontal expansion and vertical thrust; the center rises, the wings expand and then return in generous, full-rounded forms. The broad, majestic rhythm of the colossal arches above the third-floor windows flows steadily beneath the insistent, high-pitched ring of arched windows in the attic zone. An extraordinary range of decorative brickwork sustains and accentuates the basic shapes of the building. Vibrant contrasts in the color and texture of materials dazzle the eye yet subtly reinforce the building's underlying order.

Clayton's houses, churches, and commercial buildings (he never got to build a courthouse) do not evoke the remoteness, the harshness, or the deprivation of nineteenth-century Texas. Instead they attest to the florescence of Victorian civilization at the edge of the wilderness, a triumphal assertion of determination, endurance—and artistic ability.          —STEPHEN FOX

MARK PENBERTHY

# FROM DOUGHBOY TO PLAYBOY

## Pappy O'Daniel fires Bob Wills.

**1933** James Robert "Bob" Wills single-handedly invented the music now known as Western swing. It was daring music in Bible Belt Texas—an infectious fiddle-dominated syncopation that demanded dancing. In songs like the classic "San Antonio Rose," Wills drew on the Western music he had heard while growing up on his daddy's farm in Hall County, old fiddle tunes from Tennessee and Kentucky, Dixieland, and blues and jazz. In his teens he learned blues as he picked cotton alongside black workers, and that remained his most profound musical influence. His call-outs onstage drew on cotton-field hollers, like "Lawd, lawd" or "Hallelujah, amen."

Wills started to pick up a big following after he moved to Fort Worth in 1929, playing live radio shows. In 1931 his show was sponsored by Light Crust flour; Bob subsequently named his band the Light Crust Doughboys. The president of the company was W. Lee O'Daniel, who would later be governor of Texas. Known as Pappy, O'Daniel became the band's announcer and writer. A parlor moralist, O'Daniel made Wills quit playing dances and warned him repeatedly about his bouts with the bottle. Finally, in August 1933, O'Daniel fired Wills. It was the best break Bob Wills ever got.

He and his loyal band members moved to Waco (where the Texas Playboys band was born with Tommy Duncan as Bob's great lead singer), then to Oklahoma City and Tulsa. O'Daniel tried without success to keep Wills off the air and sued him for advertising his band as "formerly the Light Crust Doughboys." Wills's popularity only increased. To further gall O'Daniel, Wills even got General Mills to market Play Boy flour. —CHET FLIPPO

## 1883: Smothered Squirrels à la Ville de Bayou

**I**n 1883 the Ladies' Association of Houston's First Presbyterian Church published *The Texas Cook Book,* proudly billing it as "the first enterprise of its kind in our State." With its formulas for yeasts, vinegars, catsups, and Saratoga potatoes (a.k.a. potato chips), this earnest document bespeaks a very different Texas, one without Safeways and 7-Elevens. Simply reading the recipe for mustang grape wine is exhausting. It calls for straining grapes through thick blankets, hole-boring, and other unthinkable exertions. The frontier was still with these townswomen, judging from their instructions for smothered squirrels and broiled venison steaks. Yet theirs was clearly a cuisine of emerging affluence, calling for the occasional can of New England lobster, boasting fourteen pages of parlor-perfect

"Fancy Dishes," and even putting on airs (one contributor dubbed her creamed spuds "Potatoes a la Maitre d'Hotel").

Their recipes are foursquare in the white Southern Anglo mode, rife with corn and pork and fried things and garden vegetables cooked to a fare-thee-well (fresh spinach should boil for one and a half hours, the book advises). Save for a smattering of Louisiana goodies, one looks in vain for examples of cross-cultural pollination. There is breaded veal but no chicken-fried steak, Boston baked beans but no pintos, and nary a jalapeño to be found. Some of the recipes—like this one for green corn fritters—seem almost new again, though, thanks to the recent infatuation with regional American cooking.

GREEN CORN FRITTERS.

Grate six ears of boiled corn, beat the yelks of three eggs, and mix with the corn; add two even tablespoons of flour, season with pepper and salt, add the whites of three eggs beaten to a stiff froth. Fry in hot lard; serve upon a napkin laid on a flat dish.

—ALISON COOK

# THE
# Tastemaker
## 1907

*Carrie Marcus Neiman.*

Neiman-Marcus has always been more than a store. It was to Texas what Harrods was to London: a place where new money could learn to emulate old money, a place that supplied the taste that wealth had not. The Neiman-Marcus label became a kind of pedigree, and for generations of girls from all over Texas, the first shopping trip to Neiman's was a rite of passage.

From the day the store opened its doors in 1907, the two founding families set out to educate suppliers and customers. Their buyers gave wholesalers fits by demanding subtle refinements in fit and trim. On the floor, the legendary Carrie Marcus Neiman would not hesitate to endanger a sale if she thought a dress was not right for a patron; many women would not decide on a garment unless she was in the fitting room.

Carrie and cofounder Herbert Marcus, her brother, passed their role as tastemakers on to Stanley Marcus. In an episode that became an emblem of the store's uncompromising attitude, Stanley once killed the sale of a mink coat to a sixteen-year-old girl, saying that it was "inappropriate." The father was furious, the daughter crestfallen, but the next day the father returned to tell Marcus that he was right. The daughter got her mink, six years later, for her wedding. This time she had Stanley's blessing.

—PATRICIA SHARPE

# 1939

## The Met Does Dallas

Of all Dallas' claims to being the cultural capital of Texas, none has rivaled its status as one of eight American cities on the annual road tour of the Metropolitan Opera. Opera is to culture what Sauternes is to oenophilia: an instant badge of sophistication.

Dallas did not come by its badge by chance. From 1930 on, Arthur L. Kramer, the president of A. Harris and Company (which later became part of Sanger Harris) made frequent trips to New York to lobby for Dallas as a new tour city. Finally, in 1939 the Met agreed, but only if Kramer could guarantee $65,000 for the four performances. It seemed like a tall order. Dallas had been culturally in the doldrums, its Little Theater moribund, its symphony a low-budget, semiprofessional orchestra conducted by an SMU professor. But Kramer put together a group of donors who pledged $136,800 for the initial Met season. The first performance was Massenet's *Manon*, with Grace Moore (the Beverly Sills of her day) and Ezio Pinza, followed by Verdi's *Otello*, Wagner's *Tannhäuser*, and Puccini's *La Bohème*.

The Met continued to visit Dallas until 1985, when it suspended the arrangement for a year for budgetary reasons. Subsequently, the Met announced that its tour would be severely abbreviated in 1986 and canceled thereafter. No one suspected it at the time, but the Met's 1984 visit was probably its last.

—W. L. TAITTE

## OUR TOWN
### Arthur Temple gives Diboll to the hired help.

**1951** On April 28, 1951, employees of the Southern Pine Lumber Company's main plant in Diboll received a short, nine-line letter from the boss. "Attached you will find a deed to the house in which you live," it began. "This gift is made to you." It was signed by Arthur Temple, Jr.

When Temple took over as manager at Diboll in 1948, the little sawmill town had hardly been touched by the modern world. Diboll was a company town: every building was owned by Southern Pine. The practice of paying workers in company scrip good only at the company store had ended several years earlier; nevertheless, workers continued to buy everything at the commissary. There were no paved roads except the highway to Lufkin, but then few workers had cars anyway. Chickens and goats ran loose in the streets. All the houses were painted red and white. Unable to accumulate cash or property, workers stayed not just for years but for generations; sons labored at the very jobs their fathers, even their grandfathers, had held. But Temple understood that the modern world could not be shut out forever. In time his influence would reshape not just Diboll but all of East Texas.

Today Diboll is as spiffy-looking as any town of five thousand in Texas. Southern Pine, now Temple-Inland, is one of the giants of the timber industry. But there is no trace of the other company towns, or the companies that ran them.

—PAUL BURKA

## *Baylor brings the curtain down on*
## *Eugene O'Neill*

**1962** In 1962 Paul Baker, chairman of the Baylor drama department, got the rights for the very first university production of Eugene O'Neill's *Long Day's Journey Into Night*. He was well aware of Baylor's policy against "vulgar, profane, or blasphemous language," and he mentioned to Carlotta O'Neill, the playwright's widow, that he would like to delete the "God damns" and "Christs." She wouldn't hear of it. Baker decided to produce the play anyway, perhaps believing that the reputation of his program—*Time* called it "one of the most fertile experimental theaters in the U.S."—would forfend any crisis.

Maybe it could have, except that a Baptist minister on a visit to Waco took a group of nine-year-old boys to see the play. *Long Day's Journey* moved the minister very much. It moved him to call quite a few ministers in Waco to protest its nastiness. Then it moved him to call Baylor president Abner McCall. McCall was a good friend of Paul Baker's, but he was also preparing for a major fundraising drive aimed at the congregations of the same ministers who were now in an uproar. He asked Baker to edit out the offensive language. Baker refused. McCall had no choice but to close down the play in midrun. Three months later Baker and his entire staff resigned, removing their talents to Trinity University in San Antonio.

Baker went on to make the Dallas Theater Center a top cultural institution. Trinity's DTC-affiliated graduate program, once Baylor's, flourished for more than twenty years. Perhaps there are a few at Baylor who remember fondly the days of Paul Baker. In any case, as O'Neill's James Tyrone would say, "It's a late day for regrets."

—ALICE GORDON

# 1913 Miss Ela Hockaday opens a finishing school in Dallas and single-handedly creates the Texas ideal of what a lady should be.

# Little Women

### BY PRUDENCE MACKINTOSH

TEN YOUNG GIRLS from prominent Dallas families walked up the steps of a big gray frame house on Haskell Avenue near Live Oak on Monday morning, September 25, 1913. They were greeted at the door by a tall, uncompromising, steely-eyed schoolmistress, Miss Ela Hockaday. Texas womanhood has never been the same since.

The daughter of a rigid, scholarly schoolmaster who had established a boys' academy in Ladonia, in Northeast Texas, Ela Hockaday had strong convictions about what belonged in a young woman's education. Her curriculum included mathematics, English, history, Latin, German, French, and a liberal dose of her own high expectations and unyielding ambitions for young ladies. She based her school on four cornerstones: Character, Scholarship, Courtesy, and Athletics. Thanks to her vigorous insistence on competitive sports, three generations of Texas women have field-hockey-scarred knees and great tennis backhands.

For all of Miss Hockaday's apparent sternness, hardly any of her students remember actually being scolded. An early student recalls that she and her roommate once dared to sneak into the kitchen after lights-out for an additional serving of homemade Grape-nut ice cream. Just as their spoons were digging into the large ice cream can, the lights went on. There stood Miss Hockaday in her bathrobe with flashlight in hand. "Oh, girls," she said sweetly, "you must be hungry. Well, this is certainly no way to eat. Put those spoons down." With that she summoned a maid and instructed her to don a uniform and set the table with linen place mats, napkins, crystal bowls, and spoons. The errant girls were led to the dining room and required to choke down

ELA HOCKADAY DRILLED MORE THAN MANNERS INTO HER STUDENTS.

three bowls of ice cream before being allowed to return to their rooms.

In 1919 the school moved to a nine-acre portion of the Caruth farm on Greenville and Belmont. The cornfield was quickly transformed with Georgian buildings, playing fields, rose gardens, Miss Hockaday's own antique-filled cottage, and a boarding school known as the home department, where daughters from remote West Texas ranches gained a measure of sophistication. Miss Hockaday obliged the parents who backed her school by sending many members of her earliest graduating classes to Barnard, Smith, Radcliffe, Wellesley, Mount Holyoke, Stanford, and Vassar. She understood the implicit mandate as well. Shortly after the school opened, Miriam Morgan, daughter of a Dallas family with aristocratic roots in Virginia, joined the faculty as the ultimate authority on etiquette. Report cards as late as 1948 show that girls were being graded with an S (satisfactory) or an I (improvement needed) in such areas as "knows the meaning of joy," "speaks in conversational tones," and "behaves in a ladylike manner at all times." Green-and-white beanies called courtesy caps were award-

ed into the sixties.

Over the years the school name inevitably became associated more with money and status than with Miss Hockaday's cornerstones. Dallas' leading businessmen —among them Herbert Marcus, Jake Hamon, Karl Hoblitzelle, Eugene McDermott, and Erik Jonsson —have served on Hockaday's board. Neiman-Marcus has supplied white graduation dresses to Hockaday since 1917, a fitting alliance, since in their early days Neiman's and Hockaday were in similar businesses. In a testimonial for Herbert Marcus in 1937, Miss Hockaday said, "The women of Dallas have always felt grateful to Mr. Marcus for giving them the utter confidence that their clothing was appropriate and tasteful wherever they were." Miss Hockaday's job was to see that their confidence would not be undermined when they opened their mouths.

To the discerning, however, Miss Hockaday's legacy is much more than Idlewild debutantes. While the school can point to alumnae as diverse as Rita Crocker Clements, Sissy Farenthold, and Dorothy Malone, more important are the legions of Hockaday women who have applied Miss Hockaday's passion for thoroughness to the support of museums, libraries, symphonies, and charities throughout Texas.

Ela Hockaday retired in 1947, but until her death in 1956 she remained in her cottage on campus to give daughters the same scrutiny she had given their mothers. One remembers being summoned from a car crowded with boys and girls about to leave the school for a football game. "Miss Hockaday handed me a folded newspaper," she recalls, "and cautioned, 'If you *must* sit on that young man's lap, sit on this.'" 🌵

# 1893 AT THE CHICAGO WORLD'S FAIR, AMERICA DISCOVERS TEXAN FRANK REAUGH—AND WESTERN ART.

# LONGHORN LEONARDO

## BY MICHAEL ENNIS

PRESIDENT GROVER CLEVELAND ceremoniously pressed a button, and all around him electric motors and lights flickered and hummed, bringing to life the Chicago World's Columbian Exposition. It was May 1, 1893, and the crowds thronging the broad esplanades of the shimmering White City were eager for a glimpse of their future. But they would also see some of America's most cherished past. Thanks to Frank Reaugh, a farmer's son from Terrell, Texas, America was on the threshold of discovering Western art.

Reaugh (pronounced "Ray") was among the American artists invited to exhibit alongside Europe's artistic luminaries. In the company of such old-world aesthetes as Bouguereau, Jean-Léon Gérôme, and the American expatriate James McNeill Whistler, Frank Reaugh and his contemporary Frederic Remington represented a bold new art for an American empire that now truly stretched from sea to sea and was casting greedy eyes across the Pacific. Western art, part nostalgia, part documentary, celebrated the ethos of a frontier that had, by the 1890's, entered the mopping-up phase of its conquest. But the closing of the frontier merely whetted the American appetite for secondhand experience of the wild West; the biggest single attraction in Chicago in 1893 was Buffalo Bill's Wild West Show, which ran for more than three hundred performances just outside the fairgrounds.

Frank Reaugh could offer the first generation of Western fans the authenticity that they demanded. Born in Illinois cattle country in 1860, Reaugh and his family came to Texas by covered wagon in 1876. The Reaugh farm was the only fenced land as far as the eye could see, and young Frank found himself enchanted by the "illimitable distance" of the open range. Nothing stirred his passion, however, like the enormous herds of Longhorns that lumbered across the plains toward the stockyards of Kansas City. "No animal on earth," gushed

WESTERN ART WAS FOUNDED BY A TEXAN WHO SAW BEAUTY WHERE OTHERS SAW COWS.

Reaugh, "has the beauty of the Texas steer." Reaugh became a youthful Longhorn Leonardo; he pored over books on cattle anatomy, gathered skeletons for study, and followed the great thundering drives up the Chisholm Trail, sketching all day beneath an umbrella and at night by moonlight. Reaugh went on to study in Paris in the late 1880's, but even the capitals of Europe couldn't diminish his enthusiasm for beef on the hoof. He was back in Texas to stay by 1890.

Canvas Westerns reached their peak of popularity in the early decades of the twentieth century, and painters like Remington and Charles Marion Russell became national celebrities. Compared with Reaugh, both Remington and Russell were upstarts; Remington lived most of his life in New York and first went west in 1881, and Russell didn't even begin to paint seriously until the midnineties. But perhaps Reaugh loved his open range and Longhorns too much, and his lyrical, delicately tinted pastels—"opalescent" was his term for his palette—seemed to lack the brawn and grit that a newly muscled world power expected from its homegrown art. Remington, Reaugh protested, "knew little about cows, and was principally interested in the cowboy as a wild man." But the public wanted wild men from its wild

West, and Reaugh's star faded as his more antic rivals became the immortals of Western art.

Reaugh continued to paint Longhorns, however, even after barbed wire and the railroads had reduced the once-vast herds to memories; he found the new short-horned denizens of the fenced range—short-horned animals were easier to load into boxcars—"sadly lacking from the viewpoint of art and intellect." Reaugh moved to Dallas in 1903 and became a local legend, sallying forth from his Oak Cliff studio, El Sibil, on sketching expeditions in Cicada, a Model T converted to accommodate groups of young society girls that he instructed in drawing and the great outdoors. Tall, long-haired, and tangle-bearded, a life-long bachelor who reportedly never used language stronger than "pshaw" and "shucks," Reaugh inspired such formidable talents as Alexandre Hogue, who became the foremost Texas artist of the first half of the twentieth century, as well as several generations of women who became adoring members of the Frank Reaugh Art Club. Profusely eulogized on his death in 1945, Reaugh left his own best epitaph in a brief autobiography written in the thirties. "I like the Texas," he stated simply, "that I saw in my youth."

# 1941 EVERETTE LEE DeGOLYER – GEOLOGIST EXTRAORDINAIRE, AMATEUR HISTORIAN, DALLAS MAN OF LETTERS – BUYS THE *SATURDAY REVIEW*.

# CITIZEN OF THE WORLD

## BY MARSHALL TERRY

H E STYLED HIMSELF E. DeGolyer. He was a bright and lucky man, small with a leonine head, a poor boy born in Kansas and raised in Oklahoma, sporadically educated, finally graduating in geology at the fledgling University of Oklahoma. In 1910, at age 24, he located the fabulous Potrero del Llano No. 4 "wild" oil well in Mexico, which restored the fortunes of Lord Cowdray's Mexican Eagle oil enterprise. At 25 he was chief geologist for Mexican Eagle.

He went on to establish the Amerada Petroleum Corporation, to pioneer oil geology research and methods, to serve as a national oil administrator during World War II, and to develop extensive and important libraries in the fields of Southwestern Americana and folklore, the history of science, and early American exploration. Often he acted on apparent hunches that were really based on cold analysis of a situation. He loved research, and he loved books; his real education came from his worldwide experience and constant deep reading. He came to Dallas to live in 1936 at the age of 50, moving from Montclair, New Jersey, and rerooting himself in the Southwest. ("I was born into a red land," he wrote, "and I will always love a red land best.") Armed with the precision of the scientific method and a huge and happy appetite for life and learning, Everette Lee DeGolyer was one of the truest citizens of the world ever to inhabit Texas.

So it was that when the 25-year-old editor of the *Saturday Review,* Norman Cousins, visited Dallas in 1941 and

MR. DE PROVES THAT TEXAS ISN'T QUITE SO PROVINCIAL AFTER ALL.

asked to view DeGolyer's library collection, the two men took an immediate liking to each other. As Cousins tells the story in the foreword to *Mr. De,* a biography of DeGolyer by another of Texas' civilizers, Lon Tinkle, "De" produced original manuscripts of articles published in the *Saturday Review* and had a complete file of the magazine since its founding in 1924.

Then, wrote Cousins, "Mr. De asked me to stay to dinner. The next day I asked him if he would like to own the magazine. We really needed help in

those days: we were two months behind in our printer's bills. Mr. De held out his hand: I took it, and that was that."

For fifteen years after, in effect, saving its bacon, E. DeGolyer owned the *Saturday Review*. He saw it rise to success in content, circulation, and revenue under Cousins' editorship, proving right his hunch about the man's intelligence and drive. Reportedly he never took any profit from his share of the magazine, and in Cousins' words, "when there was no longer any question about its ability to go it alone, he transferred his ownership to the people who had the responsibility of publishing it." Altogether, according to Lon Tinkle, DeGolyer laid out about $130,000 for the magazine during those fifteen years. He thought, wrote Tinkle, "it was a small outlay for what turned out to be one of the most exhilarating ventures in his versatile life."

That moment in 1941 when the brilliant young editor and the shrewd oil entrepreneur shook hands on the deal was not only a significant but also a symbolic moment. One of the state's wealthiest citizens, who had transcended his origins and his region and the bounds of his profession, made direct contact for himself and a link for Texas with one of the chief intellectual and cultural forces of the larger nation. In so doing he fulfilled himself—for he actually wrote for and helped plan various issues of the magazine—and also gave notice to the nation and beyond that lo and behold, liberal, intelligent, nonprovincial spirits inhabited Texas.❧

# 1981 VIETNAMESE IMMIGRANT NAM DANG GRADUATES AS VALEDICTORIAN AT HIGHLAND PARK HIGH.

# NAM DANG, AMERICAN

BY PETER APPLEBOME

NAM DANG REMEMBERS many things. He remembers looking out his plane window in Saigon in 1975 and realizing that he would never see his homeland again. He remembers the refugee camps in California and the classrooms where he was taught in a language he did not yet speak. He remembers starting medical school at Harvard ten years after coming to the United States as a confused twelve-year-old. But most of all he remembers the applause.

It happened at Highland Park High School's graduation ceremonies in 1981. When his name was called, the whole graduating class —to his utter amazement— rose and gave him a prolonged ovation. The applause was for his accomplishment of being named valedictorian six years after entering this country unable to speak any English. But when the crowd spontaneously honored the only nonwhite student in the class, it also paid tribute to one of 'Texas' most enduring myths: its historic role as a haven for immigrants and transplants, nomads and strivers, people fleeing from a life that didn't work or gravitating toward the promise of a better one.

Nam Dang's family had fled before, from North Viet Nam when the communist government took over in 1954. The grandfathers, both government officials, were killed before they could escape. In Saigon, Nam Dang and his family led a comfortable upper-middle-class existence. His mother was a pharmacist, his father a mathematics

NAM DANG AT HARVARD: LEARNING TO LOVE AMERICA'S TEAM IS PART OF THE AMERICAN DREAM.

professor who was working on an advanced degree in France when the fall of Saigon suddenly became imminent in 1975. Nam Dang, his mother, sister, and brother grabbed whatever possessions they could carry and boarded a plane for California.

Despite the family's comfortable life in

Viet Nam, their entry into the U.S. was marked by the same chaos experienced by their less favored countrymen. The family was processed at Camp Pendleton and then lived at half a dozen locations in California over the next year. But the Dangs did have one thing going for them. An uncle lived in Dallas and

75

worked with immigration officials to re-settle Vietnamese immigrants. De Dang had one priority for Nam Dang's family—to make sure that the children got the best education possible. In Texas that meant the Highland Park schools. The Church of the Incarnation in Dallas, which worked with immigrant families, found the Dangs a small frame rent house with a screened-in front porch adjacent to the Dallas North Tollway on Colgate Street. The house had more in common with the working-class parts of East Dallas than with the Park Cities, but its residents had as much access to the Highland Park school system as anyone else.

Nam had been an honor student in Saigon. His first year in America had been almost wasted because of the frequent moves, but he enrolled in summer classes at McCulloch Middle School soon after the family arrived in Dallas in April 1976. His real love was math, but his first priority was learning English. "If you could plot my English on a log graph, it picked way up in that one summer," he says. By the time he entered Highland Park High School in 1977, he felt comfortable enough with his new language to begin taking mostly advanced placement courses. By the time he graduated, he had an 8.6 average on a scale in which 8 was straight A's in standard courses. He is now a first-year student at Harvard Medical School planning to go into cancer research.

He isn't the only success in his family. His older sister, Anh, now 26, graduated from Brown University and is studying at Baylor College of Medicine in Houston. His younger brother, Long, who graduated from Highland Park as salutatorian two years after Nam, is now a junior at Harvard who wants to attend medical school as well.

In many ways, obviously, Nam Dang's story is not typical. His family came from a favored background, and they must rank among the biggest success stories in the current wave of immigration. But Nam has at least two things in common with the tens of thousands of newcomers in barrios and Indo-Chinese communities across Texas. One is an abiding belief in the American dream that education and hard work will be rewarded by success. "Coming from extreme hardship makes you more mature," he says. "You've seen how it is to lose everything and start all over. You don't take for granted the things that people take for granted here." The other is an ability to assimilate the popular culture with remarkable speed. Nam says he's sometimes amazed by it himself. "I remember when I was first here, and I saw all these kids getting excited about the Cowboys' games. I thought, 'How can they care so much about a game like that?' I couldn't understand it. Now I'm the same way. My only worry is whether the offense is good enough to go all the way."✤

# 1963 TEXAS A&M BECOMES A REAL UNIVERSITY.
## (YES, REALLY, IT DOES, AND WE PROVE IT.)

# MAGGIES AND CYCLOTRONS

## BY AL REINERT

ONE OF THE MAjor controversies of Texas cultural history concerns the moment when Texas A&M stopped being a joke and became a real university, an institution of higher learning instead of a school of low humor. The reliable tradition of the chicken-fried college that for more than a century supplied us with Aggies, who in turn made for Aggie jokes—somehow that was undone, went modern, got presentable. Even preppies go there now. How did that happen?

The Agricultural and Mechanical College of Texas opened its doors in 1876 as part of the federal land-grant college program. Every state got one: Georgia Tech, Michigan State, Auburn, and Purdue all began as land-grant colleges. The program can be regarded today as a far-sighted effort to instigate football rivalries as these upstart schools took the field against their respective state universities, which were always somewhere across the tracks, richly endowed, and coed to boot.

The young hayseeds who attended Texas A&M were known from the beginning as Aggies—as opposed to students—and they quickly gained fame for their earthy pratfalls and mismannered ways. Before long they were typecast as the father or husband in farmer's-daughter jokes, as the butt of traveling-salesman jokes, as straight men in city-slicker jokes. For close to a century Aggies strove to live up to their reputation, always screwing in their light bulbs with slapstick teamwork. Yet today they are doing Star Wars research in secret government laboratories.

Texas A&M now attracts more National Merit scholars than Princeton or

A&M DISPROVES ITS REPUTATION AND BECOMES KNOWN FOR MERIT SCHOLARS.

Yale and has hired Nobel laureates to teach them. It boasts a world-class cyclotron, the nation's biggest engineering school, and a nuclear reactor that has never melted down. Despite being 120 miles from salt water, it has an oceanographic fleet larger than the Greek Navy and its very own submarine. It is so deep into space research that one of these days it's going to have its own satellite too. Who do you figure is laughing at that?

It was an evolutionary transformation with few parallels, like reptiles' turning into birds. How did it occur? What was responsible? When did Texas A&M become a real university? Scholars have struggled with this mystery for years. One early proposal fixed the date at May 6, 1943, when A&M graduated its last troops of horse cavalry officers, the theory being that normal Aggies couldn't develop without the nearby smell of horse manure. Although broadly accepted at one time, the idea has since been discredited by the obvious fact that Aggies remained unchanged for many years afterward. There were just fewer jokes about Aggie horsemanship.

Recent explanations have been sociological, based on Aggie demographics. One theory, for instance, cites the first admission of women in 1964, when Texas A&M was still the nation's largest all-male college. But the only women admitted then were the wives and daughters of resident Aggies, who were already there anyhow. It took nearly a decade before a dormitory was built for unattended coeds, who by then were known as Maggies and had inspired their own genre of jokes. (How many Maggies does it take to run a dishwasher? Four to shake it and one to lick the plates.)

Aggies didn't change because girls appeared in their midst. All that did was expand the gene pool, broaden the scope of Aggie behavior. The same was true when black students were admitted, when nonmilitary undergrads were allowed, when out-of-staters started coming. But what were they doing there? That's the real question. When did A&M become a real university?

It happened on Tuesday, May 7, 1963. By a vote of 25–6 the Texas Senate declared an emergency, a parliamentary maneuver that allows a bill to be passed without separate readings on three different days—without much consideration at all. The emergency measure was House bill No. 755, "an Act changing the name of the Agricultural and Mechanical College of Texas to Texas A&M University." The bill was signed the next day, probably with a snicker, by Governor John Connally, who had once been student-body president at the University of Texas, sometimes known as t.u.

In your face, Teasip. ♣

# THE GUARDIAN

## BY SHELBY HEARON

FOR AMERICANS, 1903 was not a time that believed in letting go a smidgen of possible profit. Clara Driscoll, however, as the daughter of a wealthy Corpus Christi ranching family, had been educated abroad when Alfred Nobel established his prizes and Cecil Rhodes his scholarships. She had seen what the preservation of shrines could do for a people's reputation and morale.

Returning to Texas, she found a second battle of the Alamo raging between developers and the Daughters of the Republic of Texas (DRT). The mission chapel, widely but erroneously believed to be where the major fighting took place, had already been purchased by the state from the Catholic Church. But the convent, the scene of the heaviest fighting, and the vast courtyard where Travis drew his legendary line were owned by the Hugo and Schmeltzer Company, a wholesale grocery firm, and in danger of disappearing. A New York syndicate was negotiating to buy the property, long buried under commercial superstructures, and erect a hotel–a prospect welcomed by many prominent San Antonians.

The Daughters had been able to come up with only $1000 of the $5000 needed to option the property. Driscoll joined the society and immediately set to work, sending out pleas through the state's newspapers, talking to old Texas families, setting up committees.

CLARA DRISCOLL PLACED THE FUTURE OF THE ALAMO IN HER OWN HANDS.

When the first payment came due, the Daughters had only a third of the money required. At that point Driscoll went to her father and told him that she was resolved to buy the Alamo for the DRT herself. He conveyed the funds to her account.

Clara was hailed as the savior of the Alamo. But the honeymoon was short-lived. No sooner had the 1905 Legislature reimbursed her than the ladies of the DRT fell to fighting over his-torical issues, such as whether the eyesore Hugo and Schmeltzer building had been built over portions of the mission wall. Driscoll finally maintained that the wall wasn't important, and she wanted it razed. Both sides were intractable. Angry not only for herself but for the women who had worked with her ("Though they may not have been fortunate enough to have been born with the ermine upon them by direct ancestry, they are all Texans"), she resigned her membership and began a long and bitter court battle for control of the society.

She poured her passion for the battleground into a collection of romantic stories, *In the Shadow of the Alamo*. In one of them, a beautiful young museum custodian speaks, perhaps, Driscoll's own sentiments: "Watch it, if you have that privilege, in the silence of eventide, when the glow of a departing day throws its radiant color like a brilliant crimson mantle about the old ruin. How clearly the old battle scars stand out, vivid and lurid in the stones, red as the blood of the men who fought and died there."

The immediate aftermath notwithstanding, Driscoll's purchase of the Alamo for public use marked a new civic awareness in the state. In tacit acknowledgment, her old rivals in the DRT saw to it that upon her death in 1945 she lay in state in her beloved Alamo. ♣

# 1955

"I SEE IN HOUSTON," SAYS CONDUCTOR LEOPOLD STOKOWSKI, "THE POSSIBILITY OF BUILDING ONE OF THE GREAT ORCHESTRAS OF THE WORLD."

# FALSE CRESCENDO

### BY FRANCIS L. LOEWENHEIM

THE INITIAL ANNOUNCEMENT, ON February 20, 1955, was sensational. "Silver-maned, unpredictable Leopold Stokowski, one of the legendary figures of the music world, will come to Houston next season as the Houston Symphony's presiding spirit," wrote Ann Holmes, then and now the *Chronicle*'s fine arts editor, in a front-page article.

"I see in Houston," Stokowski declared, "the possibility of building one of the great orchestras of the world." Stokowski's tenure as music director, which was to last nearly six years, put Houston on the national music map, as it was intended to do. But like other cultural and intellectual landmarks in Houston's history—James Johnson Sweeney's tour as director of the Museum of Fine Arts, the Ford Foundation's $2.1 million matching grant to the Alley Theatre, Edgar Odell Lovett's presidency at Rice Institute—it was marked as much by failed promise as by significant achievement.

With minimal changes in personnel, Stokowski lost no time in transforming the Houston Symphony. Within a season or so, the sound of the orchestra was dramatically changed. Recording began, with remarkable sonic results still available today. There were, until audience objections became increasingly vocal, substantial amounts of new or little-known music, including Houston, U.S., even world premieres. The old Music Hall was partly reconstructed in accordance with Stokowski's specifications.

But frustrating limitations remained. The number of permanent musicians, for instance, never rose above ninety, although the country's leading orchestras had one hundred or more. The management had no interest in national tours. By 1960 disenchantment and dissatisfaction between Stokowski and the orchestra board were mutual and inescapable.

The final break came over a nonmusical issue. In 1982 Stokowski's authorized biographer revealed what the Houston papers had never told. The conductor had wanted to engage the all-

STOKOWSKI CHANGED THE ORCHESTRA'S SOUNDS, BUT HE COULDN'T CHANGE HOUSTON.

black chorus of Texas Southern University for a performance of Schönberg's massive *Gurrelieder*. But Houston Symphony concerts remained tightly segregated, and the management refused Stokowski's request. His last Houston concert—though no one in the hall knew it as such at the time—concluded, blazingly, with one of his specialties, Shostakovich's Symphony No. 5.

Today the orchestra is larger, the season year-round, the players better. Other things, though, have not improved. Under Sergiu Comissiona, in charge since 1979, the orchestra has begun to record again, though with no great critical or commercial success. The former adventurous program policy appears a thing of the past. More than ever, Houston audiences know what

they like and like what they know. Many big-name instrumentalists—and singers, who appear with the Houston Grand Opera—seem too expensive for the symphony to engage. The board of directors wouldn't dream of supplying its string players with superior instruments that would improve the orchestra's sound, as was done for the St. Louis Symphony long before its highly acclaimed European tour last spring. If anyone around the orchestra has recently calculated how many millions it might take to move the symphony into a class with, say, the Cleveland Orchestra, it remains a closely guarded secret.

So much for musical daydreams. A generation after Stokowski, the orchestra's bright hopes and expectations of those days seem depressingly remote.♣

# TERMS OF ESTRANGEMENT

## BY DONALD BARTHELME

THE TIME WAS October 1981; the vehicle, the by-then venerable *Texas Observer.* The message was that Texas writers, at best, might aspire to the second-rate. In fact, Larry McMurtry implied, Texas had no literature that you didn't have to tie a pork chop to its head to get the dawg to read it. According to McMurtry, the Houston poet Vassar Miller was the only world-class writer in the state.

The response from the Texas literary community was striking. Four writers in Abilene stopped drinking, cold turkey. John Graves grasped his posthole digger and swore a mighty swear. Max Apple asked himself, "Am I an apple, or merely a dumb withered raisin?" Larry King considered taking the veil; he put on the veil, took off the veil, put on the veil again, and decided, finally, that the veil was not for him. Laura Furman called up Rainer Maria Rilke in heaven and asked him what to do next. Charlie Smith began running eight miles every day before dawn with a Purdey shotgun clenched between his teeth. Beverly Lowry ordered up a railroad car of vitamin B from the Upjohn concern. Shelby Hearon spit in the eye of the editor of the *New York Times Book Review,* on the theory that a certain *virtù* attaches to offending the gods. From El Paso to Hemphill, from Dalhart to Rio Grande City, it was crisis time for Texas quality lit.

I disagree with McMurtry; I think that taking the thing state by state, there are more good writers in Texas than

TEXAS LITERATURE WAS SO SECOND-RATE, IT SHOULDN'T HAPPEN TO A DOG, SAID LARRY MCMURTRY.

anywhere in the country save New York and California. New York is a special case, our Paris; you go to have your corners knocked off. When I first lived there, two decades ago, I was one night congratulated by a prominent poet on my "rural irony"; being from Texas, you're a natural target. California has movie money, and since most writers make less than a tenth-level law-

yer, that is of interest.

Those peculiarities aside, one must ask: What has Nevada done for literature lately? Who's the Alaskan Tennyson? McMurtry acknowledged the geographical fallacy in his argument (indeed, his argument, considered in this way, disappears) but wanted to make it anyhow. The gravamen of his complaint, made not for the first time, was that he had

had high hopes for us and that we had disappointed him. Perhaps his hopes were grandiose, or perhaps his definition of Texas literature was too narrowly drawn. We've done at least as well as Rhode Island, we're pushing Wyoming to the wall. . . .

The question of who is, and who is not, a Texas writer intrudes here. In 1915, in Galveston, my grandfather began building a raft. There was a terrible hurricane in the Gulf, and a raft must have looked, at the time, like a pretty good idea. My grandfather owned a lumberyard, as it happened, and had thoughtfully repaired thither to build the raft. The men laid out the two-bys and nailed them together and debated which way the planking should run, drank whiskey, and generally had a high old time, with the waters rising and the wind howling around them. The women, my grandmother among them, played cards (probably liars' poker). Fifty years ago, in 1935, my father, an architect, took his wicked pencil in hand and designed the Hall of State for the Texas Centennial Exposition. I was pulling catfish out of the Guadalupe when A. C. Greene, a much younger man, was still trying to understand those funny curly fingerlike things at the end of his feet. Am I, then, a Texas writer? Because I don't deal much in the specifics of place, McMurtry suggests (in an otherwise generous critique) that the answer is no, not really. I would hope that a more liberal definition of what is Texian would prevail—it would be healthier.

Another atmospheric disturbance, parallel in a way, blew up about a year ago when Don Graham complained, in the *Texas Humanist,* about all the new writers in the state who came here from someplace else. "Fern-bar writers," he called them, whatever that may mean. (Did he mean faggot homosexual queer pansy fairies? And if so, why didn't he say so?)

Mr. Graham seems to believe that new arrivals, new citizens parking their tired, dusty, rump-sprung Honda Civics in the back streets of Austin and Dallas and Houston, are not good for the state's literary culture, that they in some way dilute it or render it less authentic. This betrays a weak notion of historical process. Not true of America, not true of Texas. A "pure" Texas literature would probably be written in Coushatta. What we want are people who can speak a little Coushatta, a little Big Spring, a little Brit lit crit, a little Hebrew, a dash of salsa.

There's a great painting by the Armenian immigrant Arshile Gorky, who died in 1948, titled "How My Mother's Embroidered Apron Unfolds in My Life," in which the wonder of possibility and the to-be-dreaded movement of time are stunningly present. Gorky saw many things about America that no one else had ever seen, and he had to come from far away to do it. A rich and vital culture accepts all gifts.❧

# 1921 J. FRANK DOBIE GIVES UP THE RANCHER'S LIFE AND INVENTS TEXAS LITERATURE.

# VOICE OF A MYTHIC LAND

## BY BRYAN WOOLLEY

IN 1919 THE CATTLE market was booming, and Jim Dobie began urging his nephew to get into it. He offered the young man a job as his second-in-command and a junior partnership in his big ranching operation on the Nueces.

At the time, J. Frank Dobie was a $100-a-month English instructor at the University of Texas, where he didn't see much of a future for himself. He had no Ph.D. and no intention of getting one. He was loudly scornful of the pedantry that passed for scholarship in his department. The academic political winds carried no promise of promotions and pay raises for him. On the other hand, he loved the animals, people, terrain, and weather of his ranch heritage. He also loved the prospect of getting rich. In the spring of 1920 he quit UT and went south.

In Dobie's cow camp was a vaquero named Santos Cortez who often got bored with the mundane evening bull sessions of the other hands and would walk up to the house for a dose of cerebral palaver with his boss. Cortez was a wonderful teller of folktales, and sometime during the months of their nocturnal conversations, an idea crept into Dobie's head. "I seemed to be seeing a great painting of something I'd known all my life," he wrote many years later. "I seemed to be listening to a great epic of something that had been commonplace in my youth but now took on meanings. . . . One day it came to me that I would collect and tell the legendary tales of Texas. . . . I considered that if they could be put down so as to show the background out of which they have come, they might have high value."

If the boom had continued, Dobie might have become a successful rancher. He might have lost sight of the vision

DOBIE (R., WITH JOHN HENRY FAULK) RESCUED US FROM ZANE GREY.

he caught from Santos Cortez, and the world beyond South Texas would have heard little of him. But in the summer of 1920 the bottom dropped out of the cattle market, eventually causing Uncle Jim to go broke. In late 1921 J. Frank returned to the university and cranked up Texas' first literary career.

In some circles it has become fashionable to denigrate Dobie's work. The tales he collected about Longhorns, mustangs, rattlesnakes, cowboys, buried treasures, and lost mines are hardly epic, his critics say. They are simply the ramblings of old coots, provincial in their concerns, chauvinistic in their attitudes, retold in a style too direct and flinty to be considered real literature. J. Frank Dobie, they say, is an embarrassingly primitive ancestor for a modern, urbane Texan author to haul into a white-wine lunch with a New York editor.

To sneer at Dobie for not being a Texan Henry James is like sneering at Columbus for crossing the Atlantic in a little wooden ship instead of the Concorde. All writers make do with what they have, and what Dobie had was a Texas frontier ranch background, a keen

intellect, a good education, strong opinions, a deep love of great literature, and—rare in the Texas of his day—an awareness that his native place contained all the materials necessary for the creation of art. "If people are to enjoy their own lives," he wrote, "they must be aware of the significances of their own environment. The mesquite is, objectively, as good and as beautiful as the Grecian acanthus. . . . We in the Southwest shall be civilized when the roadrunner as well as the nightingale has connotations."

And what Dobie did with what he had was remarkable. He preserved thousands of Texas tales and memoirs that would have died with their tellers if he had not come along. He wrote 25 books—nearly all of them still in print and being read—and hundreds of articles for newspapers, magazines, and scholarly journals. He convinced the major Eastern publishing houses that a Texas writer, writing in Texas about Texas, could attract an audience outside Texas. He persuaded them to publish not only his own books but the works of other Southwestern writers as well and then talked the Eastern newspapers and magazines into reviewing them. He helped organize the Texas Folklore Society and the Texas Institute of Letters, both still keystones in the intellectual life of the state, and fought a lifelong battle for academic freedom and excellence against mossback UT regents, presidents, and professors. In his much-imitated English course, "Life and Literature of the Southwest," he taught generations of readers—and many future writers—that "the roadrunner as well as the nightingale has connotations."

Hell, he invented Texas literature. He rescued us from Zane Grey and fortified us against Louis L'Amour.♣

# 1963 TEXANS CRINGE AS LYNDON JOHNSON MAKES HIS FIRST TELEVISED SPEECH AS PRESIDENT.

# MAH FELL' UMMURRUKUNS

BY NICHOLAS LEMANN

IT WAS A GRAVE, SErious, tragic occasion, one burned into everyone's store of sad memories. But let's admit that there was a subtext. Here, for the first time, a Texan stood before the American people as their president, being solidly applauded by the members of Congress, the justices of the Supreme Court, the diplomatic corps, the Joint Chiefs of Staff, and so on—a Texan, consoling and reassuring the civilized world.

But then, dammit, there was that accent. Over a few years of disastrous television addresses, it would become painfully familiar. "Mah fell' Ummurrukuns." "Yew-nited States." "Further" instead of "further." "Tinnytive" instead of "tentative." "Wahr" instead of "telegram." "Prospairity." "Contribyit." And that's not to mention his whole demeanor: the hair slicked straight back; the upper teeth concealed by a flabby lip; the lower lip shooting out to the side when he talked; the nervous, false little smile; the blinking; the tidal rise and fall of his eyebrows; the dark, hooded eyes. Never mind that his intimates knew him to be a man of force, brilliance, suavity, and depth. In his public image, the most famous of all Texans was a hick.

Lyndon Johnson had a funny, and typically Texan, relationship going with hickdom. As Senate majority leader in the fifties, in a basically Southern institution and away from the glare of the TV lights, he was an object of respect, not sneering fun. Then as vice president he started slipping; in 1961, on a state visit to the Taj Mahal, he emitted a loud noise that *Newsweek* transcribed as "Yeeaaayhooo!" During his presidency, the issue of hickdom became an obsession of his, of the Eastern establishment's, and, secretly, of the folks' back

LBJ'S INAUGURAL, 1965: WE LUV YA, LYNDON, BUT STAY OFF THE TV.

home. It affected the course of history. One reason Johnson wouldn't listen to the ever-growing chorus against the Viet Nam War was that he thought it was coming from the people who were laughing at him anyway; when a trusted aide like Bill Moyers began to have doubts, in LBJ's mind it was a sign not that the war was wrong but that Moyers was going to Georgetown parties.

It's one of the paradoxes of American life that as the country has become more democratic, especially since World War II, it has also become more obsessed with sophistication. This has hit Texas hard—we think of ourselves as big-time (unlike, say, Mississippi), but the coasts think of us as unsophisticated. Since big-timeness and sophistication are now so intimately linked, being thought of as unsophisticated is code for being thought of as small-time, which is pure pain for Texans. Even with Johnson long gone, the hick issue lurks behind almost every aspect of life in Texas. Ben Love, the chairman of Texas Commerce Bancshares, puts Gerald Ford on his board of directors so that when he goes abroad

they'll know he's a real player, not just some Texan. Universities import Nobel prize winners so they'll be regarded as big-time, only to be regarded as rich but small-time for being unable to grow their own.

There's something humiliating about adopting the obvious solution, namely, slavishly mimicking the style of the East, and somehow it never quite works anyway. LBJ acquired a taste for expensive tailoring, but he couldn't get rid of his accent; he hired the then-official architect of the American establishment, Gordon Bunshaft, to design his personal monument, the LBJ Library, but it's ugly. On the other hand, handling the inferiority complex by striking a pose of aggressive unsophistication (surely that was behind the Taj Mahal episode) doesn't work either—it's too obviously forced, and it's not the way we act back home where we're comfortable.

Is there any hope, then? Yes, definitely. For one thing, time will heal; if Texas is a nouveau riche, its money can only get older. More important—the most important, the great hope—is the continued development of Texas culture. Last fall, when the Houston Ballet played in New York to rave notices, I'm sure I wasn't the only one whose feeling was, I don't know anything about ballet, but I know they're not laughing at us this time. There is something of the same feeling when Neiman-Marcus successfully maintains its arbiter-of-taste image in the East, or when Houston gets a national reputation as an architectural shrine, or when Texas food is solemnly and lengthily discussed in the *New York Times*. Those are Texas achievements, not imports; they've made life better here, and as a side effect, they've won us respect outside the borders. ❧

# HENRY B AND HENRY C

## BY PAUL BURKA

**1981** HENRY CISNEROS IS ELECTED THE FIRST MEXICAN AMERICAN MAYOR OF SAN ANTONIO AND BECOMES CONGRESSMAN HENRY GONZALEZ'S RIVAL FOR THE JUDGMENT OF HISTORY.

IT IS A WARM FALL SUNDAY, AND THE mayor of San Antonio is making his rounds. Henry Cisneros maneuvers his 1984 Chevrolet through the city's West Side, noting city hall's sins of omission: a pothole here, a trash pile there, the undemolished shell of a burned-out building. It is a long ride. The mayor stops at the sight of anyone on the street to exchange greetings, switching fluidly from Spanish into English.

The West Side spreads out beyond the abandoned Missouri Pacific railway station, whose crumbling facade and broken windows signal that you are approaching the wrong side of the tracks. To cross the rail yard is to take a trip back into time, into a forties America of aging, low-lying frame buildings where only church spires break the second-story plain. For 75 years the West Side has been a barometer of the social and political currents of a people. The Mexican Revolution was plotted here. *La Prensa,* a national Spanish-language newspaper, was published here, aimed at readers who expected to return to Mexico but never did. The first stirrings of Mexican American protest, a strike by pecan shellers in 1938, occurred here. The Raza Unida movement started here at St. Mary's University.

The West Side has produced two major public figures. One is Henry B. Gonzalez, known to all as Henry B, whose one-man stand against segregation bills in the Texas Senate made him, for a brief time in the late fifties, the most celebrated politician in the state. The other is Cisneros, who in 1981 became the first Mexican American to lead

one of the nation's ten largest cities. In the careers of the two Henrys lies not only the story of a neighborhood but also the story of a people.

Now 69, Henry B is near the end of a strange and bittersweet career. He has been a city councilman, a state senator, and, for the last 25 years, a congressman. He has known prominence and obscurity, adoration and spite, respect and derision, popularity and loneliness, but he has never known peace. At first he seemed to be on his way to greatness, just as Henry C seems now, but his first moments proved to be his best. At 38, Cisneros is already a national figure. His résumé includes service on the Kissinger commission on U.S. policy in Central America and a bridesmaid's finish for a vice-presidential nomination.

Henry B and Henry C are separated by a generation, by style, and by philosophy. But they are united by remarkably similar backgrounds—in Mexico and in San Antonio. In their similarities and in their differences are clues that may provide an answer to the overriding question about the people who chose them as leaders. A fourth of Texas will be of Mexican descent by the year 2000. To be blunt, will they be Mexicans, or Americans?

"YOU'LL MAKE THE AMERICANS MAD." Henry B. Gonzalez's mother was not exactly overjoyed when her son told her that he wanted to run for office.

His father was even less encouraging. "*Eres un fracaso,*" said Leonides Gonzalez: "You are a disaster." He added a Mexican saying: It is better to be a public woman than a public man.

It was certainly easier. In 1950, the year Gonzalez made his first political race, only two Mexican Americans held elected offices in Bexar County—a justice of the peace and a constable. Poll taxes and apathy cut down the Mexican vote. Everybody ran at large, citywide or countywide; there was no Voting Rights Act, no such thing as a safe ethnic district. To raise money for a race was impossible; the handful of big-wheel Mexicans who had it to give were totally opposed to anything that might "make the Americans mad."

Gonzalez didn't know it when he started out, but politics was in his blood. Eight generations of his forebears had been alcalde, or mayor, of Mapimí, a mining center in northwest Mexico. Before the Mexican Revolution Leonides, for all his protestations about his son's chosen career, had held a position with the blood-freezing title of *jefe político.* He kept an eye on all the other officials in his region, reported back to President Porfirio Díaz in Mexico City, and interceded on Díaz's behalf when necessary. But he didn't tell his son the family history until many years later. Leonides' disenchantment with politics no doubt began when a revolutionary band captured him and summarily condemned him to execution. He was spared, jailed, then allowed to escape, after a bribe, to the United States in 1911. He always saw himself as a temporary visitor in America and thought it inappropriate to involve himself in its politics. Much later, when [ CONTINUED ON PAGE 101 ]

# 1919

ON HIS HONEYMOON, LLOYD BENTSEN REALIZES THAT TO SUPPORT HIS NEW WIFE HE NEEDS TO GET RICH QUICK. AND AS HE DOES, HE FOREVER CHANGES THE RIO GRANDE VALLEY.

# LORD OF THE VALLEY

### BY JAN JARBOE

LLOYD MILLARD BENTSEN KNEW that he had better get rich in a hurry when his young bride, Dolly, spent $190 on a baby-blue silk dress, a matching pair of shoes, and a hat with a quarter-size patch of mink on it. She bought the outfit on her honeymoon trip to San Antonio in 1919—a seventeen-hour drive from their home that was little more than a shack on the Edinburg Canal near Mission. On the way back a worried Bentsen asked his wife why she had spent money she knew they didn't have.

"Dolly leaned her head on my shoulder, smiled, and said, 'Lloyd, I have confidence in you. That's why I did it.' Right then, I knew I had to work morning, noon, and night making an income that Dolly could live on."

Dolly Bentsen's shopping spree was the genesis of one of Texas' great empires. Lloyd Bentsen went on to become the master land salesman of South Texas and its leading citizen for half a century. More than any other person, he changed the character of the Rio Grande Valley. The newcomers who bought his land turned the Valley Anglo, but at the same time his dealings with Mexican Americans broke with the historical pattern of pure exploitation. He has seen his namesake son become a United States senator, but in South Texas he is still referred to everywhere as Mr. Lloyd.

Dolly died in 1977, but Bentsen, now 92, continues to put in twelve-hour days. A tall, lean, high-waisted man who carries himself like a baron, he oversees 41,000 acres of farmland, three large ranches, and massive holdings in oil, gas, and real estate. He has the sinewy hands of a man who knows physical toil. I had to delay my interview for several weeks because my request came at harvest time and he couldn't be away from the fields. Anyone who thinks the years might have left Bentsen less than razor-sharp is well advised to avoid a transaction with him.

On a warm day in the early fall, Bentsen drove out to one of his ranches, identifying species of exotic game mixed in with native white-tailed deer. He talked about growing up poor in a two-story farmhouse on a hundred-acre homestead in the Dakota badlands. He inherited his passion for real estate from his parents, who had come to the U.S. from Denmark looking for land. "My father used to tell me about the time he could have bought land in South Dakota for five dollars an acre but didn't because he didn't want to go into debt," he said. "I remember thinking what a shame it was my father hadn't bought that five-dollar land. I was determined to buy all the land I could get my hands on."

If war hadn't broken out in 1914, Bentsen would probably have continued following the grain harvest across the Midwest every year, breaking broncos, cutting wheat, and racing motorcycles. Instead he found himself on military assignment in San Antonio, where he struck up a friendship with a fellow soldier named Ray Landry, another man destined to father a well-known son, Dallas Cowboys' coach Tom Landry. One weekend in 1917 they set out to Landry's hometown of Mission for a weekend of hunting and drinking.

"Ray and I were walking on the board sidewalks downtown when I first saw Dolly," Bentsen said. "I wish I could tell you how beautiful she looked in her Red Cross volunteer uniform with the silver bars on the shoulder. All I can say is that she literally took my breath away. I gave her a snappy salute, but she ignored me."

But not for long. After the war, Bentsen came back to Mission with $1.50 in his pocket and married Edna Ruth Colbath, the blond, blue-eyed girl he called Dolly. "Everybody said we were a mismatch," Bentsen said, still savoring his triumph. "I was poor, and she was an orphan girl who'd lived well off her grandfather's inheritance. By the time I came around, her guardian had lost all her money playing cotton futures in the stock market. I always say she married me because she was fresh out of money and fresh out of family."

Bentsen made his first real money selling groceries, although even then he showed he understood the Valley's two major resources, land and Mexican labor. In addition to owning a general store, he got into the land-clearing business. The typical clearing contract was for $15 an acre, and it was customary for the contractor to spend half on Mexican laborers and keep the other half for himself. Bentsen, though, paid the whole $15 to the laborers—but in scrip for his store rather than cash. Both Bentsen and the workers were better off. Pretty soon all the laborers wanted to work for him, and he had a monopoly in the land-clearing business. Within six or seven years his workers had cleared several hundred thousand acres of the Lower Valley. Bentsen began buying cleared land and farming it. By 1930 he and his brother Elmer had gotten into what he calls "the immigration land business."

The Bentsen brothers were not the first large-scale developers in the Valley. At the outbreak of World War I, John Conway purchased 10,000 acres of brush country and became the first man to subdivide large parcels of the Valley.

By 1917, when Bentsen first came to the Valley, Conway had sold out to John Shary, whose daughter later married Allan Shivers. After Shary died in 1945, the Bentsen brothers bought out much of the Shary holdings.

As we drove west on U.S. Highway 83, the Valley freeway, Bentsen pointed out tract after tract that he'd sold, noting what he'd sold it for and how much it was worth today. "I've always said that the reason the Valley has turned into the lush garden it is today is because a lot of us developers solicited the most aggressive people we could find," he said.

> "I WAS DETERMINED TO BUY ALL THE LAND I COULD GET," SAYS BENTSEN, 92, WHOSE PASSION FOR REAL ESTATE CHANGED THE VALLEY.

KENT BARKER

The Bentsen brothers brought potential buyers to the Valley by train from Iowa, Kansas, South Dakota, and other places in the Midwest. On their excursions, the clients stayed at a clubhouse near McAllen owned by the Bentsens. They were either first- or second-generation Americans; many were like Bentsen's own parents. He could sell land to them because he understood their hunger.

We left the main road, driving on a thick carpet of grass behind his huge ranch-style house near Mission. Bentsen pointed out geese and ducks sitting on a 27-acre man-made lake stocked with fish. Beyond the lake was a grove of oranges and mangoes. He recalled the sales pitch he used to give. Lapsing into it easily, Bentsen said, "There was generally a crowd of fifty or so, and I'd tell them this way:

"A wealthy friend of mine taught me that the three most important words in real estate are 'location,' 'location,' 'location.' You're located right now in one of the three semitropical parts of the United States. The other two are Florida and California. The secret is to buy all the Valley land you can as quick as you can."

His memories of the sales pitch mingle with family remembrances. One summer night in the late thirties he was so convincing that his youngest son, Don, who was sitting on the front row, interrupted him with, [ CONTINUED ON PAGE 104 ]

# 1968 HIS JOB IS TO SELL CORN CHIPS. BUT MEXICAN AMERICANS AREN'T BUYING THE BANDITO'S STEREOTYPES.

# ADIOS, BANDITO

BY ANNE DINGUS

FRITO'S CHARACTER TALKED LIKE SPEEDY GONZALES, WORE A SOMBRERO, AND ENDED UP IN THE WRONG PLACE AT THE WRONG TIME.

SANTA ANNA CRUSHED US AT THE Alamo. Pancho Villa taunted us with his raids. To the list of Mexicans who have caused great consternation among their neighbors to the north, add the Frito Bandito. A cartoon huckster who enjoyed a brief but eventful TV career during the late sixties, the Bandito did as much to galvanize Mexican American political protest as to hawk corn chips.

The Dallas-based Frito-Lay company introduced the Frito Bandito in 1968. The rhyming of the two words was irresistible (though the correct Spanish spelling is "*bandido*") and so, the company thought, was the cartoon character —a dark, squatty midget who beamed out from under the requisite huge sombrero and curving moustache and sang, to the tune of "Cielito Lindo," these immortal lyrics: "Ay-yi-yi-yi, I am the Frito Bandito/I love Fritos corn chips, I love them I do/I love Fritos corn chips, I'll steal them from you."

Though no adman of sound mind would have dreamed of featuring a black man as, say, rolling his eyes and munching on watermelon, circumstances were different for Mexican Americans. In 1968 civil rights were still regarded as the exclusive political property of the black population. Mexican Americans had not emerged in the public consciousness as a pressure group.

The Bandito helped change all that. He made his debut on children's shows and proved a success, despite a few scattered complaints. So Frito-Lay forged ahead with national prime-time exposure. It wasn't long before the company regretted its decision.

The Mexican-American Anti-Defamation Committee charged that the Bandito was a racist stereotype that implied Mexicans were too lazy to do anything but eat and steal. *Newsweek* called the Bandito "unshaven, unfriendly, and leering." TV stations banned the commercials from the air. A few cynics were unkind enough to suggest that the Frito was born of exploitation. Frito-Lay founder Elmer Doolin had discovered it in a small cafe in San Antonio. He learned that the fried-snack recipe had been created by a poor Mexican national who wanted to return south of the border. Doolin tracked the originator down, paid him a hundred bucks, and went on to parlay the corn chip into a fortune.

Stung, Frito-Lay responded with its own survey indicating that 85 per cent of Mexican Americans polled liked the cartoon thief. It noted that the company had more than five hundred Mexican American employees. But the company's protestations were ineffective. Eventually Frito-Lay bowed to the rising political pressure of Mexican Americans and turned the selling of the Frito over to the Muncha Buncha gang. The Frito Bandito had stolen his last chip. ❧

THE OLD DUVAL COUNTY COURTHOUSE

MEEK PAPERS. CONNER MUSEUM. TEXAS A&I UNIVERSITY

# BURN, BABY, BURN!
## 1914: *A timely fire saves the Parr dynasty.*

As in many courthouses in Texas, there is a plaque in the redbrick Duval County courthouse announcing when it was built and who the officials were at the time. "Erected 1916," it says. "G. A. Parr, County Judge." But it gives no hint of the real story. In the summer of 1914, the six-year reign of Archie Parr, political boss of the South Texas brush country, was in jeopardy. The local judge, formerly in Parr's hip pocket, had turned against him by upholding the right of Parr's opponents to conduct an independent audit of Duval County records. That was a mortal threat; the basis of Parr's power was the county treasury, which he used as a slush fund to provide for poor *Mexicanos* and pay their poll taxes in exchange for their votes. He appealed the judge's audit ruling, but he had no intention of leaving his fate up to others. Before sunrise on August 11, the courthouse burned to the ground. The records were incinerated, Parr's opponents broken. By 1920 most Anglos had left Duval County. The fire extended the Parr dynasty by 61 years—until 1975—during which Archie was succeeded by his son George, George provided the votes that elected Lyndon Johnson to the U.S. Senate in 1948, and Duval County became synonymous with political corruption and the *patrón* system.           —PAUL BURKA

# Change, Please

### COPS invade the bank, but they don't want money.

**1975** Two hundred or so people, almost all of them Mexican Americans, descended on the Frost National Bank in downtown San Antonio one morning in early 1975. They clogged the teller lines, changing dollars into quarters, quarters back to dollars. Upstairs their leaders confronted bank chairman Tom C. Frost to complain about how city hall, developers, and bankers favored growth while allowing inner-city neighborhoods to decay. Frost, a genteel man with a sense of history and noblesse oblige, was lecturing his visitors about proper decorum when Ernie Cortés interrupted him with "That's balderdash."

A stocky, thirty-year-old native of San Antonio, Cortés had trained as a community organizer in Chicago. He returned in 1973 to assemble the group that became COPS (Communities Organized for Public Service). Soon COPS was proving that you *can* fight city hall. Using leaders drawn from PTAs and church organizations and radical tactics like invasion of the Frost Bank, COPS changed the face of San Antonio politics. It forced the city to start spending money on streets, drainage, and parks in the inner city. It brought Mexican Americans into the power structure. And it shifted the focus of Hispanic politics away from minority causes like bilingual education to bread-and-butter issues.

Seven years after the Frost incident, COPS met with local businessmen to discuss San Antonio's participation in the troubled South Texas Nuclear Project. For the first time since the bank invasion, Tom Frost and Ernie Cortés were in the same room. After the meeting, Frost went up to Cortés, smiled, and said, " 'Balderdash,' wasn't it?" —PAUL BURKA

## NOW SHOWING

**A Spanish-language theater
adjusts to a changing clientele.**

**1980** Going to the movies, like going to church, is a weekly ritual for thousands of Mexican American families. Children run up and down the aisles, the audience keeps up a running commentary on the movies, and friends gossip across the rows. All of this makes Al Zarzana a happy man. Zarzana owns four theaters in Houston that feature Spanish-language films made in Mexico. Back in Houston's glory days, 1979 to 1981, he had twelve theaters and pulled in 15,000 people a week.

Theaters like Zarzana's are one of Texas' hidden cultural and economic barometers. Zarzana's rise as a theater mogul is directly tied to the waves of Mexican immigrants—some legal, most not—who have found their way to Houston, filled with the same dreams that fueled the Italians who landed at Ellis Island and the Vietnamese who risked life and limb as boat people. And he has seen the assimilation process work its mysterious magic as well. Back in 1980, for instance, he realized that as his audience became more attuned to American pop culture, it preferred American movies with Spanish subtitles over the less polished Mexican-made films. He began booking subtitled pictures, and movies with a heavy plot-to-dialogue ratio (*Bambi, King Kong*) did a phenomenal business. The horror-violence-religion genre (*The Godfather, The Exorcist*) were also perennial favorites. But by 1983 the Houston boom was over, and Zarzana's business tapered off dramatically. Why? Because the illegal aliens had moved on, following the construction jobs to Austin and Dallas.

—LAURA FISHER

# The Moses of the Rio Grande

**Richard King rides into a small Mexican town intending to buy cattle.
Instead, he leads the villagers north and becomes the first patrón.**

**1854** Richard King referred to them as "my friends," but it was not so simple as that. They had another, more accurate designation for themselves: Kiñenos, the King people. The founder of the King Ranch may indeed have been their friend, but that friendship was only part of a complex and strange association that demanded stewardship, responsibility, submission, and pride.

Richard King was the first *patrón,* the Texas equivalent of a feudal lord. It was, to some degree, an accidental role. When he rode into a tiny village in Northern Mexico in 1854, he meant to acquire only cattle. But when the villagers sold King their stock, along with the cattle went their economic base. King saw the opportunity. He offered to relocate the whole town on his ranch. Henceforth the citizens would work for him, and he would be their protector.

He led his people north, through the Wild Horse Desert onto the Santa Gertrudis section of his ranch. The villagers prospered. They began to understand that though their share of the wealth of the great ranch was limited, their share in its destiny was profound. They became Kiñenos—legendary vaqueros and skilled managers. In later years and on less legendary turf, the *patrón* system took on more sinister forms. For a Kiñeno, however, loyalty to the *patrón* was not a craven or demeaning obligation: it was a point of honor as exquisite as anything a samurai might invent. Witness the example of the old vaquero, Ignacio Alvarado—who, on his deathbed, sent his son to explain to the *patrón* why he was missing at a roundup. "My father said to tell you he was sorry he could not come," the boy reported. "He had to die."

—STEPHEN HARRIGAN

# The Last Patrón

## 1978: Pepe Martin goes to jail.

When J. C. "Pepe" Martin, Jr., was sworn in as Laredo mayor on May 1, 1954, he became the eleventh member of his family to hold the post. The first, Don Tomás Sánchez, founded the city in 1755. Pepe Martin was the end of the line, the last *patrón.*

Martin was the boss of Webb County's political machine. As head of the Independent Club, he made the final decision on who would run for what office. He dispensed patronage—not only for the city but also for the county and the schools—to those who voted his way. He dispensed other things as well. Anyone walking into Martin's city hall office was likely to find elderly women capped in black mantillas pleading for his help in paying the rent or the light bill.

A multimillionaire with extensive land holdings and oil and gas interests, Martin didn't need to steal from the city to keep the machine running. He certainly didn't need city funds to pay for his houseboy or building materials for his ranches. But that was the way things were done in Laredo and South Texas.

The dismantling of the machine began in 1977, after a maverick named Lawrence Berry uncovered massive corruption in the city street department. Even in South Texas, officials could no longer look the other way. Twenty-four of Martin's henchmen were indicted on charges that included theft and bribery, and in May 1978 Martin himself was indicted for mail fraud—he had sent a city check through the mail to pay for $250 in building materials used on one of his ranches. Martin pleaded guilty, paid the city $201,118 in restitution for years of misusing city funds, and spent thirty weekends in an unlocked cell in the Webb County jail.

—CARMINA DANINI

# NOT FROM THIS WORLD

## 1894

He was not from the modern or English-speaking world, and thousands of South Texans still believe that he was not from our world at all. But for a month, in April 1894, he camped on the banks of modern society, just across San Pedro Creek from English-speaking San Antonio. Pedro Jaramillo was better known as Don Pedrito, the folk healer, or *curandero*. He was a native of Guadalajara, but stories of his background differ: whether he had been a gentleman or a peasant, whether he was driven out of Mexico or left voluntarily, whether he received the gift of healing from God or from another *curandero*. He had come to the Los Olmos Ranch, near what is now Falfurrias, in 1881, and by the time he visited San Antonio he was already a legend in the triangle formed by Brownsville, Laredo, and Corpus Christi.

Don Pedrito had been in town for about two weeks, charging nothing for his services and refusing any donations larger than a dollar, when the *Daily Express* began a series of articles that drew attention to his presence. He had cured the city street commissioner of neuralgia, the *Express* said, by ordering the patient to pull three hairs from his head. He'd cured an-

other notable of tuberculosis by prescribing that half of an orange be rubbed inside the patient's left shoe. In his last sixteen days in the city, according to the paper, he consulted with 11,583 supplicants, and "silk dresses were crushed against the greasy blankets of the natives. There was no distinction of class or race."

Though Don Pedrito promised to return to San Antonio, he never did. He died at Los Olmos in 1907; some said he was 106, others 77. To those who believed in his powers, though, he was ageless. His visit to San Antonio provided Anglos with a glimpse into a culture that, in its uncomplicated acceptance of the hidden world, was more alien than they could understand. For a brief moment Don Pedrito brought two vastly different cultures together, but in the end he was the very embodiment of what divided them.        –DICK J. REAVIS

# POLKA PICANTE

### 1928: Narciso Martínez buys an accordion, mixes the rhythms of Bohemia and Mexico, and squeezes out conjunto.

Narciso Martínez had wanted an accordion ever since he first saw one when he was a child growing up in the Rio Grande Valley. "It was a French model, I think," he says. "Then my brother started playing one, and I decided I liked the sound." In 1928, at the age of seventeen, he bought his own. Within a year Martínez had begun to define *conjunto*, the distinctive music with a snappy, pure Tejano beat.

Martínez had few mentors. "There was no one to copy," he says. "In those days there were no electric lights. There were no radios. All you had was what you had in your head." He quickly discovered a love for polkas, waltzes, and mazurkas—the same music enjoyed by Bohemian farmers around Kingsville, where he was living at the time—and added his own in-

LALO CAMPOS/KVET

delible stamp by concentrating on the treble tones of his button accordion. He embellished the sound with the *bajo sexto*, a twelve-string Mexican guitar, to produce *conjunto*. Today *conjunto* reverberates in dance halls from the Rio Grande to migrant communities as far away as Washington state, interpreted by such contemporary stars as Esteban Jordán, originator of the psychedelic accordion sound of the sixties, and Flaco Jiménez, son of San Antonio's greatest accordionist.

Martínez was the most prolific recording artist of *conjunto*'s formative years, cutting more than fifty titles beginning in 1935. Bluebird, his record company, took advantage of the music's cross-cultural potential. Some of his records sold under the name "Louisiana Pete" to appeal to Cajuns; others were marketed as the Polski Quartet's. In South Texas, though, he was known as El Huracan del Valle—"the Hurricane of the Valley."        —JOE NICK PATOSKI

# OPPOSITES ATTACK

*What Tocqueville was to America, Frederick Law Olmsted was to Texas. A New Englander who later in life designed New York City's Central Park, Olmsted kept a journal of his sights and insights during a trip to Texas in 1853. By that time, as Olmsted records, the antipathy between Texans and Mexicans had transcended the politics of the Texas Revolution and was firmly rooted in cultural differences.*

There is . . . between our Southern American and the Mexican, an unconquerable antagonism of character, which will prevent any condition of order where the two come together. The Mexicans, in our little intercourse with them, we found as different as possible from what all Texan reports would have led us to expect. This was, probably, as much owing to our being able to meet them in a considerate manner, and to their responsive regard, as to any difference in standards of judgment. People commonly go into Mexico from Texas as if into a country in revolt against them, and return to boast of the insolence with which they have constantly treated the religious and social customs, and the personal self-respect of the inhabitants. This arrogant disposition is not peculiar to the border class, nor to the old Texans. Nowhere is it better expressed, than in a book written before the war, by a Virginian who claims to be a friend of President Tyler, and who was appointed by him to a responsible office. The tone of condescension with which this gentleman patronizes people who are evidently much his superiors in true refinement, education, wealth, and social dignity, is not less absurd than the indignant impatience with which I have heard a ruffian of the frontier describe the politeness, incomprehensible to him, of Mexican hospitality.

# 1970

IN THE BRIEF ERA OF RADICAL CHIC, JOSÉ ANGEL GUTIÉRREZ–YOUNG, CHARISMATIC, REVOLUTIONARY– BECOMES THE LEADING VOICE OF CHICANO SEPARATISM.

# VIVA LA RAZA!

BY TOM CURTIS

THE DREAM WAS BORN in the salad days of Chicano radicalism, a time of boycotts and Brown Berets and rhetorical shouts of "Kill the Gringo!" The dream was that a third political party, called La Raza Unida–"the United Race"–would rise up all across South Texas, where at least 21 counties had Mexican American majorities. In an electoral revolution, the down-trodden masses would throw out school boards, city coun-cils, county sheriffs, district judges, and other remnants of the Anglo oligarchy and seize control for itself. Meanwhile, so the theory went, La Raza would field candidates state-wide, drawing votes away from Democrats–and if that ap-proach benefited Republicans, well, better the bastard who's out than the bastard who's in.

The dream became reality in Crystal City and surrounding Zavala County, the flat, fertile heartland of the South Texas winter gar-den that marks its status as the nation's spinach capital with a statue of Popeye. There, in late 1969, a charismatic gradu-ate student named José Angel Gutiérrez returned from St. Mary's in San Antonio to lead a school boycott. The protest was triggered by a ruling that the high school's homecoming queen had to be a daughter of graduates of Crystal City High. It was designed to eliminate al-most all Mexican American girls from contention.

Gutiérrez forced school officials to compromise. A month later he helped organize La Raza Unida. In spring 1970 the party swept the school board elec-tion, and Gutiérrez became board presi-dent. The new party soon captured the city council and the sheriff's office. In 1972 its candidate for governor, Ramsey Muñiz, came within a hair of taking enough votes from Dolph Briscoe to

JOSÉ GUTIÉRREZ AFTER HIS FALL: SEPARATISM DIDN'T WORK.

elect Republican Hank Grover. Then in 1974 Gutiérrez was elected county judge along with two Raza Unida county com-missioners. At that moment Mexican American separatism in South Texas seemed the wave of the future.

The next spring, Gutiérrez–who had begun to fancy himself a South Texas Fidel Castro–made a much-publicized trip to Cuba. The trip sealed his fate with Democratic politicians, who up to then hadn't quite known how to deal with him. His attempts to launch a feder-ally funded farming cooperative were undercut by state officials, including Briscoe, who called Zavala a little Cuba.

By that time the Raza Unida revolu-tion was devouring itself. Gutiérrez had made La Raza Unida an extension of his own personality rather than a true third party; as a result, it couldn't transcend his home territory. The party elected only a few local officials outside Zavala

County. Its chance to be a statewide spoiler began to evaporate when Briscoe failed to draw significant opposition in 1974 and vanished entirely when Muñiz was sentenced to prison in 1977 after pleading guilty to conspiring to smuggle marijuana. In Crystal City, Gu-tiérrez had divided his Mexican American base with his increas-ingly dictatorial methods and his excesses in dispensing pa-tronage (his wife was named to run a federally funded county health clinic). A growing coali-tion of Anglos and alienated Mexican Americans opposed his every move, in the voting booth and in the courtroom, where each side was trying to put the other in jail. Many who had mastered the mechanics of politics in La Raza Unida's ranks were using what they had learned to supplant the party.

Although Gutiérrez deftly managed to survive a bitter reelection battle in 1978, a judge's ruling in an election contest stripped him of his majority on the com-missioners' court. Outvoted, he quit at-tending meetings. In February 1981 he mailed in a letter of resignation from Mount Angel, Oregon, where he was teaching at Colegio Cesar Chavez. Soon after his resignation, Henry Cisneros was elected mayor of San Antonio. The high tide of separatism had passed.

La Raza Unida had helped to awaken some of South Texas' sleeping masses, but it had also served to reinforce the old stereotype that Mexican Americans are (a) too fratricidal or (b) too diverse to function effectively as a bloc. Undoubt-edly it helped speed up the process of change in South Texas; although Anglos still dominate the economy, office-holders usually have Spanish surnames. And every year since 1970, Crystal City High has had a Mexican American homecoming queen.

# 1948 A FUNERAL HOME REFUSES TO BURY A SOLDIER, AND A CIVIL RIGHTS MOVEMENT IS BORN.

# LAST RITES, FIRST RIGHTS

## BY RICHARD ZELADE

IN LIFE, PRIVATE FIRST class Felix Longoria was a bit player. In death, he was a catalyst for the modern civil rights movement of Mexican Americans in Texas. Longoria was "a pretty regular sort of a Latin American," as the *Dallas Morning News* put it. Born and raised in Three Rivers, he worked as a truck driver before being drafted at 25. He died in combat on Luzon Island in the Philippines in June 1945, leaving a widow and a young daughter. That is all the public ever learned of Longoria, the man. Only when controversy enveloped the reburial of his mortal remains was Felix Longoria thrust into the international spotlight. The disposition of his bones became a symbol of the discrimination then encountered—even unto death—by Mexican Americans in much of Texas.

The war had given Mexican Americans a new sense of confidence and power. Unlike black soldiers, they were not assigned to segregated units. Mexican Americans had the country's highest ethnic-group representation in combat service and Medal of Honor awards. They returned home expecting to reap the full benefits of their service and determined to keep their hard-won equality. To protect their GI bill benefits, several hundred Mexican Americans in the Corpus Christi area formed the American GI Forum in March 1948.

Late that year Felix Longoria's remains were shipped stateside. More than three years after his death, his family

IN LIFE HE WAS FELIX LONGORIA, SOLDIER. IN DEATH HE WAS A SYMBOL OF PREJUDICE EVERLASTING.

planned to give him a proper funeral in Three Rivers. Longoria's widow, Beatrice, had arranged for the town's only funeral home to bury her husband. But when she returned to confirm her plans with the home's new owner, she was told that the chapel could not be used for her husband's wake "because the whites would not like it."

Enter the newly organized American GI Forum. Dr. Hector Garcia, the president of the forum, organized a protest meeting and fired off a telegram to Texas' recently elected senator, Lyndon Johnson. The next day, Johnson arranged for Longoria's reburial with full military honors at Arlington National Cemetery. Johnson timed his reply telegram with that information to arrive during the protest meeting.

The mayor of Three Rivers, with the blessing of the local chamber of commerce, sent his own telegram to the meeting, saying that "some mistake" had been made and that the Longorias could use the funeral chapel and even the mayor's home if desired. Attorney general Price Daniel, Governor Beauford Jester, and Congressman Lloyd Bentsen sent messages of support for the Longorias. Beatrice Longoria related her story to the one-thousand-plus crowd and publicly accepted Johnson's Arlington offer, although she did not rule out some sort of service at Three Rivers. That night $900 was collected to send the Longoria family to Washington for the funeral. Hundreds of dollars rolled in during the coming weeks.

Overnight the story of Felix Longoria was spread hemisphere-wide. It had escalated into one of those signal events that stir consciences and alter the course of politics. On February 16 Private Longoria was reburied at Arlington National Cemetery. President Truman sent his top military aide, General Harry H. Vaughn, who told reporters that he was there because of "the stupidity of that undertaker." Mexican and U.S. diplomats also attended, as did Senator Johnson and most of Longoria's family.

The next day, State Representative J. F. Gray of Three Rivers called for a House investigation "to learn the truth or untruth of these allegations" of discrimination. The House authorized the committee by a vote of 104–20. After several days of testimony and almost a month of deliberation, the committee concluded that no racial discrimination had taken place. The ruling did not surprise the Mexican American population of Three Rivers, who had regarded the inquiry from the beginning as a sham and a whitewash.

But the matter did not quite end with the committee's majority ruling. Another representative, Frank Oltorf of Marlin, filed a minority report concluding that he "could not concur in their majority report without violating both my sense of justice and my intellectual honesty." The next day, a colleague withdrew his name from the majority report. The two dissensions destroyed the credibility of the majority report, and it was never incorporated into the legislative record. Garcia and the forum claimed victory.

The three-month-long Longoria affair helped the nascent Mexican American movement channel its discontent into disciplined activism. It demonstrated with such appalling clarity the depths of white prejudice that even politicians could not afford to look the other way. At the same moment that Felix Longoria found his final resting place, the cause that he symbolized began to hit its stride. The road ahead would be long and rocky.❧

# RIVER OF BLOOD

### BY ROLANDO HINOJOSA-SMITH

IN EARLY 1915, AT THE height of the Mexican Revolution, a Mexican national named Basilio Ramos was arrested in McAllen. A onetime beer distributor in the Duval County town of San Diego, Ramos was a follower of deposed Mexican president Victoriano Huerta. Officers found in his possession the Plan de San Diego; simply put, it was a revolutionary manifesto calling for no less than the liberation of Texas, New Mexico, Arizona, California, and Colorado. The territory had been, in Ramos' high-blown rhetoric of the times, taken over in a "most perfidious manner by North American imperialists."

Ramos also furnished the starting date of the invasion: February 20 at 2 a.m. There was a catch, though. Ramos' Supreme Revolutionary Congress had yet to appoint a military commander or to raise an armed force. That aside, the plan also called for a race war; it stipulated the death of all Anglo males over sixteen as well as "traitors to the race," meaning "disloyal" Texas Mexicans. But loyal Mexican Americans, blacks, Japanese, and Indians would be welcome to join the ranks.

Nothing much came of the plan. There was no invasion or revolt. Ramos was charged with conspiracy to levy war, and his bond set at $5000; in short order bail was reduced to $100, and he skipped to Matamoros, never to affect the course of history again.

The racial strife that followed in the lower Rio Grande Valley, however, was a far more serious and lasting matter. In the ensuing twelve months, three hundred "suspected Mexicans," the majority of them American citizens, were "summarily executed by hanging or shooting on the Texas side of the river as a result

THE RACE WAR ON THE RANGE: TEXAS RANGERS ROPE THEIR QUARRY.

of the feelings aroused by the Plan de San Diego," according to a U.S. Army report. The *San Antonio Express* reported that "finding the bodies of dead Mexicans had become so commonplace that it created little or no interest." At least that was the paper's view; one can only imagine the interests and feelings of the survivors and other relatives.

Local lawmen and vigilante groups did some of the killing, but it was the Texas Rangers—56 were operating in the Valley by 1916—whom Texas Mexicans feared the most. Ranger captain J. M. Fox put it neatly enough: "We got another Mexican, but he's dead." Another Ranger report relates that a Constable Hinojosa transporting three prisoners to jail was stopped by three Rangers. He was given a receipt for the prisoners, who were found dead the next day. The *Washington Post* noted that any Mexican found armed "was under instant suspicion." In one six-week period, nine Mexicans were killed "while trying to escape" from the San Benito jail. The South Texas word "*rinche*," for Texas Ranger, came to mean all law enforcement officers, and neither the word nor

the rancor has completely died yet.

Ramos' scatterbrained plan had lit the fuse of racial trouble. Retaliatory border raids by Mexican gangs began in July 1915. They were organized by two Mexican Americans, one a rancher, the other a grocer, who were seething at the way Rangers treated all Mexicans, American or not, with equal contempt. Following the first raid, the leaders anonymously issued the first rhetorical blast, demanding a halt to the "criminal acts and insults of the miserable Rangers who guard the banks of the Rio Bravo."

In 1916 new rumors circulated of a Mexican invasion on May 10. On May 15. On June 10. American troops pursued raiders across the Rio Grande into Matamoros. Upriver at San Ignacio more troops went into Mexico after bandits who had killed three soldiers. On June 16 General Hugh Scott directed the War College to draw up a plan for the invasion of Mexico. But in the end economic reason prevailed. So many Texas Mexicans had fled to Northern Mexico that there was a severe labor shortage. Valley mayors and other influential people issued a statement calling for the protection of "good Mexicans" on the American side of the Rio Grande. By July 1916 the raids had come to a halt and the two presidents, Woodrow Wilson and Venustiano Carranza, had reached an agreement on importing Mexican labor into America and sending economic assistance to Mexico. Still, the half-baked ideas of a fool, Ramos, had caused hundreds to die. No pain lasts one hundred years, as we say in Spanish, but in South Texas it's been seventy years now, and still counting. ❧

# 1887 HER NAME IS TULA BORUNDA GUTIERREZ, AND SHE HAS BLESSED US WITH THE TAMALE, THE TACO, THE ENCHILADA, AND THE BOUNTY OF TEX-MEX FOOD.

# OUR LADY OF THE TACO

## BY RICHARD WEST

WITH THE OPENING IN 1887 OF the first Tex-Mex restaurant, Marfa's Old Borunda Cafe, the culinary history of Texas emerged from the dark ages and entered the renaissance. Forevermore, any Texan whose imagination becomes overoxygenated contemplating enchiladas, tacos, or beans refritoed will measure life as B-NOD or A-NOD, Before and After Number One Dinner.

Tula Borunda Gutierrez took the basic Mexican diet—corn, beans, chiles—that dated back to five thousand years before the arrival of the Spanish, intermarried its flavors with a few new things, and sold the result to her astonished neighbors, who were used to nourishing themselves mainly on a stock of tortilla, bean, and red pepper. Like all good cooks, she added her own topspin, taking special care with the corn, for from corn come tortillas, and from tortillas, enchiladas, tacos, *chalupas, flautas,* and other dishes whose warmed content is like a stroll in the sun. Simple food then: robust, thermally rich, stoutly regional.

The classic Tex-Mex plate presentation is an enchilada, tamale, or taco served with rice and beans, a dollop of guacamole salad optional, known to millions as a No. 1 Dinner. At the Old Borunda it was prepared on a mesquite-wood-burning stove, and the result was an ecumenicity of smells, textures, and flavors that caused diners to experience a pleasure so intense it could have been a Pentecostal visitation. The aftereffect, lasting hours, was a blissful lethargy that lullabied as well as wind or water.

For a while the Old Borunda Cafe was the grand arcanum of Tex-Mex, but the young, vigorous cuisine traveled well. The new style suited the climate, land, and temper of Texans. In 1900 O. M. Farnsworth opened the Original Mexican Restaurant on Losoya Street in midtown San Antonio with an expanded menu that added chiles rellenos, *pescado,* and other exotica like mole poblano to Tula Gutierrez's basics.

Sixty per cent of the country's Mexi-

STEVEN PUMPHREY

CAROLINA BORUNDA HUMPHRIES, TULA'S NIECE, CARRIED ON THE TEX-MEX TRADITION.

can Americans lived in Texas before and just after World War I, and they helped spread the glory as they migrated to urban areas around the state: Delfino Martinez's Original in 1922, Austin's first (Martinez's son, Matt, would later gain Hall of Famoso status with his El Rancho restaurant and Mexican seafood); Cuellar's Cafe in Kaufman six years later, ancestor of the huge El Chico chain; Houston's Felix Mexican Restaurant on Main Street the next year, still serving essentially the same menu today; Joe T. Garcia's family-style in Fort Worth, which opened Independence Day 1935 and is still in business.

All food appeals to some senses, only great food to all senses. Along with chicken-fried steak and barbecue, Tex-Mex forms the Holy Trinity of our

state's official cuisine. It is multileveled and richly dimensional, giving us taste, nutrition, history. It is soul-binding, brotherhood food that has done more to entwine us with our Southern neighbors than any politician in history. On the darker side it is responsible for unfortunate aberrations like Taco Bell and chili cookoff warfare.

And what of the Old Borunda Cafe, the fount, the navel of the universe to any Tex-Mex fanatic? It continued to serve simple, near-perfect No. 1 Dinners at its 75-year-old location on U.S. Highway 90 in Marfa until last August, when an illness in the family forced Carolina Borunda Humphries, whose sister-in-law bought it in 1910, to at last close the doors. Bow your heads and pass the tortillas. An era has ended.❧

# 1911 AS REVOLUTION RAGES ACROSS THE NARROW RIO GRANDE, EL PASOANS VIE FOR FRONT-ROW SEATS.

# SO CLOSE, SO FAR

## BY TOM LEA

ON THE REMOTEST western edge of Texas, 585 miles from the capital of the state but just a few yards across the Rio Grande from Ciudad Juárez, Chihuahua, stands El Paso. The central business sections of the two adjoining border cities are barely two miles apart. Built that close together and isolated for hundreds of miles in all directions from any other cities of comparable size and importance, the two neighbors share an inherent interest and an inescapable involvement in each other's affairs.

But with proximity there is also distance—the vast distance in culture, institutions, and traditions that face each other on opposite sides of the Rio Grande not just at El Paso but for a thousand miles downstream. The closeness and remoteness of El Paso and Juárez were never evinced more vividly than in May 1911, when the first major battle of the long, bloody Mexican Revolution erupted in the streets of Juárez in plain sight and within rifle range of curious spectators on the American side of the river.

For months before the battle, the convenience of El Paso's location and its security from the Mexican military and police authorities had made the city on the American side of the river the plot-hatching headquarters, the arms-smuggling center, even the mustering ground, for rebel chiefs of Northern Mexico. They gathered under the insurgent banner of idealistic Francisco Madero to overthrow the ruthless regime of Porfirio Díaz, for more than thirty years president and ironhanded boss of Mexico. By New Year's Day, 1911, both sides of the river knew big trouble was on its way. Armed revolt sparked and

EL PASOANS PITCH HOMEMADE COOKIES AND CANDIES TO MEXICAN REVOLUTIONARIES NEXT DOOR.

sputtered all through Mexico. The federal commander of the plentifully armed but somewhat undermanned Juárez garrison, General Juan Navarro, realizing the importance of holding the key city of his country's northern border, set about fortifying strong points, entrenching and barricading, emplacing machine guns and artillery batteries, preparing Juárez for siege.

On February 6 the vanguard of 1500 rebel volunteer troops, mostly recruited and led by insurgent general Pascual Orozco, appeared and made camp on the bank of the Rio Grande, just beyond the northwestern outskirts of Juárez, opposite El Paso's ASARCO smelter. Shortly after, a band of about 500 gritty partisans following a former bandit and newly commissioned *insurrecto* colonel soon to make an immortal name for himself, Francisco "Pancho" Villa, rode up from the south. On April 2 Madero in person—he had proclaimed himself

the provisional president of Mexico pending legal elections—joined the encampment with more men and made a bare little adobe house on the Mexican side of the river the official headquarters of the revolution.

That spring thousands of El Pasoans walked or rode the smelter streetcar or came by buggy or bicycle or automobile, out the smelter road along the river, to see what they could see on the other side. The *insurrectos* were a real sight with those great big hats and fierce mustachios, those wild rigs with the bristling bandoliers strapped crisscross on their chests and belted thick with brass and lead around their middles, all carrying a knife and some kind of a gun, loaded and ready. El Pasoans generally approved of the courteous gentleman Madero with this remarkable collection of rebel underdogs rising up to fight tyranny. Everybody that had a Kodak came to take pictures; some pitched homemade cookies and candy and even silver dollars into brown hands across the brown shallows of the Rio Grande.

With Navarro's seven hundred regular army troops of the federal garrison in Juárez alerted, expecting attack but initiating no action, and with Madero's by-now three thousand rebel volunteers chafing in camp, itching for orders to start shooting, everybody on both sides waited. Last-minute peace negotiations held in El Paso's Sheldon Hotel, between delegates from the crumbling Díaz government and the surging party of Madero, broke down on May 7. The next morning about eleven o'clock, through the connivance of Pascual Orozco and Pancho Villa and without the knowledge or approval of Francisco Madero, the first shots were fired in the first battle of Juárez.

A small rebel detachment touched off the fight by sneaking along the cover afforded by a dry irrigation canal to where riflemen could exchange shots and insults with a federal outpost. By midafternoon all rebel forces were committed to a general assault upon a city fiercely defended by well-prepared regulars.

The battle was fought bitterly, house to house, street by bloody street, with heavy casualties, hundreds killed and wounded on both sides (no official count was ever recorded). On the morning of May 10 the beleaguered federals were finally driven to their damaged garrison on the west edge of town. Navarro surrendered that afternoon.

From vantage points as near the river as caution or sentries from Fort Bliss allowed, from crowded rooftops of downtown buildings, from foothills in Sunset Heights, from the tops of boxcars and the roof of the Santa Fe depot in the railroad yards down close to the river, El Pasoans by the scores of hundreds, using all the binoculars that could be found in town, watched for three days that first battle of Juárez and remembered it the rest of their lives. Stray bullets did cross the river. In spite of the warnings and precautions, noncombatant El Paso suffered twenty casualties, five killed and fifteen reported wounded.

The day after the surrender of the Juárez garrison, the city of El Paso gave refuge and safety from assassins to the defeated Navarro. A week after the surrender (with the deposed Díaz on his way to exile in France) the city of El Paso gave a victory banquet to Madero, with many toasts, many vivas, much goodwill.

It took several days for authorities in Juárez to find and to bury all the dead. It took many months for the city's battle damage, public and private, to be repaired. Scars remained for many years, and some still abide, reminders of that first bloodletting of a revolution that all Mexico suffered in tumult and triumph, in sacrifice and sorrow, in villainy and heroism for the next dozen years.

From very close by, El Paso watched, and still watches. ♣

THE TEXAS STEREOTYPE
# HOW OTHERS SEE US

[ CONTINUED FROM PAGE 48 ] vidual opportunity was envy and resentment. *The Super-Americans* glorified Texas and patronized it at the same time.

It was a cheap shot, but if we were an easy target we had only ourselves to blame. Since our first great real estate developer, Stephen F. Austin, the boosters of Texas have insisted that Texas was paradise with such relentless disregard of any evidence to the contrary that we became our own parody. It was tempting, and probably satisfying, for the rest of the world to doubt just about everything we said about ourselves or to turn it into mockery. But what did we care, really? We wanted them to like us, but if they didn't, too bad.

That all changed on November 22, 1963. When President Kennedy was shot in Dallas the Texas myth wasn't a laughing matter anymore. It was dangerous. Texas was the unruly American child everyone knew would come to a bad end, and finally it had happened. Kennedy, shot in Texas. Where else?

It didn't matter that his assassin was a leftist loser with shadowy connections to Cuba—the complete opposite of the Texas myth. Much of the world still saw that tragedy as the lawless, right-wing frontier's rising up to strike down the bright star of Camelot: the worst of America slaying the best.

THREE YEARS AFTER THE ASSASSInation I left Texas for the first time and went to England to study. One spring evening in 1967 I went to a party at a castle in Ireland, a real castle with turrets and battlements and an old moat. A woman in a British officer's tunic greeted me. "Oh, you're the Texan," she said, taking me inside. "Tell me, why did you shoot President Kennedy?"

Any Texan who lived in Europe in the sixties can no doubt tell a version of the same story. I spent a good deal of my time trying to point out that Texas didn't shoot JFK and neither, for that matter, did I; Lee Harvey Oswald did.

But the myth cut both ways, and the good side had kept some of its edge. My compatriots at Oxford were known as Americans. I was not. I was referred to as the Texan. It was something different from being an American—or perhaps more. We were, yes, the super-Americans, the distilled essence of the New World.

We were what Europe had once thought all Americans to be—rude, uncouth, exotic, energetic, pragmatic. In a world that was already made we were building something. We were unfinished; we lived in the realm of the possible. Our time wasn't wasted in rummaging through the past but in making the future.

The English took Texas seriously. It was a lodestone, a magnetized image that kept pulling at their imagination. It was their idea of the frontier, the leading edge of the great Westering movement that had been drawing Europe out of its civilized shell for five hundred years. In that tidy, green little island with so much history, I realized for the first time that the Texas myth, both good and bad, was more powerful than the real thing.

It didn't take me long to realize the potential of that myth, if only one was willing to risk the occasional outburst of ridicule or resentment. I put away my sweaters and loafers and sent home for my blue-jean jacket and cowboy boots. I only had one pair, some worn-out rough-outs I had bought at Stelzig's and worn during the summer when I worked as a surveyor. I had never dreamed of wearing them in polite company. Where I grew up cowboy boots were a badge of inferiority. They meant you didn't know that other people wore shoes. They meant you were a rube.

In Oxford cowboy boots meant something else. They meant you were not just another privileged upper-class twit or yet another American trying to ape the English. They meant you were special.

I wore them every day.

IN 1980 I MOVED TO CALIFORNIA. A woman who worked with me there simply couldn't believe that Texans were civilized. To her, we were racists, male chauvinists, warmongers—macho, violent, weird sickos of arrested sensibilities. She didn't say that straight out, of course, but we Texans learn to tell.

She told me a story.

"I drove through Texas," she said.

"Oh? What did you see?" I asked.

"I don't remember," she replied. "It all looked the same." Don't people always say that! "All I remember is that I was behind a man in a pickup truck, and he threw a beer can, a sack, and a candy wrapper out the window!"

She said the last words with great emphasis. A beer can . . . a sack . . . a candy wrapper. Out the window. Texans trashing gentle nature. Forget that Californians have felled ancient redwood forests, buried a canyon as beautiful as Yosemite under a reservoir, and turned a lush farming valley into a desert so that Los Angeles would have more water to fill its swimming pools. Californians are civilized. Case closed.

For her the stereotype was all there was—or would be—to Texas. Facts didn't matter. So what if we had more poor people than New York State? The image of the rich, obnoxious Texan still defined us. But that stereotype has since been swallowed up by the vast changes of the past fifteen years. As recently as the sixties, we were still on our own, proud and insecure, boastful and resentful, all at once. From the president on down, we were citizens of our own nation. The great migrations of the seventies changed all that. More than a million Americans moved to Texas from other states in the decade. Much of the old Texas rubbed off on the newcomers, but a good deal of them rubbed off on us as well.

The stereotypes of the Texas myth that were so abundant in *The Super-Americans* became harder and harder to find. Wildcatters' sons like the Bass brothers went off to Yale and studied philosophy. The Klebergs picked a colorless businessman from the East to run the King Ranch. Arthur Temple shed East Texas insularity and merged with Time Inc. Banks became holding companies, the Jett Rinks joined the Council on Foreign Relations, and the cowboys all moved to Arlington and Pasadena and became John Travolta. We were supposed to be country folk, but we were instead an urban and suburban culture, with world-class medical centers, universities, and NASA. We spent more time in shopping malls than on the ranch. "Texas Republican" no longer was an oxymoron.

The changes in Texas since 1970 have been mixed blessings. LBJ was not without his faults, but he never lived on River Oaks Boulevard or forgot what it was like for the poor, black, or out of luck. His successors, in politics, banking, business, and law, are much smoother men, more at home in New York than in Cut 'n' Shoot. No one is going to catch Lloyd Bentsen, Ben Love, or Ray Hunt lifting a shirt to show the scar from an operation, though sometimes we might wish they would. The same misguided yearnings for respectability that caused the furor over *The Super-Americans* 25 years ago has turned us against our own past. Not long ago the city of Houston hired a New York public relations firm to help the city shed its cowboy image. We're not like that, they keep saying, we're not what you've heard. We're just like everybody else.

I DON'T THINK SO. THERE IS STILL something vital about the Texas myth. Its positive side, the image of Texas as the land of beginning anew, the last frontier of opportunity, has captured the imagination and the ambitions of millions of people. It is still powerful enough to be born again, fresh and vivid, for each new immigrant who comes to the place as if for the first time.

In 1984 I stopped in Bangkok at a bar filled with a mixed bag of the American overseas empire—Viet Nam veterans who had never left Asia, multinational executives, pilots, journalists, adventurers. A balding man in a safari jacket and cowboy boots came up to me, blew some cigar smoke in my face, and began a conversation that proved how strong the myth still is.

"Where are you from?" he asked me in an accent from deepest New Jersey.

"Texas," I said.

"Hey, whaddyuh know," he replied. "So am I."

Aren't we all.✤

THE TEXAS STEREOTYPE
# LYNDON 'N' LUDWIG

[ CONTINUED FROM PAGE 50 ] the cattle pens. Mrs. Johnson complained that a trailer house set up for the Secret Service spoiled the view from the dining room picture window. Each ranch building was already fitted out with a white telephone, including the modest auxiliary house where the president's elderly cousin Oriole Bailey made her home. "Don't you pick that thing up, Oriole," LBJ had warned her. "Khrushchev might answer."

The formal Johnson-Erhard meeting took place on December 28 in the living room of the ranch house, where hung a framed letter from Sam Houston to Lyndon Johnson's great-grandfather. The main achievement of the conference, German and American spokesmen told the press, was "a close personal understanding between the two leaders"—a phrase that was perhaps a bit more significant than usual, since their predecessors, Kennedy and Konrad Adenauer, had not always seen eye to eye.

On the day of the barbecue, the chancellor was in high good humor. He passed under a "*Herzlich Wilkommen*" banner hanging by an authentic Texas chuck wagon parked there by Walter Jetton, the Fort Worth caterer who supplied the barbecue. Inside the Stonewall gym, the chancellor in his limited English assured "Frau Johnson" that "I feel at home with you." Johnson, believing that he'd scored a big diplomatic success his first time out, was in even better spirits as he bestowed thirty creamy, broad-rimmed LBJ hats on all members of the two official parties.

Van Cliburn and Salinger played a Steinway rented for the occasion; a wall had to be cut open to get it into the gym. (That wasn't the only problem. Cliburn had had to overcome the resistance of his mother, who insisted that a world-famous musician shouldn't be playing at a barn dance, until Cactus Pryor explained to her that it was the president's barn dance.) As for Salinger, he took the keyboard at LBJ's insistence to thump out a composition of his own, only after inquiring plaintively, "Is this the right thing to do after Van Cliburn?" Local dance groups performed German figures, the Wanderers Three sang folk songs and hit Broadway tunes, and the hundred or so guests sat at tables spread with red-checked tablecloths and ate their barbecue, spareribs, potato salad, and baked beans, while drinking coffee from range-style tin cups.

When it was over, the last ribs consumed, the farewell speeches made, the Germans gone home, it was clear that there was not only a new president and first lady but a new style—the breezy, informal style of the West—in the White House. The Kennedy era was past. Texas had gone East, made good, but stayed itself.✤

THE CIVILIZERS
# ICING ON THE CAKE

[ CONTINUED FROM PAGE 65 ] introduce the locals to lobster bisque and sweetbreads coquille, but she also added a crucial ingredient—style.

The niceties were a passion with Miss Alice. She did not simply serve biscuits; she served biscuits on a grand silver platter. She dyed her mashed potatoes pink, set her congealed salads on beds of pastel-tinted cabbage, garnished her desserts with fresh morning glories. Her elaborately hand-decorated wedding cakes became the standard for an entire region; she put one of her spun-sugar wonders on a westbound train ensconced in its own Pullman berth. That it would have been inedible by the time the festivities commenced was hardly the point; Alice's cakes spoke of refinement, not mere food, and refinement was what her clientele yearned for.

Miss Alice had arrived on the scene at just the right moment. San Antonio was ready for her, poised for a flowering of manners. On the one hand, until the railroads arrived in the 1870's, it had been as rough-and-tumble a town as you were likely to find in Texas, positioned on the edge of one frontier to the south and another to the west. The crude frontier ethic that marked most of nineteenth-century Texas could be found aplenty in San Antonio. (Mary Maverick, a bride fresh out of Alabama in the 1840's, gave a party at which one woman ate so much ice cream that she had to be carried home, other guests made off with roast chickens under their jackets, and some celebrants declined to leave at all.)

On the other hand, San Antonio was Texas' largest city—a position it would hold through the twenties—and more important, it was a commercial center of no small consequence. Alone among Texas cities, it had developed an established mercantile aristocracy. These people, who made up the city's defining class, were mostly German immigrants with a sprinkling of Southern Anglos, but they made the Southern style their own, a style that even today distinguishes San Antonio society at its upper levels. And there were no stronger exponents of Southern gentility than Miss Alice and Mr. Bob, what with their plantation dinner bell, their Negro staff, and their antebellum hostelry. Affluent locals dined at the Argyle on Thursdays, Sundays, and holidays—the servants' days off. Transient military swells swarmed in, and a Dr. Chaplin, locally credited with inventing the seismograph, came for one of Miss Alice's meals and stayed on for years. The table was an obvious focus for the display of social graces, but the O'Gradys expressed their civility in other areas as well. They eschewed locks and cash registers, nurtured their faithful retainers through decades of service, and made it a point of pride to furnish the hotel with antiques, fine linens, and fancy china. Mr. Bob, appropriately elected the first mayor of Alamo Heights, would spend hours on the wide verandahs in polite conversation with such guests as General "Black Jack" Pershing.

Advancing age and an excess of open-handed hospitality finally caught up with the O'Gradys, who lost the Argyle to foreclosure in 1941. Until 1956 it languished as a down-at-the-heels boardinghouse. Then some socially high-powered matrons–Betty Slick Moorman, Margaret Tobin, and Carolyn Negley–came up with a plan. They would establish the Argyle as a private, nonprofit dining club with a carefully chosen membership pledged to support the Southwest Foundation for Biomedical Research. It was a triple dip: status for the membership, the sort of charitable affiliation so dear to the leisure class, and a civilized place to entertain in the bargain. Exclusionary social clubs have played an important role in San Antonio's ritualistic, pageantry-loving society, and the infant Argyle was not immediately accepted as the peer of, say, the German Club or the Order of the Alamo or even the matriarchal Battle of Flowers Society. Yet by the early sixties, old-line San Antonians and new were clamoring to get into the Argyle. They still are.

What is the lure? To begin with, there is the powerfully nostalgic mystique of the Argyle club. The place remains as resolutely Southern as ever, dreamily suspended in time under its sentinel magnolias, enfolded by capacious porches that seem made expressly for the club's mint julep parties. The service makes members feel like pampered newborns, thanks to the largely black veteran staff and to the ministrations of Weingart, who knows the idiosyncrasies of every member, right down to whether he expects French bread instead of the club's usual watercress biscuits. The mixed bag of vintage furnishings donated by members contributes just the right note of genteel eccentricity. Insiders may quibble about this or that ("Most members loathe that sculpture by the entrance marquee, a melancholy little girl with a jug," confides one), but they take an intensely proprietary pride in the club, which in any event wears its quirks as naturally as a dowager duchess would. Nobody seems to mind that the main dining areas on the basementlike ground floor have low ceilings and exposed pipes that smack of another century; they find it rather cozy. Those who denigrate such arrangements surely must be envious outsiders who couldn't get into the club for all the Rolexes in Texas.

Then there is the food. The table Mel Weingart sets causes as much comment as Miss Alice's ever did, though members are as quick to kibitz as they are to praise. ("It *is* the best food in town," says one member, "but you still complain.") The spirit if not the letter of Miss Alice's cuisine has been preserved; Weingart confesses that once members began testing her legend-

ary recipes with a view to republishing her cookbook, they realized that "there was no way anyone would be interested in it. It was all too heavy, too thick, too fattening." The idea was quietly dropped.

Still, Weingart, a Denver native who came to the Argyle in 1965 by way of Dallas' Columbian Country Club, talks about "artistry" and "presentation" in a way Miss Alice might admire. His cuisine is at once simpler and more cosmopolitan, without ever veering into the alarming or the outré. "We stay abreast of what's current," he says, hence the blackened salmon on this season's menu. But Weingart, who can't quit fiddling with something till he thinks he's got it absolutely right, has concocted his own spice mixture that he says is "a hell of a lot better than Paul Prudhomme's. I bought some of his, but my hair almost fell out of my head when I tasted it." Ever in pursuit of complete culinary propriety, Weingart buys whole fish and has it deboned on the premises ("when it's fileted, fisheries sell you junk") and has the club's bread, rolls, cheese straws, and toast rounds baked from scratch. "We use real butter, real cheese, all of which costs a jillion dollars, and we give it away free." Somewhere Miss Alice is smiling.

Finally, there is the Argyle club's fabled exclusivity–which raises the somewhat thornier issue of what sort of test is required of one to allow regular passage through the club's hallowed portals. Or, to put it more bluntly, what values do the club members still hold dear? For starters, conspicuous consumption counts not a whit, not at the Argyle club or anywhere else in old San Antonio society, for that matter. Thus the Mercedes-and-Jag quotient in the Argyle parking lot is noticeably lower than it would be at any posh Houston or Dallas club. Nor is raw power or even merit necessarily a coin of the realm. What counts is more a matter of breeding –family connections, personal associations, and, of course, civilized behavior. "The respectable classes in San Antonio are very, very respectable," reflects T. R. Fehrenbach, Texas historian and Alamo Heights pundit. "In the upper circles, Southern attitudes, or what people think are Southern attitudes, do prevail, right down to a recoiling from vulgar talk. LBJ really put people off here."

It is indeed difficult to envision LBJ at the Argyle, where, as one member says, "If you were obstreperous, it would be severely frowned on." Certain standards still obtain: coat and tie are a must for men, save when sportsmen in field gear make prior arrangements to lunch in the Hunt Room. Once Henry Catto, Jr., former protocol chief for President Gerald Ford, arrived tieless for a luncheon with arts patron Robert Tobin; he was turned back at the door. Graver infractions must be dealt with as well. Take Count Ivan Podgoursky–"a wild man, given to drink, frightening," as one member describes him. "He was an out-of-town member, but he moved back to San Antonio, and the

membership committee told him he'd have to resign and reapply. Then they didn't elect him." Whether the count recovered we will never know, for his stepson finished him off with a brass bookend after the count attacked him with a knife.

So whom does that leave as members? It leaves 800 resident members and 400 nonresidents with names like Schreiner, Seeligson, Briscoe, O'Connor, Oppenheimer, Frost, Groos, Steves, Kleberg– practically an Olympian roster of old Texas names, old Texas money, old Texas manners. And it leaves many of those on the outside fuming at their inability to climb into this rarefied circle. True, the membership fee is a mere $2000 (not $10,000, as one hopeful yuppie told me with a perfectly straight face), but with a ceiling of 835 on resident memberships and a waiting list of more than 400, there's still room for the eating out of hearts. "My wife and I have never been able to get anybody in," frets one charter member. An old-line San Antonian reports hearing a chamber of commerce official griping bitterly that "I can get a guy to come here with a two-hundred-million-dollar industry, but I can't get him in the Argyle."

Interesting point. This song would not be sung in Houston, Dallas, or Austin, where dynamic newcomers are far more apt to find themselves embraced by the local gentry. San Antonio's upper class has always been loath to acknowledge the value of outsiders, a xenophobic tradition that lives on. If the Argyle's role as a bastion of high standards was, in Miss Alice's day, predicated on a desire to bring refinement to the populace at large, it now seems based more on a desire to separate the club's membership from the confusing stew that is modern-day San Antonio. Since mankind discovered the napkin, manners have been one of the ways the privileged class justifies its existence and distances itself from hoi polloi. Membership in the Argyle has become, among other things, a certifiable means of separating oneself from the developers, fortune seekers, and parvenus who have swarmed into the new San Antonio, making it the nation's tenth-largest city.

Nowadays the Argyle functions more as a safe house than as a setter of standards; it is a comforting and quaint anachronism in which members can do things as they've always been done. Inside, they can complain about the food and the new order. Outside, the San Antonio of Mayor Henry Cisneros and his high-tech hustlers marches along regardless.

Yet there are signs that the Argyle is moving forward, even if it is at a very leisurely pace. Doctors from the city's booming medical community are showing up on the club roster, and that's not all. "The saying used to be that Red McCombs would get into the Argyle when hell freezes over," chortles one prominent San Antonian, referring to the car dealer turned wheeler-dealer. "Well, Red McCombs is in the Argyle now."❧

[ CONTINUED FROM PAGE 68 ]
a table laden with a typical French display of fruits and vegetables—voluptuous strawberries, dewy peaches, and asparagus as big around as a man's finger. The seating was both table- and banquette-style. In the private club, members kept their personal stashes of booze in liquor lockers rather than resorting to the odious brown bag.

Bermann courted the moguls of oil, banking, and ranching, and Maxim's at lunch quickly became *the* place in Houston to do business. "All the bigwigs liked me; they called me Frenchie," he recalls. "To them I was a butler." Before long everyone with social standing or pretensions had an account at Maxim's. The patronage of customers like Schlumberger magnate John de Menil gave Maxim's social sanction. Many regulars ran up enormous tabs, and one pair of regulars had dinner delivered on nights when they didn't feel like eating out.

Maxim's was the first in Houston to bring in Belgian endive, the first to cook with wine, the first to use sauces. The fish *en papillote* was a sensation; people ordered it just to see what something cooked in a paper sack looked like. Although the menu was classic haute cuisine—Bermann had trained under Escoffier at the Ritz in Paris and Henri Soulé at Le Pavillon in New York—it was also realistic and showed that Bermann knew his customers. "At lunch the businessmen wanted to eat like their fathers and grandfathers," he says. "They ordered chicken-fried steak and a sautéed minute steak that we named Oil Trash. But at night they brought their wives and daughters and wanted to eat class."

Catering to both types of whims produced an oddly schizophrenic restaurant, but that was part of the magic of the old Maxim's. Its food was as good as its customers could get in New York, but the atmosphere never made them feel uncomfortable or put down. Some occasionally complained that the folksy touches were a little too down-home, like the rack of lamb served with Bama mint jelly *en jar* and the wine list that bore the admonition "Don't drink the water!" accompanied by an illustration of the infamous Brussels statue of a little boy urinating into a pond. Any number of customers chided Bermann for letting frumpy waitresses in hairnets and sensible shoes run the dining room instead of tuxedoed waiters. But he stubbornly refused to change. On a visit to Maxim's in 1958, his old mentor Henri Soulé took Bermann to task for offering chicken-fried steak. Bermann flashed his diamond-and-sapphire cuff links at his old friend. "When I worked for you, Soulé," he huffed, "I had to use safety pins for cuff links. Chicken-fried steak bought me these." ♣

[ CONTINUED FROM PAGE 84 ]
his son took him to the White House, Leonides Gonzalez told John Kennedy, "You're the second president I have met." Kennedy asked who the first was. "Porfirio Díaz."

Henry B (he was born Enrique Barbosa, and a few old-timers still call him Kiki) had made a name for himself on the West Side even before he ran for office. After serving in World War II, he had gone to work in the Bexar County juvenile probation office. He differed from the usual lock-'em-up-and-throw-away-the-key type the West Side was used to; he took all sorts of chances to keep kids out of trouble. The more he learned about the West Side's back alleys and street gangs and overwhelmed parents, the more the central idea that would dominate his political life began to take shape: ethnic separatism was a mistake.

"My juvenile probation job opened my eyes," Gonzalez said this past summer. He was seated at the head of a long table in the House dining room in the Capitol, eating scrambled eggs with chorizo that he had brought back from San Antonio. "I saw how wrong parents had been to hold on to the idea that we were in this country as guests. It just made the kids feel isolated." As he talked, he seemed deep in thought, an impression enhanced by three deep furrows that ran across his forehead, crisscrossed by three vertical lines that seemed to rise out of each eyebrow.

He was promoted to chief probation officer, the first Mexican American in this century to run a Bexar County department. But when the county judge insisted on making a patronage appointment in the probation office, Gonzalez quit. The second major theme of his life had made its appearance. Anyone in public life is forced to make choices between principle and effectiveness. Gonzalez has consistently chosen principle, and as a result he has forfeited effectiveness.

In 1950 Gonzalez decided to run for the Legislature. No one gave him much of a chance. But he got into a runoff and teamed up on a slate with Maury Maverick, Jr., who was running for another legislative seat in the countywide election. Maverick barely won. Gonzalez barely lost. The next day Maverick Senior took Gonzalez to lunch at the St. Anthony Hotel and, seeing the place filled with local businessmen, said in a loud voice, "These are the people who voted against you and Maury Junior."

Gonzalez finally broke through three years later. For neither the first time nor the last, San Antonio politics was convulsed for reasons that seemed unfathomable to outsiders. The downtown establishment was split. Two groups were trying to capture city hall. One called itself the San Antonians, to emphasize that the other side had brought in an out-of-towner as city manager. The San Antonians decided that they needed a Mexican name on the ballot to lure the West Side, whose votes were usually ignored in years when the establishment wasn't split. Gonzalez had two things going for him. He was known citywide for his 1950 race. More important, however, he had not run as an ethnic politician. His main issue, getting a court of domestic relations for Bexar County, was not an ethnic issue. The San Antonians put Gonzalez on their slate, and this time he won without a runoff.

The San Antonians quickly regretted their decision. At his first council meeting, Gonzalez raised a ruckus over a water rate increase. Then the prominent businessmen behind the ticket summoned the entire council to the St. Anthony for a secret meeting to discuss appointments. Only the mayor was allowed to talk to the press, the businessmen warned. But afterward Gonzalez promptly answered a reporter's question. In a few days, one of the businessmen called Gonzalez with an offer of a well-paying job. Gonzalez would have to resign, of course. Gonzalez said no. There was another meeting a few weeks later at the home of a councilman, only this time the businessman was missing. Gonzalez asked where he was. The councilman's wife replied that she didn't let Jews in her home. Gonzalez walked out. "I felt," he recalled, "surrounded by ignorance."

It was a tumultuous three years. The San Antonians' unity fell apart. Gonzalez was often the swing vote. He was shot at, threatened, framed; he changed the all-powerful city water board from a body that filled its own vacancies to one appointed by the council; he exposed back-room deals; he won a battle to end segregation of city facilities like swimming pools. But he had six children and no money, and the council took up all his time. He decided to run for the state Senate, which met for just five months every two years.

Gonzalez took on Ozzie Latimer, the incumbent, for the Democratic nomination. In Austin Latimer was best known for approaching young women and flipping his tie to reveal a gold screw tie tack. But in San Antonio he was regarded as unbeatable. Gonzalez beat him by three hundred votes and became the first Mexican American ever elected to the Senate.

He found himself in a body that was very Southern, very conservative, and very clubby. The Texas Senate of that era was sometimes venal and frequently mean, but it was an odd kind of meritocracy, where certain things could be overlooked if a man had intelligence and logic and a gentlemanly style. Gonzalez, a voracious reader of history and the son of a former landed aristocrat, won the respect of his peers he had never had in San Antonio. He was at home in the Senate; even today he wishes that it had paid enough that he hadn't had to leave. The Senate was from a different era of politics, the era when oratory was more important than TV commercials, when it was still possible to believe that a single speech might change the world. And in 1957 Gonzalez made such a speech.

It was three years after *Brown* v. *Board of Education of Topeka.* Unyielding segregationists were trying to maintain the color line in the schools. The package passed the House and reached the Senate floor, where it was certain to pass. Gonzalez met the first bill with a filibuster.

He was dressed in a light blue suit and white shoes, with a yellow tie and a yellow handkerchief. He read for a time, but for the most part he spoke extemporaneously, hour after hour, citing Herodotus, Jeremiah, Shakespeare, and others from memory. "For whom does the bell toll? You, the white man, think it tolls for the Negro. I say, the bell tolls for you! It is ringing for us all, for us all." The Senate gallery filled and stayed filled all through the night; it was emptied as a penalty for applauding; it filled again. To the argument that integration would lead to intermarriage, Gonzalez answered, "They want to be your brothers, not your brothers-in-law." A day passed, a night, a second day. Gonzalez was shoeless now, pacing in his yellow socks. Finally, at 1:45 a.m. on the second night, the segregationists agreed to give up on the rest of their bills if Gonzalez would quit talking and let this one pass. He sat down after 36 hours and 2 minutes, then the longest filibuster in Texas history.

HENRY CISNEROS' DRIVE THROUGH the West Side has taken him to its eastern border, close to the interstate highway that leads to Mexico. The area used to be a horrible slum, block after block of *corrales*—tiny houses in a square, with a single toilet in the middle. A few *corrales* remain. "Some of the finest people in San Antonio own this stuff," he says, shaking his head. But we are not here to see the *corrales*. Out of the former slums have risen office buildings, new houses, a pink shopping mall.

The new development is known as Vista Verde South. It started out as a joint project of Control Data Corporation and a Mexican American developer. Actually, it started out in Henry Cisneros' mind; it is the embodiment of his vision for San Antonio: high tech resurrecting the inner city. While still a city councilman, he went to Control Data's headquarters in Minnesota, wooed the company's chairman, and persuaded him to put up the industrial buildings. But then Control Data fell upon hard times, and the developer couldn't find tenants, and now the buildings and the shopping mall are mostly empty, the houses aren't finished, and Vista Verde is, in the words of one West Side civic leader, "dead in the water."

Cisneros is not by nature a pessimist; he believes that Vista Verde will ultimately be successful. But he is a far different man from the youth who took me on a similar drive around San Antonio eight years ago. Then he sat in front of another decrepit area, smashed his fist into his palm, and said, "It doesn't have to be this way. I know *just* what San Antonio needs." Today he has a more tempered outlook about the West Side. "We've made some progress," he says, "but it is so hard to arrest the cycle of decline."

Even Cisneros' own neighborhood has not escaped the cycle. When his grandfather Romulo Munguia moved there soon after arriving from Mexico in 1926, it was a mixed area of Germans and Mexicans known as Prospect Hill. The hill is imperceptible, and so, for most of today's residents, are the prospects. The imposing two-story residences where the Germans once lived have gone to seed, and more and more illegals are moving into the area.

For years city policies contributed to the decline of the West Side. San Antonio spent its capital budget on the fringes of the city, the growth areas, and ignored streets and drainage in the inner city. But in the early seventies, while Henry Cisneros was doing graduate work in the Northeast (he earned a doctorate in public administration from George Washington University and a master's degree from Harvard and worked toward a doctorate at MIT), the old order back home was falling apart. In San Antonio pedigree had always been a prerequisite for power; now new money wanted its turn. Meanwhile, a fledgling organization known as COPS (Communities Organized for Public Service), composed mostly of ordinary Mexican Americans who were neighborhood leaders, began making loud demands that the city start paying attention to its older sections. The political arm of the downtown establishment, the Good Government League, lost the mayor's race in 1973. When Cisneros returned for a teaching job at the UT–San Antonio in 1974, local politics was in the greatest turmoil since Henry B. Gonzalez had been elected to the council 21 years earlier.

In 1975 the Good Government League put Cisneros on the slate that was to be its last. One of the GGL's contacts on the West Side was Ruben Munguia, Cisneros' uncle, whose printing business was a hangout for West Side political types of a certain stripe: men in their late forties and fifties whose main interest was achieving representation for their people, not changing the world overnight, who wanted respect but not power or money. Munguia recommended his nephew and . . . well, there aren't many people Henry Cisneros can't charm one-on-one. Like Henry B, Henry C came to office only after being handpicked by the Anglo power structure.

That was one of many parallels in their lives. Like most prominent Mexicans on either side of the Rio Grande, each family considers itself more Spanish than Indian. The first Munguia came to Mexico in 1549; Gonzalez's ancestors arrived in 1561. Each family was important in Mexico. Romulo Munguia's great-uncle was the first archbishop of Guadalajara. Leonides Gonzalez's uncle was attorney general of Mexico. The lines converged in San Antonio when Munguia, who had run a newspaper in Puebla, went to work at *La Prensa,* the Spanish-language newspaper. Munguia ran the composing room. His boss, the general manager of the paper, was Leonides Gonzalez.

No one had ever burst upon San Antonio politics like young Henry Cisneros. Not for him the sober, "I'm a team player," make-the-rounds-of-the-civic-clubs campaign that GGL candidates had always run. He organized block parties, barbecues, walking tours; he was on the TV news constantly. In a citywide race he lost the West Side, where the GGL slate always fared poorly, but won enough Anglo votes to claim his seat without a runoff. Just 27, he was the youngest councilman in San Antonio's history. After the election he made the rounds with city workers—dashing to fires, reading electric meters, collecting garbage, always with the TV cameras present.

Almost from the start there was talk about his becoming San Antonio's first Mexican American mayor. He had the right credentials (all those East Coast degrees), the right message (economic development was the answer to San Antonio's problems), and the right accent (none). But the times turned against him. By nature a consensus politician, Cisneros found himself in a town that was polarizing. The GGL was finished. COPS was growing stronger and more militant. The city started electing councilmen from individual districts instead of citywide. The next council was, in the tangled jargon of modern American politics, a majority minority council: five Mexicans, one black, five Anglos. To avoid the label of *vendido,* a sellout, Cisneros was forced to cast vote after vote against his larger political principles. (He supported a bond package that aided the inner city and all but ignored Anglo San Antonio; it passed the council but was beaten by an army of angry Anglo voters.) He seemed at the mercy of events, unable to lead the minority coalition or leave it. He drifted with the ethnic undercurrents: "It's people like you who have had their boot on the neck of my people for generations," he erupted at a developer during a hearing.

Fortuitously for him, Anglos regained the council majority in 1979. No longer a swing vote, Cisneros could make alliances with Anglos without risk to his political base. When three-term mayor Lila Cockrell retired in 1981, Cisneros was thick with a cadre of developers and businessmen who did not hold with old-line San Antonio's traditional fear of outsiders. He won handily, running well even on the Anglo North Side.

AFTER GONZALEZ WON HIS CON-gressional seat in 1961, he posted a sign on his door on Capitol Hill: "This Office Belongs to the People of Bexar County." There are a number of such signs in the House office buildings today, and in our cynical age they seem like mundane public relations gimmicks. But to Henry B. Gonzalez, his sign—the first of its ilk, he says—was a declaration of independence from the past. "At the time I entered politics, there was only one kind of minority politician," he says, "and that was the *coyote*, a kind of ward heeler, or at best a token. I refused to accept the role of minority politician."

It was a message he had been preaching for years. In the spring of 1957, Gonzalez made a speech to Mexican American students at the University of Texas. "The overriding necessity of the minority groups is to join the mainstream of the American way," he told the students. They must, he warned, avoid "overpowering groups," "beating of the tom-toms," "the battle of the appetites." The reporter for the *Daily Texan* noted that Gonzalez, in his white summer suit, resembled a senator of the Old South.

It has been Henry B. Gonzalez's unhappy fate to be a prophet without honor. The essence of what he stood for fell out of fashion in the sixties. American politics became the politics of facile labels and caucuses and quotas—the politics of overpowering groups, the beating of the tom-toms, the battle of the appetites. Henry C's entanglement in ethnic politics lasted just two years; Henry B's has lasted a political lifetime. He has been caught up in the cruelest, most ironic transition of our time: the shift of ethnic separatism from a conservative cause to a liberal cause.

Soon after his election Gonzalez found himself at odds with the new generation of West Side politicians. At first they sought his support, but he wouldn't fight the Good Government League with them or join their ethnic political organizations or take up causes, like abolishing the Texas Rangers. He broke with, among others, county commissioner Albert Peña, State Senator Joe Bernal, and State Representative Johnny Alaniz. Each fight was bitter and public. There are any number of versions of what caused the splits, but the two camps had little in common, socially or politically. The Young Turks were dealing with a man who had made a San Jacinto Day speech in the state Senate eulogizing the Texas heroes who defeated Santa Anna. Gonzalez had allied himself with Peña a decade earlier only on the condition that Peña, then a candidate, stop posturing on the West Side as "the only Mexican in the race." He once told Peña that his Spanish was no good. It was the Mexican Revolution all over again; he was the aristocrat, they the Zapatistas.

"There's something psychological in the man," Bernal told the *Texas Observer* years later. "His family escaped the Mexican Revolution because they were pursued by revolutionaries. I think he sees the same element in La Raza Unida and anybody who starts getting militant."

His most vocal critics were the members of MAYO, the Mexican American Youth Organization. It was headed by a student at St. Mary's named José Angel Gutiérrez, who later would lead La Raza Unida's takeover of Crystal City. In 1969 Gutiérrez made a celebrated speech in which he called for "the elimination of the gringo" by social or economic means, and "if that doesn't work, we may have to resort to violence in self-defense." Gonzalez had already gone to the House Ways and Means Committee to attack MAYO's Ford Foundation funding. Now he accused MAYO of having a Cuban connection. MAYO voted to censure him. Gonzalez was called a *vendido*, a *Tío Tomás*, a white taco, a traitor to his people. In 1970 MAYO staged a walkout when Gonzalez spoke at St. Mary's. There was an altercation onstage as well. An even uglier incident occurred three years later at the University of Colorado when a Gonzalez speech was interrupted by 150 young Mexican Americans. He was kicked and spat upon. "Lice, step aside, here comes your comb," Gonzalez bellowed at his tormentors in Spanish.

But all of Gonzalez's feuds seemed to have the same ending: his opponents didn't stay in politics long. He backed an Anglo against Alaniz for county Democratic chairman in 1968. Alaniz lost. Another foe, Councilman Pete Torres, ran for mayor in 1971. Gonzalez endorsed the Good Government League's John Gatti. Torres lost. In 1972 Gonzalez's former aide, Albert Bustamente, ran against Peña, with considerable establishment backing. Gonzalez made no endorsement (he had actually fired Bustamente after learning that his aide was laying plans for a race, saying, "There is only one politician in this office, and that is me"), but Peña lost too. Bernal also fell in 1972. And on the West Side people said that what Gonzalez really meant when he fired Bustamente was, "There is only one politician in this *town*, and that is me."

He had settled into a role that is unique in modern American politics. For a parallel one has to go back to Mexico and back a generation to Leonides Gonzalez. As his father once did, Henry B keeps an eye on all the other politicians in his domain. He is San Antonio's *jefe político*.

THERE CAN BE NO WORSE FATE FOR a man who knows and loves history than to see history fail to give him his rightful place. "If I have achieved anything in Texas politics," Henry B. Gonzalez wrote me shortly after our breakfast in Washington, "it is to have established the idea that a minority politician

can represent the whole community. This different perception has made possible the success of people like Henry Cisneros, who like me always insisted on being a citywide politician." But Gonzalez has never gotten the credit he deserves.

One reason is that he has never lived up to his potential in Congress. He is too unbending, too unwilling to play by the insiders' rules to be a success at legislative politics. He has the disease of the fifties' Texas liberal, who would rather lose and remain pure than win; he is out of another era. He sends back contributions from the housing and banking industries, which are regulated by a committee on which he sits. He cast a quixotic vote against his own housing bill in 1983 as a protest against House leaders of his own party, who, to save his bill, had used a parliamentary maneuver of which he disapproved. He makes long speeches to an empty chamber—a series of speeches, really—that go on for weeks and months, with titles like "Central America: Dose of Reality" and "My Advice to the Privileged Orders." No one in the House takes the afternoon speechmaking period seriously except Gonzalez and a small band of insurgent Republicans, who use it to denounce the House leadership.

In 1977 he was chairman of a special committee probing the assassinations of John F. Kennedy and Martin Luther King, Jr. To the acute embarrassment of his colleagues, Gonzalez plunged the committee into a highly visible controversy by unilaterally firing the staff attorney. Reversed by his own committee, he fought on by refusing to sign the lawyer's pay vouchers. At one point the committee voted to adjourn rather than hear Gonzalez's side of the story. He finally resigned his chairmanship. During the battle the now-defunct *Washington Star* ran a profile about Gonzalez that described him as "the kind of congressman who would periodically introduce legislation to bring back the penny postcard."

But there is another reason that Gonzalez has been bypassed by history. In breaking with one ethnic stereotype, the *coyote*, he perpetuated another. His political style—prideful, quick to take offense, slow to forget, knowing no compromise, treating all combat as to the death—seems straight from Mexico. A *jefe político* is not the sort of person who gets credit for breaking new ground.

And so Henry B has seen Henry C become his rival for the judgment of history. Cisneros has inspired imitators in the Mexican American community in a way Gonzalez never did. Since he has become mayor the old-style Mexican politician has all but vanished from the San Antonio political scene. Cisneros has also had a greater effect on San Antonio as a whole than Gonzalez ever did. He has changed the outlook of a city that had viewed the future with pessimism for fifty years. The progression from Henry B to

Henry C is the progression of the immigrant, from first-generation American to second-generation American. For Henry B, nothing came easy, not even being an American. He went to school knowing no English; he went to the third grade believing that he was a Mexican national. His teacher told him he was an American (he was born in San Antonio), but when he told that to his housekeeper she said—in Spanish, of course—"I guess if a cat is born in an oven it makes him bread." Henry C grew up speaking English and Spanish. Henry B's cause was civil rights—political equality. Henry C's cause is jobs—economic equality. Henry B had to fight for everything he got in politics. Henry C has had to fight for very little. When he has gotten into fights, they have been passionless affairs with mixed results. As mayor he has lost more battles than he should have, including a recent fluoridation referendum he backed. He's won a few, too—most notably the awarding of an engineering school to UT–San Antonio, after his stirring speech swayed an initially hostile board—but in general he would rather negotiate than fight. Gonzalez would rather fight than negotiate.

Gonzalez is increasingly critical of Cisneros these days. He has jumped on the mayor for keeping San Antonio in the South Texas Nuclear Project and over other utility issues. (Cisneros never responds. He was careful, on first getting elected to the council in 1975, to write Gonzalez, "I will never run against you.") But their fundamental difference is one of time. Gonzalez lives by the standards of the fifties, when liberalism was in vogue and he ran for governor on $7200—and lost by a three-to-one ratio. "Henry Cisneros raised more money in one race than I have in my entire career," he said at our Washington breakfast. By fifties' standards, when bigness and business were suspect, Cisneros is a conservative. He operates in a different era of politics, one that Gonzalez cannot accept but that would not have been possible without him.

THE MORNING DRIVING TOUR IS almost over now. Henry Cisneros has one last project to show off. "Look at this," he says, pointing to a new home with an ample lot. "A couple of years ago there was a slum here as bad as anything in San Antonio. We tore it down, built a new house, moved the same people back in. Now it looks great."

But the lesson of Henry B and Henry C—indeed, the lesson of the West Side of San Antonio—is that what looks good to one generation appears in a different light when seen by the next. Just as Henry B cannot come to terms with what Henry C represents, so there will come a day when Henry C is seen as just a stop on the road to somewhere else.

In the back seat, Mercedes Cisneros, age ten, looks out the window at the house her father has been praising. "But Daddy," she says, "it's *purple*."❧

[ CONTINUED FROM PAGE 87 ] "Dad, if this land is so good, why are we selling it?"

"Well, son, I've got title to the land, but it's not paid for. The only way to pay for it is to sell to all these good people."

Some of the land deals were controversial. In 1950 several buyers filed lawsuits contending that the Bentsens had defrauded buyers by selling dry farmland that they claimed was irrigated. The test case involved an Iowa family named Polmateer, who sued to cancel a contract on a ten-acre tract. As a result of the case, the contract was rescinded and the Polmateers were paid $5000. The judge in Brownsville who heard the case did not rule on the fraud question.

Bentsen expanded his holdings beyond real estate into oil and gas (the Bentsen brothers always retained most of the mineral rights to the land they sold) and banking. At one time Bentsen controlled six Valley banks. In each town where he owned a bank, the other bank in town was owned by Doc Neuhaus, a rancher and businessman who was Bentsen's chief rival for supremacy in the Valley until he died in 1983. Bentsen and Neuhaus were a case study in the mysterious sociology of South Texas; for years they lived next door to one another, feuding by day and frequently dining together at night.

We drove up to the headquarters of the Bentsen Development Company, an unpretentious one-story building on the outskirts of Mission. The walls of his office were covered with the photographs of politicians. Most of them dated from the days when Bentsen was part of the old conservative Democratic establishment: Shivers, Sam Rayburn, John Connally, Lyndon Johnson, and, of more recent vintage, the senator known in the Valley as Lloyd Junior. But Mr. Lloyd almost wasn't a Democrat at all. When he first moved to the Valley, he went to see R. B. Creager of Brownsville, state chairman of the Republican party during its dormant years.

"I told Mr. Creager that I wanted to join the Republican party since my daddy had always been a rock-ribbed Republican in South Dakota. He said, 'Young man, do you want to do what's best for Texas?' I said I did. And he told me, 'You go back to Mission and join the Democratic party, because what's best for Texas is for every state in the union to have a two-party system and for Texas to be a one-party state. When you have a one-party state, your men stay in Congress longer and build up seniority.' I took his advice."

It was time for Bentsen to go back to work. As we left his office, we drove through a grove thick with palms. "I told the boys to stop planting palm trees after 1990," he said with a wink, "because I want to be completely out of the palm business when I'm one hundred."❧

104

# 3

# COMING OF AGE

**THE RISE OF THE CITIES** ✳ In 1940 more than half of all Texans lived on the land. We were a state of country stores and crossroads hamlets. Today four out of every five Texans live in cities, and we are a state of shopping malls and urban sprawl. **THE NEW POLITICS** ✳ We've come a long way from the days of Southern racism and one-party fratricide. But the old themes—like Yankees and unions, water and fundamentalism, and oilmen and their money—still matter, even in a two-party state. **UP FROM COLONIALISM** ✳ For years, Texas was at the mercy of Eastern money—a colony, some said, of New York. Then Texas grew into a modern industrial state and found itself with America's Team, America's fashion, and America's favorite TV show.

# WHERE ALL THE YOUNG FOLKS GONE?

### BY NICHOLAS LEMANN

**1940** FOR THE LAST TIME, A CENSUS SHOWS A RURAL TEXAS. IN TOWNS LIKE GARWOOD, THE END IS NEAR.

IT'S THE SUNDAY AFTER LABOR DAY, over a hundred degrees on the coastal prairie. The rice crop is in and mostly sold—another year of low prices. The hunters won't be arriving for several weeks. There's a breathing spell. Hay bales stand reassuringly in the fields. Small towns all up and down Highway 90A are holding their annual festivals.

In Nada, which is on Highway 71, twenty miles south of 90A and just south of Garwood (which has its Lions Club Fair in October), it's the St. Mary's Parish Festival and Homecoming. "Come when you can—Leave when you want!!" says the flier. By midafternoon it's Texas Brueghel: old ladies interminably playing bingo in the shade, benign priests wandering through the crowd, adolescent boys huddling around the game where you knock over bowling pins with a baseball; pregnant women, sheriff's deputies, kids riding at a tiny, trucked-in amusement park; men outdoors tending barbecue, women indoors doling it onto plastic plates along with coleslaw and kolaches. There is a screen against the sun, but no air conditioning. Over to one side an auction is going on, where people pay prices like $70 for items like a bag of homemade noodles to help out the church, and the auctioneer doesn't need to be told any of the bidders' names.

THE URBAN MIGRATION HAS LEFT SMALL TOWNS LOOKING AS IF A VACUUM CLEANER HAD SUCKED UP EVERYONE BUT THE OLD-TIMERS.

The first buyer is the county judge.

One reason a parish in a tiny village like Nada can draw such a good crowd is that the people who moved to the city, and there are a lot of them, come back for events like this. Rural Texas has been depopulating for almost half a century now. It peaked in population in the 1940 census, which was also the last census to show the state as majority rural; now Texas is 80 per cent urban, well above the percentage for the nation as a whole. The effects are in plain sight on any back-road drive, hamlet after hamlet slowly turning into a picturesque ruin, looking as if a vacuum cleaner had come through and sucked up everyone but the old-timers.

For two generations the move from country to city has been Texas' great mass experience and the shaping force in the history of towns such as Garwood and Nada. Urbanization is a presence in Texas life so huge that it is sometimes difficult to see it in clear perspective, and it has spawned a number of myths. The biggest holds that urbanization has damaged the essence of Texas. A smaller and currently popular myth maintains that the countryside is coming back. Rural population did stop dropping in the seventies, but this is almost completely attributable to two phenomena, the boom [ CONTINUED ON PAGE 156 ]

# 1949 THE OPENING OF THE SHAMROCK HOTEL IS THE PARTY LIZ SMITH WAS BORN TO COVER.

# IT HAPPENED ONE NIGHT

## BY LIZ SMITH

LIZ SMITH

HOUSTON, MARCH 18, 1949. The opening last night of the already famous and infamous Shamrock Hotel "combined the most exciting features of a subway rush, Hallowe'en in a mad house, and a circus fire," said the *Houston Post*'s editor GEORGE FUERMANN.

Wildcat oil king GLENN MCCARTHY's "Emerald Folly" at the intersection of South Main and Bellaire cost him $21 million. It boasts 63 shades of green in its "International Modern" decor, a thousand-car garage where visitors can tank up on four different kinds of gas, five special rooms for nightlife, ten acres of specially woven rugs, the world's biggest beds and bath towels. Even its garbage is refrigerated. But naysayers were asking, even after they learned that McCarthy had spent $1.5 million on his opening-night party, "How can anything succeed that is five miles from downtown Houston?"

Nevertheless, at least 50,000 people gawked, gaped, drove up, and stood in line to get a glimpse of the 2000 Hollywood, New York, and Texas elite who opened the Shamrock in black-tied, bejeweled, and begowned splendor. The hotel's news vendors wore tuxedos, and pretty girls passed out thousands of shamrocks flown in from Ireland. Guards made sure that the shell-shaped 165-foot swimming pool kept its emerald-green color. (Texas Aggies had

threatened to dump orange dye into McCarthy's pride and joy, which is filled from private springs beneath the hotel.) The owner himself threw a $100 bill across the pool on a bet. He casually wrapped the C-note around some heavy change and heaved it over. It's said that when the trick doesn't work, McCarthy strips to his shorts and dives in to retrieve his money.

The Shamrock was pronounced a disaster in advance by experts. The great American architect FRANK LLOYD WRIGHT took one look and asked one word: "Why?" Later, after a tour, he went on to say, "I always wondered what the inside of a jukebox looked like. It's tragic—an imitation Rockefeller Center."

But McCarthy, in his trademark glasses and diamond ring as big as the Big Bend country, walked through it all with an insouciance that comes of having been born poor in Beaumont just six years after the legendary Spindletop oil field was discovered there in 1901. This is a man who is so self-possessed that he keeps a life-size color photograph of himself in his office. This self-made diamond in the rough is barred from a number of Texas clubs because of his brawling tendencies, so he has created his own playpen.

The day before his premiere, McCarthy flew into Houston with HOWARD HUGHES, aboard the latter's private plane. But the elusive Hughes was nowhere in sight last night. He hates crowds. And the Shamrock was no place for anyone who hates crowds. The mayor of Houston, OSCAR HOLCOMBE, was trapped in the lobby and couldn't get in to dinner for two hours. He fumed: "They let people in without tickets, and they took the places of those who had bought the $42 dinner tickets. It was the worst mob scene I ever witnessed. It was

ridiculous." The highly respected JESSE JONES was trapped in the entrance like a yearling waiting to be turned into a steer. The DOROTHY LAMOUR national radio broadcast, meant to be a grand entertainment highlight, was so fraught with noise, shouts, remarks, and mayhem from onlookers that NBC canceled it at midpoint. That sent the beauteous star to her suite in tears: "I've been on the road with Bing Crosby and Bob Hope but never through anything like this."

Guests who got to dine feasted on pineapple surprise, consommé royal, blue ribbon steak à la Shamrock, stuffed artichoke hearts, peas à la Française, potato château, pâté de pheasant *en* aspic, hearts of lettuce Lorenzo, frozen pistachio mousse. But one woman, upon being served supreme of pompano Normandie, gasped: "Why, it's only fish!"

Shamrock flacks boasted that there were 175 major movie stars and big names in the crowd, including the dashing ERROL FLYNN (after whom McCarthy may have patterned some of his own life and looks) . . . the plump LOU COSTELLO . . . the gravel-voiced ANDY DEVINE . . . MGM's star VAN JOHNSON in his omnipresent red socks . . . comedienne JOAN DAVIS, who is now a blonde . . . the elegant RUTH WARRICK, ever remembered as the wife of Citizen Kane . . . the one and only GINGER ROGERS, who loves everything green and went wild for the Shamrock's ink pots . . . the woo-woo man HUGH HERBERT . . . EDGAR BERGEN without Charlie McCarthy . . . ROBERT STACK and RHONDA FLEMING (are they an item! they're so good-looking!) . . . Mary Pickford's BUDDY ROGERS . . . ED GARDNER of Duffy's Tavern . . . those great actors VAN HEFLIN and ROBERT PRESTON . . . skater SONJA HENIE . . . Clark Gable's

PHOTOGRAPHS COURTESY OF HARRIS COUNTY HERITAGE SOCIETY

perennial friend VIRGINIA GREY (he always dates her between wives) . . . creator of the WACs, OVETA CULP HOBBY . . . cowboy actor DON "RED" BERRY, who drank out of the slipper of Beaumont oil heiress ANN JUSTICE (doesn't he always) . . . the Park Avenue hillbilly DOROTHY SHAY . . . that girl-about-the-world PEGGY CUMMINS . . . columnists COBINA WRIGHT and EARL WILSON (no, they're not an item!) . . . Ireland's and Hollywood's PAT O'BRIEN . . . the famous "pick up the check" guy JOHNNY MEYERS . . . oilman SID RICHARDSON . . . EDDIE RICKENBACKER . . . the SAM MACEOS of Galveston's gambling empire . . . DEL WEBB . . . oh, I could go on and on.

Chief among the missing was McCar-

thy's good friend FRANCIS ALBERT SINATRA. But the hotel promises to bring the crooner in for two weeks in January. Rumor has it that at that time, Frankie will bring in his new love, the MGM actress AVA GARDNER, in spite of the fact that he is still very much married to NANCY, the mother of his three children. Maybe this appearance in Houston will pump up Sinatra's flagging career.

Some looked down their noses at the crush and overkill of last night's opening. One bystander commented, "It's like a nouveau riche family that has hired a butler and begins a little social climbing

CROWDS JAMMED THE SHAMROCK OPENING; LATER, CARMEN MIRANDA AND FUNNY-MAN JERRY COLLONA (BY PORTRAIT OF GLENN MCCARTHY) PACKED 'EM IN.

but always dreads that grandpa might break down and start eating peas with a knife. Last night Houston ate peas with a knife."

Yes, but at least Houston ate high on the hog along with the peas. Glenn McCarthy was warned by ill-wishers that he might well lose his shirt since his new hotel needs an 82 per cent occupancy rate to succeed. The millionaire who married a sixteen-year-old socialite in 1930 with a borrowed wedding ring and $1.50 in his pocket simply shrugged and said, "I just lent a dollar to a bum outside who once advised me to stay out of the oil bidness." ❧

# 1971 Newcomer Southwest Airlines has this funny idea that businessmen might like to fly from one Texas city to another.

# Hot Pants Special

## BY PAULA PHILLIPS

CHARLES FORD

SOUTHWEST AIRLINES PROVIDED PAULA PHILLIPS WITH HOT PANTS AND STOCK OPTIONS.

*FIRST PERSON*

With every planeload that Southwest Airlines flew out of Hobby Airport and Love Field, Texas became more and more an urban state. The airline helped make possible the growth of new institutions like bank holding companies and the diversification of countless small businesses. Equally as important, it reinforced the Texan's natural feeling that the whole state was his home. Southwest Airlines managed to shrink Texas without making it seem smaller. Yet this interview with one of Southwest's original stewardesses reminds us that in the beginning the idea seemed farfetched and fanciful.

"I'M ORIGINALLY FROM CHICKASHA, Oklahoma, and I got hired by Braniff to come to Dallas. I thought that was the cat's meow—working for a big airline, Big D, get to travel. That was '69. I worked for them for about a year, on call the whole time. They kept saying I'd be on a regular line, but I finally got fed up with all that stuff. A pilot told me about Southwest Airlines. He said there was a new airline starting up. He said, 'Haven't you read the ads in the newspapers?' They were asking for girls that looked like Raquel Welch. Well, I would never answer an ad like that. It'd be too presumptuous. No way. But the more I thought about it, the more I got fed up with Braniff. I called, got an interview, and ended up getting hired.

"I knew it was going to be a new airline, a commuter airline, whatever that was. I didn't know that businessmen would actually fly from one city in Texas to another, instead of driving from Plano to Dallas. I didn't know the planes were going to be that big, that it was going to be an actual airline!

"I began in June '71, and like, wham, bang, everything was due to start on June 18. They used all the girls for PR, anything they could get their flight at-tendants to do for publicity. We did all of our commercials, advertising, posters. We were constantly going to Lions Clubs, the Jaycees, telling them what cities we went to, how big our airplanes were, and how we were going to be an airline for commuters, for businessmen. And it was cheap. I think our cheapest fare was like eleven dollars. It was all one class. Our theory was that it was all first class. Everybody was treated the same.

"Southwest was the first airline to let girls be individuals. So whatever your best feature was they let you go with it. We had the hot pants. They were real short. I thought they were pretty hot! And go-go boots that laced up the side and an orange shirt with a white ammunition belt. We had little skirts that we had to wear over our hot pants through the terminal. Part of the secretiveness was to get people to come fly with us. If you want to see the girls, you have to fly on us. And then, on the airplane, we took our skirts off. One day I wore my skirt, but I [CONTINUED ON PAGE 158]

## 1962
# One Small Step for George R. Brown, One Giant Step for Houston

WAS THERE EVER ANY DOUBT THAT THE National Aeronautics and Space Administration would end up in Houston? So what if the Houston site was, as Tom Wolfe put it in *The Right Stuff*, "a thousand acres of cattle pasture south of Houston near Clear Lake, which was not a lake but an inlet and was about as clear as the eyeballs of a poisoned bass." What mattered was that George R. Brown wanted NASA in Houston. Brown and Root had become the largest construction company in the world by landing huge federal contracts, thanks in no small part to Lyndon Johnson, who was

then vice president of the United States, thanks in no small part to George R. Brown. Brown was a trustee of Rice University, which had recently established the Albert Thomas chair of political science, thanks in no small part to Brown's $500,000 contribution. Thomas was a local congressman who just happened to be chairman of the subcommittee that controlled NASA's budget.

NASA was a typical Houston deal. Humble Oil donated 1000 acres out of 50,000 it owned in the area. Its real estate subsidiary made a killing. Brown and Root, which (surprise) got the $250 million contract to build the space center, made a killing. Johnson crony Jack Valenti got NASA's advertising contract. Even Rice ended up with a new space science department, subsidized by NASA contracts.

It is easy to be cynical about the great Houston deals. Like the Ship Channel, the Astrodome, and Intercontinental Airport,

NASA was an inside deal that made the insiders rich. But it's also true that in 1962, the year of the NASA deal, Houston was an unsophisticated Southern town with a population of fewer than a million. National TV commentators still called it Houston, *Texas*. NASA had a lot to do with Houston's transformation into one of the world's big-league cities. The insiders took care of themselves, but they took care of Houston too. —JOSEPH NOCERA

# THE ORGANIZATION MAN
## 1936: R. L. Thornton forms the Dallas Citizens Council.

*For young liberals like Willie Morris, a visit to the Dallas of the fifties was like a trip to Dante's Hell. In his book,* North Toward Home, *Morris offered the following observations about why Dallas was his least-favorite Texas city.*

And then there was Dallas, always a cavernous city for me, claustrophobic, full of thundering certitudes and obsessed with its image. From the first I was admittedly prejudiced about the place; I would detour fifty miles to avoid it. . . .

In 1936 its leading businessman [R. L. Thornton, chairman of Mercantile National Bank], who succeeded after much effort in raising several million dollars to bring the Texas Centennial to a city which had played a smaller role in the state's history than a dozen dying hamlets, had learned an important lesson. . . . "We had to have men who could underwrite. . . . We didn't have time for no proxy people. Then I saw the idea. Why not organize the 'yes' and 'no' people?" In the late 1930s, without an election or a local consensus, the city's most powerful businessmen decided to run Dallas. The government of the city was a group called The Citizens Council, consisting of the men who on their own could commit their companies to whatever policies they chose. The consequences of this monolith had not been trivial. Civic dissent had been successfully excluded by furious appeals to community "loyalty." . . .

By 1960 a strikingly high proportion of Dallas' citizens were in managerial, professional, and white-collar work. In a city like this, almost wholly white-collar in character, standards were set by the employer. Political and social conformity worked downward, to the middling manager and below; conservatism became synonymous with social acceptability. . . . Much of this could have been said of other cities, but no other American community of this size had so mutely acquiesced in the sacrifice of diversity.

# DEATH OF THE 'DILLO
### 1 9 8 0
## THE SIXTIES COME TO AN END IN AUSTIN.

Traditionalists maintain that the sixties ended on December 31, 1969. Others say they died with Kent State or America's withdrawal from Viet Nam. But in Austin they were going strong until December 31, 1980—the night the Armadillo World Headquarters closed down.

Though the Armadillo was synonymous with hippies and innovative rock, it didn't open until the summer of 1970. According to legend, Eddie Wilson, the manager of a local rock group known as Shiva's Head Band, slipped out of the Cactus Club on Barton Springs to relieve himself. He spied an abandoned National Guard Armory nestled behind a skating rink and decided that it would make a perfect music hall. The name came from the shy, armored animal that Austin artist Jim Franklin had turned into the symbol of the hippie counterculture.

The large concert hall with the beer-joint atmosphere became Austin's musical heart and the symbol of its laid-back, mellow lifestyle. Austin's living legends hung out there: the Guacamole Queen, Big Rikke, who worked in the kitchen; the Hawaiian Prince, who spent his daylight hours on a rock at Barton Springs wearing plastic leis and floral baggies; Doug Sahm of Sir Douglas Quintet fame. You never knew who might wind up on the Armadillo's

It was far out while it lasted.

stage: young Bruce Springsteen sang for a $1 cover, the Austin Ballet Theater danced for an audience that munched on nachos, Count Basie performed to a full house, a string quartet played Beethoven before a Michael Murphey concert, Baba Ram Dass lectured on metaphysics. If you didn't want to watch the show, you could muse on Franklin's larger-than-life paintings or sit outside underneath the wisteria arbor in the beer garden, mingling with the colorful clientele.

But even in Austin, the sixties had to end. The loyal followers grew fewer and fewer. In 1977 the owners filed for reorganization in bankruptcy. By 1980 the Austin land boom had begun, and the ground the Armadillo occupied was worth more in dollars than in nostalgia. The Armadillo was razed, and the site that once was the heart of Texas music is now home to a high-rise office building, One Texas Center.—DEBORAH FANT

# THE STOLEN HEART

**1969: An episode in the DeBakey–Cooley heart wars.**

Yes, 1969—but the artificial heart stayed in for only 63 hours, after which it was replaced by a transplanted human heart, after which the patient, Haskell Karp, quickly died. That was the high baroque phase of the Texas Medical Center. Denton Cooley and his former mentor turned bitterest enemy, Michael DeBakey, were deep into their heart-transplant war, competing from two adjacent hospitals, St. Luke's and Methodist. After the artificial heart incident, the situation went from overheated to superheated. Karp's widow unsuccessfully sued Cooley for malpractice; Cooley was investigated for stealing the artificial heart from DeBakey's labs, where it had been developed, but nothing came of the investigation.

Both doctors are still practicing, and the passing years be damned; Cooley's face is suspiciously unwrinkled, DeBakey's hair suspiciously jet-black. Though the late sixties heart-transplant derby doesn't look as good today as it did when *Life* was breathlessly reporting on it as an inside-the-body space program, they both stand up as larger-than-life figures. Cooley and DeBakey can be seen now as part of a process in which it was proved that the essential flamboyant style of Houston, though developed by oil wildcatters, could be successfully adapted to other fields, such as space exploration, real estate development, and, unlikeliest of all, medicine.

Which one won? Cooley is more fabulously talented and, of no little import in Houston, has made a lot more money. DeBakey was more visionary and influential in bringing the resources of the government into medicine to create an enormous industry. In Houston today, the Texas Medical Center is the single largest employer.

—NICHOLAS LEMANN

## The MOOSEUM

*Louis Kahn finds inspiration for the Kimbell in a cow barn.*

**1966** The Kimbell Art Museum in Fort Worth, designed by Louis I. Kahn, has a magical dignity. It is a building of beauty and strength, of intimacy and loftiness. Its finest achievement, though, is that it seems so right for its place, as if the state's best art museum could belong nowhere else but in Fort Worth—a city that in a word-association test would have been linked with cattle long before culture.

That new affinity did not occur by accident. When Kay Kimbell died in 1964, he provided the directors of his art foundation with $75 million and instructions to "build a museum of the first class." Museum director Richard Brown chose Kahn

# HI, SOCIETY

The Jaycees take a deep breath, rent some tuxes, pop a few corks, and launch Houston onto the international social scene.

**1950** During the first postwar years, Houston society couldn't have been less interested in the small consular corps stationed in town. Then in 1950 the international committee of the junior chamber of commerce decided to give a ball in honor of the foreigners, hoping to show Houstonians the social and economic advantages of having such outsiders in their midst. The first Consular Ball was held at the old Houston Country Club, and the nervous Jaycees hired a consultant to make every detail conform to the formal European style. White tie and tails were required. Guests were announced, and they bowed or curtsied as part of the grand march. Following the dance, three hundred guests sampled a midnight buffet of cold ham, cuts of tenderloin, stuffed tomatoes, lobsters, and champagne.

The Consular Ball was only a year removed from the legendary party that opened the Shamrock Hotel, but it was light years removed in sophistication and refinement. In the past, society had played a far less prominent role in Houston than it had in Dallas and San Antonio. But the

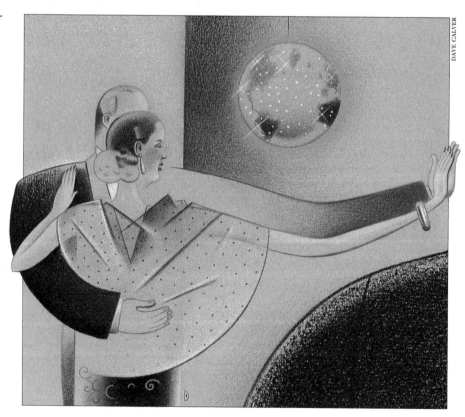

modest dreams of a few Jaycees enabled Houston to leapfrog ahead on the international social scale. Today Lynn Wyatt takes Queen Elizabeth II for barbecue when she visits the U.S., Joanne Herring Davis is honorary consul to Pakistan and Morocco, and Baron Ricky di Portanova tosses his own caviar and linguine at Tony's

and then jets off to host Houstonians in Acapulco. For certain Houstonians, the search for amusement is now a global enterprise. Oil and space exploration may be the most compelling reasons for Houston's status as an international city, but nobody can accuse the city's socialites of not doing their part. —MIMI SWARTZ

as architect specifically to get away from the predictability of a Frank Lloyd Wright or Ludwig Mies van der Rohe. Kahn had a reputation for building to a situation and for incorporating indigenous architecture. He first visited Fort Worth in 1966, and by March 1967 he had developed the basic elements of the museum: rows of rectangles with barrel vaults for ceilings, interrupted by open courts. Searching for Kahn's inspiration, academics have attributed the design to, among other things, second-century Roman baths and the ruins of Pompeii. But in Fort Worth you hear a different story, one that explains why the museum fits in so well. The repetitive barrel forms look a lot like the animal barns at the Will Rogers Memorial Center, just a block away.

— CATHERINE CHADWICK

# 1979
# DIVORCE
## TEXAS STYLE

In 1979 there appeared some cold, hard data to support the sense many people had that in Texas' transformation from a rural to an urban state, something had gone awry. The data were this: the metropolitan areas of Dallas–Fort Worth and Houston tied that year for the dubious distinction of leading the nation's 25 largest cities in divorces per capita.

Explaining why breaking up was easy to do in Texas became a cottage industry for sociologists, psychologists, and other cultural observers. Some said it was because the big cities were full of young people. Some said it was because Texas was now populated by rootless transplants from the North who inhabited the ever-growing suburbs. There were theories about the anonymous quality of city life and the loss of the feeling of community that had been the social glue of so many small towns in Texas. There was even talk that citified Texans were particularly susceptible to divorce because they saw themselves as urban versions of the lone gunslinger. In all of those large and profound theories, there was no doubt some truth.

But there was also another possible factor, a more mundane one that was somehow overlooked by many of the sociologists and psychologists. In 1969 the Texas Legislature enacted a no-fault divorce law. "Before then, a big deterrent to divorce was the dread of having a contested case and then having a jury trial," says Charles Tessmer. He's not a sociologist but another sort of urban observer, with a somewhat less cosmic vision: a prominent Dallas lawyer.

— EMILY YOFFE

# Dog Bites Man! Houston Rejects Zoning!

## 1962

On November 6, 1962, Houston voters swarmed to the polls in small numbers to soundly defeat a proposed zoning ordinance. It was not so much a pivotal moment as a reaffirmation of the city's spirit, since a straw vote was even more soundly defeated in 1948. Zoning and Houston just do not seem to peacefully coexist. Hugh Roy Cullen observed that zoning was un-American at the time of the 1948 election, and those in favor of this form of planning have not attempted another test since the 1962 defeat. The consequences are mixed.

On the one hand, practical dreamers like Ken Schnitzer and Gerald Hines have an environment in which to conceive and construct stunning urban achievements like Greenway Plaza and the Galleria complex. On the other, you might well have a fetching view of a Tenneco station from your living room window.

Lack of zoning and its consequent rigidity has helped Houston become a brash city whose excesses and vitality are equally obvious. The absence of zoning allows for cultural oddities and fine madness: the weekend melee of lower Westheimer, where strolling hookers serve as the palace guard for sleaze emporiums and nice restaurants side by side; the mini-slum of Lamar Terrace, once comfortably middle-class suburbia and now a haven for motorcycle gangs and illegal aliens while absentee landowners wait hopefully for commercial development; the proliferation of "downtowns"; the ungainly strip centers; the striking and strikingly odd architecture; the glorious residential areas of Southampton, River Oaks, and North and South boulevards as well as the despairing slums. The beautiful or the terrifying can appear anywhere.

Actually, unzoned Houston has a certain charm. Where else would you find a fundamentalist church within one hundred yards of an establishment that proclaims, "All New! All Nude!"?

Let the better man win, we always say.

— PETE BARTHELME

INSTITUTE OF TEXAN CULTURES

1928

## WHY I CAME TO THE MILAM BUILDING

The Milam Building was the world's first air-conditioned skyscraper. But judging by the apologetic tone of this ad, which appeared in the *San Antonio Evening News* for November 9, 1928, Texans didn't immediately appreciate how totally air conditioning would change their lives.

The chief reason it suited me when I came over to look was its location. I can park my car next door to the building, and be in my office quicker than I could be if I were located in any other building.

Then, too, the Milam Building seems to be a community in itself. I don't have to leave the building to reach a barber shop, cafeteria, drug store, stationery store, cigar store, telegraph office, etc. And in the neighboring offices there are lawyers, real estate men, lumber men, public stenographers, delivery service, employment bureau, and many other services.

At the time I moved in I was a little prejudiced against the air-conditioning system. I don't know why, for I never had taken time to investigate it. But after moving in I prize it above all features of the building. I feel better, and finish the day's work with more energy. Because of the air-conditioning system I can keep my windows closed and keep out the street noises. This absence of noise, together with the quiet cork tile floors, makes this the most restful building, from the standpoint of quiet, that I have ever been in.

Then, too, with the windows closed I can keep the wind out. If there is anything that is irritating to me it is to have my papers, telegrams, etc., distributed on my desk and then, momentarily forgetting a paperweight, have some of them blown out of order. Here I can lay the lightest papers about my desk without fear of having them blown about.

— EARL WILSON, R. E. WILSON CO.

**This Is the Turf That Replaced the Grass That Needed the Sun That Was Blocked by the Paint That Banished the Glare That Blinded the Player That Missed the Ball That Lost the Game That Was Played in The Astrodome That Hofheinz Built**

**1965** Like the Astrodome itself, which was the site of his terrible contribution to baseball, Kenneth Travis Johnson was big, white, and unfortunate. If he is remembered at all, it is as the poor sap who in April 1964 pitched Texas' first major-league no-hitter. The Houston club being what it was back then—which is to say, even worse than it is now—Johnson lost the game anyway.

But Ken Johnson's more important moment would have to wait a year, for the opening of the building that its publicists called the Eighth Wonder of the World. Sunday afternoon, May 23, first inning. The San Francisco Giants' third baseman, Jim Ray Hart, was batting, with two men out and two on base. Johnson served up a decent enough pitch, Hart managed ordinary contact, and the ball floated upward toward center field. There Jimmy Wynn trotted in, stopped, reached up with his glove, and then (wrote Mickey Herskowitz in the *Houston Post*) "suddenly looked wildly about him like a man caught in an elephant stampede." Wynn had lost the flight of the ball against the translucent background of the dome's latticed steel. The ball fell ten feet behind him. While Wynn chased it all the way to the fence, Hart followed his teammates home. Shooting the messenger, the Astros traded Johnson to Milwaukee during the seventh inning of the very same game.

Such is the trigger of history. The Astros' owner, Roy Hofheinz, ordered a heavy coat of paint for the dome's ceiling. It went a long way toward solving the fly ball problem, but it also kept the sun from performing its kindly magic on the hybrid Bermuda grass that covered the field. The next season, Monsanto installed a plastic carpet on the Astrodome floor. Attracted by its low maintenance cost, others followed Hofheinz into the lab and perverted the game forever. Since the need for it was established by Ken Johnson's pitch and Jim Ray Hart's swing, the awful stuff has spread like weeds. —DANIEL OKRENT

Where's the ball that changed the game?

## O GALLERIA MIA

# 1966

HINES: THE $3-A-FOOT VISIONARY.

When romantics talk about the Galleria in Houston—the shopping mall that has come to symbolize, as much as any single thing, the sprawling, glamorous, slightly chaotic city that Houston has become—they tell about the day Gerald Hines saw the Galleria Vittorio Emanuele II in Milan and decided that was what Houston needed. As the romantics tell it, you can imagine the dynamic young Houstonian in a dark business suit and dark horn-rimmed glasses strolling across the Piazza del Duomo. Pigeons scatter. Hines enters the triumphal archway to the shopping arcade, stops to take in the sidewalk cafes, the mosaics, the frescoes, the elegant shops, and—presto!—where there are radiator shops, vegetable farms, and a drive-in theater on the edge of Houston, he envisions Galleria I, II, III. He imagines three floors of shopping ("an unheard-of concept at the time") and an ice skating rink (the first ever in a shopping mall) and high-quality stores like Tiffany and Mark Cross that had never before been lured to Texas. He envisions, in other words, one of the most successful shopping malls ever built anywhere.

But when you ask Gerald Hines about his source of inspiration, he answers, "Three dollars a square foot."

"Pardon?"

"No one had ever paid more than fifty cents a square foot for land for a shopping mall," he explained. "I had paid six times that much. I had to figure out a way to intensify the development."

"But what about Milan?"

"I had been there about ten years before we started building in Houston. Then in '66, after we had drawn up plans, I stopped through to see it again. I was in the Swiss Alps on a mountain-climbing expedition, so I just dropped down for another look."

"And that was what you had envisioned for Houston?"

"I wouldn't use that word. I'm a developer, a follower of the culture, an interpreter of what people want," says Gerald Hines, "not a visionary." —JOHN DAVIDSON

# THE FAST TRACK

## 1871: LITTLE D
(POP.: 3000)
STEALS A RAILROAD.

For those who doubt for a second that Dallas was genetically coded to do bidness, consider its first two leaps toward the big time. First, Dallas made a rather preposterous try at maritime greatness. In 1868, the *Dallas Herald* crowed that the arrival of the first boat to navigate the Trinity River was "the greatest event that will ever occur in the history of Dallas." When the first steamboat made in Dallas ingloriously struck a stump and sank a year later, Dallas turned to Plan B—beg, borrow, or steal a railroad.

Towns all over Texas were bidding for railroad lines, but none with as much missionary fervor, rah-rah unanimity, and political guile as Dallas. In 1870, when surveyors laid out a north-south route for the railroad that went eight miles west of town, Dallas leaders wooed the line with a package that included a donation of depot grounds, right-of-way, and $5000 cash. Citizens approved the measure by a vote of 167–11. Suddenly Dallas, a town of perhaps a thousand people, was on the map.

Then Dallas went for the big prize, an east-west line that would make it a junction. Plans called for the Texas and Pacific's transcontinental route to go fifty miles south of Dallas. But local legislator

John W. Lane slipped a provision into the 1871 railroad law requiring the line to pass within a mile of a place called Browder Springs. Browder Springs turned out to be a mile south of downtown Dallas. Then, to make sure the railroad ran through the middle of town, Dallasites, ever on the team, voted 192–0 to pony up $100,000 and free right-of-way. (There's no record of whether the eleven losers who voted against the first project were converted, shot, or run out of town.) Two decades later, Dallas was Texas' most populous city.

— PETER APPLEBOME

## TANDY SHACK

### 1963

## Fort Worth goes high tech.

"CHARLES TANDY HAS NEVER STAYED FAR from leather," the *New York Times* said in 1963. "His career was practically carved in leather." But money, not leather, was the motivating force in Tandy's life. In the next fifteen years he pioneered the consumer electronics business and led the transformation of Fort Worth from cow town to modern city.

Tandy's father started a Fort Worth wholesale business in 1919, when Charles was one year old, supplying leather to shoe repair shops. After World War II Charles joined the business and took Tandy Leather Company out of shoes and into leather crafts by opening a chain of hobby supermarkets, with spectacular success.

Even as the *Times* article appeared though, Tandy saw the leather industry in a precipitous decline. Within a few years he bought, among others, Pier I Imports, Leonard's department stores, Wolfe Nursery Stores, Color Tile, and a floundering Boston-based retailer of electronic components that had only nine stores, called Radio Shack. At the time electronics was almost entirely a mail-order business, but Tandy opened retail stores, keeping his managers highly motivated by offering them a percentage of their stores' profits.

Tandy liked to say, "To catch a mouse you've got to make sounds like a cheese." Radio Shack was the big cheese. When he died in 1978, six months after riding an elephant into his sixtieth birthday celebration, Radio Shack had seven thousand outlets and Tandy Corporation was a billion-dollar multinational business with 20,000 employees. In a park just north of the Tarrant County courthouse, Fort Worth erected a nine-foot bronze statue, of the kind usually reserved for conquering generals, in Tandy's memory.

— SCOTT LUBECK

# Remember the Alamo?

### 1965: *A theme park in Arlington outdraws the Texas shrine.*

In 1965, after decades as the uncontested shrine of Texas tourism, the Alamo fell. All at once, the champion was Six Flags Over Texas, a new amusement park in Arlington that, in its loose and vaguely horrifying fashion, traded on the theme of Texas history.

Should we be alarmed? Does the attendance duel between the Alamo and Six Flags represent a struggle for the soul of Texas, a struggle between the sacred and the profane? Before we pass judgment on Six Flags, however, we should remember that the Alamo is itself a triumph of showmanship. There is a manufactured hush to the place, an overdone reverence in the signs admonishing gentlemen to remove their hats and visitors to "be silent." And of course, there is a souvenir shop that rivals the mercantile ambitions of its competitor.

Still, the Alamo is old; it is pure. It is Texas as Texas forevermore should be. The rise of Six Flags does not erase its significance but just points to a changing Texas. The Alamo is in the heart of the oldest city in our state; Six Flags is in a phantom metropolis between Dallas and Fort Worth. The battle between Six Flags and the Alamo is really the story of the emergence of the suburbs. Six Flags beat out the Alamo that year because it catered to Texans who were less settled, more mobile, and restless. Perhaps these new Texans—who, after all, are us—may finally prove themselves indifferent to the old weepy power of our heritage, but I doubt it. For the last four or five years the Alamo has been surpassing its rival again, pulling ahead by a few hundred thousand visitors a year. Just to be on the safe side, maybe we should rename it Alamoland and install a state-of-the-art roller coaster called the *Degüello*.

— STEPHEN HARRIGAN

# San Antonio Takes Off

## 1930: Randolph Field rejuvenates the Alamo City.

INSTITUTE OF TEXAN CULTURES

In 1926 the U.S. government wanted to build a major airfield to train new aviators. San Antonio, with an ideal climate (only fifteen unsuitable flying days a year), was its first choice. There was only one hitch: the government didn't want to pay. Good citizens from Shreveport to Dallas to New Braunfels were eager to donate land to get the base for their towns. The government told San Antonio it could have the base only if the city came up with the land.

San Antonio had been first in population in Texas in 1920 but over the next decade would fall behind Houston and Dallas. Chamber of commerce officials desperately wanted to add the military and its money to San Antonio's odd mixture of poor Mexicans and German merchants and farmers. The trouble was, the city had no land to donate and no money with which to buy a site. Over the next few months, those problems were solved in typical local fashion, involving much confusion and crankiness. A German-speaking civic leader was dispatched to persuade recalcitrant German farmers to sell their land. First attempts to raise money for an airfield ended in a ruling that the purpose was illegal. Finally, after the city raised $500,000 under a vaguely worded ordinance, the base opened in 1930.

Even its most ardent supporters could not have envisioned how much Randolph Field would change San Antonio. Another base—Lackland—followed; Brooks and Kelly were greatly expanded. The military became San Antonio's second-largest industry, providing more than a quarter of its economic base. And young men who trained there moved back to retire, bringing San Antonio the growth its boosters had always coveted.

— MIMI SWARTZ

# 1925 FEARING LABOR UNIONS AND OUTSIDERS, SAN ANTONIO'S OLD GUARD RUNS THE FORD MOTOR COMPANY OUT OF TOWN . . . OR SO THE FABLE GOES.

# THE FORD FOLLIES

BY JAN JARBOE

IN THE SUMMER OF 1925 THE FORD Motor Company opened an all-electric plant on East Grand Avenue in Dallas and started turning out 35 new automobiles every hour. The factory is long gone now, but it remains a political issue after sixty years—not in Dallas but in San Antonio.

According to San Antonio legend, Ford officials initially planned to build the assembly plant there but retreated to Dallas after being rebuffed by local power brokers. Over the years the story of how a few families ran Ford out of town has become the anecdote that best typifies San Antonio's colonial society. "Remember the Ford plant" has almost as much significance in San Antonio as "Remember the Alamo." It means remember the days when the business and political establishment feared outsiders so much that badly needed new jobs were allowed to pass to other cities.

Labor leaders like Albert Peña have used the story to illustrate the lengths to which the old guard would go to keep unions out of town. "The way I heard it, local businessmen kept Ford out by jacking up real estate prices," says Peña, now a municipal judge. "The local guys were afraid that Ford might pay higher wages than anyone else."

All hell broke loose in 1977 when word leaked out that economic development consultants had recommended that the city beware of recruiting companies that would raise wage levels too quickly. Angry Mexican American activists charged that modern businessmen were continuing the legacy of their forefathers who had blocked the Ford plant just to keep Mexicans in their place. Henry Cisneros used the story, before he ran for mayor in 1981, in explaining to national reporters that San Antonio's reputation as a sleepy border town was well earned.

Is the story true? San Antonio newspapers did not carry the story in 1924 or 1925. Dave Crippen, archivist for Ford in Dearborn, Michigan, has searched his files and found nothing to suggest that

"REMEMBER THE FORD PLANT" IS ALMOST AS FAMOUS AS ANOTHER TEXAS RALLYING CRY.

San Antonio was ever a contender for the assembly plant. Art Basse, who has worked in Ford's property management department for 33 years, says unequivocally that the incident never happened. "That plant was destined for Dallas," Basse said. "It was designed especially for Dallas." Basse says he's heard the same story about other cities and considers it a popular urban myth.

By now, though, the story has taken on a life of its own. Too many people have a stake in perpetuating it, even businessmen. San Antonio needs to come to terms with why it was the most populous city in Texas in 1920 but by 1930 had slipped to a distant third behind Houston and Dallas. The lesson of the smug insiders who liked tourism and military bases but not heavy industry and high-priced labor is too valuable to lose to a little thing like the truth. ♣

116

# 1933 FOLKLORIST JOHN LOMAX SHINES HIS LIGHT ON THE RURAL BLUES OF AN UNKNOWN SINGER AND CONVICTED MURDERER CALLED LEADBELLY.

# THE MIDNIGHT SPECIAL

BY CHET FLIPPO

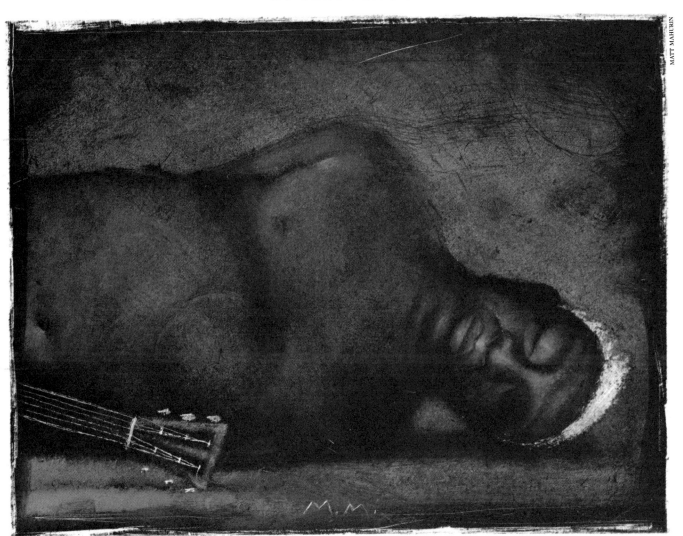

LEADBELLY WAS THE KING OF THE TWELVE-STRING GUITAR. HE REMAINS A MIST-SHROUDED GIANT IN THE PANTHEON OF TEXAS BLUES.

HUDDIE (PRONOUNCED "HEW-dee") Ledbetter got the nickname "Leadbelly," some people said, because of his powerful stomach muscles, impervious to the knife attacks that were frequent in his violent world of East Texas and Louisiana juke joints and prisons of the twenties. Others said it came about because of his awesome strength or because of his sexual prow-ess. All those legends are likely true, to some degree. Leadbelly remains a mist-shrouded, wraithlike giant in the pantheon of Texas blues. He was the self-proclaimed king of the twelve-string guitar and carried Texas blues to the world. His powerful voice made such songs as "Rock Island Line," "Good-night Irene," and "Midnight Special" part of American culture. He was also a piti-less murderer. He would have undoubt-edly remained a faceless prison inmate, his music unknown, had it not been for the efforts of pioneering Texas musicolo-gist John A. Lomax.

Ledbetter's history cannot be fully documented. He was born in either East Texas or the Caddo Lake district of Louisiana, probably in 1885. His mu-sical training came from work songs, church hymns, and voodoo chants. It is known that by 1917 he had played on the streets of Dallas and had been performing for nickels and dimes with Blind Lemon Jefferson for several years. He had a deep knife scar that ran around his neck like red pearls, and he bragged that he had killed often. In 1918 he was convicted of a barroom murder but was pardoned in 1925, after Governor Pat Neff heard him sing, "Had you Governor Neff, like you got me/ *I*'d wake up in de mornin', an' I'd set you free." But by 1930 Leadbelly was back in prison, convicted of assault with intent to murder. And that's where John Lomax found him in 1933.

Few nonmusicians have had more impact on American music than John Lomax and his son Alan. Under the aegis of the Library of Congress, the two traveled the country, ferreting out unknown folksingers and hillbilly musicians and blues pickers, authentic American musicians whose music was rooted in their own particular place and experience. The Lomaxes recorded thousands of the songs they heard. We know the work of Woody Guthrie largely because of the Lomaxes. And it was through their recordings that whites first caught a whiff of an emerging black music called the blues. The blues drew from the old rural church songs and cotton-field chants of the rural South, but it was a distinctly urban music, as gritty and hard as the city itself. And Leadbelly was the acknowledged master, as important a figure to the evolution of the blues as Louis Armstrong was to jazz.

Once they heard Leadbelly sing, the Lomaxes knew that they had discovered a true original. They eagerly recorded whatever he would play for them. On their second trip to the prison, as the Lomaxes turned on their recording machine, Leadbelly made a shrewd plea for freedom, asking them to intercede on his behalf. John Lomax did intercede, eventually winning Leadbelly's release. Lomax later wrote about what happened next: "I looked up from my newspaper as I sat in a hotel lobby in Marshall, Texas, on Sunday, September 16, 1934, to see a Negro man standing timidly by my chair. . . . In his right hand he held a battered twelve-string guitar, in his left a brown-paper sugar bag. He wore no coat; only an old hat, a blue shirt, a patched pair of overalls and rusty, yellow shoes. . . .

" 'Why, hello, Lead Belly! What are you doing here?'

" 'I'se come to be your man, boss; to drive yo' car.' "

Leadbelly went on to be the Lomaxes' driver and valet, and he became a celebrated performer in New York and Europe. He and Lomax parted ways in the late thirties, after a knife was apparently pulled during a contract dispute. Lomax objected to Leadbelly's fondness for drink; Leadbelly wanted more money. Leadbelly died in New York on December 6, 1949, after being arrested, once again, for assault.❦

# 1968 THE CONTROVERSY OVER HEMISFAIR'S DESIGN MARKS THE END OF OLD SAN ANTONE AND THE BEGINNING OF NEW SAN ANTONIO—FOR BETTER OR WORSE.

# FAIR OR FOUL?

## BY LISA GERMANY

SAN ANTONIANS STILL REGARD THE 1968 HemisFair, celebrating the 250th anniversary of the founding of their city, with remarkable warmth, considering that it left a deadening expanse of monumental buildings and moldering parking lots in the heart of their downtown. The fair has been credited with everything from getting people to realize the potential of the Riverwalk to including Mexican Americans in civic activities for the first time and thereby ushering in a new era of San Antonio politics.

Part of the fair's legacy, however, was to seal the destiny of downtown San Antonio. No longer is San Antonio like Boston and San Francisco, the cities with which Will Rogers once ranked it. Those places are peopled by residents as much as by tourists. Since HemisFair, however, San Antonians don't go downtown and even fewer live there.

The shape of the fair was determined when its backers rejected the vision of O'Neil Ford, who had built an international reputation as an architect keenly sensitive to the cultural and regional qualities that set San Antonio apart. Ford was ahead of his time in his effort to integrate the fair with about fifty of the existing buildings, retaining much of the ambience of the original neighborhoods. Those who opposed him were still thinking in terms of urban renewal; they wanted to clear 92 acres of slums.

Urban renewal prevailed. Bulldozers razed the old neighborhoods, and in their place rose the convention center, the Institute of Texan Cultures, the United States Pavilion (now a federal courthouse), and the Tower of the Americas. Most of the open area was leased by carnival operators and concessionaires. After the fair they pulled out, leaving the grounds as vacant and dispirited as they remain today.

Numerous factions disputed the design of HemisFair while it was in the planning stage. Ford sided with conservationists and lost the good fight. When it was over, he went ahead and served as

FORD LOST THE FIGHT TO BUILD *HIS* HEMISFAIR, BUT HE AGREED TO DESIGN THE TOWER.

architect for the Tower of the Americas.

HemisFair signaled a turning point. Surrounded by controversy from the start, the venture lost money in the end, and in retrospect it appears that city officials and fair executives gave little thought to the future of the site. In the early seventies the University of Texas regents rejected it as a home for the new

San Antonio campus in favor of a huge tract of land far to the northwest. The tendency to build outside downtown continued as San Antonians turned away from their distinctive past and retreated into colorless suburbia. Now, almost twenty years later, the city finds itself embarked on a $133 million plan to redevelop HemisFair Plaza.✦

# 1900 THE KILLER GALVESTON HURRICANE SWEEPS AWAY THE MOST CIVILIZED SOCIETY TEXAS EVER KNEW.

# DESTINY DENIED

## BY JOHN EDWARD WEEMS

ON A DARK, SQUALLY MORNING IN the late summer of 1900, 37,000 Galvestonians were unknowingly about to receive from nature a local answer to a worldwide question that had been debated since the year began: When did the nineteenth century end and the twentieth commence? The Vatican had declared, logically, that since there was no year zero, the twentieth century would not begin until January 1, 1901. Popular opinion favored one year earlier. But for Galveston the turn of the century would forever be dated from September 8, 1900.

That gloomy Saturday morning an issue-deciding hurricane, creeping landward from the Gulf of Mexico, began aiming its violence almost directly at the city. As wind and water rose to heights never before experienced in the storm-prone city, adventuresome people fled sight-seeing positions near the beaches where huge waves pounded ashore with incredible thunder, undeterred then by any seawall.

Local weathermen sought to warn other people in low-lying areas to seek higher ground, but the poor communications of those days interfered. By six o'clock that evening, when the Angelus rang out from St. Mary's Cathedral calling for prayer from predominantly Catholic Galveston, the rector thought it sounded "not like a salutation of praise but a warning of death and destruction." Then the cathedral towers swayed. The two-ton bell, torn from its bands and clasps, crashed to the floor.

Galveston, the whole island, lay entirely under storm-whipped sea water. From six thousand to eight thousand residents died.

The hurricane proved to be a landmark event. It is still known as the worst recorded weather disaster in North American history. For Galveston it was a disaster in other ways as well. The 1900 storm brought to an abrupt end the era during which Galveston was the premier city of Texas. It helped persuade the federal government to provide Hous-

BEFORE THE STORM CHURCH BELLS RANG "A WARNING OF DEATH AND DESTRUCTION."

ton with a deep-water channel and allowed the inland city to surge ahead in the bitter competition that had begun years earlier. That probably would have happened anyway, considering the limits nature had put on Galveston's expansion and Houston's accessibility for railroads. But the storm made Galveston's subordination swift and irreversible.

It did not kill Galveston. The city rebuilt behind a fifteen-foot seawall, raised its grade level by pumping in sand dredged from the ocean floor, and initiated a more efficient form of municipal

government called the city commission, which was copied elsewhere. But the sense that Galveston was destined to be a great city never returned; there was too much risk and too little opportunity on a sandbar exposed to the sea. Longtime Galveston residents told me in 1956, when I was researching a book on the storm, that the city never was the same afterward. An attorney who had lost his family and his home would recollect those happy earlier days and put it this way: "It seemed as a dream of a thing that had never been."✦

120

# 1949 IT'S AN ASPHALT JUNGLE OUT THERE, AND IT ALL STARTED WITH DALLAS' CENTRAL EXPRESSWAY.

# LIFE IN THE FAST LANE

BY JIM ATKINSON

CENTRAL EXPRESSWAY WAS CHRIStened with a bottle of cologne. Seven thousand Dallasites turned out on the evening of August 19, 1949, dressed in finery despite the sweltering heat. They heard a band concert and some speeches, and then Dorothy Savage, wife of the mayor, stepped to the dais and proclaimed, "From the wholesalers and retailers of Dallas comes this bottle of cologne, symbolizing, as does this marvelous highway, fashion, culture, and marketing. With it, I christen thee 'Central Expressway.' "

On that distinctly Dallas note, the assemblage retired to the barricaded streets of downtown to square dance the night away in celebration of two miles of concrete that reached as far north as Fitzhugh. Dallas always has had a way of transforming bricks-and-mortar civic accomplishments into social and cultural events.

Not that anyone there that night regarded Central as a simple civic accomplishment. The *Morning News,* never shy with hyperbole, called it a "new scientific wonder," and at that moment, before the first rush hour, it may have been. Central Expressway was Texas' first urban freeway, and in the minds of Dallas civic leaders, it proved that their city was far ahead of rivals like Houston, if not in population at least in vision, style, and modernity. Central was viewed as a space-age Main Street, along which satellites of commerce would one day thrive in environments once thought unfit for human habitation. When it was finished, linking the southern and northern city limits, it would be, in the words of chamber of commerce president D. A. Hulcy, a "great civic undertaking."

But that was just the trouble: it would never be finished. Its success soon rendered it obsolete. There was always more to be done, more lanes, more miles, more exits, more interchanges, a downtown overpass, doubledecking, and now a subway. By 1951 the normally chauvinistic *Times Herald* had begun to question whether this wonder was living

DESPITE HIGH HOPES FOR THE NEW CENTRAL EXPRESSWAY, A HORSE MIGHT BE FASTER.

up to expectations. Central quickly and forever became the most bemoaned, argued over, and analyzed swath of roadway in the state. Today the first urban freeway in Texas is the seminal example of how the city that works doesn't always.

If Central was a failure as science, it and its kin in other Texas cities have been more successful as a social force. No zoning ordinance can approach the power of an urban freeway to dictate the shape of the urban landscape. Central helped create an environment of reflective-glass high rises and shopping malls and fast-food restaurants. It hastened the emergence of suburbs like

Richardson and Plano and McKinney, and gave Dallas a new vocabulary of urban sprawl: "drive-time radio," "peak load," "bumper-to-bumper," "weaving."

Now Dallas–and Houston and Austin –have committed millions to mass transit systems that must operate, if possible, in cities that freeways have built. A drive up Central these days is a painful reminder that one of the most automobile-dependent states in the nation still has no idea how to move people around a city. Or, as former mayor Savage himself said of Central recently, "Yeah, hardly a day goes by when somebody doesn't throw that up in my face. It seemed like a good idea at the time."

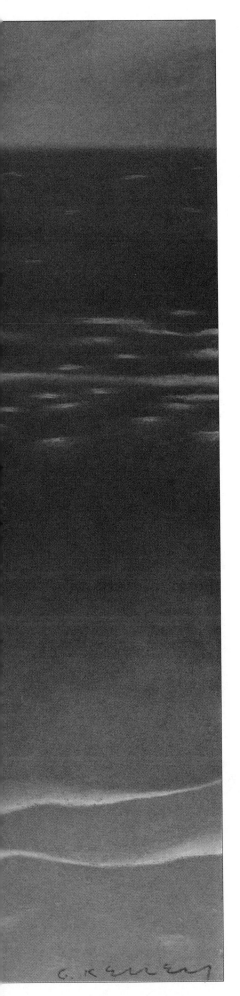

# THE TIDE TURNS

### BY LAWRENCE WRIGHT

## 1952 WHY ARE THE TIDELANDS SO IMPORTANT? AND WHY IS GOVERNOR ALLAN SHIVERS WILLING TO RISK THE DISINTEGRATION OF THE OLD ORDER TO CONTROL THEM?

**B**EAUFORD JESTER, THE LAST HAP-py man to govern Texas, boarded a midnight sleeper in Austin on the eleventh of July, 1949. As usual the governor bedded down in his opulent three-berth suite at the rear of the train. According to political legend, he suffered a heart attack and died in the arms of his mistress, who was discreetly let off the train in Bryan. The governor, dead and now alone, resumed his journey.

He was traveling across a state that no longer knew itself. Texans liked to think of themselves as a people of the land—cattlemen, oil-men, farmers—but they were becoming a people of the cities, a people of white shirts and coffee breaks and lunchbox laborers struggling to get their union cards, a people of station wagons and lawn mowers and working mothers, a people of impatient minorities, many of them just shedding their military uniforms. Oil and the war had turned Texas into an industrial state. Beauford Jester had been a part of the change—he had been a more progressive governor than anyone expected—but now he was dead and left on the train for a surprised porter to discover in the Houston station.

At eight-fifteen that morning a reporter for the *Houston Press* broke the news to Lieutenant Governor Allan Shivers. Shivers, then 41, had gone to the state senate at the age of 27. He had grown up poor, but he had married the daughter of a South Texas land inves-tor and was perhaps the wealthiest man to assume the gov-ernorship—at a time when big money was still thought to be a liability for polit-ical office. He was glamorous, charming, trim, profoundly good-looking, highly popular, and yet it was typical of Allan Shivers that [ CONTINUED ON PAGE 159 ]

> SHIVERS STOOD FIRMLY FOR TEXAS' RIGHTS TO ITS TIDE-LANDS. BUT HE WAS TOO LATE FOR THE PAST AND TOO EARLY FOR THE FUTURE.

# 1951 A GIFTED BLACK KID GROWING UP IN A SMALL TOWN SEES ONLY ONE CHOICE: LEAVE.

# GOOD-BYE TO MINEOLA

## BY WILLIE BROWN

*One of the hidden costs of segregation in Texas was that blacks with ambition and talent got out of the state as quickly as they could, never to return. Among those was Willie Brown, who left his hometown, Mineola, in 1951. Today he is an attorney in San Francisco and Speaker of the California Assembly.*

"Mineola had nothing, absolutely nothing, going for it. It was a small, very poor, very backward community, totally and completely racially segregated. It was run under the old high sheriff system, where the sheriff ran the town. The mayor was the elected official, but the law enforcement guy ran the town. Period. There was just no question about that.

"My school was a very small black school. It had five or six classrooms. When I first started, there were only ten grades in the school. They added the eleventh and twelfth grades while I was attending. Before that, you had to travel eleven miles by bus up to Quitman for the high school. They also added a wing while I was there, but the wing was only for the lower grades—first through fifth—and in the wing they added inside rest rooms. Before that we didn't have inside rest rooms. There was no gymnasium for basketball. Everything was outside.

"The white school, Mineola High, was located on the other side of town. They had a great football team, the Yellowjackets, and they had a great football stadium, in which we were allowed to play when we had a game. They had all the facilities; they had indoor bathrooms, they had indoor showers, they had all of that. They had a gymnasium in which they played basketball. They had a library—we didn't have a library. Not only that, but we only had used books, books that had already been used by the white students. All the way through school, I never touched a new book.

"I had two uncles who left Mineola, one who went off to war and the other who worked in the defense industry in California. Mineola had one method by which people earned a living—a pea house that processed pinto beans and black-eyed peas—and that was the only thing that went on in that town. My mother also left Mineola and moved to Dallas. I was raised by my grandmother, like my sisters and brothers, and my two uncles and my mother sup-

plied the resources for her to raise us. Every week money came back, and once or twice a year, those relatives would come back. This one particular uncle, Uncle Itsie, wanted desperately to get me out of Mineola.

"I had always, apparently, shown some promise in terms of thinking ability, and as far back as I can remember I had had

a lot of motivation. When I was nine and ten, I was shining shoes in Parker's barbershop and sweeping the floor for three dollars a week. By the time I was twelve I had also bought my own bicycle because I managed my money. Apparently those qualities said to my uncle, 'This is a kid who could do something. He's got a shot.' He kept insisting that I be allowed to come to California.

"Everybody in my family had always insisted that the kids had to have an education. They absolutely beat that into us —that you had to go to college. But there was no place in Texas to go besides Prairie View A and M or Texas College down in Tyler, the black colleges. My sisters all went to Texas College down in Tyler, and two of them became teachers. I had decided I wanted to become a math teacher. I was good in math, and somebody had told me that Stanford had the best math. I didn't have any counsel in that direction; there weren't any counselors at Mineola Colored High. So I came out to California with the intention of going to Stanford. When I got here, of course, I didn't have the appropriate credentials; I hadn't had the subject matter in high school. Instead I enrolled in San Francisco State College. I was not even able to pass their entrance exam because there were words and concepts I had not been exposed to. But the professor who was administering the tests said, 'I really think you could do college-level work. Why don't we admit you as a special admittee?' Within six weeks I was doing college work. I went on through and got a B.A. and a law degree with no trouble.

"It is true that whatever training I had in high school, and whatever discipline was instilled in me in Texas, stood me in good stead in my post-Texas world. The one thing I know now about my experience in Mineola was that every black

youngster in that town was required to graduate from high school. You could be twenty-three, and you'd still be in high school if you had not passed whatever minimal training they'd provided you with. No matter how inadequate it may have been, they insisted that you grasp it before you were allowed to move on. So there would be kids who stayed in the fifth grade three years; there would be kids who were twenty-three and still playing high school football—seven years they'd been playing football—but they had to complete the work.

"And those teachers! I had a professor teaching geometry who knew *nothing* about geometry. Nothing. He was a coach; he'd never completed math himself. But what he did was make us memorize the entire geometry textbook. You learned every theorem. Theorem Ninety: I can cite Theorem Ninety in my sleep. Theorem Eighty-four. Theorem Three. Every day you had to memorize a new theorem. The examination was whether or not you wrote exactly what was in the book, and that's how you got your grade. Well, obviously, that taught you not one ounce of geometry. But it gave you discipline and made you believe in yourself. It gave you confidence that you could learn.

"And that's what I learned in that black school. I didn't fully appreciate it, I suspect, at the time, but on reflection—especially now, as I see what kids are getting in California schools—I'm telling you that there is something to be said for those all-black schools. The black mothers and fathers and teachers might not have been qualified, but they knew they had to equip me to survive in this world. You learned that it was really awful to drop out. Period. We didn't have any dropouts in Mineola. It was ingrained in us that there was no such thing as people who were so totally stupid that they could not perform. That quality came from the heart and soul of the black community, and it's still there."❧

INTERVIEWED BY PAUL BURKA.

CALIFORNIA SPEAKER BROWN: "WE ONLY HAD BOOKS THAT THE WHITE STUDENTS HAD ALREADY USED. I NEVER TOUCHED A NEW BOOK."

125

## THE LAWMAN

### A black cop brings law and order to the Houston police force.

**1982** Black police chiefs these days are more the rule than the exception in big Northern cities and in heavily black Southern cities like Atlanta. But when Mayor Kathy Whitmire picked Atlanta public safety commissioner Lee Brown as Houston's new chief in 1982, the appointment represented a watershed, if not a sea change.

Houston's lawmen and black populace have always regarded each other warily, even before the Camp Logan riot in 1917, when more than a hundred black soldiers of the 24th Infantry exploded after policemen pistol-whipped two comrades. Four policemen died; 82 black soldiers were later hanged or jailed for life. In more recent years Houston cops seemed to be the last vestige of the city's redneck heritage. During the notorious reign of Chief Herman Short in the sixties, his Criminal Intelligence Division kept one file known as "Miscellaneous Niggers" that included clippings about State Senator Barbara Jordan. Short was followed by five chiefs in eight years, during which the department was sometimes mutinous and frequently quick on the trigger.

That was the setting in 1982 when Whitmire named Brown. Tall and scholarly looking, with a Ph.D. in criminology from the University of California at Berkeley, Brown was the first outsider chief in forty years. Operating more as a rulebook bureaucrat than as a classic tough chief, he established his authority by firing more than a score of officers, white and black, who had been accused of serious policy violations. He has met with groups from gays to Vietnamese to civic clubs. Both the rate of killings by police and the crime rate have dropped significantly. Today, nearly four years after he took over, the most surprising thing about Lee Brown is that he is so uncontroversial.

—Tom Curtis

# 1944: The Betrayal of Speaker Sam

Texas' turbulent politics has claimed many victims over the years, but none was more prominent than Sam Rayburn, who might have been the first Texan in the White House had he not got caught in the cross fire between warring Democrats back home.

In 1944 President Roosevelt seemed a cinch to win reelection, despite doubts that he would live much longer. The vice presidency loomed as the year's big prize. Among those eyeing the job was Rayburn, who had led the House as Speaker through three grueling war years and was enjoying acclaim rarely matched in the history of Congress. "Cold political calculations, the balancing of assets and liabilities, give Rayburn the edge," concluded the *St. Louis Post-Dispatch,* ignoring Missouri's own Harry Truman.

But in Rayburn's home state, the rifts that first appeared in the Texas Democratic party in 1940 had grown steadily worse. By 1944 there were two battling factions whose opposite social and economic philosophies drove them bitterly, irreconcilably apart. Oilmen and other wealthy conservatives set out to buy control of the state party. They dominated the state convention and approved a platform that, among other things, condemned the "communist-controlled" New Deal. And they swore to defeat any congressman they considered too cozy with the president. Rayburn was their number one target. Never mind that he was a key defender of Texas interests, including oil, in Congress.

Rayburn and all other incumbents were reelected. But without backing from his home state–Rayburn was not even picked as a delegate to the Democratic National Convention –his vice-presidential hopes were dashed. He would, for the remaining seventeen years of his life, look back bitterly at the year that his one chance at the presidency was wrecked by the emergence of Texas' new wealth as a political force. —Don Bacon

# MR. MAVERICK AND THE PINKO PECAN SHELLERS

### *Or, how standing up for the Bill of Rights costs a great mayor his career.*

*Nuts to you! Maverick tells the mob.*

**1939** It appeared harmless enough–a two-sentence letter requesting the use of a San Antonio city auditorium for a meeting. But the request came from Emma Tenayuca, an organizer for the poorly paid pecan shellers, and her group was the Communist party. Mayor Maury Maverick knew that granting the permit might be his political death knell. But he could hardly turn it down: as an attorney for the American Civil Liberties Union and a New Deal congressman, he had been an eloquent defender of the Bill of Rights.

Maverick's enemies equated his action with an endorsement of communism. Because of threats to members of his family, Maverick moved them to a friend's home the night of the meeting. Hooligans even pestered Maverick's parents. On the day of the meeting, Tenayuca led a hundred workers through a stone-throwing mob of five thousand into the auditorium. When rioters invaded the hall, breaking windows and slashing the upholstered seats, the workers fled through a rear door.

Maverick's distinguished record of public service (his greatest legacy is San Antonio's Riverwalk) couldn't save his bid for reelection. The incident heralded the emergence of Red-baiting in Texas politics and thus was a dress rehearsal for the liberal-conservative confrontations of the next three decades. Much of the opposition to Maverick was stirred up by his archenemy, Vice President John Nance Garner of Uvalde, whose challenge to Franklin Roosevelt's third-term bid in 1940 would formalize the split of the state Democratic party into two permanently divided camps.

Not long after his defeat, a lady of some prominence approached Maverick after church services and said, "I hear talk all over town that you're a communist. But if you come to church, well, you can't be a communist." Maverick answered, "I hear all over town that you're a whore, but I don't believe that either."

— Kaye Northcott

126

REGAN DUNNICK

# CHICKEN LICKIN'

## 1978: Bill Clements makes a campaign pledge.

John Hill's speech was about what one could expect to hear at a political banquet. Invited to the 1978 Amarillo Industrial Exposition, the Democratic nominee for governor praised local civic leaders for overcoming the loss of an air base by attracting industry. He finished by displaying a laurel wreath to honor his hosts. Then it was Bill Clements' turn.

The Republican nominee, it developed, had a display of his own. To the astonishment of the crowd, he produced a limp chicken–plucked, dressed, with its head still on–waved it aloft, and announced, "I'm going to hang Jimmy Carter around John Hill's neck like a dead chicken." Then he tossed the bird to Hill. It fell short–splat!–into the dinner plate of a dignitary's wife. The bird bounced; it wasn't dead, after all, but a novelty item made of rubber.

At the time, just seven weeks after the May primaries, Clements' vow seemed like wishful thinking. Texas was a one-party state; no Republican except John Tower had ever won a statewide race. Polls showed Hill with a three-to-one lead. Clements was largely unknown. But the next day, the rubber chicken story was in every paper in the state and Clements had begun to turn the race his way. He had done what no Republican had been able to do before but what more and more have done since–nationalize Texas politics by linking state Democrats to the national Democratic party. In November, helped by a low statewide turnout and a $7 million campaign budget, he nipped Hill at the wire, and suddenly Texas was a two-party state.

—Paul Burka

# A FOOTHOLD FOR FUNDAMENTALISM

### God calls, and W. A. Criswell answers.

FIRST BAPTIST CHURCH

**1944** George W. Truett died in 1944, three years short of the half century he had hoped to serve as pastor of the First Baptist Church of Dallas. The world of Southern Baptists was stunned when First Baptist called a little-known preacher in Muskogee, Oklahoma, named W. A. Criswell to succeed the denomination's most beloved and respected preacher. Criswell recalls that one man, on hearing him preach, observed that the church had "traded a beautiful sunset for an atomic bomb." The metaphor is apt, in terms not only of visibility, impact, power, and message but also of fallout whose effect is yet to be measured. Criswell's encouragement of and participation in business— "The Lord blessed me," he has observed, "with a sixth sense for making money"—has helped foster a distinctive free-enterprise piety that marks a substantial segment of Dallas commerce. Menachem Begin's acceptance of the pastor's invitation to visit First Baptist— though the visit was canceled when Begin's wife died—symbolized Criswell's key role in developing the oft-noted ties between Israeli leaders and Christian fundamentalists. And inviting Criswell to pronounce the final benediction at the 1984 Republican Convention was a way for Ronald Reagan to pay some political debts to the fundamentalists.

The lasting impact of Dr. Criswell, however, is likely to stem from his role in the fundamentalist movement that threatens to split the Southern Baptist Convention into at least two separate bodies. His stature as an elder statesman and his staunch insistence that every word of the Bible is inspired of God and without error have lent dignity and weight to the effort by strict fundamentalist elements to wrest control of denominational boards, agencies, and schools from more-moderate hands. When asked, as he often is, about retirement, he speaks of new opportunities, vowing to leave retirement decisions in the hands of the Lord and quoting the words of the song that opens most Sunday morning services at the church: "All who will, come and go with me. I'm bound for the promised land." —William Martin

ACCUSED ASSASSIN SAYS "OH!" as Jack Ruby calling him an S.O.B. fires a bullet into his abdomen — 11:30 AM CST.

ALAN COBER

OH!

You Son of a Bitch!

— Alan E. Cober —

JFK's Alleged Killer Slain — Kennedy Admirer Plays "Executioner" — OSWALD is Dead of PISTOL SHOT Beneath Heart. Ruby says "I couldn't help it"; Millions Witness Murder on TV.

# 1963: "Oswald's been shot!"

When Jack Ruby emerged from a crowd and fired a lethal bullet into Lee Harvey Oswald, the shame of Dallas was complete. Those who were saying that John Kennedy had been killed by the climate of hate in Dallas could no longer be ignored, not even in Dallas. Oswald may have been a loose thread, a lone gunman unaffected by the infamous WELCOME MR. KENNEDY TO DALLAS ad that ran in the *Morning News* on the last day of Kennedy's life—but Ruby, a police character and nightclub operator, was undeniably woven into the fabric of his city. The terrible weekend seemed to be the natural outgrowth of all that had gone before: a mob jostling and spitting on Lyndon and Lady Bird Johnson during the 1960 campaign while U.S. congressman Bruce Alger carried a "Lyndon, Go Home" placard nearby, another mob spitting on U.N. ambassador Adlai Stevenson, a handbill showing mug shots of the president under the headline WANTED FOR TREASON. And now, Oswald and Ruby. Dallas had to change. The word went out to Mayor Earle Cabell that for the good of Dallas he was to step down and run against Alger, the darling of the Minute Women and the John Birch Society. The Johnson landslide of 1964 swept Alger out of office and Cabell in. Hatred and nuttiness were no longer respectable. Dallas had reentered the political mainstream. —PAUL BURKA

# HARD LABOR
## Strikebreakers build the Capitol.
### ★ 1883 ★

At the end of Reconstruction the Texas Legislature, in its wisdom, deemed it appropriate to construct a new capitol building, the old one having been rendered unfit for further use by virtue of its long occupancy by Republicans. The Legislature was at somewhat of a disadvantage, however, since Texas in those post–Civil War days was impecunious to the max. Ah, but it had land, lots of land. So in 1879 the state sold three million acres to pay for its new playhouse. A contract was signed in 1882, the proceedings hastened by the old capitol's having burned a few months earlier.

The plans called for the new capitol to be built of nearby limestone, but a shortage forced a change. The exterior would be granite, free of charge courtesy of Burnet County quarry owners. The granite, however, would be much more expensive to transport. Enter Governor John Ireland. He made available five hundred prison inmates to build a railroad from Burnet to the quarries and to cut and dress the stone. Not amused was the International Association of Granite Cutters. The union voted 500 to 1 to boycott.

The contractors also secured the services of 62 Scottish granite cutters. The Knights of Labor attempted to head them off at Galveston harbor, but the canny Scots had debarked in Virginia and gone to Texas by train. Eventually the contractor was found guilty of violating federal laws against importing foreign workers and assessed a small fine. But the new capitol was built anyway, and forever after in our state the voice of labor has been but a peep. The episode is one of the few in Texas history in which the state did not take organized labor for granite.          — MIKE KELLEY

# 1873: SEMICOLON SELLOUT

**A rigged court decision gives Republicans a bad name.**

It sounds more like a law-school teaser than the hottest political issue of its day. Suppose the state constitution provides that "all elections shall be held at the county seats, until otherwise provided by law; and the polls shall be opened for four days." The Legislature sets an election on a single day. Is it constitutional?

In 1873 Reconstruction had run its course. The hated Republican governor, E. J. Davis, was at the end of his term; a Democrat, Richard Coke, had won the

election and was ready to take office. But Davis attacked the single-day election law in court—and if the law was invalid, so was Coke's election.

The fix was in. The Texas Supreme Court, made up entirely of judges appointed by Davis, declared the law unconstitutional. The decisive factor was a semicolon. It cleaved the disputed constitutional provision in two, the court ruled, and the crucial phrase "until otherwise provided by law" applied only to the first clause. The Legislature could not alter the requirement that polls had to be open for four days.

Coke's backers, unpersuaded by grammatical nit-picking, armed themselves and occupied the legislative chambers in the old capitol building. Rip Ford, the grizzled ex–Texas Ranger, led a contingent toward the Capitol singing "The Yellow Rose of Texas." On January 19, 1874, the Texans charged the governor's office. They found it empty; Davis had fled.

The shadow of E. J. Davis still falls on Texas today. The state constitution, adopted two years after his abdication, made the governor relatively powerless, as he has remained ever since. Judicial reform, sought for at least half a century, has run into an entrenched prejudice against appointed judges. And the decisions of the Semicolon Court, as it quickly became known, have been ignored as precedents, and neither judges nor lawyers will acknowledge them to this day.
          —PAUL BURKA

## Lyndon's Lucky Number

**1948** This isn't the real Box 13—just a replica of the infamous ballot box that won the 1948 Democratic senatorial nomination for Lyndon Johnson. But these are indeed the real partisans (that's Alice police chief Stokes Micenheimer at the far left) of South Texas political boss George Parr, the man who made Box 13 a permanent part of Texas political lore. This picture is thought to have been taken in celebration of Johnson's uphill victory after a long and bitter post-election fight. Three days after the voting, the Texas Election Bureau declared Coke Stevenson the winner over Johnson. But after three more days, Jim Wells officials found a discrepancy of 203 votes in the bureau's returns for Box 13. Remarkably, all 203 voters had signed the polling list in alphabetical order, in the same handwriting, and in a different color ink from the previous voters. All but one of them voted for Johnson, enabling him to win the election by 87 votes out of more than a million and start on the road that was to lead to the presidency.          —PAUL BURKA

# Texas Politics Gets a Conscience

**1955** The *Texas Observer*'s first excursion into investigative journalism in 1955—an account of the killing of a black youngster by joyriding white youths and the dismal law-enforcement response—drove off most of the subscribers the new paper had inherited from the *State Observer* and the *East Texas Democrat,* political organs that had reflected old Southern views not just on party politics but also on race. Pressure from the *Observer*'s bankrollers, a group made up mostly of prominent lady Democrats, resulted only in an article titled "The Devastating Dames," which promptly reduced the bankrollers to one. The *Observer*'s one-man staff, 24-year-old, Oxford- and UT-educated Ronnie Dugger, soon had Texas politicians and journalists wondering how one little low-rent tabloid could make so much trouble.

The *Observer* reported what the rest of the press consistently ignored—migrant workers, Freedom Riders and sit-ins, university political shenanigans, life's unfairness in its abundant forms, and, above all, the way Texas politics really worked. If it unfailingly viewed events from a liberal perspective, it did so with an evenhandedness that raised its editorial influence far out of proportion to a circulation that has rarely gone above a poverty-level 12,000. Among its staff writers have been Bill Brammer, Willie Morris, and Bob Sherrill in addition to Dugger, who is now its nonresident owner and publisher; its pages have carried the writings of Dobie, Bedichek, and Webb, along with those of William Goyen, John Graves, and Larry McMurtry.

The *Observer* has charged its share of windmills, embraced dubious strategy (it urged liberals to support Republican John Tower for the U.S. Senate, not once but twice), and sometimes sounded like a newsletter for Texas liberals. But it has also pricked consciences, raised the standards of Texas journalism, and thorned the side of the establishment. After thirty years, all against the odds, it continues to do so.
          —WILLIAM J. HELMER

# 1944 UT PRESIDENT HOMER RAINEY LEARNS
THAT SOMETIMES THE TRUTH SHALL GET YOU FIRED.

# RAINEY AND THE REGENTS

## BY RONNIE DUGGER

ON THE DAY OF HIS inauguration as University of Texas president in December 1939, Dr. Homer P. Rainey declared, "We are making, or are about to make, here in Texas, a momentous decision." A committee of faculty members had accepted as fair a statement that there was not one first-class university south of the Ohio and east of California. Yet there in the Texas constitution was the unavoidable specification that UT would be "a university of the first class." Rainey now said to the regents, politicians, and powerful alumni who were assembled in the crowd before him: "Remove as far as practicable all hampering restrictions," do not keep "too close a control," provide "freedom of action," and the university could be great.

The firing of Homer Rainey five years later was a defining event for higher education in Texas. In 1946 the educator suffered a second rejection, in his campaign for governor, that set the mold of Texas politics for the entire postwar era until 1982.

In conjunction with his inauguration Rainey had arranged a series of discussions about the university. One of the speakers was Harry Weiss, the president of Humble Oil and Refining, the largest producing oil company in the United States. What, Weiss asked, should the university do? He answered his own question: inspire students "to the ambition to do each job" necessary for "the satisfactory operation of the system as a whole.... Train specialists.... Conduct fundamental research of problems in the natural resource industry." Education, Weiss continued, had been

STUDENTS WANTED RAINEY. THE REGENTS DIDN'T. GUESS WHO WON.

contributing to "dissatisfaction and unrest," attracting people "to try any form of economic, social, and governmental panacea," and perhaps that had happened because there had not been enough research in "basic principles of a sound economy."

So there was the choice: freedom of thought and inquiry at the state university, or a state university that would serve industry and train good and satisfied employees who would fit into the system without being attracted to new ideas for social change. And a grim struggle did then begin for control of the university that set the standards for the rest of the public schools and colleges of the state.

Born in Red River County, Rainey

was a serious Christian and a populist liberal in the rural traditions of East Texas. He had been the presidential choice of J. R. Parten of Madisonville, a wealthy oilman and Roosevelt Democrat who was chairman of an enlightened board of regents appointed by the moderately liberal New Deal governor, Jimmy Allred. But by the time Rainey took over, the governorship was in the hands of archconservative W. Lee O'Daniel. Soon the board of regents was too.

In about 1940, according to Parten, "a certain definite political activity was started ... to eliminate from our institutions of higher learning so-called radical teachers." Parten received dozens of letters criticizing Dr. Robert Montgomery, a professor of economics at UT who believed in competitive free enterprise but also in public ownership of public utilities. A lawyer told Parten of having attended a meeting of several businessmen and attorneys who were "after" Rainey and who had laid plans to get O'Daniel to appoint regents who would eliminate "all radical elements in the faculties." Former Speaker of the Texas House Robert Lee Bobbitt later testified that "certain monopolists, corporation executives, and rich industrialists [were] seeking control and supervision of what the youth of Texas may be taught" under the guise of patriotism.

At the first meeting of the board after the businessmen had hatched their plan, Rainey was seated across the table from one of the regents, movie-house lobbyist D. F. Strickland. According to Rainey, "He took from his pocket a small card and passed it across the table to me. It contained the names of four full professors of economics. . . . He said, 'We want you to fire these men.'" Amazed, Rainey asked the regent why. "We don't like what they are teaching," he replied.

Bob Montgomery, Clarence Ayres, E. E. Hale, and Clarence Wiley—these esteemed professors had been on the faculty fifteen years or longer. Rainey refused to fire them. For the next several years, while millions were dying in the world war abroad, the regents warred against freedom of thought at the University of Texas. By 1944 Rainey had taken all he would take. Deliberately, the East Texan provoked a public confrontation with his O'Danielized superiors.

Calling the faculty into assembly before him, Rainey listed sixteen instances of what he called improper behavior by regents or by the whole board, "a long series of restrictive actions." The faculty gave him a prolonged ovation and later a unanimous vote of confidence. The regents fired him by a vote of six to two. Eight thousand Texas students marched to the Capitol and struck the university for a week, but Rainey was out.

Governor "Farmer Jim" Ferguson's abuses of UT in the teens of the century and regents' chairman Frank Erwin's in the sixties and seventies bracket the firing of Rainey but do not approach it in perfidy. Corporate leaders who feared and opposed freedom of thought had fired President Rainey, and a miasma of ideological pressure and intellectual caution descended upon the state university. The firing of Rainey signified the corporate domination that continues still over the UT system and the rest of the state's higher education.

In 1946 Rainey tried for governor, but the issues in the campaign were the same ones he had found at UT, and there was an obscene pile-on. Teams of schoolboys were sent across the state by commercial bus to tell the voters that Rainey's daughter walked along the university drag holding hands with Negro boys. A candidate named Grover Sellers held "men only" political rallies at which a supporter pulled on white gloves, picked up a copy of John Dos Passos' great novel *USA* (which Rainey was blamed for letting Texas students study), and gave racy stag readings from it. Beauford Jester crushed Rainey in a runoff, and in due time Jester was succeeded by Allan Shivers, Price Daniel, John Connally, Preston Smith, Dolph Briscoe, Bill Clements.

The cycle has begun, perhaps, again, with the election in 1982 of the moderately liberal governor Mark White. But whether it has or whether it hasn't, walk down the Drag, across to the front of the university tower, glance up to the motto there about knowing the truth that is supposed to make you free, and remember Homer P. Rainey of Red River County, telling the board of regents, in his polite, educator's way, to go straight to hell.❧

# 1969 WHEN A TREE FALLS AT UT, YOU HEAR THE SOUND OF FRANK ERWIN'S HANDS CLAPPING.

# CHAIRMAN, SPARE THAT TREE

## BY SUZANNE WINCKLER

THOSE WERE CONFUSING TIMES for us native Texans who were coming of age in the sixties on the University of Texas campus. I'm not referring to the Viet Nam War but rather to the matter of trees. On October 22, 1969, a bunch of us got in a big fight with Frank Erwin, chairman of the board of regents, over trees. He wanted to cut some down—about forty stately old oaks, cypresses, and willows growing on campus along Waller Creek—so he could add 15,000 seats to UT's football stadium. We thought otherwise. We outnumbered him, but he won. I was so mad about it for so long that it has taken me many years to sort out what was truly important about that day. It wasn't the trees.

The first question, looking back, is why would a bunch of kids from Texas care about trees in the first place? Take me, for example: I was born in Colorado City, a town on the flat, brown plains west of Fort Worth. Like most good Texans, I had never given much thought to trees. Even though I've since come to have a real appreciation for them as individuals, a big stand of them still makes me nervous, which is why whenever I have to go to East Texas I hotfoot it out to the prairie as soon as I can. Yet here I was in the autumn of 1969 taking a graduate English course in, of all people, Henry D. Thoreau. At the time, a lot of what Mr. Thoreau had to say made sense, and some of it still does. But I see now that I could have learned more about my own neck of the woods from Mr. Erwin.

I suspect my colleagues and I cared about the trees on Waller Creek not because of some deep affinity we had for them but because it was fashionable to care about green things. We represented the new Texas, Erwin the old; he had inherited what historian T. R. Fehrenbach called Stephen F. Austin's "sincere and boundless joy at the destruction of the wilderness." Just as "each crashing tree along the Brazos gave Austin pleasure," so did each crashing tree along Waller

THE SIXTIES ARRIVE: PROTEST UT STYLE.

Creek please Erwin. Lesson number one: Be true to your place. While we were bending like willows to every breeze of the times, Erwin was as ram-rod as an oak for what he saw as a minor infraction against Mother Nature and a major improvement for UT.

A weaker individual would have bent just a little. Even seventeen years later it is hard to find many people who were on Erwin's side in this fight, from the then-president of the university, Norman Hackerman, to the wildest, woolliest hippies who took such glee in swinging from the trees that day. He might have had more allies if he hadn't been so dis-agreeable. In the entire history of Texas, a place where being an S.O.B. is a re-spected art form, there are few finer ex-amples of arrogance on the rampage than Erwin clapping his hands as the trees fell. He seemed to isolate himself on purpose. Lesson number two: You can move quicker when you work alone. While a great many of us—students and professors—were running around filing injunctions, trying to raise money, going to rallies, writing editorials in the student newspaper, Erwin was dealing with the only people who really counted: the men driving the bulldozers. While he was talking to them we were bumping into each other. Our only victory was Pyr-rhic—the restraining order went into ef-fect after the biggest trees were lying in a heap on the ground.

Erwin handled the tree debacle the way he did all his business—like a ranch hand who sees a tick crawling across his arm and dispatches it with one swift flick of his finger. Three days later he was re-ceiving with equanimity a Distinguished Axe Award at an alumni luncheon. When his foes handed out "Dirty Noth-in" buttons to commemorate Erwin's characterization of protesters ("I'm dis-turbed that a bunch of dirty nothins can disrupt the workings of a great university in the name of academic freedom"), he wore one on his lapel. He put the bump-er sticker "Pray for Rosemary's Baby and Frank Erwin" on his car. Lesson number three: Don't look back. It is a lesson that his adversaries, at least this one, have been slow to learn. I still bridle when I drive past the corner of San Jacinto and Twenty-first Street, even though that stretch of Waller Creek looks green and tranquil, pretty much as it did before October 22, 1969. ❧

# 1965 THE HOUSTON POWER ELITE TOPPLES A *CHRONICLE* EDITOR WHO DARED TO BE HIS OWN MAN.

# FINAL EDITION

## BY SAUL FRIEDMAN

THE PURGE OF STEVEN ENDS THE *CHRONICLE*'S BRIEF INDEPENDENCE.

WHEN I CALLED THE newsroom at the *Houston Chronicle* to report the death on Thanksgiving Day, 1984, of one of its former editors, Robert T. Cochran, the young reporter did not recognize the name. That was understandable but sad, for reporters on today's *Chronicle*—and in Houston in general—ought to know about that time when the largest newspaper in the South's most populous city was not merely an aging handmaiden of the Houston establishment.

Cochran was the chief of the *Chronicle*'s editorial page from 1961 to 1964. He was part of a brief renaissance led by the paper's new editor, William P. Steven. Before Steven arrived, the paper had fed Houstonians an unrelieved diet of right-wing columnists like Fulton Lewis, Jr., and Paul Harvey, diatribes against the United Nations and the Warren Court, and pious incantations on free enterprise and states' rights. Cochran opened the op-ed page to the leading national columnists like James Reston and Max Freedman. His elegant editorials sympathized with the civil rights movement in the South. His aim was less to change Houston's politics than to change its thinking, to broaden its perception of what was respectable in current affairs.

Steven was brought in, in 1961, after the *Post*—flourishing while its publisher, Oveta Culp Hobby, was off serving in the Eisenhower Cabinet—captured the circulation lead. In her absence the *Post* vigorously examined the influence of a group of political vigilantes known as the Minute Women. The *Chronicle* studiously ignored controversy. Envious of the competition, younger *Chronicle* reporters, of whom I was one, began a union movement. That along with the

*Post*'s growing circulation lead prompted unprecedented action by John T. Jones, Jr., who had inherited from his uncle, the storied Jesse Jones, command of the Houston Endowment foundation that owned the *Chronicle*. The paper's long-time editor, M. E. Walter, was kicked upstairs and replaced with Steven, who had been the editor of the well-regarded Minneapolis papers.

Steven recruited religion editor James Clements, a former Episcopal bishop in Houston who had stirred up controversy with his theological liberalism and commitment to integration. He purchased the *Los Angeles Times–Washington Post* and *New York Times* news services. And he ended the fledgling union movement by promoting union leaders and raising salaries across the board. (Mine went from $120 to $165 a week.) Most important, he began covering the news with an even hand. Local liberals challenging conservatives for office no longer were ignored. Reporters like myself were allowed to report on the John Birch Society and to cover the civil rights movement. Soon the *Chronicle* had

pulled ahead of the *Post*.

Make no mistake, Steven was not as aggressive or as liberal as grumbling conservatives supposed. He supported desegregation because it was the law. But the *Chronicle*, aiming to help downtown businesses avoid trouble, joined the *Post* in deliberately ignoring the integration of local hotels and restaurants. Steven's closest political friends were John Connally and Lyndon Johnson. His (and Cochran's) editorials were cautious and designed to negotiate the minefields of Houston's business establishment.

Steven's big mistake was his support of the construction of a domed stadium in the city's southwest suburbs —against the interests of Houston Endowment's real estate and banking holdings. And the displeasure of Endowment trustees and their friends increased as the *Chronicle*'s new posture was accompanied by the awakening of Houston's large but lethargic black community. Despite the nervousness, Steven authorized and worked with me on a four-month study of how it was to be black in Houston. But the series itself was destined never to see print.

On September 2, 1965, just before the series was to run, the Endowment board met without Jones's knowledge and fired the *Chronicle* board. It then constituted itself as the new newspaper board and replaced Steven with Everett Collier (one of Walter's protégés). In the manner of a Kremlin purge, Steven's name disappeared without explanation from the masthead. Soon Jones, a gentleman who never forcefully used his clout in Houston, was out of power at the Endowment as well. The *Chronicle*, like the *Post*, slipped back into mediocrity. The Houston establishment had closed ranks.❧

# 1954 WEST TEXAS LANDOWNERS WIN A COURT BATTLE TO PUMP WATER OUT OF THE GROUND. AND A DECADE LATER, COMANCHE SPRINGS IS DRY.

# SILENT SPRINGS

## BY STEPHEN HARRIGAN

I F YOU VISIT FORT STOCKTON TODAY and ask to see Comanche Springs, you will be directed to a municipal swimming pool in Rooney Park. The pool is large but unremarkable; it does not seem to warrant the two-story bathhouse and pavilion that towers above it.

But when the bathhouse was built by the WPA in 1936, it stood over a different body of water, a natural pool that was fed by the prodigious discharge of a spring called the Comanche Chief. The Chief was the largest of the outlets that made up the Comanche Springs system. Together they pumped 60 million gallons a day of clear and slightly alkaline water onto the dry earth, forming a desert oasis that the people of that country –back to the Jumanos and before–had relied upon for many thousands of years.

The springs–along with the pools, creeks, and marshlands that they fed– quit flowing for good sometime in the early sixties. There is no mystery to it. Farmers who owned land higher on the water table drilled so many wells that the springs were simply pumped dry.

People downstream saw it coming. In 1952 a group of them filed suit against Clayton Williams, Sr., and a few other "pump farmers," seeking an injunction against further drilling. The legal action was long and bitter, its concerns vital but arcane. The central issue was who owned the groundwater. The plaintiffs argued that the water that fed Comanche Springs ran in well-defined underground channels and therefore constituted a subterranean stream. According to the plaintiffs, a stream was a stream, whether it flowed on the surface or below it. In each case, under the doctrine of riparian rights, the water belonged to everyone along its course. The pump farmers argued that the water beneath their land did not flow, but percolated, and was therefore theirs to keep.

The case ultimately reached the Texas Court of Civil Appeals, where the flowing-versus-percolating argument turned out to be a moot point. Underground water, the court said, belonged

THE SPRINGS FED AN OASIS THAT PEOPLE HAD RELIED UPON FOR THOUSANDS OF YEARS.

to the landowner, and that was that. Knowing full well that its decision would seal the fate of Comanche Springs, the court ruled for the defendants. The verdict helped set the stage for the haphazard groundwater policies, depleted aquifers, and water crises that would henceforth be fixtures of Texas life.

The immediate effect on Fort Stockton was devastating, at least to those families whose land, previously watered by the springs, slowly turned to desert. There is no precise date for when the springs stopped flowing. For a few years after the Court of Civil Appeals decision they would dry up in summer and return in winter, but always with less force. By the early sixties they were gone entirely. There were no more water hazards on the golf course, and Fort Stockton children no longer learned to swim in the spring-fed wading pool just downstream from the Chief. But the annual Water Carnival continued in the concrete pool,

and for a short time an effort was made, for sentimental reasons, to pump city water through one of the old dried-up spring openings.

Today the Chief is a deep, dry crevice, so wide that one can stand above it and marvel at the explosive force with which the water must once have rushed forth out of the earth. Long ago, a cage was built over the spring opening to prevent swimmers from exploring its dangerous passages. The cage is still there, as if containing some fitful, invisible presence. A few years back a group of cavers squeezed in through the mouth of the Chief and discovered an extensive cave system. They found a few pools of water, but mostly the caves are dry, and most people expect them to stay that way. Just in case, though, the concrete bottom of the pool rests on stilts above the bedrock. That's to leave room for the water to flow if the springs ever come alive again.❦

# 1958 STRIPPER CANDY BARR, BROUGHT TO TRIAL FOR SHOWING DALLAS WHAT IT REALLY WANTED TO SEE, POSES FOR THE JUDGE.

# Say "Cheesecake"

## BY GARY CARTWRIGHT

ON VALENTINE'S DAY, 1958, DALlas checked its conscience, found itself woefully deficient, and sent Candy Barr to prison for fifteen years. The charge was possession of less than an ounce of marijuana, but Candy's real crime was shaking her behind at the establishment, which heretofore had paid handsomely for the sight. That's how the can-do city solved its problems in the fifties. Someone with a dark sense of humor called that decade the age of innocence, but in Dallas at least it was the age of hypocrisy.

The good citizens of Dallas had been trying to get their hands on Candy for some time, and a few had succeeded—at upward from $100 a pop, it was said. Long before her name was a household word, Candy peeled at smokers sponsored by the Jaycees and SMU fraternities. Her infamous stag film, *Smart Aleck,* was a classic. This was no threadbare hooker sweathogging on a bare mattress; this was a stunningly beautiful fourteen-year-old nymphet. This was America's sweetheart: the pouty mouth, the tropical green eyes, the body that could stop a corporate board meeting. When Candy took her clothes off, generations of guilts and sublimated fantasies came into sharp focus.

It might have gone on like that, except Candy got discovered by a master showman named Abe Weinstein, who made her a headliner at his Colony Club. After that she was a daily item, not only in newspaper ads and columns but wherever society matrons gathered. Shoppers strolling along Commerce in front of the Colony Club were confronted with a lifesize cardboard cutout of Candy in her cowboy outfit pointing a toy pistol under a cocked leg. When Candy shot her exhusband as he kicked down her door, that poster came to life. Always quick to seize the moment, Abe Weinstein managed to get her bond increased from $5000 to $100,000 before he paid it, and citizens flocked to watch the gun moll strip.

The Dallas cops went to a lot of trou-

WHEN SHAPELY STRIPPER CANDY BARR WENT ON TRIAL, ALL OF DALLAS GOT THE PICTURE.

ble to nail Candy. They maintained constant surveillance from a rented apartment and tapped her phone. They may have planted the evidence. Less than two hours before the bust, another stripper who was having trouble with the cops asked Candy to hide a small stash for her.

The trial was a four-day farce. While the all-male jury pondered the larger question of how they could explain anything less than a long prison sentence to their wives, sisters, and mothers, the public leered and Judge Joe B. Brown borrowed a news photographer's camera and took shots of what the papers called "the shapely defendant" for his personal collection. Lawyers were certain the verdict would be overturned, but in the meantime Candy moved to Las Vegas, where, according to newspaper reports back in Texas, she shacked up with mobster Mickey Cohen and appeared as a bridesmaid in the wedding of Sammy Davis, Jr., to a white actress. The State Court of Criminal Appeals voted two to one to uphold the conviction, and Juanita Dale Slusher, alias Candy Barr, a runaway from Edna, served three years and four months.♣

# THE TEXAS WATERGATE

## BY MOLLY IVINS

YET ANOTHER INDICA-tion something is wrong with journal-ism is that it has coined the expressions "a good mur-der" and "a great scandal." Ah, but the Sharpstown scandal, fellow Texans, was a *great* political scandal. What fun. What a spectacle. Practically everybody with any pretension to political respectability turned out to be guilty of something. And the rest of the bums we threw out.

The Sharpstown scandal was to Texas as Watergate was to the nation, but Sharpstown came first and consequently seems now to have occurred in a gentler, more trusting time. Because the public level of cynicism about government was low-er then, the outrage over the revelations of Sharps-town was keener.

It was the governor's in-augural ball, 1971, and Preston Smith of Lubbock, just reelected by a thumping margin, should have been frivoling the night away. Instead the governor, who at the best of times bore a striking resemblance to Dopey of the Seven Dwarfs, looked like somebody had just run over his pup-py. Rumors that the mother and father of scandals was about to break were all over the hall; it was a minor league ver-sion of the Duchess of Richmond's ball the night before the Battle of Waterloo. The next morning there were huge black headlines in every newspaper in the state. The Securities and Exchange Commission was investigating the col-lapse of the financial empire of Frank Sharp, and the SEC wanted to know how many state officials Sharp had paid off to prevent that collapse.

Frank Sharp was a wheeler, a dealer, and a windmill fixer, banker, real estate

A SPECTACULAR SCANDAL BREAKS, AND SHARPSTOWN TOPPLES ALMOST EVERYBODY IN TEXAS POLITICS.

developer, insurance mogul, board and commission member galore. Busier than a cranberry merchant was Frank Sharp. (The cast of characters in the Sharps-town scandal all seemed to have been named by Charles Dickens.) The trou-ble with Sharp's many enterprises was that they amounted to a giant Ponzi scheme. He looted his Sharpstown State Bank in Houston to make insider loans to his confederates so they could buy stock in Sharp-owned companies and then use the inflated stock as collateral for loans. Those practices did not escape the attention of federal bank examiners. Because the money in the Sharpstown State Bank was insured by the Federal Deposit Insurance Corporation, the feds demanded that Sharp shape up. Instead, Sharp bought two bills from the Texas Legislature that would have replaced the

FDIC with a state deposit insurance cor-poration, thus ridding himself of federal interference.

It is an axiom among politicians that you should never let a scandal drag on; a pol caught in the cookie jar is best advised to confess everything at once, beg for public forgiveness, and possibly find Jesus on the spot. The matter then becomes a mere one-day wonder. The public's attention is hard to catch, its memory short. But once people get hooked, they follow it like a soap opera, and that's what happened with both Wa-tergate and Sharpstown.

The Sharpstown soapie played itself out for an entire legislative session—the governor, the Democratic party chair-man, the Speaker of the House, two of the Speaker's associates, and assorted state legislators had all gotten loans from

Frank Sharp's bank, which they then used to buy stock in Frank Sharp's companies. That is not to mention two former attorneys general, a former insurance commissioner, the mayor of Houston, some astronauts, and assorted other dignitaries and numskulls who had roles in all this. Some of them made money, some lost it, depending on how soon they sold out. All of them wanted it forgotten, ASAP. Those members of the Legislature who (a) had nothing on their own consciences and (b) had the courage to buck the entire political leadership of the state turned out to be precious few. When it finally came to a vote on the House floor as to whether the Legislature should investigate its own members and leaders, only 30 out of 150 House members voted for the measure. "Those thirty dirty bastards," said a member loyal to Speaker Gus Mutscher, and the name stuck. The Dirty Thirty, a coalition of the liberals and the few Republicans in the House, began a struggle that lasted for months. "In those days, if you voted against slavery and stealing, they called you a liberal," says Dirty Thirty alum Bill Bass, now a state judge in Tyler. In retrospect, it is clear the Dirty Thirty were helped by the clumsy brutality with which the Speaker tried to suppress them, culminating in a redistricting plan so grossly unconstitutional it was enough to gag a maggot. Mutscher's attempts at vengeance made political heroes of them and particularly of their leader, Frances "Sissy" Farenthold of Corpus Christi.

One little-noticed effect of the Sharpstown scandal was that it galvanized the state press. Before the scandal, the attitude of Texas newspapers toward the state's political power structure might most kindly be described as supine. Sharpstown was such a wonderfully rich and complex set of doings that every paper could get hold of a piece of it and find an exclusive somewhere. They were not content merely to print what the pols had to say in their defense; the press thought more answers were required and started digging for them. Most uncharacteristic behavior. In response, the politicians tried to blame everything on the press. To read their statements today is to be amazed by how often they tried to divert the public's anger into shooting the messenger.

As a matter of ethics, the response of the pols caught in the Sharpstown scandal was especially instructive. What they said, one and all, in various ways, was, "Who, me? What do you mean I'm in trouble? I can't be in trouble. *Everybody does it.*" Now the everybody-does-it excuse is not acceptable in Ethics I, much less to the average mother of a seven-year-old, but the citizenry shrewdly perceived that the real Sharpstown scandal was that almost everybody in Texas politics *did* do it. The problem was the whole system. Frank Sharp's banking bills passed the House of Representatives by 120–8 and the Senate by 24–2. Sharp didn't bribe all those people—they didn't even know what they were voting on. The Speaker wanted it; that was all they had to know, that was the way it worked.

Fourteen months after the scandal broke, former Speaker Gus Mutscher was convicted in Abilene of conspiracy to accept a bribe. The prosecutor was Travis County DA Bob Smith, a man with a manner as plain as his name. Smith told the jury in his summation, "Y'all keep hearing about the mess in Austin. Y'all keep talking about the mess in Austin. All over this state we keep asking, 'Why don't they do something about the mess in Austin?' Well, this is your chance to do something about the mess in Austin."

The people had their chance to do something about it on Election Day 1972. They elected a new governor, a new lieutenant governor, and 85 head of freshman legislators, every one of them running hard on a platform of reform. Of course the new bunch didn't clean up the Augean stables in Austin. They passed a little ethics legislation, some financial disclosure laws, lobby registration, and a few procedural reforms, and that was about the end of the post-Sharpstown "ree-form." But it was real, visible progress. Whattaya want, blood? Besides, if we took all the fools out of the Texas Legislature, it wouldn't be a representative body anymore.✦

# GONE TO TEXAS

BY GRIFFIN SMITH, JR.

1969 IN SEARCH OF LOWER TAXES AND SIMPLER LIVING, SHELL OIL ABANDONS MANHATTAN AND MOVES TO HOUSTON. HENCEFORTH, TEXAS WOULD HAVE PASTRAMI, OPERA, . . . AND CLOUT.

MODERN TEXAS BEGAN ITS JOURney up from colonialism in 1969, when Shell Oil moved its operational headquarters lock, stock, and barrel from midtown Manhattan to downtown Houston. Shell's corporate hierarchy followed in 1970. The decision instantly made Shell the largest corporation in the Southwest (a position it still holds by a comfortable margin—compare its $23.7 billion in assets with the $18.2 billion of its nearest Texas rival, Tenneco). It also transformed Texas, Houston, and the lives of Dick Bauer, Bob Dunphy, and John O'Driscoll, three of the hundreds of Shell employees who dutifully joined the unprecedented migration.

The effect of all this on Houston is writ large in the contrast between a newspaper photograph published a week after the move and a view of the same scene today. In the photograph, the then-tallest office tower west of the Mississippi dwarfs the Tenneco Building, the Bank of the Southwest, the First City National Bank, and the Exxon Building, rising grandly above six lanes of Allen Parkway where, on a bright midday, fewer than a dozen cars can be seen. "The giant One Shell Plaza dominates the Houston skyline," the caption exults. Fifteen years later, One Shell Plaza is merely one peak

> WHEN BOB DUNPHY ARRIVED, HE WAS CALLED A DAM-YANKEE. NOW, "NONE OF MY KIDS HAS ANY INTEREST IN RETURNING EAST," HE SAYS.

among many in downtown Houston's High Sierra of corporate skyscrapers, and a current photograph of the parkway would likely show more automobiles than pavement. In the city's profile and in its intricately changed ways of life, of which congested traffic is but one particularly irksome example, the consequences of Shell's decision are inscribed.

M. W. Kellogg followed Shell from New York. U. S. Home came from Florida. So did numerous subsidiaries, divisions, and sections of larger firms, such as Esso Standard Eastern and Esso Exploration, two affiliates of Standard Oil of New Jersey. Soon, those who wanted to sell things to Shell and the other giants followed; like pilot fish alongside sharks, advertising agencies and suppliers and even law firms moved—or opened Texas branches—to service their clients. In the 1980's the Dallas–Fort Worth area has attracted even more corporate migrants than Houston, ranking third in the country (behind New York and Chicago) in the number of corporations with over $1 million in assets headquartered there (more than 1700). Among them are such colossi as Caltex Petroleum and American Airlines from New York and Diamond Shamrock from Cleveland.

It is hard [ CONTINUED ON PAGE 161 ]

# 1975 Drew Pearson Makes a Miraculous Catch, and the Cowboys Become America's Team.

# HAIL MARY

## BY DREW PEARSON

FIRST·PERSON

*On December 28, 1975, the Dallas Cowboys trailed the Minnesota Vikings 14–10 with time running out. A desperate Dallas drive culminated in the most famous play in the Cowboys' history, the Hail Mary pass from Roger Staubach to Drew Pearson.*

"The thing about that whole sequence of happenings in the last, I guess, minute and twenty-four seconds, the most surprising thing was, we were so down. We were out of that game and everybody was on the sideline, frustrated, mad, upset, because we figured we had lost the game. So when we hit that field to try to salvage the game, we had no idea we could pull it off. Even though Staubach had the ability to pull games out, we still didn't have the confidence as a football team that it could happen.

"I was very frustrated because I hadn't caught any passes and had had only one ball thrown to me, and I was really pissed off. But this was a whole different situation because Roger's not getting plays from Landry and he's calling plays on his own. He asked me and the other receivers what we could get open on. I told him I could do the turn-in routes, and we hit a couple of them. They were giving us that. That got us near midfield, and we felt good because we'd started ninety-one yards away.

"But then the drive started to bog down, and we wound up with a fourth and sixteen. I came back to the huddle and Roger said, 'Is there anything you can get open on?' I thought, 'Fourth and sixteen, you don't have a lot of plays that'll work in those situations.' But since we had had success running the inside route, I told him I'd fake it inside and take it outside.

"What I ran was a post-corner. Roger told everyone to stay in to protect him because he needed at least three and a half seconds to throw the pass because

my route needed time to take effect. Roger was going to look at the post and even pump it there to get the defensive back leaning that way, and then I would break it back out to the corner. I closed the gap between me and cornerback Nate Wright real quick, and so when I broke outside I was a little ahead of him. The ball was thrown way out to the sideline, and as I made the catch I was hit and knocked out of bounds. I never got my feet in bounds, and the only reason it was a legal catch was the defensive back hit me and carried my momentum out of bounds and didn't give me a chance to get my feet down.

"There was snow all over the ground and I slid about ten feet. There were some security guards there, and I landed at the feet of one of them, and the thing I remember more than anything was that he kicked me. To me, that play was the real Hail Mary, because you had fourth and sixteen and you make the first down on a play that could have been real controversial. To me it was the biggest catch of the drive because it made the real Hail Mary possible.

"So we're about at the fifty, but we're inside a minute. I came back to the huddle and Roger asked me, 'Are you ready to go deep?' and I said, 'No way, I need to catch my breath,' because I was really winded. So he threw a quick sideline route to Preston Pearson; it was incomplete, and I think there were about thirty-two seconds left. I dogged it that play, gave it a good ten-yard sprint, and then tried to get my breath.

"Roger asked me if I was ready to go, and I said, 'Yeah, we got no choice.' I told him I was going to give the guy another good move to the inside, and then I told him to pump it, and then I was going deep. What really gave the play its timing was that Staubach dropped back and pumped it to the other side of the field, and that left me

one on one with Nate Wright.

"I was shakin' and bakin' on Nate Wright, and my thinking was the main thing was to close the gap between me and him as quickly as possible, because if I'm even with him, I have a fifty-fifty chance of catching the football. So I really came off the line with a lot of explosion, and when I got up on him, I gave him a move to the inside, and he bit to the inside, and that gave me a chance to come around him to the outside. He spun around, and as he came out of his spin, we were about even; maybe I was a little ahead of him. If Roger had just laid the ball out there, there wouldn't have been any controversy about whether Drew Pearson pushed the guy.

"But in a way, the blessing to the whole thing was that the ball was thrown short. I was able to turn around and see it. I was just coming out of my break, twenty-two yards or so down. Then I looked back, and at first I thought I needed to take off, but five or six steps later I realized it wasn't going to make it. So I just kind of put on the brakes, and meanwhile, Wright was just looking at me and hadn't seen the ball. As I came back, we collided a little, and I kind of looped my arm over him to get through him, and as my arm came down, the ball was just there.

"I wasn't really worried about interference, because at that point in the game it can't hurt your situation that much more. You've got to make whatever play is necessary to get to the football. The ball just came to my hands, but I thought I had dropped it. I hadn't grabbed it. But it hit my hands, and it slid back and lodged between my hip and my elbow. I just took a couple steps back and still thought I had dropped it, and I looked down and realized, 'Damn, it's still there.' You catch as many balls as I did, and you have a sixth sense for whether you've caught it, without looking, and I

> "THE FOOTBALL JUST CAME INTO MY HANDS, BUT I THOUGHT I HAD DROPPED IT. THEN I LOOKED DOWN AND REALIZED 'DAMN, IT'S STILL THERE.'"

was just sure I'd dropped it.

"So I just backed up into the end zone, and the first thing I'm looking for is that flag. I saw this orange blur come flying out there, and I thought, 'Oh, no, they got me.' But then I thought, 'Flags don't roll'—it was a hat or something—and then I saw the ref signal touchdown.

"I remember Nate Wright had fallen down and that Paul Krause, the safety, came over pointing at me that it was pass interference. If he hadn't been doing all that refereeing, he could have made the tackle at the five- or six-yard line, because I just backed into the end zone.

"My team mobbed me. I couldn't believe it. I don't know why I couldn't believe it, but I just never had made that kind of play before. I even saw Landry jumping up and down and carrying on. But the bad thing was, in Metropolitan Stadium both benches are on the same sideline. So after we had our celebration, I had to walk past the Viking bench to get to mine. Nobody said anything, but the looks were threatening.

"I kind of held my breath until I got to the Cowboy area, and then the celebration kept going. We play a lot of basketball in the off-season, and all my teammates were saying I had used an old basketball trick, which is where you just swing that arm over and then give them a nudge in the ribs to move them. To this day, if you look at those films, you won't see any extension of my arms, which is what refs are looking for. I used the move before then and I used it after then. And if I did give a nudge, it was subconsciously. It was nothing like where I said, 'Okay, here's what I'm going to do.' I was just trying to get to the ball and keep it from being intercepted.

"When I came down from it a week later, I realized, 'Hey, we hadn't made the play-offs in '74, and we had to struggle to make them this time.' That game catapulted us into success in the rest of the seventies. We went on to the bowl in '75, and we went twice after that. In fact, that catch was probably the seed of the whole America's Team thing."❧

INTERVIEWED BY JIM ATKINSON

# LONE STAR SHTICK

BY LARRY L. KING

PART OF IT WAS MY FAULT. But I insist on sharing the blame with Tommy Tune, Judi Buie, Dan Jenkins, Mort Cooperman, Dandy Don Meredith, *New York Daily News* gossip columnist Liz Smith, a terrible—and now mercifully defunct—restaurant called the Dallas Cowboy, numerous Texas-based kicker-pickers like Willie Nelson, Jerry Jeff Walker, and Kinky Friedman, and any other sinners who come to mind.

I'm talking about those who contributed to Texas chic, that virulent strain of cultural herpes that afflicted New York City a few years ago, when oil prices were high and Texas was booming and the Big Apple was on the verge of bankruptcy.

I don't know who started it; maybe New Yorkers thought if they'd *act* like legendary Texans, then perhaps some of the legendary Texas money might rub off on them. Some say Texas chic began when a Fort Worth lass, Judi Buie, began hawking expensive cowboy boots from a posh East Side address. I first noted the impact in 1972 with the publication of *Semi-Tough*, the best-selling Dan Jenkins novel featuring one-liners from the mouths of two fictional macho pro football players from Fort Worth, Billy Clyde Puckett and Shake Tiller, along with a supporting cast of cosmic cowboys and "awl bidness" primitives. Soon a Manhattan waddy couldn't mosey over to Elaine's without hearing Billy Clyde and his buddies quoted. The sports bunch at P. J. Clarke's drinking emporium picked it up; such jocks as Frank Gifford and Don Meredith plugged *Semi-Tough* on ABC's *Monday Night* [ CONTINUED ON PAGE 164 ]

FROM THE BOARDROOMS TO THE SUBWAYS, NEW YORKERS WERE DOLLED UP LIKE RODEO COWBOYS.

# THE GIZMO

*TI's Gordon Teal reaches into his pocket and pulls out the invention that changed the world.*

### 1954

The entire electronics industry knew that a gold mine was waiting for the company that could make the first high-temperature transistor. The first commercial transistors had been made of germanium, an element that starts to break down in high heat. A transistor made of silicon, a related element, could theoretically operate reliably regardless of temperature. But on May 10, 1954, at a technical conference in Dayton, Ohio, speaker after speaker reported that no progress had been made. As it happened, the last presentation that afternoon was by Gordon Teal, Texas Instruments' research and development director. Like most other R&D types in the industry, he had been working for the last few years on the task of building a silicon transistor. Unlike all the others, he had succeeded.

"Our company," he told the audience, "now has two types of silicon transistor in production. I just happen to have some here in my coat pocket." An assistant brought out a standard record player, one that used a common germanium transistor. Teal put on Artie Shaw's swinging rendition of "Summit Ridge Drive." As the record played, he dumped the transistor in a vat of boiling oil. The sound stopped.

Next Teal wired in one of his silicon transistors. He started the record again and dumped the transistor into the same hot oil. The band played on. Reporting on the session, *Fortune* magazine said that an executive from Raytheon was heard shouting into a telephone, "They've got the silicon transistor down in Texas!" It was not clear whether the achievement or the location was the bigger surprise.

— T. R. REID

---

# CONGRESSMAN QUIXOTE

**Wright Patman impeaches Treasury Secretary Andrew Mellon for the crime of being a rich Eastern banker.**

**1932** Wright Patman was a second-term congressman from Texarkana when he introduced articles of impeachment against Andrew Mellon, secretary of the treasury under three Republican presidents and one of the country's three or four richest men. The issue quickly became moot when Herbert Hoover appointed Mellon ambassador to the Court of St. James's, but what's interesting about the incident is how inconceivable it is now. Patman represented the historic Texas outlook on the political economy, a view based on poverty, outsider status, and hatred of the rich. In his 1934 tract *Bankerteering, Bonuseering, Melloneering,* Patman gleefully charged that Mellon's personal fortune was "equal to entire value of all property in Texas." The articles of impeachment focused on alleged conflicts of interest by Mellon, but the emotion behind it was pure little-guy populism. In the introduction to *Bankerteering,* Patman wrote, "If the masses could only pierce the 'Smoke screen of secrecy' and see what is actually going on behind closed doors in the financial world; could understand the plots and plans of these 'MONEY CHANGERS' in their efforts to fleece and filch an innocent and unsuspecting public; things would be changed in the twinkle of an eye."

Today the ironies are delicious: Patman became chairman of the House Banking Committee and was dethroned as an old man by the young, liberal, rebellious Democratic freshman class of 1974. Andrew Mellon's father was an immigrant and a completely self-made man of the sort sanctified in Texas. The incumbent treasury secretary is a rich Texan, James Baker. And last year the Republican party, which proclaims itself populist these days, targeted Patman's old district as fertile ground for realignment and almost won. —NICHOLAS LEMANN

# THE MILK BOTTLE THEORY OF TEXAS HISTORY

**1933** In 1933 a couple of Texas engineers wanted to make milk bottles in Texas, for Texans, from Texas raw materials. Prospects were good. At the time, milk bottles were shipped into the state and sold at an exorbitant price—$8 a gross; they were only $6 in St. Louis. The engineers built a plant in Santa Anna, near Brownwood, and began operations. But soon the mighty Hartford Empire Glass Company in Connecticut accused the Texans of violating Hartford's patents on all glass-making machines. Unable to afford a long lawsuit, the Texans submitted to a six-month lease. It was not renewed. One of them told the president of Hartford Empire, "In Texas within my lifetime I have seen men hanging in trees for doing less than what the Hartford Empire is trying to do to my small company." But it was to no avail. After trying to make milk bottles by hand, the Texans gave up.

The episode of the milk bottles inspired Texas historian Walter Prescott Webb to write a small book called *Divided We Stand.* The book contended that because of devices like tariffs and patents, "the South and West cannot establish industry and . . . are coming more and more under the control of the North," although the South and West "have within their boundaries most of the natural wealth of America." Webb's friend J. Frank Dobie fulminated in a review, "It illuminates the bleak walls of a boxed canyon into which the march of time and the linked chain of events have herded more than 50 million people occupying 80 per cent of the territory of the United States."

—PAUL BURKA

## *Roll Over, Tchaikovsky*

### 1958: Van Cliburn knocks 'em dead in Moscow.

When 23-year-old Harvey La-van Cliburn from Kilgore walked away with the gold medal at the Tchaikovsky piano competition in Moscow in 1958, he became an American hero. President Eisenhower gave him a White House reception, Manhattan gave him a ticker tape parade, and *Time* put him on its cover and proclaimed him "The Texan Who Conquered Russia."

Van, as he was always called, was a six-foot-four-inch, curly-headed blond whose playing caused women to sob and faint away in their chairs. The national press played up his Texanness–"Ah swear," he was quoted as saying, "ah just can't believe all this is happenin' to li'l ol' Van." He was very religious, a teetotaler and a 20 per cent tither to the Baptist church, and carried a well-thumbed Bible everywhere. He was, in short, the sort of boy any Texan could be proud of. And Texas was proud. The Dallas Symphony booked him for an unheard-of $9000 concert fee. In 1962 Fort Worth sponsors announced a major new international piano competition and, worried that their city's name would not be a big draw, named the event after him.

Van Cliburn stopped performing publicly in 1978. Today his name is heard primarily because of the competition in Fort Worth. But Texas is still fighting the same old battles. A Fort Worth woman doing some fundraising in Manhattan told the *New York Times,* "We know the Van Cliburn award is the best, but if you don't come to New York and say it, nobody knows you've got it." Van Cliburn may have put Texas on the culture map, but it sure hasn't been easy staying there.

—DOMINIQUE BROWNING

Texas. Instead, most got the hell out. But the law had another consequence that proved to be one of the building blocks of modern Texas. By serving as a protective tariff for homegrown companies like W. L. Moody's American National Insurance, the Carpenters' Southland Life, and Carr P. Collins' Fidelity Union Life, it helped build Texas' first financial empires and turned Texas into an insurance center.

Too much of an insurance center, it turned out. One in every three life insurance companies in the country came to have headquarters in Texas, with its loose regulatory climate. In the decade after World War II an estimated half-million Texans lost coverage as dozens of companies failed. In 1963 the Robertson Act was repealed, but even today national companies can get state tax breaks by investing in Texas.

—PAUL BURKA

## The First of the Big-time Spenders

**1901** John Henry Kirby could have hoped for no more fitting tribute than to have the main street through Houston's River Oaks named in his honor. He was the spiritual ancestor of all that River Oaks stands for, the pursuit of wealth and grace and exclusivity and prominence. Kirby was Texas' first industrial millionaire, a timber baron who lived the part–wheeling and dealing with Boston investors, vowing to become the richest man in the South, breaking the unions in the Piney Woods, and hosting parties at his elegant mansion. The late Gus Wortham, another leading Houston figure, said of Kirby, "He taught us all how to spend money."

On July 8, 1901, the *Houston Post* devoted its front page to his biggest deal. REPRESENTS FORTY MILLION DOLLARS, the headline read, and underneath, LARGEST IN THE WORLD. Texas had never seen any deal like it. Kirby formed the Houston Oil Company to woo Northern investors looking for another Spindletop. Yankee money bought a million acres of East Texas, but oil was only the lure; Kirby really wanted the timber. He simultaneously formed the Kirby Lumber Company

and acquired eight billion board feet of Houston Oil's pine trees.

In his later years things went downhill. Friends took advantage of his generosity. The New Deal soured him on politics; he became a national spokesman for the embittered Right. The Depression found him deep in debt–too deep. He lost his company to his chief creditor, the Santa Fe Railway. When he died in 1940, the first of the big-time spenders left nothing behind but a street.

—PAUL BURKA

## PROTECTION RACKET

### [ 1907 ]

IMAGINE THE HUE AND CRY THAT WOULD ensue if any company doing business in the state–Air France, Bloomingdale's, Texaco –was required by law to invest in Texas real estate and municipal bonds at least 75 per cent of its profits from Texas business, or get the hell out. That's exactly what the Legislature did to the life insurance industry in 1907. What's more, we got away with it–for a while.

The Robertson law, as it was known, was meant to force the big Northern insurance companies to invest in capital-starved

## THE DAY THE MUSIC WAS BORN

### Buddy Holly meets the King.

**1955** In early 1955, during rock and roll's nascence, the Cotton Club in Lubbock booked Elvis Presley. As Elvis' band approached the edge of town, they were met by a young local musician named Buddy Holly, who took the as yet uncrowned King on a tour of his hometown, then just a dusty agricultural center of 110,000 people.

Holly had already melded his early influences—country, Western swing, blues, rhythm and blues, bluegrass—into an embryonic rockabilly sound. But after meeting Elvis (who was essentially what Holly wanted to be, a white performer who sounded black), Holly worked more black styles into his playing. He called the new sound Western and bop.

At first he was billed as a country singer. Never mind that onstage his shy demeanor gave way to frenetic raving. The teenagers at the Lubbock County Center, where he played his first concerts, heard something unforgettable in Holly's rollicking tunes and signature hiccup. When he jumped into his six-syllable "We-eh-eh-eh-ella" at the beginning of "Rave On," they knew this was music they could dance to.

In Texas Holly bridges the gap between Bob Wills and ZZ Top, but his influence extends far beyond Texas. He was one of the first rock musicians to write his own songs. The first song the Beatles recorded was a 78 rpm version of his "That'll Be the Day," and even their name was a play on his group's name, "the Crickets." Holly merged Texas music with rock and roll and set the world dancing to a West Texas beat.—LAURA FISHER

145

# THE INDUSTRIAL REVOLUTION

*A Yankee defense contractor moves to Dallas, and Texas sees its future.*

**1947** When Chance Vought decided in 1947 to move its airplane plant from Stratford, Connecticut, to a war-surplus factory twelve miles west of Dallas, the term "corporate relocation" was unknown. Texas was struggling to build an industrial base; the state's economy still depended more on agriculture than on oil. The move, then the largest industrial migration in the nation's history, changed everything. The arrival of Chance Vought established the Dallas area as a defense center, which in time led to high tech and, in the sixties, to high finance as well, when Chance Vought became part of Jimmy Ling's conglomerate empire, LTV.

The Navy, eager to relocate key military installations in less vulnerable locations around the country, had prodded the move. The company's top executives were won over on a tour through the Texas facility, so vast that during World War II its roofs had been camouflaged to simulate an eighteen-hole golf course. When the plant's runways proved to be too short for Chance Vought's new generation of jet fighters, the Dallas City Council anted up $256,000 in public funds to lengthen them. Back in Stratford, trying to convince its employees that they were not moving to the ends of the earth, Chance Vought filled its in-house newsletter with dispatches on the new city, beneath such headlines as DALLAS HAS SYMPHONY and FLYING POSSIBLE 98% OF YEAR.

Over eighteen months the company shipped 30 million pounds of equipment in railcars halfway across the country. Caravans of trucks towed fighter planes along highways. Fifteen hundred employees were transferred to Texas. Sixty-five hundred Texans got the jobs of those who were not.

— PETER ELKIND

# TURNING THE TABLES

### 1982: Boone Pickens goes to Wall Street.

Boone Pickens was strolling down Park Avenue, his hands stuffed in his pockets, his tie fluttering in the wind, a man who seemed not to have a care in the world. He had just eaten at the "21" club and was walking back to the Waldorf-Astoria, where he would remain for the next two weeks while his company, Mesa Petroleum, made a bid to take over Cities Service, a company twenty times Mesa's size. But on this cool June evening in 1982, he was reminiscing about the old days, about what it was like for a struggling young oilman from Texas to come to New York.

"The hardest thing," he said, "was just to get those people to take you seriously. You'd get in to see some analyst or some moneyman you wanted to invest in your deals—that's assuming you got past the secretary, which was not always the case—and you'd sit down and start to explain the deal. And when finished, you'd look at them and you'd see their blank faces, and you knew exactly what they were thinking. They were thinking, 'Who is this guy?' "

Generations of Texans had felt the same frustration at having their destinies controlled by people thousands of miles away. But Boone Pickens had changed all that; *his* decisions were controlling *their* destinies. Ahead lay not just the Cities fight but Gulf and Phillips and Unocal and all the rest of it: the reshaping of the world's most important industry. Pickens allowed himself a quiet and self-satisfied smile. "Yeah," he said, "I guess they know who we are now."

— JOSEPH NOCERA

# THE TECH TREK

### 1983: Austin goes gaga over MCC.

The announcement was called the new Spindletop. On May 18, 1983, the Microelectronics and Computer Technology Corporation revealed that it had selected Austin as its headquarters over 56 other U.S. cities. The news couldn't have come at a better time. With Texas in the throes of an oil slump, MCC's arrival was touted as the beginning of a new era in which high tech would replace oil as the state's glamour industry.

MCC's decision set off a real estate boom in Austin. High-rise office buildings sprouted along Congress Avenue, obscuring landmarks like the Capitol and the University of Texas Tower, as speculators envisioned the advent of a brave—and highly profitable—new world. But grand visions have a way of being caught short by reality. With just under 400 employees and an annual budget of $50 million, MCC has yet to prove its mettle against established U.S. think tanks like Bell Communications Research, with 7200 employees and an annual budget of $900 million, much less give any indication that it can outdo the Japanese. Even before MCC got geared up, high tech was ailing from the same symptoms—layoffs, a worldwide slump, foreign competition—as oil. So far the only lasting consequence of MCC's announcement is that laid-back Austin will never be the same. —HARRY HURT III

## Curse or Cure?

### 1882: Did robber baron Jay Gould kill Jefferson — or save it?

The women of the Jessie Allen Wise Garden Club of Jefferson have an uneasy relationship with the robber baron Jay Gould.

Gould is held personally responsible for the decline of Jefferson from a once-thriving inland port to a quaint town of 2600 people. Versions of the legend have Gould passing through town sometime between 1872 and 1882 demanding a right-of-way for his Texas and Pacific railroad line. The town fathers, smug with the prosperity that came from the port, turned him down. In fury Gould vowed, "Jefferson will see the day when bats roost in its church belfries and grass grows in its streets." He also skipped out on his hotel bill, but not before adding below his name on the register, "End of Jefferson Texas." The T&P tracks detoured around Jefferson, and the glory days ended.

For a century the story of Gould's curse has been cited to show how Texas has been at the mercy of

Terry rides the Gould car.

Eastern money interests. The problem is that it's not true. In 1983 Fred Tarpley, a professor at East Texas State University, published a commissioned history of Jefferson. In it he knocks the stuffing out of the Jay Gould story. For instance, he found that Jefferson had a railroad in 1873, eight years before Gould bought the Texas and Pacific.

That has presented a big headache for the Jessie Allen Wise Garden Club. The club has restored many of the town's historic buildings, it runs the Excelsior House hotel, and it bought Jay Gould's private railroad car, which now sits in the center of town. You could say Jefferson today is the town the Jay Gould curse built. So the garden club doesn't know quite what to do with the ghost of Mr. Gould (which is said to haunt room 215 of the Excelsior). "I was ready for the truth," says Lucille Terry, a member since 1942. "But I don't want to burst any bubbles. The story has been good to us." —EMILY YOFFE

# 1980 J.R. TAKES A BULLET, DALLAS TAKES THE RAP, AND *DALLAS* TAKES NUMBER ONE IN THE RATINGS.

# SOUTH FORK CAMELOT

BY JAMES WOLCOTT

ONE THEORY TO ACCOUNT FOR the extraordinary hold *Dallas* has on America (and the world) is that the Ewing saga is really the Kennedy saga transplanted. Jock Ewing, so the theory goes, is the Joseph Kennedy figure, a begetter of ambitious sons. Barbara Bel Geddes' Miss Ellie is the Rose Kennedy matriarch, down-home and plumped up with biscuits. Larry Hagman's J.R. is JFK, a JFK without a visionary gleam in his eye or the winds of history mussing his hair. Like Paul Newman's Hud in the 1963 film based on Larry McMurtry's novel *Horseman, Pass By,* J.R. is a crumb-bum package of Texas hormones who chases around with loose women, prefers oil to cattle, and believes that in an amoral world you've got to take that extra edge. But while Hud grew up unsoftened by a mother's devotion ("My momma loved me but she died") and saw his father as a barren tree in need of uprooting, J.R.'s parental affection is Kennedyesque. He loves his daddy–loved him in the wrinkled flesh, loves him as preserved in that awful oil painting at South Fork.

So when J.R. stepped out of his office at the end of the 1979–80 season and took a bullet, it was a video replay of JFK's assassination. Once again the world was absorbed by the spectacle of violence in Dallas, and once again the climate of the town was partially to blame, except that the reprehensible atmosphere of hate of 1963 had evolved into the glamorized business ethos of 1980. Laid up and forced to mend, J.R. reluctantly surrendered the power levers of Ewing Oil to younger brother Bobby, the Bobby Kennedy stand-in played with a pained squint by Patrick Duffy.

All summer in 1980 the press and the public took part in the "Who Shot J.R.?" debate, running down the suspects as if they were characters in that parlor game, Clue. The day before the seventeenth anniversary of JFK's death, J.R.'s would-be killer was unveiled, and to almost no one's surprise, it was Mary Crosby's Kristin, she of the long brown mane and

LOU BEACH

THE SHOOTING OF *DALLAS*' J. R. EWING WAS A VIDEO REPLAY OF JFK'S ASSASSINATION.

no-good lips. The ratings that night were stratospheric.

What was the fallout? J.R. was soon up and scheming to retake control of Ewing Oil. Kristin was discovered floating face down in a swimming pool. After a long heartbreak tango, Bobby and Pam packed their laundry into separate bags, a split fueled in part by Pam's frustration at seeing Bobby turn into another J.R.– another Ewing son trying to prove himself worthy of Jock's loins. And in the world beyond the television set, *Dallas* gave Dallas a new identity.

J.R.'s shooting threw the whole Ewing world out of whack, and the show itself seems to have suffered ever since from postoperative jitters. As if to follow yet again in Kennedy footsteps, *Dallas* had Bobby fall victim to an assassin, an echo of Bobby Kennedy's plight. (To paraphrase Karl Marx, history appears on television first as tragedy, then as schlock.) But the final straw came when the show's producers tried to pass off Donna Reed as Miss Ellie. Even J.R., rubbing the brim of his Stetson, looked confused. He seemed to be blinking in code, "I want my real momma back." My daddy loved me but he died.♦

147

# 1937 IN HIS LECTURES ON ECONOMICS AND HIS TALKS WITH LBJ, BOB MONTGOMERY PREACHES ONE THEME: TEXAS IS A COLONY OF NEW YORK.

# PROFESSOR BRIMSTONE

## BY DICK J. REAVIS

IF TODAY'S ACADEMIC STANDARDS had been in vogue fifty years ago, chances are that Robert H. Montgomery would never have made the grade. An economics professor at the University of Texas from 1928 to 1963, Dr. Bob, as he was known, wrote his doctoral thesis on the Aggielike subject of cotton producers' co-ops. His contributions to professional journals were few and thin, and his chief written work, a book about the sulfur industry called *The Brimstone Game,* was little more than an antimonopolist propaganda tract. When he stood at the lectern, exaggeration, hyperbole, and plain old reminiscence were among the tools that he used. "If Bob wanted to make a point, and a million was the figure in the record, he didn't mind adding a few zeroes to it," says a current member of the department.

What made Bob Montgomery important was his theory. He preached it to his students and his readers. "Texas," he would say, "is the largest—and incomparably the richest—foreign colony owned by Manhattan."

Like historian Walter Prescott Webb, Dr. Bob was a liberal but also a regionalist. "We have the world's richest deposits of oil, natural gas and sulphur," he wrote. "But the ownership rights are vested in giant holding companies in the financial centers, and the profits flow to these centers." According to Dr. Bob, the profits drained from Texas by Northern interests also included those from the salt, carbon black, flour-milling, meatpacking, timber, and cement industries, and even those from cotton and cattle. In 1937 economist Bob even went so far as to blame Yankee ownership—he called it "foreign" ownership—for the Great Depression. Because of America's internal colonialism, he said, "the Northeast cannot sell its wares. . . . We cannot sell our bacon and beef. . . . End result: we have a depression."

Montgomery's influence reached far beyond the classroom. In 1936 a legislative anticommunist committee subpoe-

DR. BOB TAUGHT TEXAS LIBERALS TO HATE YANKEES. WHERE IS HE WHEN WE NEED HIM?

naed him (for advocating the nationalization of monopolies). More than a thousand people, including the governor, came to wish the professor well. His teachings helped divide Texas into two political camps: those who thought developing an industrial base was worth the price of Yankee exploitation, and those who thought the price was far too high. Young Lyndon Johnson lived at Montgomery's house in the mid-thirties, and forever after Johnson dealt only with homegrown business interests, not Wall Street. A generation of Texas liberals came out of Montgomery's classes to fight the Northern railroads that resisted industrial safety laws and the big oil companies that opposed higher taxes.

Texans don't think like Bob Montgomery anymore—especially the liberal intellectuals who ought to be his spiritual heirs. Many of them have committed what Montgomery and Webb would have regarded as the ultimate surrender. They've moved to New York, whence to preach what's wrong with Texas. ❧

148

# 1933 JESSE JONES, THE MOST POWERFUL MAN IN HOUSTON, JOINS THE NEW DEAL AND BECOMES THE MOST POWERFUL MAN IN WASHINGTON.

# CITIZEN JESSE

BY JAMES FALLOWS

THE NEW DEAL HELPED MAKE the names of such master Texas politicians as Sam Rayburn and Lyndon Johnson, but the Texan who did most to make the New Deal was a man who never ran for office, Jesse Holman Jones.

Jones was born in Tennessee in 1874, the son of a middling-prosperous tobacco farmer and merchant who schooled him in the disciplines of the commercial world. At age fourteen Jones served as buyer for his father's warehouse, rejecting substandard leaf from farmers who had driven into town with their year's harvest—and then running behind the barn to cry. At twenty he went to Dallas to work for his millionaire uncle's lumber firm. By his mid-thirties, having moved to Houston and launched a career in lumber, real estate, and banking, he was a rich man himself. His formal explanations for his success ran to Ben Franklinesque chestnuts: "I have been brought up in the belief that the three most necessary things to a satisfactory life were family, religion, and money." In practice, Jones—who married late in life, never had children, and spent Sunday mornings at the office—seemed to have boiled those three necessities down to one.

Jones pioneered in Houston the style of businessman's civic leadership that is now most frequently associated with Dallas. His protective attitude toward the city may have been fostered by his ownership of the biggest newspaper, the biggest buildings, and the biggest bank. He helped raise money for the Ship Channel and became chairman of the board overseeing its completion. He acquired the *Chronicle* and wrote editorials about Houston's exciting future. His construction companies were responsible for most of Houston's significant prewar structures. (Later, when visiting Paris, he said that he was sorry he had not kept Houston a ten-story city.) He shunned partnerships—and the oil business, which he regarded as a crapshoot. His dramatically proffered personal check for $200,000 lured the Demo-

THE TEXAS TRINITY: JESSE JONES (C.), GOVERNOR ALLRED AND SON (L.), AND VP GARNER.

cratic party to Houston for its national convention in 1928. Shortly afterward, according to Senator Tom Connally, he "scurried about Texas raising money in order to reimburse himself."

Jones was called to service in Washington on the Reconstruction Finance Corporation (RFC) by Herbert Hoover, another successful self-made businessman, to whom Jones always felt spiritually closer than to Franklin Roosevelt. But the RFC floundered until Roosevelt took office and made Jones its chairman.

At the time of Roosevelt's inauguration, every bank in the country was closed. During the next two years the RFC invested more than $1 billion in more than six thousand banks; all but two of them eventually paid the government back. Jones went from city to city and challenged the remaining strong bankers to put their own money at risk helping the weak local banks. He bore an abiding hatred for New York bankers after they refused. Over Roosevelt's opposition, he promoted the single most important step toward bank stability: federal insurance of bank deposits.

For a dozen years his empire grew. He oversaw agricultural production through the Commodity Credit Corporation; he rescued the railroads as he had the banks; he assumed responsibility for all federal loan activity; he became Secretary of Commerce on the side. His impact on Texas was no less immense. The RFC made possible the first diversification of Texas industry away from agriculture and oil by investing in the state's first steel mill, Sheffield Steel near Houston, and in the first mill to make newsprint from Southern pine, Southland Paper near Lufkin. In lending some $50 billion, his RFC embraced nearly every tenet of what would now be called industrial policy. It picked winners by looking for businesses that were viable though temporarily distressed; it preferred to take equity in companies rather than simply making loans, so that taxpayers could share the profit; and it insisted on concessions and public-spirited behavior in exchange for public help. It did all that with remarkable efficiency and freedom from taint.

Six foot three, burly, of dignified mien, Jones was fully appreciative of his accomplishments and seemed to view Roosevelt as at best an equal. When the president issued an order that Jones considered misguided, he ignored it; when Jones made decisions that stretched his already considerable authority, "I would try at first opportunity to tell the president about it, but after the fact." Roosevelt took to calling him Jesus H. Jones.

As the most prominent conservative in the administration, Jones was constantly at odds with the liberal brain trusters. During the war his instinctive aversion to wildcatting made him reluctant to expand production as rapidly as Roosevelt and many others thought the arsenal of democracy required. His bitterest enemy was the increasingly leftish Henry Wallace, vice president during Roosevelt's third term. Their feud over procurement of wartime supplies grew so embarrassing —Wallace wanted to pass out free food in the Amazon jungle, where natives were harvesting rubber, while Jones thought such charity would erode the work ethic— that Roosevelt had to take both of them off the job. In the end, Wallace had his revenge. A few hours before Roosevelt was sworn in for a fourth term, the president sent Jones a note saying that Wallace had campaigned hard for the ticket, even though he had been dumped as vice president, and he deserved any job he wanted. The job he had chosen was Jones's, so would Jones please quit?

Jesse Jones resigned the Cabinet, returned to Houston, where he supported Republican presidential tickets, wrote the occasional editorial for the *Chronicle,* and died in 1956. Until Lyndon Johnson came to power, no Texan in public service had done more to change American life.❧

# 1936 IN THE DARKEST DAYS OF THE DEPRESSION, TEXAS THROWS ITSELF A BIRTHDAY PARTY.

# CENTENNIAL!

## BY BENJAMIN CAPPS

I WAS FOURTEEN YEARS OLD WHEN I attended the Centennial Exposition in Dallas in 1936, a real simple country boy from Archer County, south of Wichita Falls. We knew that there existed a large town called Fort Worth, for we had shipped cattle there by rail and by truck. Also, from reading and general agreement, we knew there must have been towns like Houston, San Antonio, New York, London, Paris, Rome. But what wonders they might hold was uncertain. It may be that the impression put on my two brothers and me by the crowds and the architecture of a city would have been enough of a thrill without the glories of a fair.

We went with a school group from Decatur, where three of our cousins lived. The logistics of the trip are dim now after half a century, but it seems that we entered Dallas from the west on a train or on the old interurban trolley. We had tickets, somehow acquired through the school system, to get into the fairgrounds and take a few rides. I remember riding the one-man bumper cars, which ran around in a pavilion, drawing their electric power from a wand that brushed the ceiling; an attendant kept yelling at the kid drivers to keep them from having a serious accident. And I remember getting free a small green plastic pickle to pin on your shirt. It said "Heinz" on it. I kept it for years.

The high point in the exposition was the Cavalcade of Texas, staged outdoors in the evenings on the old state fair racetrack. It's hard to remember all the battles and confrontations, but there were costumes aplenty. And cannon going off! For a curtain a spray of water shot up with lights shining on it so that the audience could not see the stagehands changing scenery.

A kid could not take in all the exhibits and attractions. I remember seeing an open touring car full of bullet holes; it was the death car of Bonnie and Clyde. I remember a big glass case, like a movie ticket booth, with a shelf covered with money, including real silver dollars. A

THE CENTENNIAL EXPOSITION SHOWS THAT TEXAS IS A PLACE TO BE RECKONED WITH.

sign invited you to take one, but a panel always rose up to block you, reading, "Foiled again."

But in a big building, now called the Hall of State, we got our most serious impression—history became real and awesome both. People like Austin and Houston had been just pictures and words in a book, and here they were tall bronze statues, even Travis, who died at the Alamo, and Fannin, who died at Goliad. Kids my age talked in whispers. The biggest pictures you ever saw were painted on the walls, showing scenes from all over the state. I don't know what

the others were thinking, but I had a secret wish: that I could tell those like Travis and Fannin how it all turned out, with the new nation and new state.

The centennial was a brave and confident statement that told the nation and the beleaguered rural people of the state that Texas was, after all, a place to be reckoned with. It might have seemed a wrong time to have a celebration, in the heart of the Great Depression, but kids from the country and from the city, and maybe old gray-haired kids, walked out of the fairgrounds taller and straighter.❧

# 2036: A BICENTENNIAL ODYSSEY

BY STEPHEN HARRIGAN

## A MAN, HIS HORSE-A-MATIC, AND A WILD, UNTAMED LAND

I WAS SITTING ON THE PORCH PICKING off whooping cranes with a .22 when my grandson Buster drove up in an ancient Honda Civic with a pair of longhorns attached to the hood. I hadn't seen one of those old fossil-fuel cars in thirty years, and it was just like that fool boy to dig one up.

"Where'd you get that contraption?" I asked.

"The car that won the West," he said, slapping the hood. He was wearing a ten-gallon cowboy hat and furry chaps. "I suppose you want to know why I'm dressed this way."

"Not especially," I answered, taking aim at another whooper.

"It's on account of the bicentennial. I'm celebratin' the heritage of our great state."

Buster always was a little excitable when it came to Texas lore. When he was a little boy he'd sit on my knee and listen raptly as I told him stories about the old days, the days of chili cookoffs and wraparound deals, of cruising the Silicon Prairie in a peppy little Japanese car under a wide blue Texas sky—the days when they would throw you in jail for shooting a whooping crane instead of paying you a bounty.

"I aim to drive this sucker all over Texas," he said now. "I want to get to Dallas in time for the big bicentennial celebration."

"How do you plan to do that? You can't buy gas for that thing."

"Wanna bet? I got a whole tank of super-premium unleaded from this dealer who specializes in petroleum collectibles. Come on, Tex, what do you say? Are you going to come with me or not?" Buster always insists on calling me Tex. It annoys me, but I suppose it doesn't do any harm, since to him I'm the embodiment of that long-gone Texas he knows about only by hearsay.

The fact was, an automobile trip across Texas didn't sound like such a bad idea, as long as we stayed out of the big population centers like Floydada or San

> "AN AUTO TRIP ACROSS TEXAS DIDN'T SOUND BAD, BUT THE LAST THING I NEEDED WAS TO BE DODGING AIR RICKSHAS AND HOVERBOARDS."

Benito. The last thing I needed at the age of 87 was to be dodging air rickshas and trying to find my way in those god-awful vacuum tunnels beneath the cities that made me feel like I was lost inside a prairie-dog town.

"Okay," I said, easing myself off the porch. "Crank her up."

I got into the passenger seat. Buster took off his hat and plugged in an ancient cassette tape.

"Like it?" Buster said. "It's *Mel Tillis' Greatest Hits.*"

"Don't you have any Willie Nelson?"

"Who was he? Oh, I remember. He was one of the sidemen when Tillis recorded his legendary 'Whataburger Theme.' "

"Shut up and drive," I said. There were no standards anymore.

We bounced along on the weedy, buckled ruins of Interstate 10, on the way to Houston. On the side of the road Vietnamese were toiling in the rice paddies, and farther in the distance I could see a herd of feral Santa Gertrudis thundering along through the dikes.

But Buster was more enthralled with the evidence of the past. "They say that back when Texas was a raw, untamed state, a road like this would have a Stuckey's every fifty miles."

"They weren't exaggerating," I said. "It was something to behold."

"Tell me about Stuckey's again," he pleaded.

"They had pert' near everything a man could want. Saltwater taffy, giant fly-swatters, denture motels. It was a wild, invigorating country back then, Buster."

After a few hours we arrived in Houston. The air rickshas buzzed about the city like a swarm of gnats, and traffic on the Cyclotron—known in my day as Loop 610—was furious. We created quite a sensation as we cruised down Westheimer in front of the Galleria National Historic Site. There were kids on hoverboards, a few daredevils from the Houston Pedestrian Club, infants in robot prams, and a crowd demonstrating beneath a banner that read "Multi-Gender Pride Week." All of them stared openmouthed as we passed, and Buster kept honking his horn that played "The Eyes of Texas."

We were driving by the site of the original Houston Medical Center when I spotted a Baylor Heart-Stop. "Stop in here," I told Buster.

"You startin' to wear down, Tex?" he asked.

"Never you mind," I said, slamming the car door. The truth was, I was feeling poorly and wondering why I'd ever allowed myself to start out on such a big trip without a complete systems analysis.

"I need a replacement kit for a left ventricle," I told the guy working the counter.

"What year?"

"1948."

He looked at me in mild surprise. "Cheaper to replace the whole heart."

"I know," I said, meaning to sound surly, "but I'm partial to the original equipment."

After I installed the new ventricle I felt better and realized that I was hungry. Buster said he knew of a great Mexican restaurant down in Little Borneo, but when we got there we saw that it had gone out of business and been replaced by a Kelp Kitchen. We decided to eat there anyway. They had a new item on the menu called Chili 'N' Sargasso that wasn't as bad as it sounded, even though I could tell the sargasso chips were imitation.

"I bet Houston has changed a lot since your day," Buster said, his mouth full of seaweed. Looking around, I had to admit he was right. Who would have guessed, back in 1986, that the population of Houston would one day be dominated by immigrants from Borneo?

It had all come about because of a visionary from Balikpapan named Bif Tangkulap who happened to visit Houston in 1988. Everywhere he looked he saw condominiums, hotels, office buildings—all vacant. Tangkulap knew his Texas history. It occurred to him that Houston had the same problem Mexico had had back in the early nineteenth century, when Texas was a remote and almost uninhabited province. Mexico had solved its problem by issuing land grants to foreign colonists. Tangkulap seized on the same idea. He had the city of Houston proclaim him an impresario, promising to fill the vacant space with responsible citizens in return for clear title. He went back to his native Borneo, recruited thousands of potential colonists, most of them the descendants of headhunters, and shipped them to Houston to fill the vacant living space.

The Borneans prospered, even as Houston went into decline. With the invention of vacuum tunnels and the great technical leaps forward in pedal power, the price of oil crashed to such a degree that it was cheaper to pump it back into the ground than it was to sell it. But then, against all expectations, Houston boomed again. The city's chronic subsidence problem had remained unchecked for decades, and by the turn of the century large sections of town were underwater. But what could have been a disaster turned into a triumph. Overnight, aquaculture replaced oil as the keystone of Houston's economy. The tunnels beneath the downtown area became natural holding pens for vast schools of tuna and mackerel. Homeowners became small businessmen when they discovered they could grow krill in their front yards.

Suddenly the buildings owned by the colonists became some of the most valuable real estate on earth. Certain members of the Houston ruling elite decided that this property was too lucrative to remain in the hands of foreigners. They wanted the Borneans out, and when the newcomers wouldn't sell, they saw to it that their air conditioning was cut off. The colonists rebelled, seizing the strategically important RepublicBank Center and vowing to hold it, as one of them unforgettably put it, "until hell freezes over, or we get our air conditioning back—whichever comes first."

But from the camp of the besieging army came the eerie strains of Dean Martin's rendition of "Houston," the signal that no quarter would be given. The rebel leader assembled his men and drew a line on the marble floor with a Magic Marker, offering them the choice of escape or certain death. Marvin Zindler, who had joined the Borneans in their fight for freedom, was the first across the line. The next morning the RepublicBank fell, but out of defeat came victory. Two weeks later the rebels, under the command of Dr. Red Duke, defeated the Houstonians at the Battle of Sharpstown Mall.

On the way out of town we paid a visit to the RepublicBank, which is now a shrine maintained by the Daughters of Borneo. We entered the hushed lobby and walked over to the glass case containing the most famous relic in Texas—the silver toupee said to have been worn by Zindler during the furious battle that changed the course of history.

Buster was somber as we continued on our journey. I knew that this encounter with our great past had affected him deeply. But he had perked up by the time we got to Austin. What he wanted to see first was the Museum of the Hippie, which had been erected at the former site of Barton Springs, a giant spring-fed swimming pool that in my youth had been Austin's holy of holies. It had of course long since disappeared, since it stood in the way of an immense retail, residential, and toxic-waste storage complex named Walden Pond. Nevertheless the chief attraction of the museum was a vial of Barton Springs water, perpetually venerated by a series of Austin hippies in traditional costumes.

Next stop was the state capitol. Our legislative tradition had not changed much in the last fifty years. I noticed, as we passed through the senate chamber, that some forlorn legislator was still carrying on the hopeless battle to pass some form of gun control. Actually, it wasn't guns he was worried about anymore, it was PNDs. The PND—short for Personal Nuclear Device—was the ultimate handgun. Though it could deliver only a tiny fraction of a megaton, it could reduce a victim to a shadow on the sidewalk. Currently it was possible to buy a PND in any convenience store. "When PNDs are outlawed," an opponent of the bill was shouting, "only outlaws will have PNDs."

Buster and I snuck out of the debate and wandered through the seat of Texas government. The state was a much less governable place than it had been in my day. The governor had to contend with constant border skirmishes along the

Comal, where the newly independent Republic of Tex-Mex was flexing its muscles under the leadership of its octogenarian president, Henry Cisneros. The once smooth and forward-looking mayor of San Antonio was now a barefoot mystic who sequestered himself in the National Palace—the old Saint Anthony Hotel—and passed along cryptic pronouncements that appeared on the screen of an ancient Macintosh computer that the populace reverently referred to as El Viejo. The latest such message—"Gig 'em Aztecs"—had been particularly unsettling. Nobody knew what it meant, but the Texas State Guard had immediately been mobilized.

On the way out of the Capitol we ran into Governor Dong. He was dwarfed by two surly-looking men carrying ivory-handled PNDs and wearing bright orange tam-o'-shanters, which gave them away as Texas Rangers. "How yew?" the governor said, automatically shaking our hands as he walked past. "Like to stop and talk to you boys, but I gotta head on out to my ranch."

Buster was dumbstruck. There was no denying that the governor had a certain presence. He was one of the finest examples of that uniquely Texan type, the Vietnamese redneck. Dong was a self-made billionaire. In the early teens he had scored big with a chain of antigravity parlors, places where kids could go and float around and listen to music. That business went bust when President Springsteen's surgeon general issued a report on the hazards of weightlessness to growing bodies. Undaunted, Dong invested heavily in video implants and was well-positioned when the brain movie boom transformed communications. When he decided to run for governor, he had a base of 20 million subscribers into whose skulls he could send a signal at a moment's notice.

We stayed in Austin long enough to watch a football game between the Texas Longhorns and the Iceland Auks. I snoozed through most of it. I haven't much cared for football since the Texas legislature sanctioned genetic enhancement of linemen. It changed the whole complexion of the game. Back in the old days, when the colleges had to go out and actually buy players instead of building them from scratch, football had more integrity.

Buster cheered raucously as a Texas defensive guard, launching himself sixty feet into the air, blocked an Auk field goal.

"Damn mutants," I muttered.

"Don't be such a stick-in-the-mud," Buster said. "If you had your way, they'd probably still be playing on AstroTurf."

The next day we headed west, following the old abandoned highways out onto the plains.

"This is real cowboy country—right, Tex?" Buster asked.

"Used to be," I said. "Course that way of life died out a long time ago." But no sooner had I said it than I saw a cloud of dust on the horizon. Drawing closer, we saw it was a trail drive, a herd of shorthaired yaks being delivered to market by cowboys on Horse-a-matics. When the ramrod saw us, he dismounted and moseyed over. In the background, his mount shifted and settled on its pneumatic legs. It resembled one of those mechanical bulls they used to have back in the eighties, though of course those were just dumb machinery. The Horse-a-matic had an on-board computer that gave it the intelligence of a six-year-old child.

"Howdy," the ramrod said, much to Buster's delight, since it gave him the opportunity to say "Howdy" back.

"Fine lookin' yak herd," I said, to be sociable.

"Thanks," he answered. "But if I were you two, I'd turn back now."

"Why's that?"

"Quanah Bob's on the warpath."

Quanah Bob! At the mere mention of the name I felt the hair stand up on the back of my neck. The leader of the Comanche Liberation Organization was an old man, but he was still a fierce warrior. In his younger days he had been a brilliant lawyer who had filed suit after suit demanding the restitution of Comanche lands. When the courts failed him, he assembled an army, seized a large part of West Texas from prawn farmers, and announced the formation of the nation of Comanchería. He guarded its borders fiercely, and his warriors were said to be the finest cavalry in the world, capable of entering data into their Horse-a-matics with one hand and firing off bursts from their PNDs with the other.

"I reckon we'll take our chances with Quanah Bob," Buster told the drover, meaning to impress him.

"It's up to you, pilgrim," he answered. "But he don't like intruders. The only reason he lets us through is we give him trinkets—old silicon chips, that kind of thing."

The ramrod left, and Buster and I watched as the herd moved slowly north.

"Well," Buster said, getting back into the car, "we're burnin' daylight."

"You're not serious," I said. "You're not really planning to drive right smack through Comanchería?"

"A true Texan don't never turn back," he said. "That's what you told me."

I got into the car and slammed the door. If Buster wanted to see the wild West that bad I figured nothing I could say would stop him. We headed off toward a distant mesa, and sure enough, it wasn't long before we saw a line of Comanche warriors topping the rise.

"Let me do the talking," I said to Buster as they approached. Quanah Bob himself was in the lead. He was a gaunt old man dressed in a London Fog raincoat and wingtips. When I raised my hand in greeting he merely grunted.

"Let's kill them now," a young warrior shouted.

I could see Quanah Bob was thinking it over. He dismounted and began inspecting the car. After a moment he discovered the Mel Tillis tape and held it aloft to his followers, who sighed approvingly. Then he fixed me with a compelling stare.

"We are old men," he said. "We have seen many summers." He clapped me on the shoulder and regarded the cassette reverently. "This tape tells me that your heart is true, that you respect the old ways. Therefore we will not kill you."

That was mighty nice of them, but they did take the Civic, leaving us with a broken-down Horse-a-matic that we had to ride double on. The horse said its name was Dangerous Dan and that it was looking forward to serving us with complimentary coffee and soft drinks. "Please enter your destination," it requested.

"Okay, cowboy," I said to Buster when the Comanches had ridden off. "Where to now?"

"Dallas," he said. I punched it in, and Dangerous Dan began to lumber along. It took a while to get used to his uneven gait, and by the time we camped that night, we were both saddle-sore.

We traveled all the next day, and it was night again by the time we approached Dallas. Under the full moon we could make out the ruins of Las Colinas. Little was known about this once great community, though a recent popular book called *Suburbs of the Gods?* argued that it had been the home of some vanished superrace. It was certainly an eerie spot, and as we camped beside the canals and watched the moonlight play upon the water and empty buildings I thought of it as a modern Stonehenge.

Suddenly I saw a gondola cruising down one of the canals. It was filled with a dozen grim-looking men with cork-blackened faces. They were clad in fatigues and were heavily armed.

"Get down," I said to Buster.

We took cover behind a mesquite tree as the gondola passed silently in front of us.

"Who are they?" Buster whispered.

"Terrorists," I said. "Members of the Dallas Citizens' Council. I imagine they're going out to make a raid on city hall."

The Dallas Citizens' Council was a tough bunch. Long ago they had controlled the city, but over time their influence eroded to the point where they were driven underground. As terrorists, they had had their share of successes. They had once kidnapped a city councilman and threatened to execute him if the city did not immediately "renew its commitment to valet parking."

Tough as they were, it was obvious to anyone that their day was over. Dallas, the most notoriously laid-back city in America, had passed far beyond their grasp. It was a beacon for bohemians, misfits, and cranks of all stripes, a casual place where status and breeding counted for nothing but a good laugh.

Riding into town the next morning, we saw the results of the guerrillas' nighttime mission. Spray-painted on a dozen buildings was the legend "Dallas: The City That Doesn't Work." Already city work crews were busy responding to this latest attack, writing beneath the graffito a message of their own: "Who cares?"

We had ridden Dangerous Dan hard, and he finally collapsed next to a housing project on Preston Road. His last words were "Bury me deep." Buster removed his hat, but I wasn't as sentimental about machines as he was. As he pointed Dan's head toward the setting sun, I flagged down an air ricksha, and soon we were settled in against the upholstery as the driver pedaled high above the city.

"Where to?" he asked. He was a nice young Rastafarian with dreadlocks and bib overalls, probably an honor student at SMU.

"The fairgrounds," I said.

The rickshas were stacked up over the Hall of State, and we had to go into a holding pattern around Big Tex until we got clearance to land. When we finally got on the ground, the crowd was terrible. People surged through the Hall of Heroes, admiring the new statue of Twinkle Bayoud, the former Dallas socialite who had renounced all worldly goods and gone on to become known as the Mother Teresa of Texas. "I don't like crowds," I said to Buster. "I want to go home."

"Shush," he said. His eyes were fixed on Governor Dong, who was opening a time capsule that had been sealed fifty years ago during the sesquicentennial. He held the items up one by one as the crowd looked on in puzzled silence. There was a bottle of Liquid Paper, a bumper sticker that read "Oilfield Trash and Proud of It," an armadillo purse, a postcard depicting a jackalope (long thought to be a mythical animal until scientists turned up a skeleton near Terlingua in 1997), a menu from the Dobbs House at the DFW airport, and, finally, a horny toad—still alive, of course.

"One thing about Texas," Governor Dong told the crowd, as he watered the thirsty horny toad from an eyedropper, "it ain't never gonna change."

The crowd—Rastafarians, Borneans, Vietnamese, Comanches, even a few Baptists—roared their agreement.

"Admit it," Buster said, "you're proud to be a Texan."

"Well, gol-dog it," I answered, "I suppose I am."

While the air rickshas circled overhead, the governor led the crowd in singing "Texas, Our Texas." I could see there were tears in Buster's eyes as he stood there with his cowboy hat over his heart. I guess I blinked back a few myself. Hell, even Texans should be allowed a good cry about once every two hundred years. ❧

# WHERE HAVE ALL THE YOUNG FOLKS GONE?

[ CONTINUED FROM PAGE 106 ] in early, well-off retirement and the movement of manufacturing plants to small towns. The idea that yuppies are also moving to small towns has an incredible hold on our imagination, considering that there are no numbers to support it. In Texas the towns where the working, white-collar exurbanite population is big enough to make a difference can be counted on the fingers of one hand: Waxahachie, Fayetteville, Wimberley. The booming small towns are the ones with interstate-highway exits and Wal-Marts; past them, beyond the reach of the suburbs, it's still the same old story.

In the sixties 146 of the 254 counties in Texas lost population, and only 74 counties had a net in-migration of people. In the seventies the large overall increase in population and the spread of the Houston and Dallas suburbs into the countryside obscured the trend, but 46 counties still lost population. Most of them were in West Texas, especially the big empty stretch between Lubbock and Abilene—Last Picture Show country. Colorado County, where Nada and Garwood are, grew 6.7 per cent in the seventies, but most of the growth came in the county seat of Columbus, which is on I-10 and near the Austin Chalk oil boom. The Garwood census tract lost 3.5 per cent of its population, continuing a long, steady decline.

When people leave rural West Texas, they scatter—to Midland, Lubbock, Fort Worth, Albuquerque, Austin, Los Angeles. From small-town Colorado County they overwhelmingly go to the same place, Houston, which is eighty miles to the northeast. Houston, in turn, is largely made up of people who moved there from places like Garwood. Chicago was populated from Eastern Europe and Mississippi; Boston, from Ireland; Los Angeles, from the Midwest. In Texas, although illegal aliens and Michiganders get all the hype, the crucial fact about urbanization—the thing that makes Texas cities peculiarly Texan—is that Houston and Dallas drew the population that made them among the nation's biggest cities from their own hinterlands.

The mythology of urbanization grew out of the experience of Northern industrial cities, and it portrays moving from country to city as traumatic, even tragic. Think of Dreiser's Sister Carrie or Ralph Ellison's Invisible Man, of a thousand homesick old country songs, or of the electric blues; the move to the city uproots people and sets them down, after a hard passage, in a faraway place with a different value system. Big-city sin beckons, tempts, ruins. A wonderful capsule of

it all is the chilling climactic line in the song Detroit City, in which a hillbilly talks about his letters home boasting of the success he's become: "But by day I make the cars / And by night I make the bars / If only they could read between the lines!"

To understand urbanization in Texas fully requires resisting that pull and constructing a whole new paradigm in which, rather than the city swallowing up the country people, the country people conquer the cities. Sorry, Mr. Dreiser, and you too, Mr. Ellison, but I think the person who really has mastered the concept of the country boy gone to the big city as it is in Texas is Mac Davis. This came to me one night while I was watching the Tonight show in my hotel room in Houston after interviewing migrants from Garwood all day. Most of them lived in brand-new homes in subdivisions at the western edge of Houston, that is, the edge closest to Garwood, so they could go home a lot. Those homes, for the moment, had recreated the small-town feeling of living at the edge of town: on one side would be a development called something like Kings Crossing, A Totally Planned Community, and on the other side, open fields. The homes were comfortable, airy, and affordable. The nearby brand-new shopping centers were full of exactly what isn't in small towns anymore and what people miss: movie theaters, cheery crowded restaurants serving country-style Texas food, dry cleaners, banks.

On the Tonight show Mac chatted with Joan Rivers awhile and then got up to sing a song. It was about how, even though he's a success in the big city today, he still misses his little old hometown in Texas. He smiled, winked, looked soulfully at the camera. There was something exultantly phony about it; in Detroit City there is real pain, but in this song just a ritual obeisance was paid to the convention that moving to the city is supposed to be painful. Its real emotion was nostalgia. We, the audience, knew Mac wasn't about to leave L.A. and move back to West Texas, and he knew we knew. From the vantage point of Houston, why should he? It's not just that there isn't anything to do back home; it's that one can live a quasi-small-town life in the big city.

GARWOOD, NÉE RED BLUFF, WAS founded in 1901 at a bend in the Colorado River by three local businessmen who planned to build an irrigation system and create a rice-farming community. Their dream came true, though less by dint of their own efforts than by those of their bookkeeper, William S. Lehrer, who with his son, William K. Lehrer, bought out the original partners in 1926 and whipped things into shape. Today the Lehrers run Garwood. They own two hundred miles of irrigation canals, the town's rice dryer, substantial farms and ranches, a fertilizer and chemical business, and a propane and butane business. The only church in town is Lehrer Memorial Methodist, the cemetery is Lehrer Memorial. When William K. Lehrer died a few years back, he left a sizeable fortune.

The town peaked in the mid-thirties, just as rural Texas as a whole was peaking. It had a bank, a doctor, a realtor, a movie theater, a livery stable, a hotel, a drugstore, a baker, two butchers, three grocers, a small-scale department store, two cotton gins, a railroad depot, a white school system through high school, and a black school system through the eighth grade. Small towns like Garwood were the collective seat of civilization in Texas in those days. They were self-sufficient; they meant something.

The beginning of the end was the coming of paved highways. Situated as it was, in rainy, low-lying rice country, on the banks of a river then prone to flooding, with dirt roads as its link to the outside world, Garwood could be completely cut off by a big storm. When Highway 71 was paved in 1938 (at about the time the Colorado River was flood-proofed), Columbus, twenty miles to the north, and El Campo, twenty miles to the south, became quickly and reliably accessible. (Eagle Lake is thirteen miles to the northeast, but the road there wasn't paved until 1954.) Garwood's institutions, opened to competition from bigger towns, began to wither away.

Then, after World War II, came the combine, which arrived in Garwood in 1946, and the rice dryer, which the Lehrers built in 1947; they effectively eliminated the resident farm-labor class. Before the war, rice had been harvested by hand. Large teams of workers would go out in the fields, cut the stalks of rice, gather them into shocks, and leave them out to dry. Then they would go back to the fields and pitch the dried shocks into wagons pulled by mules, which would take the shocks to threshing machines that separated the rice grains from the stalks and sent them out a chute into sacks. During the war, German prisoners of war had to be brought in from a nearby camp, or there would have been no rice harvest. Now the combine, powered by a gas engine, both cuts the stalks and separates the grain; the rice dryer, right on Highway 71, dries and sacks the rice under controlled conditions. Harvest crews today are a fifth the size they were in the days before the combine and are mostly made up of migrant labor. People who used to do that work either had to become farmers or move to the city.

The third major blow to Garwood has been the bountiful crops that agricultural technology has produced in the United States and much of the rest of the world over the last ten or fifteen years. In 1973 Garwood rice was selling for $25 a hundredweight; this year, in the medium grades, it's about $8.80. Farmers aren't going broke, but their children are figuring out, after four years at Texas A&M or

even two years at Wharton Junior College, that they can do a lot better in a different field. When a farm does pass on to a new generation, the story one often hears is that it goes to one child, where in the past two or even three might have gone back and made a living from it.

Garwood's doctor, baker, butcher shop, movie theater, cotton gins, and railroad depot are long gone. So is the bank, the victim of too many robberies in the Depression, though its building–one story, two rooms, clapboard, with an arch over the door for a touch of grandeur–still stands on the main street. G. W. Carver, the black elementary school, closed in 1968 when the school system was integrated. Garwood High School closed in 1970, when Rice Consolidated High School opened outside Altair, ten miles up the road. Priesmeyer's department store threw in the towel a few years ago. So did the second grocery store in town and the Lehrers' feed-and-implement store. The Dairy Queen closed. The Chapman Hotel converted to a private hunting lodge, the Bucksnag Club, now used in the fall duck-and-goose season. There's one beer hall in Nada, so traditional that it still doesn't serve mixed drinks; old-timers remember when there were three or four in Garwood.

Today there are two gas stations and the rice dryer out on the highway and, back on Main Street, a grocery store, a lumberyard, a rice merchant's office, a blacksmith shop, a barbecue shack, and the City Cafe, of which William N. Lehrer, who now runs the family businesses, says, "That poor lady tries to close every once in a while, but the old people don't know where they'd eat, so she stays open." The houses are neatly kept up, but there aren't any new ones. The population is down to perhaps six hundred (because Garwood isn't incorporated, that's a guess). It is a lovely, green, friendly town. Except for a few details–some new siding here, an abandoned building there–it is so nearly untouched by the events of the last fifty years that it feels a little like a movie set.

It was Garwood's good luck that just while its economic base was seriously eroding, Houston was booming. To the extent that there has been economic development in Garwood outside of rice farming, it has come as spillover from Houston. The hunters come from there, a Garwood gravel boom supplied Houston construction, and one of the rice farmers has turned to growing St. Augustine grass to supply the suburban lawn market. Houston has helped stave off the feeling of isolation that comes from being in a small town, too; except for a few diehards, people from Garwood go there frequently, to shop at the Galleria or see a game at the Summit. Garwood is too far away to be a suburb, but it's only a little more than half an hour *from* the suburbs.

Most important, Houston has so far provided an inexhaustible labor market– and one conveniently close to home–for

the displaced children of Garwood. The kids' moving away, usually to Houston, is almost a universal experience in Garwood; I didn't meet anyone over fifty who didn't have a child there. While I was interviewing William N. Lehrer, his secretary typed up, after asking around the office, a list of 68 people from Garwood who had moved away; 42 of them had gone to Houston.

IN DALLAS, THE RESIDENTS' SMALL-town origins manifest themselves in the desire to give the whole place a small-town atmosphere: orderliness, a sense of community, respect for the city fathers, a certain conformity of thought and behavior. In Houston, the small-town immigrants create their own little small towns within the city and don't worry about the whole. There are older neighborhoods in Houston that correspond to particular parts of the countryside–Kashmere Gardens to East Texas, Missouri City to the southeastern plain. In the old days people from Garwood and Nada would gravitate toward Thirty-fourth and Studemont, then the center of the Czech subculture in Houston. "They had dances, and it was just like the country," says James Hopkins, Garwood's rice merchant, who lived there back in the thirties.

Today about all that remains of that world is the Bill Mraz Ballroom, on Thirty-fourth; urban Czechs are much too assimilated to maintain a neighborhood. People from Garwood move as if by tropism to whatever suburb is the farthest west at the time they migrate. The ones who moved in the fifties are in Sharpstown and Alief; the latest wave landed in Katy, Addicks, and Richmond. It is difficult to find anyone among them who will describe city life as painful, alienating, or corrupting–this is Katy, not *Sister Carrie*. The closest it gets is the amusing story everyone has about his first apartment in a slightly chaotic complex. Divorce? Drugs? Yes, but they have those in Garwood now too. Crime? None in Garwood, and little in their parts of Houston. Sex? Never underestimate how much of that there is in a small town.

People in Garwood today work either for themselves, on a farm, or for a small business in one of the bigger towns nearby. People from Garwood in Houston usually work for big corporations: Shell, Tenneco, InterFirst. In Garwood, during the several slack times of the year, it's easy to pop down to Palacios on a nice weekday and go fishing. Surely that must be hard to give up. "Well," people from Garwood say, "yes, maybe, but back home there isn't that regular paycheck either, or the pension or the medical plan." The long hours and the commuting and the competition notwithstanding, country people know that the corporate life is a much better deal than farming. The country-to-city migration is lucky for the corporations too– country people make good employees. They respect authority, work hard, and live stable, family-oriented lives. They don't have the urban feeling that if you act important people will think you *are* important, because they don't know who you really are; they're too used to a world where you can't put anything over on anyone for that. People from Garwood, in their free time, seem to go not to smoky, anything-goes honky-tonks but to church, to suburban shopping centers – and back to Garwood.

The exception to the rule of a smooth transition is black people, who make up about 20 per cent of Garwood's population. Their degree of upward mobility is much more spectacular, frequently from poorly educated field hand to skilled craftsman or white-collar manager in one generation. But the idea of the city streets not only as an opportunity but also as a trap that can drag you down is real in a way that it isn't for whites. Stroll down Eldridge in West Houston, then Lyons Avenue in the Fifth Ward, and you'll see why.

Most of Garwood's blacks live just north of town in an area known as Vox, short for Vox Populi, which was its name back when it was a separate community like Nada. The blacks and whites know each other because the town is so small, and they mingle when business calls for it but never socially. Viewed from Vox, Garwood seems much less a totally benign little town. "When I came along," says Tonie Williams, who is 68, "we just had a little old schoolhouse, and one teacher taught four or five grades. If you were going in eighth grade you might not have books, because the white children were still using them. So you'd stay in seventh. I don't know if I finished high school or not. And the school board didn't furnish desks or fuel. We only had six or seven months, never nine months. The school board was all white farmers. They'd fix the school year so it would let out just about the time they needed you in the fields."

Tonie Williams' oldest son, Wilbert, went to Prairie View A&M at his father's insistence and then to Houston, where at first he had trouble finding a job. He ended up in Austin as an executive in a state agency. He is entirely nostalgic about Garwood and even about segregation – black teachers cared about black students, pushed them and kept them in line, he says. But his father isn't. "Opportunity just started here in '64, '65," Tonie says. "And it wasn't on a humanitarian basis. It wasn't on the goodness of the people, because if it was left to them we'd still have segregation." To that, Wilbert says, "My father is a whole lot more bitter than I am because he experienced a lot more than I did. He always sheltered us from it. He always told us there'd be a better day."

WHAT PEOPLE FROM GARWOOD think of as the true shocker about city life isn't the hours or the traffic or the money but the privacy. "Everything you do in a small town is common

knowledge," says Daryl Hunt, the son of a rice farmer, himself a bank officer. "Let's say you go in the hospital; in a day, everybody knows you did and why. Some things that people would like to keep private become major topics. An affair. A foreclosure. They meet in the City Cafe and get the gossip from the *Eagle Lake Leader-News*. In Houston I don't even look at the foreclosure section."

To give small-town closeness its due, there's a good side. Every business in Garwood extends credit, not for its customers' convenience but because at certain times of the year the customers don't have much money; when they do, they'll get caught up. Pat Berger, a fire protection technician from Nada now living in Pasadena, told me about his father, who worked in the rice dryer, lost a leg, and couldn't work anymore. Mr. Lehrer continued to pay him full wages until he died. Wilbert Williams talked of his aunts and his teachers who checked up on him when his parents weren't around. That doesn't happen in Houston. But the sense of liberation from being constantly watched and talked about is powerful, enough so to be the greatest of all the city's advantages. To have your life be yours and no one else's, to be able to sit nursing a beer in a dark bar after work without anyone's needing to hear about it, to know that all your neighbors don't know much about your marriage and your finances – these things are what is really different about living in Houston.

First-generation immigrants to the city in Texas always think about moving back. It's almost a convention. Maybe, with a hometown as close as Garwood, they could stand the commute. Maybe they could get a job nearby or buy some land, thinking ahead to retirement. The second generation is different, though. The country is just where they go to visit Grandma, and their parents' stories about butchering pigs and waking up at dawn have become the next thing to family jokes. The references to rural life that assault the senses in the suburban sprawl of West Houston – every subdivision advertised as providing "country living," every restaurant called a cafe – can't mean much to them and will surely fade away in time. In that sense the victory of the country people in Houston is incomplete; the city will get their children in the end.

At the St. Mary's Parish Festival in Nada, I met a man named Lawrence Krenek who works for an oil company. He was sweating and beaming as he roamed around the dusty ground from auction to bingo to barbecue pits, trailed by his two teen-aged daughters. He told me he had gone to Houston seventeen years ago because his father, a rice farmer, told him it was easier to make it there. It was good advice, but he still comes home once a month. I asked him if his daughters were excited about being at the festival. He rolled his eyes. "Oh, yes. They wanted to know if it was air-conditioned." ❧

THE RISE OF THE CITIES
# HOT PANTS SPECIAL

[ CONTINUED FROM PAGE 110 ]
forgot to put my hot pants on underneath. And I got to work and started to take off my skirt and I was standing there in my underwear. I mean I didn't get it all the way off, but I went, 'Oh, my God.'

"When I went into it I was scared that Southwest might not make it. But everybody worked so hard. There were only twenty flight attendants and maybe twelve pilots, and you knew everybody in the office. And they knew you, from the president on down. Everybody was family.

"My very first flight was to Houston from Dallas. We had two planes, one going to Houston, one going to San Antonio, and I used to just go back and forth to Houston all day long. Back and forth. And then all of a sudden they had a new route between Houston and San Antonio, and that was a big deal. That first year we would have anywhere from three to twelve people on the airplane, and there were times when we left with no people. Still, you had to get the plane down to Houston for whoever might show up. But anybody that flew with us definitely came back.

"We just had fun with them. It was party with them all day, you know, kid with them, get them drunk, sit down and talk to them, play cards, anything to pass the flight away. They didn't have a chance to be left alone because we didn't let them. We'd introduce a lot of men to each other, and sometimes our passengers ended up having business deals together. We still have passengers that have been with us since the first day. We know them by name and they know us by name, and we know each other's little habits. You learn a lot about people. They have different personalities from different parts of the state. Like Austin people – it's always orange juice. Houston and Dallas were always coffee.

"It got real successful within two years, it was so cheap, and all the flights started to get full. That's when you realized, 'Hey, we're going to make it!' Now we're a larger carrier. We fly to twenty-five cities and have fifty-six planes. It's just amazing to me how many planes there are.

"There are nine of us originals left. This month I'm flying with the girl who is number one in seniority. I'm three out of a thousand. It's really neat for me because the employees have profit sharing and I'm totally vested now. I was flying out to L.A. with another original flight attendant, Mary, and a new girl. And this passenger, being from California, didn't know the Southwest story – that we started in Texas as a commuter airline. He was having a pretty good time, and he asked the new girl, 'Who owns this airline?' And she just stood up and said, 'Paula and Mary.' " ❧

INTERVIEWED BY CATHERINE CHADWICK

# THE TIDE TURNS

[ CONTINUED FROM PAGE 123 ]
on the morning he became governor few people knew him well. Certainly no one expected that Shivers, whose major talent seemed to be a gift for inoffensiveness, would become the toughest and most powerful governor in the history of the state, and that in his seven years in office–longer than any other governor–he would be the pivot that turned Texas from the rural populism of the past to the modern, urban, two-party politics of the future. It is the tragedy of his career that the first victim of that political revolution would be Allan Shivers.

One person who thought he knew Shivers was a young public relations man in Austin named J. J. "Jake" Pickle, now the congressman from Texas' tenth district. Pickle was looking for a candidate to run for statewide office, and he had approached Shivers while Shivers was still lieutenant governor. "Within a few weeks Beauford Jester was dead," Pickle recalls. "Shortly thereafter Allan called me in and said, 'Jake, if you want to get in this fight, let's do some talking.' " For the next six months Pickle found himself on the road, setting up a political organization from scratch.

Texas at that time was composed of warring political tribes–labor, liberals, Dixiecrats, Texas Regulars–all competing for supremacy in a single chaotic, deeply divided, wildly antagonistic Democratic party. The organization that Pickle put together for Shivers' first race for governor was a political miracle, brought about in part because no one knew Shivers well enough to understand his politics. He had been elected state senator from Port Arthur with labor support, and although he had voted for antilabor bills, he had voted against the right-to-work law. Businessmen felt at home with him because he was rich and voted against a state income tax. He was a careful segregationist in public, although one of his sons attended the only integrated school in Austin. "In a one-party state you have to have a personal organization," Shivers later observed. His was never surpassed.

Shivers moved quickly to establish himself. Just six months after taking office, he called a special session of the Legislature to overhaul the state's mental homes and tubercular hospitals. "I have seen epileptics eating in bathrooms for lack of dining space," Shivers told the Legislature. "I saw seventy-seven aged and mentally ill women locked up in a condemned building." His speech was the first note of the modern era of Texas politics. "None of us likes special sessions, nor do we like to talk of treasury deficits and tax measures," he continued. "But when the only alternative is to close our state hospitals and turn out the helpless insane, the needy seniles, the epileptics and the feeble-minded to fend for themselves, then no choice exists." He went on to describe the state in terms seldom heard from the governor's office: "Texas, the proud Lone Star state, first in oil, forty-eighth in mental hospitals. First in cotton, worst in tuberculosis. First in raising goats, last in caring for its state wards." It was Shivers' finest moment. In 1950 he won the Democratic primary nomination by a landslide.

"Allan was born a strong person," Pickle says. "You didn't snow him; you didn't excite him or slap his back. You could see him make decisions as you were talking to him. He might give you a little laugh or a chuckle, but other than that there was not much drama to Shivers. He was a cool hombre. He wasn't mean, he was just tough."

As Texas entered the fifties it was burdened with all the problems of an emerging nation. There were roads to be built, and cities. Veterans demanded housing and jobs. Hospitals and schools and public institutions were breaking down from chronic underfunding. Mexican Americans and blacks lived in a state of peonage. But Shivers made none of those his chief cause. The people he had gathered around him were Texas' business elite who saw the expansion of the state's growing industrial base as the answer to every problem. To them, and to Shivers as well, there was really only one issue. That was the tidelands.

The question was simple. If you were standing on the beach at low tide and took a step into the Gulf of Mexico, were you walking on federal land or deeper into Texas? That question had never interested the federal government until the thirties, when Texas began selling oil and gas leases in the Gulf. Secretary of the Interior Harold Ickes announced in 1937 that the federal government owned the minerals in the coastal waters. In 1947 the U.S. Supreme Court agreed. In Texas, revenue from the offshore leases went into a fund to support public schools. "Don't let them take the tidelands from the schoolchildren of Texas," said the billboards, which were backed by oil companies that preferred paying state royalties of 12.5 per cent rather than the 37.5 per cent federal royalty. In the meantime Congress passed two bills returning the tidelands to the states. President Truman vetoed both.

Another blow soon followed. Since the days of the Republic, Texas had defined its coastal boundary as extending three leagues into the sea, a distance of about ten and a half miles. But the Supreme Court ruled in 1950 that Texas had entered the Union on an equal footing with the rest of the states, and therefore its seaward boundary extended only three miles, the same as other coastal states. In one stroke Texas became smaller by 2.6 million acres. "The tidelands was the spark, the catalyst that caused the state to split," says Pickle. "That was the beginning of the effort by an organized group of conservatives to give leadership, and Shivers was their man."

The tidelands provided an ideal issue for Shivers. His political vision was limited to Texas; he had none of the national interests or ambitions of Lyndon Johnson, soon to become his rival for power. Shivers had chances for national office; three times in his career he turned down offers of Cabinet positions. By choice and by temperament he was strictly a regional figure. His governorship represented the high-water mark of the one-party system and its "Texas first, last, and always" approach to politics. But the high irony of Shivers' stand on the tidelands is that it led him straight to the national Republican party and thus put Texas on course to becoming the two-party state it is today.

In 1952 Shivers broke with the national Democratic party over the tidelands. He endorsed Republican Dwight Eisenhower, who supported Texas' position, for president instead of Democrat Adlai Stevenson. Even before the Democratic convention in Chicago, Shivers had shown little enthusiasm for Stevenson. (Upon meeting Stevenson earlier that year, Mrs. Shivers had observed, "No one who wears white shoes will ever be elected president of the United States.") Texas liberals went to Chicago suspecting that Shivers would bolt the national ticket. They formed a rival delegation led by former San Antonio mayor Maury Maverick, who warned the credentials committee that the Texas Democratic party was a hotbed of schismatic movements with no loyalty to the national party, including Texas Regulars, Dixiecrats, states' rights Democrats, and "now Shivercrats"–giving title to a movement that was as yet unborn.

Lyndon Johnson met Shivers at the airport and took him to Sam Rayburn's room in the Blackstone Hotel. As Rayburn, the convention chairman, told the story, the two men struck a deal. Shivers gave his word that he would support the ticket, and Rayburn agreed to seat the Shivers delegation, which was filled with some of the most conservative men in Texas politics. Shivers' side of the story was that he had told Rayburn only that he had no *intention* of not supporting the nominee. Their misunderstanding led eventually to the bloodiest party fight in the history of Texas politics.

That fall the Shivercrats carried Texas for Eisenhower, who signed the tidelands bill during the next session of Congress. In a single election Shivers had changed Texas political tradition. Ticket-splitting was acceptable; the long exile of the state Republican party was at an end.

Shivers himself was at the highest point of his popularity. HE HAS TEXAS IN THE PALM OF HIS HAND, said the *Saturday Evening Post*. But back in Washington, Sam Rayburn was fuming. He believed

Shivers had lied to him, and once Rayburn hated a man he hated him thoroughly and forever. He threatened to purge his library of every book with Shivers' name in it. More to the point, he began to scheme about getting the state Democratic machinery out of the governor's hands before the 1956 presidential election.

Shivers was having trouble of his own in his reelection campaign in 1954 against Ralph Yarborough, the candidate of the labor-liberals. Yarborough had run poorly against Shivers two years before, but now Shivers was breaking precedent by running for a third term. The first of several scandals in Shivers' administration was just surfacing—this one concerning the bankruptcies of some insurance companies in the state, including a firm that had a former Shivers aide on its payroll at $1000 a month. In addition, Yarborough had discovered a curious financial transaction in Shivers' own background. At a rally in Belton, while Shivers was on the platform, Yarborough flourished a deposition showing that in 1946 Shivers had purchased a $25,000 option on a piece of land from Lloyd Bentsen, Sr., then sold it back to a Bentsen-controlled company for an astounding profit of $425,000. "This transaction is one of the most unusual business deals ever made in Texas. . . . What did the governor sell for $450,000? Was it land? No, he didn't own any land. Was it an option? No, the option had already expired. Was it mineral interests? No. . . . Was it water rights? No." When Yarborough finished, the crowd was roaring with cynical glee.

The big issue in the campaign, however, came out of Shivers' hometown of Port Arthur, where retail clerks and waitresses who had been earning $25 for a 44-hour week decided to go on strike. Because some of their leaders were avowed communists, Shivers called a special session of the Legislature to make membership in the Communist party a crime punishable by death. That was too much even for the Texas legislature, which decided that twenty years in prison and a $20,000 fine was a sufficient penalty. Shivers asserted that communists were supporting Yarborough and that "the pushing of a single button in Moscow" would bring the state to a halt.

Early in the campaign, before anyone else knew he was headed for a runoff, Shivers had made a tour of law offices in Houston, which were always a source of supporters for him. He returned to the capital depressed. He had breakfast with his friend Horace Busby, a reporter who had gone to work for Lyndon Johnson. "You know, Buzz, we're in trouble," Shivers told him, "and we're in trouble with the kind of people who have always supported me. When I go into those law firms, the senior officers make all over me, they talk about running me for president. But when I say, now I'd like to meet some of your juniors, it's a different story. They

resent me; I can see it in their faces. They want their chance. They're tired of the kind of people who've always controlled things in Texas, and they're going to take that control away."

"He was aware," says Busby, "that Texas was changing, becoming a metropolitan, sophisticated state, and that his politics were from another era."

But Allan Shivers was not going to be pushed aside by Ralph Yarborough and the labor-liberals. One Sunday morning during the strike a camera crew appeared in downtown Port Arthur just after dawn. It filmed the deserted streets, the littered gutters, the closed stores, and produced what is still Texas' most famous political spot. The message of "The Port Arthur Story," as the ad was called, was that labor had turned Port Arthur into a ghost town. In reality, the town simply was not awake. "This was in the early days of television," remembers Jake Pickle, whose firm, Syers, Pickle and Wynn, produced the film. "TV was very young then, but it was powerful." Shivers, who had led Yarborough by just 23,000 votes in the first primary, won the runoff by 92,000 votes and eased into his third full term.

IT'S BAD LUCK IN POLITICS TO STAY IN one place too long; you grow bored; you lose your edge; you are held accountable for others' mistakes. The last term of the Shivers administration opened with the land commissioner, Bascom Giles, declining to take the oath of office. Soon he would be in prison, convicted of conspiring with landsharks to bilk the state out of millions of dollars in connection with the veterans' land program. Another insurance company went bankrupt, months after the do-nothing state insurance board had known it was insolvent. During the Shivers administration nearly half a million people lost money they had invested in shaky insurance companies, while Shivers' appointees on the insurance board were accepting fat tips and Hawaiian vacations from the companies they were supposed to regulate.

The lowest point of his reign came at the very end, when he had already decided to retire and might have redeemed himself without worrying about political consequences. The U.S. Supreme Court ordered the little North Texas town of Mansfield to open its high school to black students. The mayor and the chief of police fled as a mob took over the town, seizing the newspaper, blocking the highway, and surrounding the school with angry, violent protestors. Instead of using state power to enforce the law, Shivers dispatched the Texas Rangers to uphold segregation and to prevent blacks from entering the school.

Shivers hinted about running for a fourth term, and the silence that followed was humiliating. The newspapers that had routinely endorsed him stayed mum. His phone did not ring with pledges from sup-

porters. At the end Allan Shivers was as puzzling a figure as he had been when he first assumed office.

Who was he really? Was he the man who built the hospitals, reformed the prisons, brought roads to the farmers, increased old-age pensions and created the Texas Employment Commission, helped bring education to mentally retarded children—the man who had been the most progressive and enlightened governor Texas had ever known? Or was he a racist who used state power to preserve segregation; a demagogue who welcomed Senator Joseph McCarthy—"a real American"—to Texas; an influence peddler who rewarded his friends and overlooked their crimes; a tool of the lobbies and the big-money boys; a phony reformer who financed his social programs with increased consumer taxes and higher tuitions, while letting the valuable mineral resources of the state be piped away, virtually untaxed, wastefully squandered, making the few rich and keeping the many poor? In the end, no one really knew Allan Shivers. "He might have been a good governor," Ronnie Dugger wrote in the *Texas Observer*, "but he was too late for the past, and too early for the future. It is too bad."

Before he left office Shivers had one last fight in him. He wanted to lead the Texas delegation to the 1956 Democratic convention in Chicago that August. First, however, his supporters had to control the precinct meetings across Texas in May. Whoever won in the precincts would control the party machinery, which had been in Shivers' grasp since he became governor. State party chairman George Sandlin, a Shivers man, sent out letters asking Democrats to back the governor. But Sam Rayburn had been waiting four years for this moment. "I'll have to take that boy's pants down before I'm through," he vowed.

The trouble was, although Rayburn was Speaker of the House, he was not a figure of power in his own state. He had no organization. Moreover, Rayburn knew that even a weakened Shivers was a formidable opponent. There was only one man who might beat Shivers on his own ground, and that was Rayburn's protégé, Lyndon Johnson.

"Johnson always figured, since back in the thirties, when Shivers became the youngest state senator, that the two of them had a rendezvous," says Horace Busby. "He figured Shivers would be the principal challenger in his life." Johnson himself once remarked, "Allan and I understand each other. We cut each other with the same knife."

Rayburn leaked to his hometown paper, the *Bonham Favorite*, that he wanted Lyndon Johnson to head the Texas delegation as a favorite-son nominee for the presidency. That little squib, as Rayburn called it, was later selected as the Associated Press's story of the year in Texas. Certainly it was news to Lyndon Johnson.

Rayburn hadn't asked him if he wanted to run for president. But he had correctly gauged Johnson's ambition. "I repeat what I have said many times in the past," Johnson said publicly. I am not running for any office."

He had no quarrel with Shivers—in fact he had been doing his best to avoid one—but Rayburn had put him on the spot. "The minute I turn my back on Rayburn, I am destroyed," Johnson agonized. "They'll say the rabbit in him is coming out." He decided to fight.

The squeeze was on. Politicians all over the state began to dread the sound of the telephone. For most there was really no choice. Johnson was Senate majority leader; Shivers was a lame-duck governor; one man waxed as the other waned.

Shivers and Johnson entered the ring reluctantly, talking compromise. Shivers would accept Johnson as favorite son if Johnson would give him the delegation. But Rayburn wanted Shivers crushed. Johnson later described what followed as "a campaign of hatred and prejudice . . . without equal in modern times."

For Shivers there was something exhilarating about this last campaign. He had always been a cautious man, and he had never lost an election. But now he was in a fight he knew he was going to lose, and he was swinging free. Johnson was trying to hold onto his dignity—after all, he was running for president—but once Shivers started digging up bodies there was no holding back.

"Senator Johnson," Shivers cried in Dallas, "do you favor segregation in the public schools? Answer yes or no." Johnson dodged: he was against forced integration. Shivers resurrected the oft-told tale that Johnson had stolen the 1948 senatorial election and warned that "George Parr will not be counting the votes at the Texas state convention." Johnson suggested that Shivers was responsible for the attempted suicide of the president of a failed insurance company. "If he wants to know about a suicide," Shivers shot back, "let me call one to his mind," referring to the mysterious death in prison of a George Parr hand who had promised to tell the truth about the 1948 election.

Voters couldn't believe it. These two men knew every arcane, dirty secret in the state, and they were tearing the lid off. In the meantime Johnson had been quietly making deals with the labor-liberals. On May 5, 1956, the precincts voted, giving the labor-liberals, who had been organizing since Yarborough's defeat in 1954, 1100 votes, Johnson 800, and Shivers just 620. The labor-liberals had pledged themselves to Johnson, Shivers had lost. "The voice of the demagogue has been heard throughout our state," Johnson crowed. "The people listened, then voted for the path of moderation. Let demagogues everywhere listen and take notice."

But the Shivercrats survived. That fall Eisenhower carried Texas again. Johnson

and Rayburn conspired with old Shivers hands to steal the party machinery from their erstwhile allies, the labor-liberals.

IN DECEMBER OF THAT YEAR JOHNSON got a phone call. It was Allan Shivers. He said, "Get your own bottle of red whiskey and come down here."

Johnson related the story a few years later to a group of young aides. They were spending the weekend at the plush Virginia estate of Johnson's patron, George R. Brown. Among the aides was Billy Lee Brammer, whose soon-to-be-published novel *The Gay Place* would include a major character modeled after Lyndon Johnson. They were all relaxing after "another enormous meal with servants hovering all over," Brammer wrote his wife, while Johnson told his audience how he and Shivers had sat from three in the afternoon until midnight, Shivers with a fifth of bourbon, Johnson with a fifth of scotch. "We sat there throwing lances at each other, dodging, jumping like stuck pigs when we was hit."

And then, wrote Brammer, "Somebody said too bad about Shivers. LBJ said, yes, he had everything, almost. He had the head and he had the heels, and he knew how to use them, but he didn't have a heart. No emotion. Didn't love the people. Somebody said he used to love the people, and LBJ said yes, but doesn't anymore. LBJ waved his arm about the room and said, 'Here's how you forget. You sit here at a big dining table before a crackling fire and carpets three-inch thick. Now tell me. Are you very worked up about the suffering in the world at this moment? That's what you have to watch out for.' "➤

UP FROM COLONIALISM
**GONE TO TEXAS**

[ CONTINUED FROM PAGE 139 ] now to remember that Texas for all its pride once felt powerless, and for all its independence, inferior. Not without cause, Texas darkly saw itself as little more than a colony of the all-powerful East. Texas supplied the resources—the cotton, the cattle, the oil—but the fundamental economic decisions were made elsewhere. As late as 1956, only 7 of *Fortune*'s 500 largest publicly owned industrial corporations were based in Texas. None was in Houston. Only Dresser Industries in Dallas ranked among the top 200. The image that Texas newspaper cartoonists used for generations to depict their state was a white-haired, white-suited Southern gentleman known as Old Man Texas. He was courtly, genteel, and nobody's fool, but he seemed a bit tromped on, coping as best he could with the schemes of far-off robber barons. Old Man Texas must have squared with popular conceptions, else the cartoonists would not have kept on using him. Today, when 38 of the Fortune 500 are in Texas, his appearance and behavior would leave readers mystified.

Before 1969, most people who moved to Texas did so because they wanted to. After 1969, many came because they *had* to, because their companies told them, as Shell told John O'Driscoll, "Your desk is moving to Houston. If you want to be behind it, you'll go too." The consequences of that are still with us—in pastrami, sailboats, Italian restaurants, the opera, and the Texas Republican party. What happened is bigger than Shell, but Shell is the one that started it.

WHY DID SHELL LEAVE NEW YORK? And why did it choose Houston? Taxes and the cost of living, for a start. The documents outlining the corporate thought process are lost, but by 1967 Shell had grown discontented with New York's high tax rates. The company was also having difficulty attracting employees to Manhattan, where prices were among the highest in the country and commuting was so time-consuming that workers routinely spent only seven hours a day on the job. Rents in midtown New York were approaching $13 a square foot, more than double the going rate of less congested cities. Shell commissioned Stanford Research Institute to look for other sites, emphasizing those in the Central Time Zone, where communications and transportation were cheaper for a company with nationwide interests.

The principal contenders were Tulsa, New Orleans, Atlanta, Dallas, and Houston. The finalists were the two Texas cities. Houston was chosen, according to reports published at the time, because of its growth potential, its climate (a fact that would later astound employees experiencing their first Gulf Coast summer), its schools, its labor supply, and its abundant office space, as well as such social amenities as the symphony and what the *New York Times* called "the intellectual oasis" around Rice University. Perhaps most decisive was what Shell Oil president Harry Bridges described, with an ominous lack of foresight, as Houston's "broad-based and healthy economy." The fact that Shell already had 5500 employees in the area could not have been a disadvantage.

In 1969 Harry Bridges's predecessor summoned Shell executive Richard Bauer to his office and asked him to coordinate a move of such staggering proportions that author Vance Packard would later use it as an illustration of American rootlessness in his book *A Nation of Strangers*. Shell then had 2200 employees in New York. Two thousand of them would go forth to Houston under the tutelage of self-described wagon master Bauer.

Now retired, Bauer lives in Houston's Wilchester West, one of those developments whose names seem to have been constructed by reshuffling the syllables of various fashionable New York suburbs. It is a sedate neighborhood where the houses—somebody's dream home, every one—are interspersed with still-young magnolia trees.

"We did it in summer, because of school," he recalls. The aim was to move two hundred families each weekend: household goods, office furniture, everything. "The trucks showed up Friday at New York—we brought in moving vans from all over the country—and the employee was in his Houston office on Monday." Families and personal effects followed, so that just one workday was lost in the move. All summer long, the vans flocked southward like migratory birds.

Before moving, each employee was given a week-long, expense-paid trip to Houston, spouse included, to select a new house. The company paid resettlement allowances to underwrite the cost of carpets, utility deposits, even Texas driver's licenses. It paid commissions and closing costs on the sale of the old houses and the purchase of the new. In all, the move cost Shell about $35 million, an expense recouped by the company in just four years.

That $35 million included severance pay for the few employees—mostly secretaries—who chose to stay in New York even if it cost them their jobs. "Everyone was given the option of moving, from the top right down to the porters and the clerks in the mailroom," says Bauer. "It was the only fair thing to do." Ninety-five per cent of the professionals went along. For most, the Texas vaccination took. In 1972 the *New York Times* reported that "no more than a dozen employees have disliked Houston enough to quit and return to New York." The final to-tal was probably fewer than fifty. Bauer himself plans to spend his retirement years in Fulshear.

The immigrants met Houston, and Houston met the immigrants. To go back and read accounts of that era is like unlocking a time capsule. The family of one employee sent monthly "CARE packages" of New York goodies to supplement the dozen loaves of Italian bread she carried back from Manhattan at Christmas. Another expressed surprise at finding trees in Houston instead of the expected desert. A third informed the *Chronicle* of a bug at her apartment "so big and frightening that I called my boyfriend over to kill it." The newcomers were uniformly gleeful at Houston's low real estate prices, the availability of domestic help, and the amiability of Texans. "I don't get mad all day most days here," one said, "but in New York you usually didn't get past nine-thirty before getting mad at somebody." Their dissatisfaction focused on the steamy weather, the minuscule home lots ("smaller than in Connecticut," groused one buyer), the comparative scarcity of weekend getaway spots, and the quality of the beef ("tougher than in New York"). Outright derision was reserved for the Texas liquor laws. In those brown-bag days, open saloons were forbidden by the state constitution and evaded by ubiquitous private clubs. But not coincidentally, those laws were among the first to go when migration from the East accelerated. The new Texans' presence rippled across the state in unexpected ways. Perhaps their palates could not distinguish good barbecue from bad, but they knew excellence in a bagel when they saw it. Perhaps they said "root" for route and "seerup" for syrup, but by 1978 Austin had its first Republican governor in a hundred years and the conservative Democratic Bourbons were on the ropes.

P AST THE OLD VENETIAN RESTAU-rant, past McGinnis Rolls-Royce, past the soccer teams practicing on the grounds of St. John Vianney Catholic Church, past the entrance gate to Nottingham Forest VIII, Bob and Joan Dunphy's house is the one with the flagpole and the Lone Star flag.

"We're Texas football people," Bob explains redundantly amid the photographs of three sons in gridiron garb, all veterans of Spring Branch high schools. It wasn't always so. Dunphy grew up in Massachusetts; his wife inherited one of the oldest houses on Cape Cod; in their lives as corporate gypsies with Shell, they spent a happy year in Wilton, Connecticut, from where he commuted daily to the company's marketing office in Queens.

The genial Dunphy, whose job at Shell is now community relations, vividly remembers his first encounter with the community. At a neighbor's house party the weekend after he arrived, a young lady politely inquired where the family was from.

"We just moved down from Springfield, Illinois," he answered.

"You Yankee," she said with a smile.

"Oh, you don't know the half of it," he said, rising to the bait. "What would you say if I told you I was born and bred in Boston?"

"Well then you Damyankee."

The verb "to be" wasn't used in those statements, he recalls. "And her timing was as though Jack Benny had worked on it."

Damyankees or no, Dunphy and his sons all now own boots. "I think it's very interesting none of my kids had any interest in returning to the East," he says. "We developed some professional Texans in a hurry." One works for Shell, another is a lawyer for Exxon, and the third attends Southern Methodist University.

For Joan, the first tremor of culture shock came when a store clerk called her Hon. In 1970 only one other Shell family lived nearby, but now the neighborhood "is a Shell ghetto," brimming with New Englanders. The commercial centers of this suburban quadrant are Town and Country Village the new West Oaks Mall, where a spiffy branch of Saks Fifth Avenue is the anchor store. For groceries, Joan says, "everyone I know goes to Randall's." (Sure enough, there at the market, over by the lobster tank, were two cast-iron crocks full of New England clam chowder from a company called Abbott's of New England. Jot that down as proof of the new dispensation Yankees brought.)

The schools, with their quality academics and their strong discipline, were a pleasant surprise. "The attitude was, you *will* show honor, you *will* show respect," Dunphy says. "It was quite a change." But the biggest difference has probably been time, which for the Dunphys translates into leisure and community involvement.

"In Wilton," he says, "the living was gorgeous, but the fact is, you did not have access to the amenities of the big city. Here I curse the Houston traffic, but we can go to the theater and the ball games. When you retreated up to Connecticut, it took a major operation just to get back into the city. You just didn't *do* it. If you went to the theater, you had to catch the last train back, and woe betide you if you didn't. Now, provided I start early, I'll allow forty minutes to an Oilers game."

Dunphy drove the eighty-five-mile round-trip to Queens every day rather than waiting at Wilton's picturesque little red frame station "for the New Haven Railway's latest breakdown." (The New Haven is long gone, and Wilton's service has dwindled to two through trains each way these days.) In Houston he carpools with four friends—circling the neighborhood at 6:25 a.m., arriving at One Shell Plaza by 6:55, heading back at 4:10 p.m., when their "flex-time" day ends. The trip is eighteen miles each way. If work keeps him late, a Metro bus runs within a few blocks of his house.

Thanks to the one-way carpool lane on Katy Freeway, "I'm usually home by four-thirty-five or four-forty," he adds. "Think of the implications of that. You can coach Little League, practice your backhand, tend the garden. In New York your fanny would still be in a train seat for hours."

Even though Shell employees in Houston spend an hour more in their offices each day than they did before the move, shorter commutes have changed their relationship to the community, Dunphy thinks. "There are only two things a corporation can offer, people and money. We contribute four million dollars a year in Houston. In New York we gave money to good causes, too, but at five p.m., whoosh, everybody pours out of the buildings and into trains and subways. They're *gone*. Here we have more sense of a corporate hometown. Our people are involved much more." Among the projects he oversees is SERVE, the Shell Employees and Retirees Volunteerism Effort, designed to match unused employee skills ("let's say teaching deaf children to read") with charitable needs. The project fields 1300 requests a year. "I don't know how to say this except to blurt out what I think," he says. "It's in our interest to play a proportionate part in making Houston a better place."

The drive from Dunphy's old office in Queens to his former home on Old Range Road in Wilton hints at how profoundly the daily life of an executive on the East Coast differs from life in the Southwest. As one heads north, the skyline of Manhattan soars to the left, and the peaceful waters of Long Island Sound stretch out to the right. The bumpy highway soon becomes the meandering Merritt Parkway, an extended answer to the wooded sections of Houston's Memorial Drive, with granite outcroppings, reddening willows and maples, momentary glimpses of lakes and small waterways—but seldom any hint that urban development lies beyond those trees. By Greenwich the road is in deep forest. New York City seems a continent away.

Texans like to think they are still close to the land. But the tranquil drive to Wilton is far more rural, more soothing, than the freeway combat that constitutes the homeward journey of most Houstonians. And at the end is a picture-postcard New England village, with stores like B&G ("outfitters for the country life") and the Saddler (stocked with riding gear), and hilly residential neighborhoods like Old Range Road: secluded, wooded, private. Texans are wont to ask how New Yorkers can endure Manhattan; for many the answer is, they don't. The lucky ones like Bob Dunphy pass through a time warp like Merritt Parkway and emerge in an altogether different place that they consider their real home. It is an astonishing transition, far sharper than from One Shell Plaza to Memorial. For a businessman in

Wilton, going to New York to work is like going down into a mine for a coal miner. It's not home. It's just a place to spend a few hours earning a living.

In the crisp autumn air Wilton seemed a world apart, not just from Manhattan but from Texas too. But at Palmer's supermarket there was one last lesson to be learned about the amalgamation of cultures in modern America. Beside the meat counter sat two familiar-looking, steaming cast-iron crocks. Sure enough, they were from Abbott's of New England. Sure enough, one said "Clam Chowder." But the other one was labeled "Chili."

NORTH PLEASANT STREET IN Ridgewood, New Jersey, has a deeply settled look. Gradually the blocks of steep-gabled two-story houses diminish to ones more modestly proportioned. Toward the end is number 363, a frame cottage with dormer windows that was home to John and June O'Driscoll and their nine children when he worked in New York City as an engineer for Shell.

The tidy bedroom community of Ridgewood is a long way in spirit from the section of the South Bronx where O'Driscoll grew up—146th Street and Third Avenue, a proper Irish neighborhood once, Fort Apache now. North Pleasant Street is the sort of place many in the city aspire to reach. But there, he recalls, "you knew the names of the people who lived in the houses, and that's all."

In the mornings, he walked four tree-shaded blocks down East Glen and caught a bus that took him across the George Washington Bridge as far as 168th Street in Manhattan. There he descended into the subway for the thunderous 120-block ride down the IND line to Rockefeller Center. "I only worked seven hours a day in New York," he says, "but by the time I came home I'd been gone eleven." Life with Shell gave every indication of being an uneventful, Clark Kent existence. But surprises lay around the corner.

"We were living in a forty-six-year-old house that was beginning to bulge with bunk beds and had one hell of a tax bill on it. We had college education for nine kids coming up. New Jersey had only one state university, Rutgers, and it had room to admit only half the kids who applied. We paid three income taxes—federal, New York state, and New York city—but because we lived in New Jersey our kids couldn't even get into the New York state university system." Balding, bespectacled, cherubic, O'Driscoll reflects for a moment on the implications of taxation without representation.

"When the boss called our department into his office to announce the move," he continues, "my reaction was: When? How soon can we go? We came to Texas, bought a wonderful home with low taxes, and found twenty-one state schools with much lower tuition. There was just no question about it, financially."

When the O'Driscolls moved into their home on Pecan Creek off Katy Freeway in August, the street seemed oddly quiet. "There were fifty-eight kids in sixteen houses on this one block," June remembers. "But we didn't know it until school started, because everybody was indoors to get away from the heat."

In due time the outdoors was discovered. "Coming down here with teenage boys, we were ready for them to want driver's licenses and motorbikes," O'Driscoll says. "They didn't ask for those. They asked for .22 rifles—to go hunting for armadillos behind the Addicks Dam. They'd walk over, camp out, and shoot at anything that moved. In New Jersey you can't even fire a gun." Back East, the family's traditional group outing had been the annual Christmas show at Radio City Music Hall. In Texas, it soon became summer visits to the Peaceful Valley Dude Ranch near Bandera.

THE LAST REMNANT OF SHELL'S New York dominions is suite 4225 in the RCA Building, Rockefeller Center. From such heights the view below is as arresting as ever: the spires of St. Patrick's Cathedral, the prosperous bulk of Saks Fifth Avenue, *Newsweek*'s tower, the Empire State Building. It is Manhattan as seen on an isometric map.

Only three employees are left in suite 4225. The other rooms are neat but oddly and unmistakably vacant, the desks polished and waiting for the occasional company executive who drops by on business in the city. In the boardroom Shell's directors still convene three or four times a year around the great oblong table ("so as not to get trapped in the oil patch," it's whispered). It all must have looked very much like this the day before the movers came: the same paintings, the same stately grandfather clock, the same quaint old motor oil bottles from the twenties decorating a side table, emblems of continuity. The baby-blue carpet, spotless, muffles every footfall.

The keeper of this lonely corporate legation, Shell's New York consul if you will, is Claire O'Connor, executive secretary. She has been with Shell for 35 years. She remembers when 47 people worked in suite 4225. She has never set foot in Houston.

When Shell decided to make the move, it occupied eight floors in Rockefeller Center, two at Time-Life, two at Sperry-Rand, two at the J. C. Penney Building. Seventeen years ago this suite was one of the nerve centers of the corporate world. Decisions were made here that allocated billions of dollars, influenced the fate of nations, touched the pocketbooks of a tenth of the people on the planet. Now, this morning, there is just Claire and nobody else—no ringing phones, no voices, nothing to suggest that anything ever mattered here, nothing but the measured ticking of the grandfather clock.❧

## LONE STAR SHTICK

[ CONTINUED FROM PAGE 142 ]
*Football.*

Meredith already had begun singing "Turn Out the Lights," cracking his good-ol'-boy wisecracks, and swaggering through Manhattan in Larry Mahan hats and Judi Buie boots. Dallasite Mahan, several times World Champion Rodeo Cowboy, began peddling a line of Western wear to Yankees and himself posed for underwear ads while swinging a lasso and wearing only a big cowboy hat, boots, and snug-fitting briefs.

Herman Gollob, unrepentant Texas Aggie and New York book-publishing mogul —he unleashed Jenkins and Billie Clyde Puckett—began to take authors, ad men, agents, and other editors to lunch at a new restaurant. The Dallas Cowboy featured leggy waitresses done up in costumes like they'd just come from a hard day of barrel riding, and some of the worst alleged chili, ribs, and other Texas tasties ever foisted off on an unsuspecting public. Herman, given that he is an Aggie, may not have known how dismal the food was; if he did, he didn't tell his guests, and so the dumb Yankee bastards thought it was good and began steering *their* friends there.

I myself began swaggering through Manhattan's stone canyons in cowboy clothes about 1965; never mind that I had not been on a horse since 1947 and then only long enough to fall off. Fellow writer and old friend Bud Shrake, himself writing Texas stuff in novels, films, and magazine articles, played cowboy with me. At six feet six before putting on his high-heeled boots, he fit the role perfectly. When he came to New York from Austin and the two of us made our nightly fun runs— asking one another loudly if he had the dope, the other one saying naw, dammit, he guess he'd left it in our Learjet—people didn't know if the rodeo was playing Madison Square Garden or if we were on a buying spree for the Texas Mafia.

One afternoon in early 1978, shortly before the Off-Broadway opening of *The Best Little Whorehouse in Texas* (by yours truly, Peter Masterson, and Carol Hall), I was walking down a Greenwich Village street and spotted a new bar bearing the name "Lone Star." Curious, I entered to find longneck Lone Star beer, something resembling chili, and Mort Cooperman, who said he intended to bring in live country-and-western bands from Texas and make a fortune. I thought, "This New York Jew's gotta be crazy to open a shitkicker joint in the Village!" Next thing I know, *Whorehouse* is holding its first cast party at the Lone Star. Soon you couldn't get in the place unless you begged.

Willie Nelson's music began to take over the jukebox at Elaine's and elsewhere. When he visited New York they let him in Sardi's wearing his braids, patched overalls, sweaty bandanna, and scruffy tennis shoes. Everybody in the place wanted to meet him; people in tuxedos sprang to open doors for Willie and snapped their gold cigarette lighters in front of his face. The former Michigan State wrangler and Dallas Cowboy Pete Gent wrote *North Dallas Forty*, a novel full of Texas craziness that went on to become a big movie.

I think the real flowering of Texas chic occurred when Tommy Tune turned the dancing Texas Aggie football players into cowboys in a show-stopping number in *Whorehouse*. Almost immediately, New York disco dancers began to show up dressed like those Aggie cowboys. Soon the craze spread to the heterosexual community as well. It was the sight of a Wall Street dude dolled up like a rodeo cowboy —carrying his briefcase down Fifth Avenue —that inspired my nineteen-year-old son, Brad, who had dressed Western all of his life, to abandon his cowboy regalia. "When everybody else gets out of my costume," he said, "then I'll put it back on."

We liked it, of course, even as we snickered at Damn Yankees trying to say "y'all" in acceptable accents and looking silly in cowboy hats. Imitation, after all, is said to be the sincerest form of flattery, and for many, many years New Yorkers hadn't flattered Texas at all. We had to go hat-in-hand to New York banks for really big money, we had to romance New York editors to get our writing published, and too many haughty French waiters looked down their noses like maybe we'd come in wearing Big Mac overalls and brogans fresh-dipped in cow plop. Hell, we gave 'em a president of the United States, and they laughed at him because he said "*A*-rab" and showed everybody his operation scar and liked barbecue sauce. They treated us like a bunch of country bumpkins until they woke one day to realize we had snuck around and got chokeholds on their TV networks and publishing houses and had infiltrated their executive boardrooms and law offices. We stole airline headquarters from 'em and some of their better bank customers. New Yorkers, on the other hand, couldn't seem to clear Queens streets of snow or get their garbage hauled or make their subways run on time. Those fool Yankees were imitating a fantasy Texas, of course, a Texas that never was or maybe barely had been—or at least one that failed to reflect our poverty pockets and ignorance or other shortcomings because we were careful to cover up our sins with whoopees and brags. And them suckers' falling for our Camelot bullshit was maybe the sweetest thing of all.

Texas chic is gone now. Nobody knows why for sure. Perhaps when our rig count nose-dived we lost a certain advantage, though more likely it was simply time for the fad to end. The death of Texas chic was pleasing to many, Texans and non-Texans alike. Only those of us who got about half-rich off it feel like mourning. ♣

# INDEX

NOTE: Names in capital letters indicate authors. Page numbers in italics indicate a photograph or illustration.